D1571038

The Franco-Americans of New England
A History

Armand Chartier

The Franco-Americans of New England
A History

Translated by Robert J. Lemieux and Claire Quintal

Revised and Edited by Claire Quintal

ACA Assurance and Institut français of Assumption College
1999

Cover concept, photo selection, and captions: Paul M. Paré

Cover photos. Center: New Hampshire Franco-American girls during World War I. Below, left to right: Saints-Pierre-et-Paul Church in Lewiston, Maine; gallery opening at the Franco-American Centre in Manchester, New Hampshire; "Jeter le Pont" - traditional musicians from Vermont; wedding portrait from the Antonio Prince Family Files; Franco-American grandmother with a Little League baseball player; young textile workers captured on film by Lewis Hines. Photos ACA Archives.

ACA ASSURANCE
P.O. Box 989
Manchester, NH 03015

INSTITUT FRANÇAIS
Assumption College
P.O. Box 15005
Worcester, MA 01615

ISBN 1-880261-05-7

TABLE OF CONTENTS

Chapters   Page

A Claire Quintal l'incontournable experte ès matières franco-américaines.

A Eugène Lemieux qui a émis l'idée de traduire cet historique

A Denis Vaugeois sans qui il n'y aurait pas eu de version française à traduire.

Acknowledgments

Obviously, I am most grateful to ACA Assurance (formerly the Association Canado-Américaine) and to the Institut français of Assumption College for undertaking the publication of the present volume.

Professor Robert J. Lemieux, as the first translator of the text, showed enviable patience and persistence in transposing the idiosyncrasies of my French style into comprehensible English. For his role in this venture, I am deeply in his debt, and I thank him wholeheartedly.

Professor Quintal, Directress of Assumption College's Institut français, soon became co-translator, editor, advisor, a source of documentation, and a pillar of support. Until our collaborative effort in this translation, I had seldom had the privilege of working with someone who has raised the virtues of meticulousness and conscientiousness to veritable art forms. My indebtedness to her is staggering. For now, I can only articulate a profound *merci*, hopeful that the future will provide opportunities to begin the lengthy process of "returning the favor."

Special thanks are due to Paul Paré for his pertinent comments on the Postscript and for his input on the cover design and the choice of photographs; to Rev. Alexis Babineau, A.A., and Robert J. Lemieux for the final proofreading of the entire text, to Carmella Murphy for her technical expertise, Sylvia Desautels for coming to our rescue when time was tight and deadlines looming, and Amandine Blanc, living proof that the French university system turns out well-trained and highly disciplined graduates.

For demonstrating to me the growing appeal and strength of genealogy among *today's* Franco-Americans, Sylvia Bartholomy of Rhode Island, Albert Hamel of New Hampshire, and Albert Marceau of Connecticut also deserve my heartfelt gratitude. My contacts with them have yielded much information and numerous insights. To all of them, un *grand merci*! And to Albert Marceau, who went far beyond duty's call in obtaining documentation for me, I owe an extra special *grand merci*!

I also extend my thanks to Richard Belair, Sister Clarice Chauvin, S.S.A., and George Ouellette for their close reading of the first version of the translation and to Sr. Alice Aubé, R.J.M., Elizabeth Aubé, Adèle Boufford Baker, Professor Eloïse Brière, Robert Cormier, Richard L. Fortin, Professor Joseph Garreau, Lisa Ornstein, Rhéa Côté Robbins, Madeleine Roy, Professor Madeleine Giguère, and to the officers of the many "French" genealogical societies, all of whom, in some way, contributed to making this a better volume than it might otherwise have been. Once again, to each of them, *Merci*!

A. C.

About the Publishers

ACA ASSURANCE

ACA ASSURANCE, one of the organizations often referred to as pillars of Franco-American *survivance,* is proud of its participation in making the history of the Franco-Americans better known through the publication of this book.

Founded in 1896 in Manchester, New Hampshire, as Association Canado-Américaine, ACA ASSURANCE is a fraternal benefit society that serves the economic needs and cultural interests of persons of French Catholic heritage in both the United States and Canada. In recent years, it has been one of the fastest growing fraternal societies in North America and among the most innovative in meeting the needs of its members and the larger community.

The more than 69,000 members of ACA ASSURANCE reside in New England, Louisiana, and Eastern Canada. As a fraternal benefit society, the organization is member-driven with a democratic structure that allows members to participate fully in the life of the association at various levels, from the monthly local lodge meeting or chapter activity to the international convention held every four years. ACA Assurance is not only the oldest but also the only surviving independent fraternal benefit society among those founded by and for Franco-Americans. The others have either ceased operations in the United States or have merged with non-Franco-American fraternal organizations.

ACA ASSURANCE provides financial security for its members and their families through a variety of up-to-date, competitive and guaranteed issue insurance plans. ACA ASSURANCE has always subscribed to a cautious investment philosophy and remains financially strong. At the end of 1998, it had assets of $44.3 million, a surplus of $5.5 million with $328 million of insurance in force.

Although member delegates to ACA's Centennial Convention in 1996 changed the name of the Society to ACA ASSURANCE, the organization remains as committed as ever to the cultural and language goals of the founders of Association Canado-Américaine. ACA's cultural programs include various activities organized by local chapters, a quarterly French-English magazine, financial aid for college studies, a classroom exchange program between New England and Canadian schools, group travel opportunities to various destinations, a French-language television program available throughout most of New England and parts of Louisiana and the Maritime Provinces, as well as privileged access to its genealogical and historical research facilities.

ACA's international headquarters is located in Manchester, New Hampshire, and the Canadian office is in Trois-Rivières, Québec. Further information can be obtained by writing ACA at Post Office Box 989, Manchester, NH 03105-0989,or by calling 1-800-222-8577. The E-mail address is aca@inc-net.com or you may visit their Web site at www.acaassurance.com.

Eugène Lemieux is the current president.

Paul Paré

L' Institut Français -The French Institute

The French Institute, which is a self-supporting entity under the aegis of Assumption College, is both an academic research facility and a resource center for persons interested in francophone questions. Founded in 1979, the Institute has continued and expanded the French tradition at Assumption College. It organizes colloquia, publishes books, and has initiated a variety of cultural projects. Through its specialized research and outstanding collection of Canadiana and Franco-Americana available on-line within the college catalog, it seeks to increase awareness and promote knowledge regarding the French fact in North America.

The Institute, which maintains ties with similar research centers in France, Canada, and the United States, has published the following titles: *Steeples and Smokestacks; The Beginnings of the Franco-American Colony in Woonsocket, Rhode Island; The Franco-American Woman; Franco-Americans and Religion: Impact and Influence; Franco-American Literature: Writers and Their Writings; Le Journalisme de langue française aux États-Unis; Les Franco-Américains et leurs institutions scolaires; Le Patrimoine folklorique des Franco-Américains; L'Émigrant acadien aux États-Unis; The Little Canadas of New England; L'Émigrant québécois vers les États- Unis,* and *Situation de la recherche sur les Franco-Américains.*

The French Institute has hosted many distinguished visitors. Among the most notable are the French Minister for Francophone Affairs; the Vice-Minister for International Affairs of Quebec; the President of Quebec's Laval University; scholars from France, Canada, francophone Africa and Haiti, as well as French ambassadors and senators.

The Institut français/French Institute is located at Assumption College in Worcester, Massachusetts. Further information can be obtained by writing to: P.O. Box 15005, Worcester, MA 01615-0005 or calling (508) 767-7414. The Fax number is (508) 767-7374 and the e-mail address is instfran@assumption.edu.

Claire Quintal

Foreword

When, during the preparation of the present volume, I began reviewing documents accumulated since the completion of my *Histoire des Franco-Américains de la Nouvelle-Angleterre, 1775-1990*, published in 1991 by the Éditions du Septentrion in Sillery, Québec... I was quite surprised in a heartwarming way.

Agonizingly aware of the grievous losses incurred by *my* ethnic group, I had initially believed that updating this work for publication in the late 1990s would mainly entail a lengthy recitation of regrets and lamentations.

Not so. To offset the losses, there had been gains, especially in the area of genealogy. After skimming through sample issues of journals published by the genealogical societies, several facts became apparent, two above all: the vigor and enthusiasm evident in these societies and their evolution from genealogy to an interest in social and cultural history, which fulfilled a long-standing hope of mine.

There has been forward movement in other areas also between the late 1980s and the late 1990s. Under the adroit leadership of its president, Eugène Lemieux, a new Franco-American Centre has been established by ACA Assurance whose funding is making the present publication possible. The Institut français at Assumption College, sagaciously directed by Professor Claire Quintal, has begun publishing a variety of scholarly works, while maintaining a grueling schedule of activities, including the publication of its own colloquia proceedings.

In a word, le peuple *franco—américain*—or at least some major elements of it—was showing signs of vitality, as substantiated in our Postscript, Appendices, and Bibliography. All of this indicates to me that there is an even more extensive Franco-American life "out there" than what is summarized in the present volume. Long may it last!

A. C.

I

THE GREAT MIGRATION
1860-1900

The first Franco-Americans, in the broadest sense of the term, are probably to be found among the Pilgrims aboard the *Mayflower,* which landed in Plymouth, Massachusetts, in 1620. These colonists, mainly of English stock, were the first to settle the New England region. What is less well-known is that among these pioneer families one at least was French: that of Guillaume Molines. Like the Molines, other French Huguenots in search of religious freedom also established residence in the thirteen original colonies during the seventeenth century. These settlers of French origin might be called "Franco-Americans," were it not more or less agreed upon to reserve the term for Americans of Québec or Acadian origin.

In the seventeenth and eighteenth centuries, explorers, missionaries, soldiers, and *coureurs de bois* from Canada roamed freely across what is today the United States. Some remained for long or short periods of time, and their frequent voyages to and fro established an early precedent for frequent comings and goings across a border which, at first, did not exist, and whose exact line would not be drawn for quite some time.

So, except for an unknown number of Canadian soldiers who, without leaving a trace, crossed into American territory upon the signing of the Treaty of Paris in 1763, there was no French-Canadian presence to speak of either in New England or the Northeast before 1775.

When the thirteen colonies rebelled against England in 1775, the French Canadians viewed the American rebels in a favorable light. But their sympathy was never strong enough to induce more than a handful of them to join the thirteen colonies in revolt. Still, some of them did help the insurgents and thereby contributed to emigration into the United States. When, at the end of 1775, the Americans invaded Canada, they were able to recruit enough French Canadians to form two regiments. And when the American troops withdrew in June of 1776, they were accompanied by one hundred and fifty French-Canadian soldiers. These soldiers were in fact emigrating, because the British authorities would never have allowed these "traitors" to return to Canada. As to the role played by Quebecers and Acadians in the War of Independence, historian Virginia DeMarce has identified more than 1800 French Canadians who fought on the side of the rebels. Some of their names are known to us, such as: Lieutenant Colonels Pierre Régnier and Jacob Bruyère and Captains Auguste Loiseau and Philippe Dubois, among others. It is also a fact that some battalions composed of Canadians fought in Washington's armies and that a regiment under the command of Major Clément Gosselin, a Knight of the prestigious Society of the Cincinnati, saw action at the Battle of Yorktown in 1781.

In return for their services, Canadian and Acadian volunteers were given land in upper New York State along Lake Champlain. And, in 1789, New York granted additional lands in the same region to some deported Acadians. Such was the origin of two villages: Corbeau, which has become Coopersville, and Rouse's Point, named after Jacques Roux, a veteran of the War of Independence. So even before 1800, two hundred and fifty or so Canadian and Acadian families had settled in northeastern New York State, and they would be numbered among the founders of the future diocese of Ogdensburg.

History provides us with very scant details and, all too often, remains mute regarding the emigrants from Québec and Acadia of the late eighteenth and early nineteenth centuries. A few bits of information have, nonetheless, escaped oblivion. Immediately following the Revolutionary period, sporadic immigration into the northernmost areas of New England and New York State took place. Often some of these early immigrants came to Maine to work in the logging industry. Others signed on as dock workers when, around 1820, navigation on Lake Champlain began to stimulate the development of regional trade. Still others found work as farm hands here and there near the Canadian-American border. Before long, newcomers joined the "old-timers" in Corbeau, while other New York villages like Champlain, Chazy, and Split Rock Bay also received their share of *Canadiens*.

This entire region on both sides of Lake Champlain, in Vermont as well as New York, was considered missionary territory by the Catholic hierarchy of French Canada from the very beginning of the nineteenth century. The area was served by the pastor of Chambly in Québec, Rev. Pierre-Marie Mignault, an uncommonly energetic and zealous priest. From 1819 to 1854, Rev. Mignault traveled by cart and canoe, following the topography of a region more richly endowed with lakes and forests than with suitable roads. Refusing all remuneration, he administered the sacraments and celebrated mass, often in private homes when there were no churches nearby. For, not only were the churches widely scattered, they were under the direction of Irish priests, no small drawback for immigrants who spoke no English.

Little by little, the Catholic Church would seek out these immigrants. But the efforts of this heroic period were nothing compared to the great religious expansion that would occur a half-century later. If, during the early years, the Franco-American church was slow to develop, this was due as much to the bishops of Québec, who hesitated to send priests into a foreign country, as to the Irish-American bishops, who were reluctant to found separate parishes. According to Bishop Jean-Octave Plessis of Québec, French-Canadian Catholics were fully capable of establishing a parish in Burlington in 1815 but would have to wait until 1850 to have one of their own. This early resistance was a harbinger of the difficult battles that lay ahead.

There were no doubt other immigrants, individuals as well as families, scattered throughout the Northeast. But, outside the Burlington-Winooski, Vermont, and the Madawaska, Maine, regions, there were no significant concentrations of immigrants to be found. So, it took considerable courage for those rare nonconformist pioneers to venture into southern New England: the François Proulx family settling in Woonsocket, Rhode Island, around 1814; Charles Benoit arriving alone in Worcester, Massachusetts in 1820; the Abraham Marois family living in Southbridge, Massachusetts, in 1832—not to mention those who were drawn to the Midwest and to the West, ranging from Michigan to Oregon by way of Illinois and Wisconsin.

It is true that the Rebellions of 1837-38 against English rule forced a certain number of rebels called *Patriotes* to seek refuge in the United States. But it is equally true that the disastrous economic situation of those terrible years contributed at least as much to the migratory movement. Thus, before 1840, some French Canadians were already plying various trades in Vermont: in forests, in quarries, in the lumber trade, and in agriculture. Others found jobs in New York State's public works projects.

And even before their insurrection had been crushed, several *Patriote* leaders, along with an undetermined number of their comrades in arms, were obliged to flee across the American border to avoid prison or the scaffold. Louis-Joseph Papineau settled in Albany, Doctor Robert Nelson in Plattsburgh, and Ludger Duvernay in Rouse's Point, all in New York State. Actually, the *Patriotes* scattered throughout the

Northeast and could be found here and there in Michigan and Missouri, and even in California.

For a time at least, the rebel leaders hoped to interest the American government in their goal of national independence. But, less than a half-century after its own revolution, the United States had adopted an anti-revolutionary policy, and the hopes of the *Patriotes* remained unfulfilled. The amnesty of 1842 allowed many of the rebels, who had endured considerable hardship while in the United States, to return to Canada. Although their emigration was, by and large, only a temporary one, its importance lies in the fact that it gave birth to two typically Franco-American institutions: a newspaper and a parish.

Founded in Burlington by Ludger Duvernay, *Le Patriote canadien* had a very brief life span. The first issue of this eight-page "political, historical, literary, and industrial weekly" appeared on August 7, 1839, the last on February 5, 1840. But several characteristics of the many Franco-American newspapers of the nineteenth and twentieth centuries could already be found in this first-born among them. As the offshoot of a rebellion, this newspaper, as short-lived and argumentative as many of its successors, thrived on controversy. During its brief career, it dared to criticize the clergy, printed excerpts from the writings of the unorthodox French priest Lamennais, who had broken with the Church when the Pope condemned his work, and succeeded in irritating the future Prime Minister, George-Étienne Cartier, by publishing some poems that he had repudiated. In doing this, the editors were pursuing no less a goal than that of Canadian independence. The newspapers which followed this one would also devote themselves to an equally high-minded and difficult cause: warding off assimilation.

Rather than return to Canada after the amnesty, some exiles chose to remain with the Canadians in the Corbeau region. This created a population large enough to allow for the founding, in 1842, of the first

Franco-American parish in the eastern United States: Saint Joseph de Corbeau in Coopersville, New York.

Most early immigrants were isolated individuals, so silent and invisible that their history cannot be written, engulfed as they were in the great American vortex as soon as they crossed the border. The years from 1800 to 1840 constitute a shadowy period in the history of Québec emigration to the United States. Although the immigrants were too few in number to make known their presence by founding parishes, societies, or newspapers, these people—history's forgotten ones—continued, nonetheless, to "come to the States." In fact, enough of them did so that Lord Durham, in his notorious Report of 1839, underscored the threat that this migratory movement posed for Canada.

This flow of an increasing number of inhabitants from Lower Canada at the end of the eighteenth and the beginning of the nineteenth centuries would turn into a veritable torrent resulting in grave consequences for Canada in the 1840s. Reduced to its simplest terms, the situation was as follows: in Quebec and Acadia, a growing surplus of unemployed workers; in the United States, an industrial revolution of such dimensions as to attract immigrants from all the nations of the world. From 1815 to 1914, more than thirty million immigrants would come to the United States, hundreds of thousands of them from French Canada.

Emigration Fever (1840-1860)

Given that the predominantly agricultural province of Québec was in a state of perpetual crisis throughout the nineteenth century, it is surprising that *la fièvre des États* (stateside fever) did not spread sooner. One can hardly imagine a scenario more conducive to emigration than the prevailing agricultural conditions in Québec during this period.

First, there was widespread ignorance of agronomy. Little effort was made to familiarize people with agricultural practices which could have improved crop yields. The lack of any scientific information on seeding techniques or crop rotation led to a progressive decline in production on land that was all too often poorly prepared for cultivation. Additionally, these farms that were expected to provide food for ever larger families were continually being subdivided from one generation to the next. Compounding the problem was the shortage of arable land due to the seigniorial system of land tenure as well as the wholesale acquisition of property by powerful English absentee landowners. Huge estates were thus removed from agricultural development.

In short, everything—a lack of roads and bridges, a shortage of markets, a credit system controlled by heartless usurers—contributed to the creation of the worst possible situation. Usury was common, and farmers confronted by predictably poor harvests and lacking any governmental protection were forced to borrow at prohibitively high rates of interest.

Colonization efforts in wilderness areas proved to be only a palliative. The strategy was much discussed, but little was done, at least with any degree of efficiency, since too few lands had been opened to colonization. Given the overpopulation in the St. Lawrence Valley, the logical solution would have been to colonize the Eastern Townships, the least remote of the populated regions. Alas, those lands remained in the hands of speculators like the British American Land Company which sold only at exorbitant prices.

Other possible solutions to the agricultural crisis existed only in an embryonic state. Industry was not expanding rapidly enough to create the jobs needed to offset rural overpopulation, and trade was hampered both by England's elimination of preferential tariffs (1846) and by the failure of the United States in 1864 to renew the Treaty of Reciprocity of 1854.

To this already lengthy list of obstacles and difficulties must be added the negligence demonstrated by a succession of governments which made no appreciable effort to assist the young in acquiring either Crown Lands or those in the hands of speculators. Nor did they seek to improve a primitive road network or curb the shameful greed of the usurers. Meanwhile, throughout the entire century, the population continued to increase at a truly extraordinary rate, giving rise to almost constant overpopulation.

Since those most affected by these conditions—farmers and their families—have left no written accounts, it is impossible to assess the impact, in human or emotional terms, of these harsh economic realities. One fact, however, is particularly revealing: from 1840 to 1930, nearly a million Quebecers and Acadians left for the United States. The disarray, anguish, and despair which led to this exodus will never be fully known.

Luckily for them, geography offered immigrants from Québec and Acadia a great advantage over their European counterparts. From 1835 to 1850, the expansion of the railroad system greatly facilitated their travel back and forth between the two countries, as an increasing number of them spent anywhere from a season to a few years in New England.

While poverty seemed to be taking root in Canada, New England was experiencing a profound transformation from an agricultural to an industrial region. This phenomenon was about to disrupt forever the demographic equilibrium by producing waves of immigrants that would have been inconceivable in 1840. The successful combining of technology and capital with a labor force from various countries gave rise to the prodigious economic development which continued with little interruption until around 1930.

It seems only right to give here a partial listing of the major industries whose founding led to this immigration of Quebecers and Acadians into the Northeast.

1790   Pawtucket, Rhode Island: establishment of the Slater Mill, the first mechanized factory in the United States.

1813   Fall River, Massachusetts: construction of the Troy Mill; one of the leading manufacturing centers was being developed even then.

1822   Lowell, Massachusetts: founding of the prototype of American industrial cities.

1822   Chicopee, Massachusetts: founding of the Chicopee Manufacturing Company.

1838   Manchester, New Hampshire: the first stage in the development of the colossal Amoskeag Corporation which would eventually employ 17,000 people, a large percentage of whom were   Franco-Americans.

1844   Blackstone River District: ninety-four factories were located within a fifty-mile stretch between Worcester, Massachusetts, and Pawtucket, Rhode Island, by way of Woonsocket, Rhode Island.

Even before 1850, a number of localities destined to become major industrial centers and magnets for French-Canadian immigration could already boast of factories operating at full capacity. Expansion was imminent.

Factories had to be carefully sited near waterways that could provide the energy needed to power the machinery. Very often canals had to be dug to divert rivers and streams, numerous in the region. Projects of this kind sometimes proved to be highly complex undertakings, as in Lowell, Massachusetts, and Lewiston, Maine.

Moreover, these large-scale enterprises required an enormous amount of capital. A small group of Yankees, on the cutting edge of New England capitalism, took control in the first half of the nineteenth century. Known as the Boston Associates, the group included members drawn from the most prominent families of the time: Amory, Appleton, Cabot, Dwight, Jackson, Lawrence, Lowell, Lyman, and Perkins, among others. Together, these patricians controlled various corporations, including many banks and insurance companies, and they also wielded considerable political influence.

Sensing, early on, the fortunes that could be amassed as a result of the new technology, these Yankee capitalists dedicated themselves so vigorously to industrial empire-building that they provided the impetus for one of the most significant achievements of nineteenth-century America: the prodigious expansion of the textile industry. Not surprisingly, with their factories in Waltham, Lowell, Chicopee, Holyoke, and Lawrence, Massachusetts; in Dover, Manchester, and Nashua, New Hampshire; and in Biddeford and Saco, Maine, the Boston Associates were able to maintain their dominance for several decades during the industrial expansion they had themselves been largely instrumental in bringing about.

On a smaller scale, other equally shrewd capitalists were able to profit from the Industrial Revolution. Throughout New England and New York State, plants and factories of all kinds sprang up to produce axes, coaches, chairs, boilers, etc. But it was the textile industry, both cotton and wool, that led the way, especially in southern New England, where, around 1850, some 900 factories employed over 100,000 people. The leather industry, mainly boots and shoes, also played a major role in this unprecedented economic boom. Lynn, Massachusetts, alone, was producing over nine million pairs each year around 1850.

The very first industrial workers, both men and women, were Yankees of course, the most famous being the "Mill Girls" of Lowell. In the 1820s and 1830s, these young women would leave their farms to spend a few years in the spinning mills where they found job security, a healthy moral atmosphere in group homes under the watchful care of stern matrons, and the opportunity to enroll in courses in their spare time. These cultured young women also published a literary magazine, *The Lowell Offering.* The immigrant experience would turn out to be vastly different.

This period of untrammeled growth came to an end in the 1840s. Seeking to maximize profit in a competitive environment, owners increasingly imposed harsher working conditions on the workers. The ensuing job dissatisfaction led to strikes and, for many workers, to permanent job changes as new opportunities arose, due to an expanded job market and the American West.

This instability benefited the immigrants who quickly filled the vacancies. The Irish, scorned by Yankees as "an ocean of ignorance," were the first to do so. Forced to flee famine in their homeland, successive waves of Irish had already filled many factory jobs during the 1840s.

The relatively slow rate of immigration by French Canadians is not easily explained, given the economic situation in Québec and its proximity to New England. Was it due to their general lack of information about the industrial development occurring in New England? Or to the hope that their lot would eventually improve? Or to their attachment to their homeland? Given the present state of knowledge, there are, as of now, no good answers to these questions.

Yet from 1830 to 1850, thousands of Quebecers and Acadians had already found employment in more and more diversified occupations throughout the northeastern United States. It was agriculture, lumbering, and the construction industry that drew them here, and they found seasonal, temporary, or permanent jobs, first in Maine, New Hampshire, and Vermont, and soon in southern New England.

The urbanization spawned by industrialization encouraged the building of residential areas, often adjacent to the factories. This was the case in Manchester where the Amoskeag Corporation built row upon row of brick houses, known as corporation housing, for their workers. At the building sites, there was an ever-growing need for manpower in all the trades. It was not uncommon to find French Canadians among the masons, bricklayers, and carpenters in Manchester or Cambridge.

These early immigrants remained in contact with Canada. When they returned, dressed in their finery and sporting handsome gold watches, their visits spurred others to come and "test the waters." There arose an information network which was expanded after 1850 by recruiters (sometimes Canadian immigrants themselves) who were hired by the mills to entice their countrymen to follow their example. These agents, who traveled through Québec from the Montréal area to the lower Saint Lawrence, were living proof of the high regard which their employers now had for the Canadians. Though skeptical at first, these employers now had to admit that the Canadians were hard workers who put their heart into their work and were not inclined to "rock the boat." They were quite docile, lived nearby, and could easily be recruited.

Sporadic at first, then intermittent and often only temporary, the level of immigration remained stable after 1850. Before the Civil War, i.e., before the 1860s, the immigrants were constantly on the move in search of jobs. As a result, they tended to be seen as nomads, forever setting out for the Midwest or returning to Canada. This coming and going reflected their experience in the job market. But, as the century advanced, the immigration of the Quebecers, followed by that of the Acadians, was linked increasingly to the vast movement of industrial expansion that involved all of the New England States as well as northeastern New York State.

The government of Canada did little more than voice its concern over this migratory phenomenon. However, some observers, including the editors of *La Gazette de Québec* and *La Minerve*, early on warned of the danger that emigration mania, caused by the lure of the United States, posed for the country. The government studied the problem and in 1849 and 1857 published reports prepared by special committees of the Legislative Assembly. Although the reports successfully identified the real causes of emigration, its scope, and its severity, they failed to persuade the government of the need to create programs that could effectively stem the rising tide of departures.

Toward a Permanent Settlement (1860-1880)

Despite the Civil War, the economic crisis, and the repatriation campaign in the 1870s, emigration, which until then had been only temporary, became permanent during the years 1860-1880.

At the beginning of the 1860s, in an atmosphere laden with uncertainty and filled with the echoes of bloody battles, there was a lull in the exodus from Québec. The Civil War, which had then just begun, was to last for nearly five years. Either in search of adventure or attracted by recruitment bonuses, some 20,000—the exact figure is unknown, and some historians have put the figure as high as 40,000—French Canadians enlisted as volunteers, especially in the Union Army. Some braved the wrath of Canada's civil and ecclesiastical leaders and emigrated in order to enlist. Others, who were already in this country, joined the ranks of those battalions in which French was the predominant language. Two of the best known Canadians in uniform were the young Calixa Lavallée, the future composer of "O Canada," that country's national anthem, and Rémi Tremblay, the author of *Un Revenant* (1884), a fictional account of his adventures as a cavalryman.

While the agricultural crisis continued in Québec, an entirely different economic situation developed after 1863 in the United States, where a shortage of mill workers favored the immigrants. Once peace had been restored, this worker shortage was felt in all employment sectors, the war having claimed hundreds of thousands of victims. Freed at last from wartime constraints, industry again began to expand. The American West also helped create jobs in the mills by attracting Anglo-Americans who preferred the life of the pioneer to that of the factory worker.

This industrial revival led to feverish activity in New England. There was construction everywhere: mills, canals, railroads, houses. In Québec, the good news was carried from village to village by recruiters from the textile companies as well as by the immigrants themselves, happy to announce that the age-old sufferings of the Québec farmer could at last come to an end in the mills of New England. Industry became increasingly diversified, and seasonal employment was available, especially in brickyards and lumber camps.

The postwar emigration out of Québec showed several signs of widening as well as deepening. Emigrant families were larger, and more of them than ever before were seeking to settle permanently. And, an important fact for the advancement of the group, the educated classes joined the workers on the road to exile. Henceforth, as the French-Canadian presence in New England became increasingly multidimensional, immigrants were absorbed into a more structured environment. For instance, there was virtually uninterrupted contact with Canada through the clergy and members of religious orders—born and bred in Canada—as well as through Canadian newspapers and French-Canadian emigrant journalists, influenced, for quite some time, by their Québec counterparts.

The period of institutional establishment began around 1870. These institutions were so numerous that they have yet to be completely inventoried. There was an immense burgeoning of organizations as parishes and societies were founded. No less impressive than their number was the spirit which they embodied.

The immigrants worked in such close collaboration that the next half-century could well be called the age of solidarity. Naturally, some of them, albeit a minority, refused to join in the common endeavor. What is undeniable, however, is the enthusiasm with which the vast majority of immigrants worked for the common good, each according to his own ability. Workers, shopkeepers, and tradesmen were ready to support the professionals who assumed responsibility for the social and cultural advancement of the group. As the number of immigrants grew, population centers from Lewiston, Maine, to Waterbury, Connecticut, would come to include a physician, a lawyer, a dentist, a pharmacist, many small businessmen, and often even a journalist. One of these, Dr. Louis Martel, became the acknowledged leader in Lewiston; in Woonsocket, it was Dr. Gédéon Archambault; and in Worcester, it was Ferdinand Gagnon, known as the "father" of Franco-American journalism whose influence was felt throughout New England.

In each village, town, and city, the *curé* (pastor) was at the apex of the social pyramid. Around 1870 the Bishops of Québec no longer viewed New England as a land of iniquity, to which it was hardly worth the trouble of sending priests. Religious authorities now understood that priests were urgently needed there. Still, the most effective spokesman for this initiative was not a Canadian but a Breton, Louis Joseph de Goësbriand (1816-1899), Bishop of Burlington since 1853. He was among the first to realize that immigration would be permanent and that, without French-speaking priests, immigrants would abandon their religion. In 1854, he went to Canada in an attempt to obtain priests. But the Canadian episcopate did not agree with "*Monseigneur de Burlington*," as he was then called. The following year he journeyed to his native Brittany and brought back seven missionaries. Soon these priests were gathering congregations wherever a chapel could be improvised. They said masses and administered the sacraments in homes and in barns. Though these surroundings were less than ideal, they nevertheless served to keep the practice of religion alive, and before long, parishes were being founded. In 1869 Bishop de Goësbriand again approached his colleagues in the Canadian episcopate, and this time he was successful. Believing that there might be as many as a half-million Canadian immigrants, he issued an impassioned appeal for priests of their own nationality. Published in *Le Protecteur canadien* in Saint Albans, Vermont, on May 13, 1869, this important article would become the doctrinal basis not only for religious separatism, but also for French-Canadian *messianisme* in America, topics to be treated later. An extract from the document reads as follows:

> In this astonishing immigration, Divine Providence, which rules the world, has designs which are hidden from us. Let it do its work. It will know how to bring good out of what we take to be evil. We believe that these immigrants are called by God to cooperate in the conversion of America, just as their ancestors were called to implant the faith on the banks of the St. Lawrence. But no matter what Providence intends, we must come to the aid of our dear *immigrés*, a multitude of people who have settled outside their homeland. . . . It is part of God's providential plan that, in general, nations be evangelized by apostles who speak their language and who understand their habits and predispositions; it is God's plan that they be evangelized by priests of their own kind.

"We believe that these immigrants are called by God to cooperate in the conversion of America. . . " is an astonishing statement given the poverty and lack of education of these men and women, but others—bishops, priests, laymen—echoed the thought, and the messianic tradition would survive in New England into the 1960s. Bishop de Goësbriand was both an idealist and a realist. Wiser, shrewder, and more compassionate toward the immigrants than most of his contemporaries, he clearly saw that the Church would be a great comfort to newcomers in their struggle to adapt to a new environment. Moreover, he realized all too well that if the Church failed to act, it would suffer the irreparable loss of some 500,000 immigrants already settled in the United States, as well as those who would follow them into exile along with all of their descendants. The stakes were high, but Bishop de Goësbriand persuaded the skeptics, and so the Canadian Church established itself in the United States so firmly that its influence would be felt well into the next century.

The stimulus given in Vermont would soon gather momentum and spread throughout New England. Although this period of the 1870s was not yet that of the cathedral churches, it was the era of the wooden ones, as plain as they were numerous. After 1900, once the immigrants were more firmly entrenched in their new environment, many of the wooden churches would be replaced by more impressive structures.

But why duplicate the efforts of the Irish-Americans whose parishes were also proliferating in the same region? The answer to this question is a complex one, and it goes beyond the notion of *messianisme*. One very practical problem was language: the immigrants barely understood English. It was impossible for them to communicate, even in a most rudimentary way, with a clergy that spoke only English. Then there was the old concept of the Canadian parish, firmly rooted in the Canadian collective psyche. In nineteenth-century French Canada, the parish was an organic whole, the mainstay of social organization.

It was nearly as essential for every Catholic as was the family for each of its members, or the *rang*—a rural subdivision—for each farmer. The parish was an integral part of the immigrant's mindset and that of his children. And it remained so for almost a century, as subsequent religious conflicts would clearly demonstrate.

This traditional notion of the parish also included a body of cultural practices that would only gradually disappear. For example, the *curé* was not only the spiritual leader of his flock but was also their confidant, the one whom they consulted before making important decisions. For his part, the *curé* understood the souls entrusted to him. He knew that his parishioners preferred the well-defined system of tithing to the "Irish system," with its disconcerting number of collections. He knew, too, that even in America, they would continue to cherish their plain chant, which the Irish did not use, and the pomp of religious ceremonies, which the Irish tended to avoid. The Irish did so out of consideration for the puritanism of the Yankees and to allay the latters' fears of a papal takeover of the United States. Finally, the Canadian *curé* could comprehend, perhaps better than anyone else, why the immigrants were sometimes tempted to burn an Irish pastor in effigy as they actually had done in Woonsocket, Rhode Island, around 1873.

A number of these priests have taken their place in history, both as parish builders and as *patriotes*. Whether or not one shares their religious convictions, their contribution to the sociocultural development of the people remains noteworthy.

—Rev. André-Marie Garin, Oblate of Mary Immaculate (1822-1895). A native of France, he founded, in 1868, Saint Joseph of Lowell, the first French-Canadian parish in the Boston diocese. In just three weeks, this persuasive leader was able to raise $3500 from his parishioners to buy a church. And this was in 1868! He later built the church and school for Lowell's Immaculate Conception parish and, simultaneously, the cathedral-like church of Saint Jean Baptiste, also in Lowell. He is credited with a host of achievements, including the building of several other churches, even Irish ones.

—Rev. Louis Gagnier (1830-1908). With the permission of his ordinary, Bishop Ignace Bourget, he left Montréal in 1869 to work among the New England immigrants. From 1869 to 1875, he founded eleven parishes in Vermont and Western Massachusetts, including his major achievement, Saint Joseph parish in Springfield, Massachusetts, in 1873. He is rightly credited for having established New England's first Franco-American school in East Rutland, Vermont, in 1869.

—Rev. Pierre Hévey (1831-1910). Born in Saint-Jude, Saint-Hyacinthe County, Québec, he founded Saints Pierre et Paul in Lewiston, Maine, in 1871 and established Maine's first Franco-American school. He moved on to Manchester, New Hampshire, where, under his leadership, the new Sainte Marie Parish (1880) became one of the most successful in the region. This priest-pioneer, a first-rate organizer and administrator, founded in both Lewiston and Manchester an impressive number of institutions—schools, an orphanage, a hospital, and several religious societies—that encouraged the spiritual, social, and cultural development of his immigrant compatriots. This "human dynamo" was the first Franco-American priest to be named an Apostolic Protonotary in 1890.

—Rev. Charles Dauray (1838-1931). Born in Marieville, Québec, he came to Rhode Island in 1872 "to recuperate" and stayed for fifty-eight years. After having founded the parish of Notre Dame du Sacré Coeur in Central Falls (1873), he moved to Woonsocket to found Précieux Sang in 1875, where he served as pastor for fifty-six years.

—Rev. Pierre-Jean-Baptiste Bédard (1842-1884). A native of Saint-Rémi d'Iberville, Québec, he arrived in Fall River in July of 1874 accompanied by his friend Father Dauray, who said to him, "Bédard, here is your kingdom." He founded Our Lady of Lourdes, which became one of the largest "Canadian" parishes in southern New England. This consummate priest-patriot, in his ethnic zeal, provoked many conflicts with his bishop. This mesmerizing individual is also remembered for the constant concern he displayed for the immigrants as he helped them find housing and jobs.

—Rev. Jean-Baptiste-Henri-Victor Millette (1842-1917). Born in Sainte-Anne-de-Yamachiche, Québec, this cleric is recognized as the real founder of the parish of Saint Louis de Gonzague in Nashua, New Hampshire. Appointed pastor in 1871, he led the parish out of its early difficulties into a period of prosperity. He is credited with a host of good works including an orphanage and a hospital. His pastorate spanned fifty-five years.

—Rev. Joseph-Augustin Chevalier (1843-1929). A native of L'Assomption, Québec, he arrived in Manchester, New Hampshire, in 1871. For about ten years he was the only "Canadian" priest in the city and New Hampshire's first French-speaking pastor. In 1871 he founded the parish of Saint Augustin which he headed until 1924 when, after having served as pastor for fifty-three years and two months, he resigned for health reasons. His biographer has described him as "the quiet and unfailing defender and protector of the rights of his people."

The immigrants preserved the parish spirit and founded new ones as soon as they were numerous enough to do so. This feeling was so ingrained that even a century later it is still an astonishing feat, especially considering the constant struggles with the hierarchy which accompanied the founding of many of the 150 "national" parishes for French-Canadian immigrants from 1850 to the 1930s. Since there is no extant documentary evidence, no one knows what specifically motivated the immigrants in their relentless efforts to establish separate parishes. Nothing suggests that they acted exclusively, or even primarily, out of fear of their own clergy's wrath, although pastors were well-known for their authoritarian attitude. In truth, the circumstances in Burlington's Saint Joseph parish would be repeated so often that the only hypothesis which explains the people's behavior in this religious matter is that of a deep, albeit simple and medieval-like, religious faith.

At Saint Joseph in Burlington, as elsewhere, immigrants of Irish descent arrived before the Canadians. So, in spite of their linguistic and cultural differences, both groups belonged to the same parish until there were enough Canadians to form a separate one. Despite the fact that the Irish feared the loss of funds which the parish needed if it was to progress, the Canadians pushed ahead and bought property. The Irish immediately objected. The Canadians purchased another site, built a church, and in June 1851 dedicated it to Saint Joseph. It was under such circumstances that the French-Canadian immigrants, in 1850, founded their first parish in New England. It should also be noted that even older parishes existed in the Madawaska region of northern Maine. Similar obstacles and difficulties would often arise again.

As soon as a parish was established, the first priority was to find a building in which to worship. In some places a hall was rented; in others, a Protestant church was purchased and alterations were made; in still others, where feasible, a church was soon under construction. The second task was to establish a bilingual parochial school, so as to avoid at all costs attendance at public or even Irish parochial schools. As the essayist Edmond de Nevers, himself an immigrant to Central Falls, Rhode Island, stated, ". . . it is especially in school that the immigrant's son learns that his race is contemptible and that his parents are vulgar; it is there that he begins to be ashamed of their name and to hate anything that reminds him of his native land." Moreover, in 1875 the Vatican, with some allowance for exceptional situations, condemned attendance at public schools.

The need to open Catholic schools explains the massive influx of the French-Canadian religious teaching orders into New England. Early on, certain pastors had anticipated the urgent need for women religious teachers. The Sisters of Saint Anne were in Oswego, New York, as early as 1866, and the Sisters of the Holy Names of Jesus and Mary were in East Rutland, Vermont, around 1869. During the 1870s, the following religious communities were established in New England: in Lewiston, the Gray Nuns from Saint Hyacinthe; in St. Johnsbury, the Dames de la Congrégation; and in Fall River, the Religious of Jesus and Mary.

Leaving their Canadian province, the Oblates of Mary Immaculate were the first religious order of men to arrive in New England. As of 1868, the influence of their parish mission program extended beyond their own parish, St. Joseph in Lowell, and into several other centers. Over the next several decades, Dominicans, Marists, and others arrived as well.

In addition to churches, schools, and fraternal benefit societies, which will be discussed below, French-language newspapers formed part of that ensemble of activities devoted primarily to *la survivance*. Throughout the century, from its earliest years in the 1860s to its decline in the 1960s, Franco-American journalism would ardently protect and defend the faith, the French language, and the traditions of French Canada. Franco-American immigrant newspapers, much like their precursor, which Ludger Duvernay had founded in 1839 in Burlington, were militant from the outset. In 1869, for example, it was a St. Albans newspaper, *Le Protecteur canadien,* that published Bishop de Goësbriand's public appeal for a French-Canadian clergy. This brand of journalism was as devoted to protestation as it was to news, if not more so.

In close collaboration with clergymen, who had often been their classmates in Québec's classical colleges, journalists waged an endless battle for the founding and, subsequently, for the preservation of "national" parishes that would be administered by priests of Canadian origin. In its role as "national guardian," the press, often with the assistance of the Saint-Jean-Baptiste Societies that were being founded almost everywhere at this same time combated assimilation in all of its guises.

If Ludger Duvernay is the precursor, Ferdinand Gagnon is seen as the founder of Franco-American journalism. Born in Saint-Hyacinthe, Québec, on June 8, 1849, he attended the local seminary before emigrating to New Hampshire in 1868 at the age of nineteen. A precocious leader, he was soon busy giving speeches in support of Canadian independence and founding French-language newspapers. In 1869 he moved to Worcester, married Malvina Lalime, and the year after, founded a newspaper, *L'Étendard national*, which the following year became the American edition of Montréal's *L'Opinion publique*. Its obvious goal was to maintain "constant communication" between the "exiles" and the people at home.

In 1874 this "communication" assumed a special dimension due to some articles in *Le Foyer canadien*, which Ferdinand Gagnon and his associate, Frédéric Houde, had founded in 1873. In its July 21 and 28 issues, this paper published a summary of the history of the Métis community in western Canada which Louis Riel had presented to an immigrant audience during a trip through Worcester. Riel had quietly recounted the major events that marked the evolution of his people, men and women of mixed French and North American Indian blood. On behalf of his oppressed countrymen, he had appealed for protection from "France's eldest daughter," the Province of Québec. Below is an excerpt from Frédéric Houde's editorial:

> One could not have spoken more sensibly, more to the point, more tactfully, nor more wisely at one and the same time. Mr. Riel is not an orator who uses grand words or high-flown rhetoric. With unerring accuracy, he gets right to the point. He expresses himself correctly and easily. In short, he is an entertaining and interesting speaker. But when he began to speak of the mission of the French-Canadian people, his voice and demeanor, until then calm and composed, became noticeably more animated. Here was a man moved by conviction and overwhelmed by emotion, so profoundly did the subject matter stir the very heartstrings of this son of Canada and of Catholicism.

Without a doubt, 1874 was a banner year in Franco-American history. In addition to Louis Riel's visit to Worcester and the Société St.-Jean-Baptiste's anniversary meeting in Montréal, attended by thousands of Franco-Americans, the year marked the founding of *Le Travailleur*, Ferdinand Gagnon's foremost journalistic endeavor, the one to which he devoted all of his fiery energy until his untimely death in 1886. A truly national newspaper for the immigrants, *Le Travailleur* was published for the first time on October 16, 1874. Its motto would become: *"Fais ce que dois."* (Do what you must).

"The old *Travailleur*," as Gagnon affectionately called it, lasted until 1892, a remarkably long time for that period. It dealt with all the important issues of the day, particularly repatriation and naturalization. On these issues, Ferdinand Gagnon wanted everyone to take a stand, either for or against. A Franco-American before his time, he pleaded with his readers to participate fully in the political life of their new country so as to avoid becoming permanently marginalized.

His death on April 15, 1886, was observed as a day of "national" mourning and elicited the following comments from a fellow immigrant journalist, Godfroy de Tonnancour:

Like Raphael and Mozart, Mr. Gagnon has died at the age of thirty-six. He, too, was an artist, an artist of the mind. His thoughts were sculpted out of the granite of duty and devotion, his works modeled on those of Christ.
. . .

Few Canadians, either in the United States or in Canada, could match his oratorical skills. He had a strong and pleasant voice that spoke directly to the heart. Due to his rousing and persuasive eloquence, Mr. Gagnon enjoyed several oratorical triumphs. . . .

As a writer, his reputation is secure. He wrote articles which had repercussions even in France. His style was compact, robust, lively, always clear and energetic. The profound philosophical lessons which he imparted with such simplicity in all his articles deserve to be pondered by all of us. (Belisle, *Histoire de la presse franco-américaine*, p.78)

Although far from complete, the following list of newspapers founded after the Civil War illustrates the range of journalistic activity just as emigration was becoming permanent:

1867—*Le Public canadien* was founded in New York by *l'Ordre des Dix*, an association campaigning for the independence of Canada. It can hardly be called a Franco-American paper since the editors considered the United States to be a "foreign country." The editor, Jean-Baptiste-A. Paradis would move on to found *L'Étoile du Nord* in Saint Paul, Minnesota, in 1870. *Le Public canadien* lasted ten months.

1868—Founded in St. Albans by Antoine Moussette and Rev. Zéphirin Druon, vicar-general of the diocese of Burlington, *Le Protecteur canadien* carried Bishop de Goësbriand's appeal for a national clergy. The paper lasted until 1871. Its motto was: "Love God and go your own way."

1869—There were only four or five issues of *L'Idée nouvelle* founded in Burlington by Médéric Lanctôt. Its primary concern was Canada's independence.

1871—*L'Avenir national*, founded in St. Albans by Antoine Moussette and Frédéric Houde, dealt with immigrant issues. It had a tumultuous existence, in part because one of the editors was generally considered to be a non-believer. This newspaper appeared until 1876.

1873—*L'Écho du Canada*, with its Boston and Lowell editions, was founded in Fall River by Doctor Alfred Mignault and Honoré Beaugrand. Naturalization and the national societies were among the most frequently discussed topics. It was last published in 1875.

1875—Of all the newspapers of that era, *Le Jean-Baptiste* lasted the longest. Founded in Northampton, Massachusetts, by Pierre-C. Chatel and M. Burleigh, it changed hands frequently. Finally, in 1894, it was moved to Pawtucket, Rhode Island, where it remained until its demise in 1933.

1875—*La Lanterne magique* was a short-lived humorous newspaper founded by Doctor J.-N.-O. Provencher in Worcester.

1875—*Le Journal des Dames* was founded in Cohoes, New York, by Virginie Authier. Presumably, it was the only publication intended for a female audience prior to the *Bulletin de la Fédération féminine franco-américaine* (1953-1991). It survived for six months.

1875—*La République* was founded in both Fall River and Boston by Honoré Beaugrand. This is where he published his novel, *Jeanne la fileuse*, the first fictional account of the emigration. The paper ceased publication in 1878.

Although a great many newspapers were founded around this time, often as not their existence proved to be ephemeral. These were times of such high hopes and aspirations that, in the years 1873-1876 alone, twenty French-Canadian newspapers were founded.

Much the same can be said of the charitable organizations and mutual benefit societies at whose meetings the issues of patriotism and *la survivance* were also often discussed. In some areas, these organizations predated the Canadian parish, and they lobbied in support of the founding of such parishes. As early as 1848, there was a Société Jacques-Cartier in St. Albans, Vermont, and a Société Saint-Jean-Baptiste in Malone, New York. In 1850, in New York City, Gabriel Franchère presided at the founding of the first American Société Saint-Jean-Baptiste. These groups, modeled on Montréal's Société Saint-Jean-Baptiste, founded in 1834 by Ludger Duvernay, would come and go in succession with no apparent loss of interest. In 1869, when there were seventeen of these societies, their leaders sought to federate them in order to enhance their social, economic, and political influence, but this dream would be realized only at the end of the nineteenth century.

While seeking primarily to care for widows and orphans, these mutual aid societies also pursued fraternal, social, and patriotic goals. Meetings were devoted to fraternizing but also to bickering, all the more so when everyone knew everyone else by name. It was here that one could find the "model member," the one who reveled in meetings with their discussions, their minutes, and their motions "made and duly seconded." The type is only just beginning to die out.

Among the many needs filled by these societies was that of ethnic solidarity. Membership was restricted to Catholics of French, i.e., French-Canadian descent, and remained so for over a century. This reflected the wishes of a clergy seeking to protect its flock from Anglo-American secret societies whose dangers had already been expounded upon as early as 1872 by Rev. T.-A. Chandonnet in his book entitled, *Notre-Dame-des-Canadiens et les Canadiens français des États-Unis.*

These societies soon assumed other responsibilities, particularly the annual celebration of Saint John the Baptist Day. In 1868, the

Oblate Father Garin wrote from Lowell to his religious superior: "Our little celebration of Saint John the Baptist was a success. Everything went well, no hard liquor and no fights." The practice spread. In 1868 there were impressive celebrations held in St. Albans, Vermont, and Watertown, New York, as well as in Lowell and Worcester, Massachusetts, among other cities. The Worcester celebration, featuring a parade of 800 Canadians, was the object of a lengthy report by Ferdinand Gagnon, reprinted by Alexandre Belisle in his *Histoire de la presse franco-américaine*. One comment in particular reveals a great deal about the mentality of the period, a comment that, in its own way, was the highest possible compliment: "It was just like in Canada."

La Saint-Jean was observed throughout New England. As soon as there were enough fellow countrymen, a solemn high mass was celebrated, followed by a stately procession of society members with their insignia and their badges, ending with an evening of fun and music. Pomp and ceremony were highly prized, and there was much discussion over the banners, the marching bands, and of course, over the choice of the child selected to portray *le petit Saint-Jean-Baptiste*. This is how Richard Santerre sums up Lowell's 1872 celebration:

> The Société Saint-Jean-Baptiste and the Union Saint-Joseph joined in celebrating the feast of the patron saint with a picnic sponsored by the various *Saint-Jean-Baptiste* societies at Spaulding Grove near Nashua and Merrimack, New Hampshire. On Monday, June 24, at 9:30 A.M., 800 members from the two organizations, accompanied by two marching bands, paraded to the Middlesex Street station on their way to Nashua. Once there, they were joined by delegates from Marlboro, Haverhill, and Nashua, and all then marched through the main streets of the city before going to the picnic grounds.

Societies organized other activities which were aimed more at the élite, like the mass meetings which they called "general conventions." From 1865 to 1901, there were about twenty such meetings to which organizations sent their delegates to discuss issues of concern to all

French-Canadian immigrants from New England to the Midwest. These meetings were held in different places and with varying frequency. The first was held in New York in 1865, the fourth in Detroit in 1869, and in the 1870s the movement reached its zenith with nine conventions.

It is obvious that a family spirit linked the immigrants of the East with those of the Midwest. As members of the same ethnic group, they felt the need to come together, to support one another, and to stand shoulder to shoulder in the battle against assimilation—viewed by them as a loss of identity, or even as a betrayal—and to reminisce about the homeland.

When the time came for Confederation, Canada's future appeared uncertain, and the more recent immigrants worried about it. Hence the many newspaper articles and speeches on the possible annexation of Québec by the United States, on Canadian independence, and on repatriation. Talk of repatriation gave rise to its corollary: naturalization. There was a continual insistence on the need to settle either on one side of the border or the other so as to avoid what Ferdinand Gagnon called "social hermaphroditism." Since most people seemed to want to settle in the United States, albeit without totally committing themselves, naturalization was usually recommended over repatriation. And despite all the campaigns advocating repatriation, the results always fell below expectations.

Fortunately, Félix Gatineau compiled a voluminous *Histoire des conventions générales des Canadiens français aux États-Unis*, a treasure trove of information on these nineteenth-century immigrants. These reports reveal in great detail the penchant of the educated class for solemn masses, banquets, concerts, and dances. They also reflect the seriousness of purpose, social awareness, and sense of responsibility with which this élite sought to serve the people. Far from scorning or forgetting ordinary folks, these men were keenly aware that one of their most important duties was to guide and educate them, and to help them materially by assisting the poor, as well as morally and culturally by raising their sights. This is how we must understand even the most high-sounding speeches: on the merits of temperance, frugality, and education; on the need to purchase life insurance; on the pressing duty to support "Franco-American" newspapers. Another aspect of the then-current mentality was also revealed when, for example, Ferdinand Gagnon deplored the "denigrating spirit" of some leaders and the the jealousy which he claimed was "the cause of our unfortunate divisiveness."

"National" parishes, French-language newspapers, patriotic organizations, general conventions, these were some of the many social forces working constantly to renew the ties with Canada. With almost every passing year, this infrastructure was being strengthened by immigration while the élite followed, on a day-to-day basis, the political, economic, and cultural evolution of the homeland.

Canada occupied a special place in the minds of these expatriates. Some events, like the first Riel Affair, strengthened the emotional bonds on both sides of the border. It cannot be ascertained at present that the people were as profoundly affected as were the members of the educated class, but the latter were gripped by the Riel story right up to its tragic conclusion. Canadian newspapers in the United States carried detailed accounts of each episode of this life-and-death struggle. On June 2, 1874, Ferdinand Gagnon published in his *Foyer canadien* a letter from an eyewitness in Saint Paul, Minnesota:

> The esteemed Louis Riel, the brave champion of the rights of our co-religionists and compatriots in the Northwest, is visiting with us these days. On Pentecost Sunday, we saw him approach the altar and receive communion with a reverence and piety that even a non-believer might find edifying. He honored me with a visit to my home. He appears to be in good health. His conversation is spirited and shows not the slightest trace

of discouragement. He can be seen at mass every morning. . . . He is said to be utterly devoted to the cause of his unfortunate compatriots.

Riel would again be the topic of discussion at the mass meeting in Montréal on June 24, 1874. Montréal's Société Saint-Jean-Baptiste, wishing to highlight the celebration of its fortieth anniversary, issued a call to "our brothers in the United States." It was answered by 18,000 of these loyal brothers, including marching bands and representatives from a number of Saint-Jean-Baptiste Societies. Without a doubt, the 1874 "gathering of the clan" marked the high point in the history of Franco-American/French-Canadian relations.

This memorable celebration, an "explosion of brotherhood," attracted many distinguished personalities. Among them were Ferdinand Gagnon, whose rhetorical talents were uniquely suited to such grand occasions; Judge Joseph Le Boeuf of Cohoes, N.Y., known as "the Chapleau of the United States" [The lawyer, Sir Joseph-Adolphe Chapleau (1840-98), became premier of Québec and lieutenant governor of the province]; Honoré Beaugrand, novelist of the emigration movement and future mayor of Montréal; Major Edmond Mallet, hero of the Civil War; and members of the clergy, including their future dean, Father Charles Dauray, of Woonsocket, Rhode Island.

Because the Riel Affair had become so politicized in Canada, it was impossible for the delegates in Montréal to reach a consensus during the debates of the 1874 convention. Some argued in favor of amnesty for Riel, whereas others opposed it. The Americans favored amnesty, but the debate turned acrimonious, and the discussions became so entangled that, in the ensuing confusion, the assembly was unable to adopt any resolution on the issue.

Ferdinand Gagnon returned home to share his joy and his pride with his "brothers in the United States," exclaiming: "Praise be to all of you, patriots of June 24, 1874!" And there would be yet another reason for him to feel proud when, during a July visit by Riel to Worcester, its citizens adopted resolutions in favor of granting amnesty to the Métis, Riel's people. A guest of Rev. Jean-Baptiste Primeau, pastor of Notre Dame des Canadiens, Riel was so well received by his compatriots that he returned to visit them once again in December 1874. There were more meetings and speeches following another equally enthusiastic welcome.

When Louis Riel arrived in Worcester in December 1875, he did so in unhappy circumstances. He had suffered a mental breakdown while visiting Major Mallet in Washington. Mallet decided to take him to the asylum at Longue-Pointe in Québec. Along the way, he stopped to visit his friend Father Primeau who, at that time, had as his guest Honoré Mercier, the future Premier of Québec, who had come to Worcester to deliver a lecture. To date, researchers have not been able to find any details of this historic meeting; but it is scarcely conceivable that no one would have made a record of what was practically a mini-summit of the leaders of French-speaking North America. And it is just as unthinkable that Ferdinand Gagnon did not drop by Father Primeau's rectory to welcome the visitors. What we do know is that when Louis Riel and Major Mallet resumed their journey to Canada, they did so by way of Suncook, New Hampshire, and Keeseville, New York, a rather puzzling itinerary unless one remembers that Mallet had influential friends in these places.

Canada was also present in the lives of the emigrants as a result of the appeals it launched for their return, appeals that became more pressing in the decade from 1870 to 1880. Viewed as a patriotic solution to a serious demographic problem, the repatriation campaign was discussed by the group's leaders at general conventions and in newspapers. The people also talked about it, and several hundred of them answered the call by returning to Canada. Some were encouraged to do so by Ferdinand Gagnon himself who, in 1875, had been appointed a repatriation agent by the Québec government. He resigned the following year, apparently discouraged by the indifference of the vast majority.

Debated at length, repatriation was still of interest to a small percentage of the population, at least until the 1930s. Due to Québec's proximity, some continued to travel back and forth. The repatriation campaigns succeeded in deepening Canada's influence on the daily lives of the people, and by recruiting a few brave colonists the effort sought to counteract the flood tide of loss of its people. By discouraging naturalization, the campaigns may also have delayed assimilation, since repatriation efforts worked to the advantage of *la survivance*.

A New Nationalism (1880-1900)

The collective life of the immigrants between 1880 and 1900 evolved during a period of phenomenal growth that extended from 1870 to around 1910. A virtually uninterrupted flow of immigrants swelled the numbers of Quebecers and Acadians in the Northeast. Along with this growth in population, there was a remarkable increase in the number of supporting institutions: parishes, newspapers, as well as many diverse organizations.

This period of growth was also, at least for the professional classes, one of conflict over what could be called the "nationalist question." The most spectacular of these ethnoreligious clashes erupted during the 1880s and reached a climax with the Sentinelle Affair (1923-1929), which will be discussed in the next chapter. Accounts of these confrontations and of what was always at stake—the establishment and administration of ethnic French-language parishes—have dominated Franco-American historiography.

Another conflict, more muted and less dramatic, developed especially after 1880 and lasted into the 1960s. It pitted the supporters of *la survivance* against those favoring Americanization. But it was rare for these foes to clash openly. For example, an individual might simply anglicize his name, enter it on the roles of an Irish parish, and with barely a nod to his ethnicity, disappear along with his progeny from the "Canadian" scene.

For almost a century, the debate over the ethnic question, with its discussion of *survivance* versus assimilation, together with notions of individual and group identity, would consume a great deal of energy, or so it seemed. In fact, it consumed less and less. As the number of *patriotes* diminished with each passing year, the ties to Canada slowly weakened, and the very memory of the great migration was almost entirely lost.

Between 1880 and 1900, a new nationalism arose among the immigrants. Leaders insisted more and more on the need for a dual allegiance: allegiance to Canada, of course, but to the adopted country as well, since loyalty to one did not exclude loyalty to the other. Ferdinand Gagnon epitomized this new attitude in his call for "naturalization without assimilation." Naturalization clubs were established here and there, and an increasing number of immigrants became citizens. Once naturalized, they acquired the right to vote and participate in American political life either by running for office or, as did the enterprising Benjamin Lenthier with his chain of newspapers in the 1890s, by supporting Yankee candidates.

But Canada remained very much present in the lives of the immigrants, and it did so in various ways. Though fewer than in 1874, a goodly number of "Canadians from the States"—both from the Midwest and New England—responded to Québec City's invitation to take part in the 1880 celebration of Saint John the Baptist Day. Most of the notables attending took an active part in the discussions. They included Rev. Pierre-J.-B. Bédard, the *curé-patriote* from Fall River; Major Edmond Mallet, a senior Washington official; the young and promising Hugo Dubuque, the future judge from Fall River; Gédéon Archambault, the indomitable Woonsocket physician; the well-known journalists Léon Bossue and Benjamin Lenthier. However, had there been a prize for oratory, it would most certainly have been awarded to Ferdinand Gagnon.

In his address, he began by praising the accomplishments of his immigrant countrymen:

> When they compared the glittering prosperity of the United States to the humble appearance of our Canadian hamlets, they had every reason in the world to become Americans and forget Canada. But just the opposite occurred. At the call of their leaders and their journalists and with the clergy's cooperation, our compatriots in the United States, united in their patriotism, have banded together to strengthen the bonds of their nationality. . . . At the call of their priests, they have built Canadian churches as beautiful and as sumptuous as the temples of wealthy Protestant sects. These humble craftsmen have formed literary societies; carpenters, whose ears are more attuned to the pounding of heavy hammers and the noisy tools of their trade, have joined musical organizations. And that's not all they have done. In some places they have even built convents, and the movement continues to spread. And all of this they have done without wealth, but with their sacrifices born of devotion.

After this glowing report about his compatriots in the U.S., Gagnon complained about their treatment by their former countrymen:

> During the past two days, in both Montréal and in Québec, I have been speaking with educated men: priests and physicians. But no one here knows the names of our parishes; no one thinks about us. The Province of Québec is forgetting its children living in exile. When the Canadian press does mention the emigrants, it is only to note their departure from the country. No one worries about us or cares about our achievements or our efforts to remain Canadians.

In a final exhortation, Gagnon pleaded with his countrymen on both sides of the border:

> Let us love one another more and come to know each other better. On both sides of the 45th parallel, let us raise the banner of our nationality on high. And on it, let us inscribe the motto: "Union and Respect."

In 1882, the same Ferdinand Gagnon found himself pleading the cause of his people before another tribunal, that of the Commonwealth of Massachusetts, and in point of fact, that of American public opinion. This time, the theme was not the indifference of the mother country but the denigrating attitude of the adopted one. The episode has been remembered as that of the "Chinese of the Eastern States."

The 1881 Annual Report of the Massachusetts Bureau of Labor Statistics written by the bureau chief, Colonel Carroll D. Wright, contained three paragraphs about the ways in which Canadian immigrants were hindering efforts to improve working conditions. The reader can judge the negative tone and bias of the report from the following paragraph:

> With some exceptions, the Canadian French are the Chinese of the Eastern States. They care nothing for our institutions, civil, political, or educational. They do not come to make a home among us, to dwell with us as citizens, and so become a part of us; but their purpose is merely to sojourn a few years as aliens, touching us only at a single point, that of work, and, when they have gathered out of us what will satisfy their ends, to get them away to whence they came, and bestow it there.

Such a belittling of two ethnic groups revealed an unmitigated arrogance if not racism. True, immigration in 1881 had not yet achieved the permanence of the late 1880s and 1890s, but between 1850 and 1881, the immigrants had founded some forty parishes, a host of service organizations, and a number of newspapers. In addition to revealing the scorn felt by the Anglo-Americans vis-à-vis the immigrants, the report also showed just how much they felt exploited by foreigners who, in their opinion, had neither the decency nor the clearheadedness to recognize the advantages offered by the "civil, political, or educational institutions" of their adopted country, and who, moreover, refused to participate in a political and economic system deemed sacred to the Anglo-American élite—a system based on the Constitution of the United States, with its guarantees of "life, liberty and the pursuit of happiness" for everyone.

These Americans believed that the immigrants were weakening the country's institutions. And it is equally plausible that they were annoyed for another reason. By refusing to integrate into mainstream America, the immigrants were avoiding the control and social pressures of the dominant culture and seemed to be thumbing their noses at them. This kind of resistance is seldom tolerated by majority groups. The rest of the text seems to support this interpretation:

> They [the French Canadians] are a horde of industrial invaders, not a stream of stable settlers. They care nothing about voting with all that it implies. Rarely does one of them become naturalized.

These last three sentences should dispel any lingering doubts about what has been already stated: Anglo-Americans were appalled at the refusal of the Canadians to integrate into this young and booming country with so promising a future. But the Canadians themselves took a different view of the matter, and the report provoked a general outcry among them.

Journalists wasted little time in answering Colonel Wright, emotionally at first, but afterwards in a more balanced manner. After the protests in the newspapers and the resolutions adopted by various groups and assemblies, came the confrontation with Colonel Wright himself. The leaders agreed to organize a delegation of about sixty people who went to Boston on October 25, 1881, to respond to the charges. Among those banding together for this delicate and indispensable attempt at restoring the reputation of their people were Attorney Joseph-Henri Guillet of Lowell, J.-Misaël Authier, a journalist from Cohoes, New York, Rev. Pierre-J.-B. Bédard and Hugo Dubuque from Fall River, and, of course, Ferdinand Gagnon.

Armed with statistics compiled by Gagnon, the spokesmen reviewed the accomplishments of the Canadians: their parishes, their organizations, their newspapers, and their increasing involvement in the political life of their adopted country. Colonel Wright listened, conceded a few points, and promised that the 1882 report would offer a more balanced view. In fact, it would contain a retraction. But today, a century later, what is even more striking is the warning Colonel Wright gave to his Canadian audience on that 25th day of October in 1881. Among other things, he said:

> . . . you cannot at the same time be loyal Americans and loyal French Canadians. I am inclined to believe that the prejudices people have against French Canadians stem from their obvious determination to live a distinct national life in the midst of the Republic. If this same report which they condemn helps them to understand that becoming citizens in the full sense of the word means their progress and advancement, the Bureau will have rendered them the greatest possible service.

This struck at the very heart of both the ethnic question and the notion of group identity, at least from the Anglo-American point of view.

The issue of cultural separatism, with its goals and *modus operandi*, would remain controversial for the next hundred years. It would divide the Franco-Americans among themselves just as it had divided the Canadian immigrants from their children and from the Yankees as well as the Irish immigrants. The issue was of crucial importance, for the integration of the Canadians into American society hinged on its solution. Should they integrate or stand apart? If so, how far apart? Too few people grasped the full import of the words uttered by Colonel Wright on that October day in 1881. In fact, he was telling the representatives of the French-Canadian community that the immigrants were marginalizing themselves by remaining outside of the social and political mainstream of American life. What other conclusion could he draw? America was reaching out to talented people everywhere, and this group refused to respond.

Of course, Colonel Wright's analysis could have been more subtle. To deny that someone can be both a loyal American and a loyal Canadian is to ignore the fact that human beings evolve slowly, especially when emigrating from one culture to another. It also disallows the possibility that one's native culture can enhance the development of one's adopted country. Colonel Wright was too harsh, too rigid, and not enough of a psychologist. Franco-American history is replete with examples of individuals and groups who successfully integrated their American experience with their French-Canadian origins.

After having responded to Yankee prejudice against them, the Canadian immigrants soon had to confront an assimilationist episcopate in the Diocese of Providence, Rhode Island. The "Flint Affair"—named after the Fall River neighborhood in which it unfolded from 1884 to 1886—centered around the parish of Notre Dame de Lourdes where thousands of parishioners were in open opposition to their bishop, Thomas Hendricken. Rev. Pierre-J.-B. Bédard had repeatedly rejected the Irish curates whom the bishop had sought to impose on him. On August 24, 1884, this *curé-patriote* died, stricken by apoplexy, and his parish went into deep mourning. Even during his lifetime, he had become a legendary figure because of his deep concern for the material and spiritual well-being of his kinsmen and for his involvement in all the Canadian patriotic movements of his day.

Father Bédard's relationship with his ordinary had been strained in the extreme. Bishop Hendricken had found Rev. Bédard to be too patriotic and too little inclined to Americanize his parish. Was this not the *curé* who had had the audacity to adopt the Canadian parish system, permitted under Massachusetts law but forbidden by the Irish episcopate?

After the death of Rev. Bédard, the bishop attempted to impose, not just an Irish curate, but an Irish pastor, Father Samuel McGee! He had badly misjudged the attitude of the parishioners who were well aware that one of Rev. Bédard's dying wishes had been that the bishop name a Canadian priest to succeed him.

A delegation, led by Hugo Dubuque, met with the bishop to work out a solution, but this proved to be a waste of time. The bishop argued that in ten years time all the Canadians at Notre Dame de Lourdes—as well as everywhere else—would be speaking English. The delegates expressed their firm conviction that French was the guardian of their faith, but the bishop would hear nothing of the kind. And so the watchword went out to all the parishioners: reject the Irish pastor, and attend mass at one of the other Franco-American parishes in the city.

Father McGee eventually left the parish after having been treated rudely by some parishioners. He was replaced by another Irish pastor whom the Canadians also rejected. On February 13, 1885, the bishop imposed a ban on the parish; in response, the parishioners drafted an appeal to Rome. Pending Rome's decision, there were more meetings and more articles in the local newspapers. It was in the midst of this turmoil that on March 27, 1885, *L'Indépendant* was born. After serving as the vehicle for the struggle "in the Flint," it was destined to become one of the great Franco-American newspapers.

Already deeply troubled by these disturbances, Franco-American public opinion, in Fall River and throughout New England, was even further aroused by the arrest of Louis Riel whom the Ottawa government was planning to execute. In this frenzied atmosphere, a few Protestant pastors, including the apostate priest Charles Chiniquy, came to preach in Fall River, hoping to make some converts; but they were not very successful. Rémi Tremblay, a French-Canadian writer and journalist who had served in the Union Army during the Civil War, became editor of *L'Indépendant*. Along with Hugo Dubuque, he waged two battles: one for the pardon of Louis Riel and the other for a decision from Rome that would favor the French Canadians.

Hoping to restore calm in the Flint, the Sacred Congregation for the Propagation of the Faith announced a prudent and adroit decision. And peace did return when, in March of 1886, the bishop named Rev. Joseph Laflamme, who had been serving as its curate since December of 1885, as pastor of Notre Dame. Better yet, the assimilation campaign was suspended, and the Canadians had obviously won, since the very principle of the so-called national parish was preserved, not just for Canadians, but also for immigrants arriving in Fall River from southern and eastern Europe.

On the other hand, Riel's death sentence aroused furious opposition in all the Franco-American centers, in the Midwest as well as in the East. Canadians in the United States voiced their outrage in meetings, newspaper articles, and letters to the Ottawa government. A prescient Major Mallet uttered this prophecy: "If Riel is hanged, the children of his executioners will erect monuments to his memory." The execution by hanging of the leader of Canada's half-castes in Regina, Saskatchewan, on November 16, 1885, unleashed a series of indignant protests culminating in a resolution adopted at the general convention of Canadians in the United States held in Rutland, Vermont, in June

1886. Formulated by Major Mallet and unanimously approved by the delegates, the resolution stated:

> It is the duty of this Convention to intervene by declaring that it condemns and repudiates, in the strongest possible terms, the unjust and cruel behavior of the federal government of Canada towards our compatriots in the Northwest and, in particular, the judicial murder of Louis Riel which was carried out on 16 November 1885 by order of said Canadian government.

This resolution marked a red-letter day in the history of the spirit of solidarity that existed between Québec, the Canadian Northwest, the American Midwest, and the Eastern United States. Never again would there be a moment of such close collaboration among the continent's four major francophone regions.

As has been shown, the sources of nineteenth-century Franco-American history reveal much more about the educated class of Franco-Americans than about the people. This is why historians, in any synthesis of the current state of the knowledge of this period, must of necessity focus on the attitudes and accomplishments of the militant élite and attempt to trace the evolution of the institutions they founded between 1880 and 1900. Of all these institutions, only the general conventions had disappeared by the turn of the century, specifically by 1901.

The following list of topics proposed for discussion at the general convention held in Nashua, New Hampshire, in 1888 represents a typical agenda for these meetings. It reveals a great deal about the chief concerns of the intelligentsia from 1865 to 1901:

I - National Alliance

Would it be appropriate to establish a National Alliance of Franco-American groups in the United States? If so, on what foundations should such an alliance be constituted?

II - Educational Issues
How can we best guarantee the existence of our French Catholic schools in the United States while increasing their number? Would the adoption of the same curriculum and the reading of the same authors not be a powerful force for preserving the homogeneity of our ethnic group and guiding the minds and hearts of our young people toward the same end?

III - Information Center
The need for a centralized permanent clearinghouse for general information and statistics on Canadians having been recognized by previous Conventions and such a bureau becoming more necessary as a result of the constant increase in our population in the United States, has not the establishment of such an agency become a matter of urgency?

IV - Federation of Societies
What do the delegates think of the proposal to unite, by means of a powerfully constituted federation, all of our fraternal benefit societies in the United States?

V - Libraries and Lectures
In order to promote the enjoyment of reading and the love of learning among our compatriots, would it not be worthwhile to establish libraries and organize lecture series? Do the delegates have any practical suggestions to submit in this regard?

VI - Permanent Board

Would it not be helpful to name a Standing Committee to supervise the implementation of the various resolutions adopted by our Conventions?

VII - Naturalization
Can naturalization campaigns be made more effective? If so, how?

VIII - The Press
How can we best increase the influence of our newspapers as well as their chances of survival?

IX - The French Language
How can we best guarantee the preservation of the French language in our families?

(Félix Gatineau, *Historique*, pp. 239-240)

The general convention served as a crossroads for Franco-Americans from both East and West. It sought primarily to unite the immigrants in spite of the distances between them, distances which were considerable even by today's standards, for example, the 1400 miles between Minneapolis and Boston. This is one reason why geographical considerations were so important when, after having assembled at the designated convention site, the delegates allocated honorary functions and appointments. At Nashua in 1888, for example, when they named Father J. Goiffon of Centerville, Minnesota, Honorary Chaplain, it was in recognition of the candidate's age, his great merit, and the region he represented. When the secretary of the convention, Emile-H. Tardivel of Lewiston, introduced him to the assembly, he did so in the following manner:

The man whom you have just chosen as your Chaplain is no stranger to you, though this is his first National Convention. Monsieur Tassé writes of this missionary in *Canadians of the West*. He is the one whom the intrepid Nolette rescued from certain death in the snows of Minnesota, carrying him on his back to the opposite shore of the Red River. Father Goiffon is an historic figure, one who commands the respect of all Canadians, especially those in that part of the West where he has exercised his holy priesthood for over thirty years. He it is who, in 1859, placed the sacred host on the lips of Gabriel Dumont for the first time. [Dumont was the military commander of both the Métis and the Amerindians of Canada.] You could not have made a worthier nor a finer choice than this one. It pays the highest possible tribute to this venerable missionary who has grown old enduring the trials of the apostolate and has confronted death itself—his wooden leg is ample testimony of this—to bring the last rites to his compatriots and the Amerindians of his far-flung missions. (Gatineau, *Historique*, p. 253)

So it was that in June of 1888, in Nashua, one could hear the account of an entire chapter in the history of the French Canadians in the American Midwest.

The conventions also facilitated contact between French Canadians in the United States and those in Canada. Five hundred of the latter attended the 1882 Cohoes convention. Though not always so numerous, the delegations often included well-known men: among those speaking in Cohoes were Bishop Louis-François Laflèche of Trois-Rivières the author, journalist, and legislator, L.-O. David Faucher de Saint-Maurice, newspaper editor, author, and legislator and Honoré Mercier.

The highly symbolic participation of Canadian dignitaries at conventions that attracted primarily the élite had little effect on the daily lives of thousands of immigrants. But Canada itself was a dynamic presence in the lives of the people, sometimes through these influential leaders. One among them whom the immigrants—people and élite alike—held in the highest regard was Premier Honoré Mercier.

Mercier displayed a keen interest in the immigrants. A frequent visitor, he often defended them in the lengthy dispute over emigration. For example, at the celebration of Saint John the Baptist Day in Québec on June 24, 1889, he declared: "I visited New England and I have returned filled with enthusiasm, having seen well-dressed Canadian workers marching proudly in the Saint John the Baptist parade, ready to celebrate our national holiday with such pomp as to command the respect of other ethnic groups." Aware of the ill repute in which the immigrants were held by some of their countrymen who remained in Canada, he uttered his famous appeal: "Let us put an end to our fratricidal struggles! Let us unite!"

Responding to the ovation given him by the Canadian emigrants, Mercier appealed to their sense of history: "You must fight against great odds. Do not despair; you are in no worse a position than our fathers were under the military regime imposed on Canada after the country had been ceded." Even after he had left office, he remained very popular with the immigrants. He visited the various centers, advocating Canada's independence which, if the people so wished, could lead to annexation with the United States. Thus did he revive a long-standing debate.

Canada's presence in the daily lives of the immigrants also persisted in the parishes they continued to found in order to meet the needs of the more recent immigrants as well as those of the earlier settlers and their ever-increasing progeny. Whereas one part of the institutional framework, the factory, was a Yankee phenomenon, the church remained very Canadian, with its clergy born and bred in Canada; this would continue to be the case for quite some time.

As new parishes were being founded, some "old" parishes entered the second phase of their history; they had now acquired the means to replace their modest wooden chapels with impressive cathedral-like churches. Erected at the end of the nineteenth and at the beginning of the twentieth century, these buildings were the purest expression of the triumphalism that characterized the Catholic Church in Québec and, by extension, in New England. Often flanked by massive brick schools, sturdy rectories, and sometimes by well-designed convents, these churches were built by pastors whose business acumen was as well-developed as their piety.

The increase in the Canadian population in the United States and the development of religious institutions—schools and hospitals—required an ever-increasing number of priests, brothers, and sisters. Hence the arrival in New England's "Little Canadas" between 1868 and the beginning of the twentieth century of some thirty religious orders from Canada or France. Around 1890 for example, about forty parochial schools were being administered by sisters. These included the Sisters of Saint Anne, the Sisters of the Good Shepherd, the Sisters of the Presentation of Mary, the Grey Nuns, and the Sisters of the Holy Cross. The Marist Brothers could be found in the Lowell-Lawrence area where the missions of the Oblate Fathers were flourishing. In Lewiston and Fall River, the respective parishes of SS. Peter and Paul and St. Anne were staffed by the Dominicans. There has been no systematic study of these communities, neither of their educational activities, nor of their charitable work in orphanages, hospitals, and hospices. But what is certain is that for over a century they exerted a powerful influence on the lives of the immigrants and their descendants.

The presence of Canada in the lives of the immigrants was also revealed in their repeated and insistent requests for Canadian priests and bilingual parochial schools. During the 1890s, these demands provoked new conflicts between Canadian parishioners and Irish bishops in several New England areas. In Danielson, Connecticut, for example, the immigrants refused to accept the La Salette Fathers whom the bishop tried to impose on them: they were French and considered to be as assimilationist as the Irish episcopate. Their attitude was unequivocal: "What our people want is a priest who speaks the same language, shares the same blood, and is of the same race. It is their right." Encouraged by the victory of the Fall River Canadians in the "Flint Affair," as well as by the separatist activities of Americans of German descent in matters of religious observance, the Danielson Canadians called upon Rev. Jean-Baptiste Proulx, pastor of Saint-Lin in Québec, to plead their cause at the Vatican. Another conflict erupted in North Brookfield, Massachusetts, where the bishop refused to grant Canadians a separate parish. Other crises were looming on the horizon even before the earlier ones had been resolved.

The immigrants were constantly running up against the assimilationist policies of the Irish-American bishops, and the latter "played rough." A parish would be officially "Irish," for example, even if twenty percent of the parishioners were Canadians; English would be the language of the liturgy, and the pastor would be Irish. In areas where the proportions were reversed, over 75% of the population being Canadian, the parish would be designated as "mixed," with the same result: services in English and an Irish pastor.

The tendency of living one's faith in a conflict situation was so characteristic of Franco-American life at the end of the nineteenth century that it came near to becoming a tradition. And, all the while, the groundwork was being laid for the most tragic of these conflicts: the Sentinelle Affair (1923-1929). Throughout these struggles, French Canada was the continuing presence, dominating the collective psyche of the immigrants. This was the case in such critical situations as Honoré Mercier beseeching Rome to name a Canadian bishop in Ogdensburg, New York, or Bishop Antoine Racine of the Sherbrooke diocese submitting a report to the Holy See on the Canadians of the United States.

But Canada's influence was even more noticeable in the very attitude adopted by the people and their leaders, both lay and religious. By demanding separate parishes administered by a Canadian clergy and in which French would be the official language of both the church and the school, by insisting that the parish preserve the old Canadian religious customs and traditions, and by requiring that these parishes be organized on the Canadian model, these nineteenth-century immigrants were expressing what for them would remain a fundamental truth: the place that religion occupied in their lives was too intimate, too sacred, for them to allow it to be invaded by strangers. This was the bedrock principle in the mindset of these immigrants, a principle that the Irish episcopate failed to understand.

Aside from these painful struggles, often heart-wrenching for the immigrants, it can be stated that at the end of the nineteenth century the prospects for the success of the group were encouraging. They continued to establish parishes along with newspapers and various organizations bent on pursuing both cultural separatism and dual patriotism: American and Canadian.

Among the many newspapers founded in the last quarter of that century some would eventually prove to be quite influential and long-lasting; they would readily lend themselves to an extended study:

—*Le Messager* of Lewiston, Maine, 1880-1968.
—*L'Indépendant* of Fall River, Massachusetts, 1885-1962.
—*L'Étoile* of Lowell, Massachusetts,1886-1957.
—*L'Opinion publique* of Worcester, Massachusetts, 1893-1931.
—*L'Avenir national* of Manchester, New Hampshire, 1894-1949.
—*La Tribune* of Woonsocket, Rhode Island, 1895-1934.
—*La Justice* of Biddeford, Maine,1896-1950.
—*L'Impartial* of Nashua, New Hampshire, 1898-1964.
    In 1898, there were four Franco-American dailies in New England: *L'Indépendant, La Tribune, L'Étoile,* and *L'Opinion publique.*

The journalists of the period are even less well-known than their newspapers, and they have been undeservedly forgotten. Many of them were born in Canada and returned to their native land to pursue their careers:

—Benjamin Lenthier (1846-19—). Born in Beauharnois, Québec, he owned sixteen Franco-American newspapers which, in 1892, he placed at the service of Grover Cleveland, the Democratic candidate for the presidency of the United States. After Cleveland was elected, most of Lenthier's newspapers—having served their purpose—disappeared.

—Virginie Authier (1849-1899). Born in Saint-Hilaire, Québec, she founded and published *Le Journal des dames* of Cohoes, New York. This short-lived newspaper (it lasted for less than six months in 1875-1876) was devoted entirely to women's issues and was the only one of its kind in the nineteenth century.

—Louis-J. Martel (1850-1899). A physician born in Saint-Hyacinthe, he founded *Le Messager* of Lewiston and was its guiding light for many years.

—Godfroy de Tonnancour (1863-1933). Born in Saint-François-du-Lac, he was the editor of *L'Indépendant* of Fall River for over twenty-five years. He was called the "Dean of the Editors."

—Jean-Léon-Kemner Laflamme (1872-1944). A native of Sainte-Marguerite de Dorchester, he was a journalist in Lewiston, Fall River, and Woonsocket before returning to Québec to found *La Revue franco-américaine* (1908). His writings, like those of Godfroy de Tonnancour, deserve to be anthologized.

—Joseph-Arthur Favreau (1873-1933). Born in Spencer, Massachusetts, he was for several years (1894-1902) editor of *L'Opinion publique* of Worcester. He is also known as a historian.

—Olivar Asselin (1874-1937). A native of Saint-Hilarion-de-Charlevoix, who, after emigrating to the United States in 1892, worked for a few years as a "Franco-American" journalist at the *Protecteur Canadien,* the *National,* the *Jean-Baptiste*, and *La Tribune*, among others, before returning to Québec.

The lack of more detailed studies makes it impossible to offer an overall evaluation of these end-of-the-century journalistic endeavors. Certain observations can, nonetheless, be formulated about them. These newspapers were obviously of service to their subscribers, bringing them local, regional, and sometimes even national and international news. They were indispensable for unilingual readers, all the more so since editors, by publishing their own opinions on current affairs—repatriation, naturalization, a "national" clergy, the cultural orientation of the parish—encouraged the discussion of these issues at the local level. These journalists, who were also fully "committed," in the modern sense of the term, helped propagate the ideology of *la survivance*. For example, Godfroy de Tonnancour wrote in 1901 on the role of the press:

> Even if it had succeeded only in preserving the French viewpoint, respect for our forefathers, love of our language and our faith, it [the press] would already have several claims to our gratitude. But, it has done more than this; it has also made us aware of our strengths and resources, and for this we must be especially grateful.

We would readily add that the press was revealing these "strengths and resources" to the immigrants at a time when they were the butt of criticisms from their own countrymen who had remained in the motherland as well as the object of the scorn, denigration, and incomprehension of both Yankees and Irish-Americans. French-Canadian newspapers in the United States played an important role in the massive counter-propaganda campaign that the immigrants were obliged to mount in order to respond to their detractors on both sides of the border. In fact, were it not for the work of two or three generations of knowledgeable and profoundly dedicated journalists, including the generation that took over at the end of the nineteenth century, the already difficult task of Franco-American historiography would probably have become impossible due to a lack of documentation.

Just as the French-Canadian newspapers of New England were constantly revivifying their ties with Canada, several organizations founded at the turn of the century were likewise modeled on those of the old country. Saint-Jean-Baptiste Societies, and other patriotic organizations which doubled as mutual benefit societies, continued to make their appearance. By around 1890, these organizations had recruited over 30,000 members in New England. In some areas, the Saint-Jean-Baptiste Society predated the national parish and encouraged its founding through the petitions and census information it submitted to the bishop.

Despite their obvious Catholic orientation, these national societies seldom gained the approval of the American episcopate. At their congress in Baltimore, Maryland, the bishops declared that ethnic associations had no reason to exist within the American Catholic Church. French-Canadian newspapers in the United States protested, and societies continued to be established, despite the fact that they were denounced as the "freemasonry" of the French Canadians.

But it is easier to found societies than to federate them, despite the fact that such a proposal had been discussed for many years, especially at the general conventions. The project finally reached fruition, however, with the founding, in 1896, of the Association Canado-

Américaine, with its home office in Manchester, New Hampshire, to be followed in 1900 by the Union-Saint-Jean-Baptiste d'Amérique, headquartered in Woonsocket, Rhode Island. In 1897 the Société des Artisans Canadiens-Français opened ten or so branches in New England as the basis for a projected federation. The Acadians soon followed with their Société l'Assomption. Through their social and cultural activities—meetings, conventions, and publications—as well as their commercial operations (life insurance), these federations helped preserve links between the Franco-Americans of the East and those of the Midwest for over fifty years, much like the general conventions had done in the past.

There was also a proliferation of new organizations at the purely local or parochial level. By 1875, the Ladies of Saint Anne were performing charitable works in Saint Joseph parish in Lowell, and soon there were other religious organizations based upon Canadian models in almost all immigrant areas. Men enrolled in the Sacred Heart League, boys in the Guardian Angels, and girls in the Children of Mary. Music organizations were formed: in 1882, the town of Manville, Rhode Island, had its Canadian marching band; in 1889, Lowell had its Cercle Lavallée, so-named in honor of that famous "Franco-American," Calixa Lavallée, the composer of Canada's national anthem; and, in 1892, Providence had its Saint Cecilia's Choir.

At this time there was also an increasing number of marching units, the pride and joy of the citizenry. Here is how one observer described Lowell's Salaberry Guard in 1891:

> The name Salaberry [he defeated a superior American force at Châteauguay], the Canadian Leonidas [King of Sparta, hero of Thermopylae] still lives in the memory of French Canadians in the United States, as evidenced by the founding in Lowell of a large troop of cavalry named after the hero of [the War of] 1812.
>
> The Salaberry Guard was founded on February 17, 1888. Its goal is to participate in all national celebrations to enhance their splendor, for their dazzling uniforms are sure to brighten any grand procession. The Guard,

sixty-five members strong, arrayed in their black uniforms and plumed hats, with gaiters and gauntlets and all the accoutrements of cavalrymen, will be on parade for this splendid celebration. (*Pamphlet-Souvenir de la Fête patronale des Canadiens français de Lowell, Mass., le 24 juin 1891*, p. 65)

These military-like organizations often pursued several goals. For example, the New Bedford Sharpshooters, founded in 1891, sought to "unify the French-Canadian residents of New Bedford, organize fraternal meetings, establish a mutual fund to assist sick members and the heirs of deceased ones, provide members with recreational and educational opportunities, and help members in the preservation and improvement of their French language."

Many of these organizations—religious, musical, cultural, and "military"—lasted for sixty to seventy-five years, and some even longer. They responded to a whole range of needs, from the ascetic to the recreational.

It will always be difficult to depict the cultural life of Canadian immigrants without having read their many newspapers and analyzed a widely scattered documentation: souvenir-programs, brochures, fliers, etc. Based upon the current state of our knowledge, the cultural activity is primarily reflective of the aspirations of a professional class, but one that mingled with the people at concerts, plays, and lectures.

Early on in fact, chorales, orchestras, and marching bands were quite commonplace. Although they enjoyed varying degrees of success, it is no exaggeration to say that because of them, French-Canadian musical life lasted until the end of the twentieth century, while a great many other aspects of the life of the community have long since perished.

In the nineteenth century, the most famous Franco-American name in music was that of the diva Emma Lajeunesse (1847-1930). Known as "L'Albani," she was also called "the little French-Canadian warbler." Born in Chambly, Québec, she emigrated to Albany, New York, around 1864 and became an international star, hailed in all of Europe's concert halls, from London to Saint Petersburg, by way of Paris, Brussels, Vienna, and Florence, etc. After settling permanently in London, she made several triumphant returns to Montréal.

The immigrants also displayed a particular affection for the theater. The first known drama club was organized in 1868 in Marlboro, Massachusetts, and all the large population centers had their drama or literary societies before 1900. The public was especially fond of comedies and melodramas; the plays of Molière were staged in Southbridge as early as 1877. From 1868 to 1930, about one thousand plays were performed. In addition to indigenous theater groups, French and French-Canadian troupes toured New England.

Lecture halls, too, were often crowded, and the most popular speaker by far was Honoré Mercier. Around 1878, Louis Fréchette was warmly welcomed in Fall River, in turn by his friend Honoré Beaugrand, by the Cercle Montcalm, and by a group of admirers who attended the lectures at which he read his poetry. Later, the historian Benjamin Sulte; the journalist and legislator, Israël Tarte, owner of *La Patrie* of Montréal; and the Jesuit, Father Louis Lalande, were also well received in the area, as was Father Édouard Hamon who, after having preached many retreats throughout New England, would become one of the first historians of those who lived in exile. In 1899, La Société Historique Franco-Américaine was founded; it would become a Mecca for French, French-Canadian, and Franco-American guest speakers. The immigrants' love of oratory guaranteed that every general convention would be a cultural event of the first magnitude.

Literature and Ideology

The main body of Franco-American literature remains poorly delineated and badly known since no one has yet undertaken the task of analyzing or indexing the newspapers in which most of the works first appeared. This much is certain—the first novel, *Jeanne la fileuse,* dates from 1875. Written by Honoré Beaugrand (1848-1906), it is subtitled, *An Episode of the Franco-Canadian Emigration to the United States.*

Beaugrand was an immigrant who lived for a while in Fall River prior to returning to Canada where he would become mayor of Montréal. He first published *Jeanne la fileuse* in *La République,* a newspaper which he himself edited, and then in book form in 1878. The work was part of a publicity campaign—the counter-propaganda effort which we have already referred to—that sought to rehabilitate the reputation of the emigrants in the minds of the French Canadians.

Without blatantly defending the prevailing *survivance* ideology, the author tells the story of a Québec family which emigrates to the manufacturing center of Fall River. *Jeanne la fileuse* is both a sociological study and an historical novel which also includes a love story. In his preface to the first edition, the author admitted that the work was more of a tract than a novel. In an attempt to respond to the critics of emigration, Beaugrand offers the reader a wealth of statistics along with "true information on the material, political, social, and religious status" of the emigrants.

Beaugrand was not only a novelist and a polemicist; he was also a folklorist. His interest in folklore is shown in the first part of *Jeanne la fileuse* where he inserts his version of "Le Fantôme de l'avare" (The Miser's Phantom), a legend that conjures up images from the *pays d'en haut* (lands to the North and West) around 1825. He also includes the lyrics to "Canot d'écorce qui vole" (Birchbark Canoe That Flies

Through the Air), as well as a description of a haying scene. The novelist also manages to weave in a family feud from the 1837-38 Rebellions to indicate that these tragic events had touched some families more deeply than official historiography might suggest. These various elements indicate just how firmly the work was rooted in nineteenth-century Canada.

In Part Two, without entirely abandoning the plot, the author focuses on the economic dimensions of emigration, resorting to techniques and procedures borrowed from polemics and the field of social history. There are a great many digressions: on the history of Fall River, the efficiency of American railroads, and the socioeconomic progress of the emigrants. To all intents and purposes, this section constitutes a thinly veiled defense of American capitalism. But Beaugrand did not neglect ethnic issues: he devotes several pages to the development of Fall River's Canadian community and to the important Saint-Jean-Baptiste convention held in Montréal in 1874.

If one applies only the traditional criteria by which novels are usually judged, the weaknesses of this work are readily apparent. But, when approached from a wider perspective, that of the intellectual history of Québec and Franco-American New England or that of the sociocultural history of francophone communities in America, *Jeanne la fileuse* can then be viewed as one of the key documents on emigration. If, as it is the case from a purely aesthetic perspective, Beaugrand did not always succeed in integrating the disparate elements of his work into an entirely harmonious whole, he has, nevertheless, bequeathed to us a host of facts and insights on the early generations of French-Canadian emigrants.

No true Franco-American novelistic tradition came into being in the nineteenth century due to the dearth of such works. After *Jeanne la fileuse* came *Un Revenant* (A Ghost), 1884, in which Rémi Tremblay

(1847-1926) gives a fictionalized account of his military adventures during the Civil War. In 1888, Anna-Marie Duval-Thibault (1862-1958), after having emigrated from Montréal to New York, published *Les Deux Testaments*, a novel of "manners" about emigration that provides information about New York's French-Canadian colony in Yorkville's Saint John the Baptist parish. If we add to this enumeration, *Bélanger, ou l'histoire d'un crime,* a novel published in 1892 by Georges Crépeau, the list of Franco-American novels published in the nineteenth century is complete. The author, who lived from 1868 to 1913, was a native of Sorel who had emigrated to Lowell.

As for poetry, some of the verses first published in newspapers deserve to be unearthed. Apart from these and some occasional poems which appeared in souvenir pamphlets, the nineteenth century has left us only a few slim volumes. In 1892, Anna-Marie Duval-Thibault published *Fleurs de printemps* (Flowers of Spring*)*, the first collection of Franco-American poetry. Prefaced by Benjamin Sulte, the volume contains twelve poems in English and forty or so in French in which the author evokes, among other themes, a tragic love affair and the absent homeland.

The poetry of Rémi Tremblay is of a totally different order. Only a part of his work is based on his life and observations in the United States. Since his *Boutades et rêveries* (Sallies and Daydreams) was published in volume form in Fall River, it can be called the second collection of Franco-American poetry. Other works by the same author are of interest to the historian of Franco-American society because they include comments on contemporary events. For example, in the collection of poems called *Coups d'aile et coups de bec*, (Feather-Like Blows and Biting Attacks) one of them, *La Cyriade* [a word play on Voltaire's *La Henriade*], satirized attempts by the Protestant pastor Narcisse Cyr to convert unhappy immigrants during the religious conflicts which took place in Fall River between 1884 and 1886.

But the most important segment of the nineteenth century Franco-American canon was nonfiction. It included all the genres and sub-genres generally associated with the concept of the "prose of ideas" in the literary tradition of France and French Canada: essays, oratory, both sacred and profane, and history.

The origins of this type of Franco-American literature can be traced back to 1868 with the founding of the first newspapers by Canadian immigrants. Because these papers were often established to support causes deemed to be in the interest of the immigrants, they contain a host of articles in which a point of view is defended with vigor, conviction, and eloquence. Without arguing that these newspapers contain a great many unknown masterpieces, they certainly include many articles that deserve to be published once again.

This literary category, that of nonfiction, dates back to the beginning of the great migration. One of the first names worth recalling is that of Ferdinand Gagnon, the true founder of French-Canadian journalism in New England. Others would follow in his footsteps and develop variations on his most cherished theme, that of *la survivance*, an idea of such importance that it would continue to be debated without interruption throughout the entire century.

A rapid perusal of the period's newspapers or of the rare works that mention them provides sufficient proof that they include some pages which, though essential to a better understanding of Québec and American history, are teetering on the edge of historical oblivion. From the viewpoint of literary history, everything, or almost, remains to be studied. For example, just the question of contacts and exchanges between the first generation of Franco-American writers and the literary, religious, and political figures of Québec would deserve a lengthy chapter, if not an entire book. It is to be hoped that the thematic content of these works will be analyzed. This could then lead to a more balanced appreciation of their overall qualities than has been the case up to now. The pages which follow may suggest some general approaches for future research.

The members of the educated class who emigrated from Québec to the United States, starting in the 1860s, had been educated in an intellectual milieu which accorded an ever-growing importance to its national history. Some of the best-known authors—François-Xavier Garneau, Rev. J.-B.-Antoine Ferland, and Rev. Henri-Raymond Casgrain—through their teaching and writings had succeeded in persuading the people of Québec that, even as a conquered nation, their past could be "utilized," for it could be a source of pride, and from it a great deal could be learned. This tendency to glorify the past, transforming the era of New France into a golden age, revealed the craving for heroes and heroines. This need would in turn have a profound effect on the writings of immigrant leaders, both lay and religious, who would be influenced also by the notion of racial antagonism propounded by F.-X. Garneau.

The Catholic Church, omnipresent in Québec, was another essential aspect of this nineteenth-century milieu that, at least to some extent, tended to look back and, in its role as mentor, to focus the mind of the people on the past. The influence of this "clerical-nationalist" ideology, well-entrenched before 1850, would last for a century. In the everyday world, the Church controlled the schools, the hospitals, and for that matter, all the social institutions of any importance, including an ever-growing number of organizations and societies for men and women, both young and old. The phenomenon of the Church as the final arbiter in all aspects of life, even in the intellectual sphere, would remain part of the immigrants' world view, and their writings would seldom be free of ecclesiastical influence.

With its markedly reactionary and clerical tendencies, nineteenth-century intellectual life in Québec was directed more towards a utilitarian outcome than towards the creative imagination. Shaping the consciences of both the people and the élite and, in so doing, consolidating the Church's position were the main thrusts of most of the writings of the period. And thus would the works of the immigrant authors also be of a largely didactic nature.

Since the country into which thousands of Quebecers and Acadians had immigrated proved to be rather unfriendly, one can understand why some of them longed to return to the village of their birth. Scorned by the Anglo-Americans, who looked upon them only as a source of cheap labor, the immigrants also found themselves at odds with the Irish-American bishops who, seeking to implant Catholicism in a Protestant country, were anxious to avoid any complications arising from a desire to preserve a language and traditions which others deemed to be foreign.

Constrained as they were by the need to use polemics—in defending their people against Yankee insults and having to struggle against the assimilationist maneuvers of an episcopate which had to be both resisted and respected—Franco-American journalists and writers alike became highly adept at affirming their loyalty to ecclesiastical authority, all the while demanding a clergy of their own kind and the right to administer so-called "Canadian," i.e., national parishes.

It was thus in a doubly hostile environment that the first Franco-American writers were called upon to exercise their creative talents. Because Americans felt less threatened than the Irish bishops, they required fewer polemical efforts, but this was only a difference of degree. Though American xenophobia was not always virulent, ambivalence towards the Canadian immigrants lasted well into the twentieth century before finally lapsing into indifference. For the Irish, however, Canadian immigrants were seldom a matter of indifference. Led by their priests and journalists, the immigrants had to wage a relentless struggle against them, first to acquire and then preserve what they considered to be their rights. This antagonistic attitude would last until the 1960s.

If to this we add that the emigrants were sometimes branded as "deserters" by priests, government officials, and journalists in Canada, it becomes clear why the leaders, in places like Worcester, Manchester, and Woonsocket, felt the need to defend themselves from that quarter as well. And, if it was not George-Etienne Cartier who uttered the outrageous insult: *"Laissez-les partir, c'est la canaille qui s'en va"* ("Let them go, it's the rabble that's leaving"), someone else said it, and it was widely repeated and disseminated. In an incisive and unforgettable way, it summarized an attitude. The immigrants truly believed that the words did in fact come from the lips of this statesman whom they had previously held in such high regard. So, whether they were being charged as "deserters," treated as "rabble," called "stubborn" by the Irish episcopate, or "Chinese of the Eastern States" by the American establishment, the immigrants found themselves constantly on the defensive. Such a situation could lead only to the production of literary works far removed from "art for art's sake," as a thematic analysis of these works will immediately confirm.

In considering the major themes of Franco-American literature before 1900, it is essential to underscore once again a basic truth that has often been overlooked: the readers whom the authors sought to reach lived on both sides of the Canadian-American border. No one was more keenly aware of this than Ferdinand Gagnon who sought unceasingly to strengthen the ties between the immigrants and their compatriots in the homeland. Gagnon was as much a man of action as he was a writer, and he ardently pursued his goal of solidarity among French Canadians with a perseverance which never wavered.

This can be seen in his understanding of the homeland, one of the major themes of this literature. Having declared the land of one's birth to be "everything, after God," he went on to define it as follows:

> The Homeland, for all other men, as for us, is the sky under which we were born, the land of our forefathers, the cradle of our youth, the roof which sheltered our fragile infancy. The Homeland is the glowing family hearth, a father's generosity, a mother's smile, a sister's tenderness, and a brother's affection. The Homeland is also the untainted blood coursing through our veins, the glory of our people, the sacred tomb of our ancestors, the blood of our soldiers, the nobility of our flags, those tattered standards wrested from the heat of battle. The faith and the courage of our fathers: that is the Homeland.

This notion, which combines piety with patriotism, was a common one for this generation of immigrant writers. Orators and journalists proclaimed their loyalty to the mother country, and an unmistakable hint of nostalgia, often of homesickness, tinges the writings of these immigrants who were prevented by circumstances from returning to their native land.

That this theme would retain its topicality until the end of the nineteenth century, and even beyond, can be seen in a passage from a speech given in Chicago in 1893 by Rev. J.-Roch Magnan:

> Gentlemen, in discussing our privileges and duties in and to the United States, I have been guided especially by reason, cold reason. But when I take up our relationship to the motherland, I sense that the subject is closer to the heart. Memory does not die. True, we have left our homeland to attach ourselves to this Republic, much as a young man bids his father's house adieu to unite with his wife. But a son whose heart is in the right place remains true to his mother's memory; likewise, dear compatriots, can we ever forget the land of our birth? This would be impossible. Our heartstrings are tied to the walls that sheltered our joys and the excitement of our youth, and nothing can ever erase those impressions. (Gatineau, *Historique*, p. 322)

Loyalty to Canada was a given. It was often linked to other themes: repatriation, naturalization, the destiny of the French in North America, and group identity. In point of fact, both repatriation and naturalization are central to the question of individual *vs.* group identity. Decisions taken at the level of the individual were bound to affect the future of the French on the American continent, a fate that preoccupied most Franco-American intellectuals of the nineteenth century.

Many of these intellectuals tenaciously sought to prove that one could become an American citizen without betraying Canada. Hence the many arguments in favor of naturalization which, while directed primarily at skeptical immigrants, were formulated in such a way as to reassure government officials, journalists, members of the clergy, and other leaders in Canada. Here is an example, among many, formulated by Dr. J.-H. Palardy:

> Naturalization, after all, is not to be equated with degradation, nor can it be considered a national apostasy. Since our nationality has no official status and since we really do not have a country we can call our own from the viewpoint of our own preference for one or the other, it matters little to us that we be incorporated with the Anglo-Saxons of the British Empire or those of the United States. We will simply be exchanging our condition as subjects for that of citizens, and our new status would make us no less French than we could be under the tutelage of the English. Far from ceasing to be ourselves, by becoming voters in our adopted country we would acquire the means to fully exercise our natural rights as free men. (Gatineau, *Historique*, p. 418)

". . . no less French. . ." Time and again, what surfaces in these texts is concern for *la survivance* or the destiny of French Canadians as a people. "Messianic" is also used to denote this vein of nationalistic thought relative to emigration, often without making a clear distinction between the two terms. *La Survivance* connotes the preservation in North America of the ancestral heritage composed of the Catholic religion, the French language, and a certain number of French-Canadian traditions. The term "messianic," on the other hand, refers more properly to a spiritual mission entrusted by God to the French Canadians as a people, namely to pray for the conversion of Anglo-Saxon Protestants. To these two thematic constants in early Franco-American literature should be added a third major theme in immigrant writings: that of the belief that emigration was a response to the plan of Divine Providence. In 1901, Joseph Guillet could state with conviction: "Gentlemen, Divine Providence, which governs all men and all nations, has instructed us to leave Canada and to settle in the United States."

At the same general convention held in Springfield, Massachusetts, J.-C. Hogue, president of the Société Saint-Jean-Baptiste of New York, declared:

> Gentlemen, this is not the place to try to understand God's intentions in the obvious fact of French-Canadian emigration, an event that nothing could prevent: neither family ties, nor love of one's village steeple, nor the many other close bonds to one's native land, nor even the many legitimate apprehensions or considerable fears that might arise at the thought of leaving one's country for a strange land. I accept this fact at face value and see God's hand in it. (Gatineau, *Historique*, p. 486)

Since the destiny of the French Canadians, their group identity, *la survivance*, the messianic theme, and the role of Divine Providence in their emigration were the major preoccupations of the intellectuals, it is not surprising that they would become the principal themes of the first Franco-American texts. This set of concerns led orators and essayists to hold forth at length on related themes, especially the notion of loyalty. To remain faithful to one's Catholic and French past—this was the first commandment, the rule of life from which no exception could be permitted, for what was at stake was not only one's personal salvation, but also that of one's homeland.

Almost all of the immigrant writers would harken back to these topics, to the point where they became commonplace in the literature of the period. Related subjects included faith, language, and traditions, constantly glorified and continuously called to mind for a seemingly forgetful public. Moreover, these three questions went hand in hand: language was considered almost as sacred as faith, since it is, in fact, the means by which faith is expressed, and it is in French that one speaks to God. Hence the writers sought to instill in the people a mystique of the French language.

French had been the language of prayer as well as that of daily life since the earliest days of New France. So for the French-Canadian élite of 1870 and 1900, both in Canada and in the United States, it had remained a sacred component of the ancestral heritage as well as an immutable part of the collective identity. To abandon it would have been tantamount to being exiled from the group; nay, it was the equivalent of apostasy since protecting the faith depended upon it. This is the meaning of the oft-repeated phrase: "*Qui perd sa langue perd sa foi.*" ("He who loses his language loses his faith.")

Convinced of the profound truth of this doctrine, the members of the intelligentsia clung stubbornly to its belief. Did they not detect among the immigrants a dangerous drift towards assimilation, a tendency to rid themselves of cultural baggage deemed to be outdated? And did they not sense on the part of these immigrants an indifference towards their ethnic history? The fact that they did accounts for the constant return to these topics in the literature of the day. Since faith and language were at the very core of the value system advocated by the writers, they made every effort to convey their message to the people, for, very early on, they detected apathy, slippage, even outright loss which, according to them, the group could ill afford to allow.

The history of Canada as a source of lessons, models, and examples was another abundant source of subject matter for the first generations of Franco-American writers. And for good reason. The very existence of French Canada in the nineteenth century was in fact *the* miracle of *la survivance*, the model to be proposed to readers and audiences alike. According to this same élite, the seventeenth century had been the golden age of the French in Canada. With names such as Champlain, Bishop François de Laval, Dollard des Ormeaux, and Madeleine de Verchères, the seventeenth was the heroic century *par excellence*, and writers constantly drew upon it to remind the Canadian immigrants of their noble origins. For *"bon sang ne saurait mentir"* ("good breeding always lives up to expectations") even if *"bon sang"* just happens to be living—perhaps providentially—in New England.

Taken as a whole, the topics of these texts often constitute a constantly renewed defense of the dominant ideology. The writers were reacting to a given situation after having developed a vision of the world in which the essential component was the need for striving to ensure *la survivance*: first by struggling against the slanders and insults being spread about the immigrants in their own land; next, against the indifference and the defections taking place at the very heart of the vast immigrant community; then against the contempt of Americans; and finally, the need to battle against the Irish episcopate's assimilationist policies.

It should, therefore, surprise no one that this literature oscillated between pleas for the defense and polemical diatribes. Its most obvious characteristics were those commended by Rev. Raymond Casgrain in his 1866 study of Canadian literature: "[Our literature] will be serious, reflective, spiritualistic, religious, evangelizing like our missionaries, as generous as our martyrs and as energetic and persevering as our pioneers of yesteryear. . . . But, most of all, it will be essentially faith-driven and religious."

This literature was also fundamentally utilitarian, serving a cause deemed to be sacred. That is why its major themes were social and rarely personal. It was a literature that often lapsed into proselytizing, and its favored means were the article that was an exhortation, the sermon, and the speech—or the speech that could be mistaken for a sermon. By discussing the so-called "nationalist question," group identity, and *la survivance*, writers created what might be described as a "theology" of nationality wherein one can easily discern several subdivisions of Catholic theology: dogma, apologetics, and ethics. This literature also contains traces of mysticism, asceticism, and hagiography because the cultural heritage was a sacred treasure for these writers.

This "prose of ideas," as it is called in French, supported the campaign that was being waged simultaneously on several fronts against the gossip and slander coming from all sides. In short, it was an attempt to vindicate the good name of the immigrants by demonstrating their loyalty to a cultural heritage based upon faith and language. These same immigrants were, at one and the same time, being urged to become more and more loyal so as to achieve both eternal as well as ethnic salvation for they also needed to "deserve the respect" of an absent homeland, all the while adapting intelligently to their adopted country.

Seen from the vantage point of the end of the twentieth century, this literature seems indeed to be an affirmation of the collective self by the literary élite, repeated time and time again in an environment fraught with uncertainty; hence the sense of anguish, urgency, sometimes even alarm, which it conveys. This also accounts for the impression that the writers derived a much needed sense of security from a cult of the past which today, a century later, prevents some readers from reaching a fair assessment of writings that are, in fact, fascinating in their own way.

A more detailed study would reveal the literary origins of these writings. The obvious starting point would be to examine the influence of the great French classical and romantic authors on the development of these writers. One might also investigate the role played by the leading French-Canadian intellectuals. It is known that Bishop Bourget of Montréal, Bishop Laflèche of Trois-Rivières, and Honoré Mercier exerted a readily discernible influence on the emigrant writers. Could Louis-Joseph Papineau, leader of the French-Canadian patriots during the 1837 uprising, not have left his mark on them as well? Is it conceivable that the powerful influence of Cardinal Taschereau of Québec stopped at the border? And what of Arthur Buies, the anti-clerical journalist, Jules-Paul Tardivel, who was also a journalist, and Sir Wilfrid Laurier, Prime Minister of Canada?

The Franco-American Psyche Around 1900

It has been estimated that by 1900 there were over a half million French Canadians in New England, equivalent to ten percent of the region's population. The new term to designate them—Franco-Americans—was beginning to take hold, sign of an evolving identity. For while they remained loyal to Canada by preserving the faith, the language, and the traditions of their homeland, these men and women demonstrated their loyalty to the United States by adopting American ways and the English language, becoming citizens, and participating in the political life of their chosen country.

The role played by them in the economic life of their adopted country obviously contributed a great deal to their evolving identity; it also had a significant impact on the industrial development of the Northeast. In the textile mills, one-third of the work force was of Québec or Acadian descent. And slowly but surely, Canadian immigrants were being "promoted," advancing to the level of skilled workers and even foremen. There was also a growing number of tradesmen, businessmen, and professionals among them.

In October of 1890, a New York newspaper, the *Commercial Advertiser,* expressed the fears that Yankees were experiencing over immigration. "The inhabitants of Canada are pouring over our borders. The victory won on the Plains of Abraham by men of the English race is being avenged by the women of Montcalm's race. New England is vanquished." Most Americans looked unfavorably upon anything Catholic or foreign, making life more difficult for the Canadian immigrants.

The Nativist movement, organizations like the American Protective Association, magazines like the *Protestant Crusades*, and even the pages of major newspapers like the *New York Times*, gave voice to the Yankee fear that their survival was in jeopardy, for their dream of a country that would remain Protestant and Anglo-American seemed about to turn into a polyglot nightmare. Yet, a century later these same White Anglo-Saxon Protestants (WASPs) would still be setting the pace and leading the country, a sign that the efforts of their nineteenth-century ancestors had been successful after all.

Americans were opposed to the cultural separatism of all immigrants, viewing it as an abuse of hospitality, a failure to conform, even as anti-American. Oblivious to the contradiction inherent in their viewpoint, they rejected out of hand the loyalty of the Canadian immigrants to *their* religion and *their* language and *their* customs, on the pretext that this idea ran counter to the individual freedom advocated by the Founding Fathers and the leading thinkers who had fashioned the American soul. They denounced the French-Canadian immigrant community as inaccessible and thus culturally closed off and impervious to modern ideas, including the principles of a democratic republic. Moreover, they feared a widespread plot by the clergy to bring New England under the control of the Pope.

These Anglo-American fears would evolve over time. In their 1881 report of the Massachusetts Bureau of Labor Statistics, Colonel Caroll D. Wright and his colleagues had denounced French-Canadian immigrants for being "migratory birds." By the 1890s, the menace of their permanent settlement had become worrisome. Now it was feared that one day, by means of the ballot box, they might gain control of public institutions, especially the schools.

It is true that, in some respects, the collective behavior of the immigrants was hardly reassuring to Yankee purists who had vowed to preserve the identity of the nation faced with millions of immigrants from the four corners of the globe. French-Canadian efforts at repatriation, their reluctance to be naturalized, the often temporary nature of their immigration, the messianic nature of their ideology aimed directly at the Anglo-Saxons, their establishment of a network of separate institutions, and the continuous as well as multidimensional presence of Canada in their lives, all of this pointed to the fact that the French Canadians were not about to be easily integrated, much less to become thoroughly Americanized in the near term.

As a result, Yankees and immigrants lived through some difficult times. The Yankees demanded that immigrants from all countries convert immediately and totally to their way of thinking, acting, and feeling. But for the French-Canadian immigrants, everything was a stumbling block to such a radical revision of their way of life: religion, language, customs, and perhaps most of all, history, since French Canadians could not forget that Yankees belonged to the same people who had conquered Canada. This historical awareness would weaken over time, and the immigrants would learn to adapt to this situation by concentrating on their livelihood as they sought to improve their economic status. In the end, Anglo-Americans also adopted a pragmatic approach to the situation. From an economic point of view, they needed a work force; and in the political sphere, they needed the votes of the newcomers to prevent the Irish from winning all the elections. Moreover, Canadian immigrants would soon have money to spend, and all things considered, they would become good citizens known for their exemplary docility.

This docility of the French-Canadian immigrants was considerably less evident in their contacts with the Irish. These two groups opposed one another on all fronts: at work, where the Irish feared displacement by the Canadians; in politics, where the Canadians began to run for office in municipal elections; and especially in the area of religion, where from the start the Canadians resisted the assimilationist policies of the Irish-American bishops.

The vast majority of Catholic bishops in the United States were of Irish descent. This advantage derived not from their having implanted Catholicism on American soil, but from sheer numbers and the fact of their earlier arrival. As a result, the Irish clergy was solidly entrenched by the time the French Canadians began to immigrate into New England in significant numbers.

Invoking the principle of a unifying order, the episcopate argued that the use of a single language would facilitate both its ministry and ecclesiastical administration. In their view, uniformity could reduce ethnic conflict within the Church and curb the anti-Catholicism of some Americans who, in time, might even come to respect the Church. It is rather ironic that Irish-Americans would adopt such an attitude toward immigrants for as Edmond de Nevers pointed out, "In the United States, Irish clergymen are the most ferocious enemies of French, German, Polish, and Italian Catholics. . . . The Anglo-Saxons should be amazed, if that were possible, to find that the most ardent champions of English assimilation are the very same people they have themselves beaten, ruined, and ridiculed."

In Québec, emigration was denounced both from the pulpit and in the newspapers. The topic would be debated for almost a century. Since emigration reduced both the Church's flock and the country's population, it caused great concern even among government officials. Still, no one seemed able to stanch the flow to the South.

In addition to governmental reports, an entire literature was devoted to debating the issue. In 1851, twelve missionaries from the Eastern Townships published a brochure, *Le Canadien émigrant, ou pourquoi le Canadien francais quitte-t-il le Bas-Canada?* (The Canadian Emigrant, *or* Why Is the French Canadian Leaving Lower Canada?) It was a plea for an energetic plan of action to reverse emigration by encouraging colonization. Around 1866, the future bishop Louis-François Laflèche spoke for most of the clergy when, in painfully memorable terms, he reproached the emigrants: "You have shrunk from the sacrifices your country asked you to make. . . ." In 1881 Jules-Paul Tardivel decried the scourge of the recruitment agents who traveled throughout Québec to hire employees for the American factories they represented. In order to discourage emigration, the life of the exiles was often painted in the darkest of colors.

Isolated and misunderstood, the emigrants were accused of every crime imaginable: love of luxury, laziness, an adventurous spirit, loose morals, etc. To combat these prejudices, the immigrant leaders launched a counter-offensive. As early as 1872, Rev. T.-A. Chandonnet, in his *Notre-Dame-des-Canadiens et les Canadiens aux États-Unis*, devoted several pages to disprove the accusations and repudiate the insults that were being widely disseminated in Québec against the emigrants. The following is typical of his approach:

> . . . what is crystal clear to anyone who has eyes to see is that the Canadians of the United States are really intelligent, energetic, skillful, and industrious. This is revealed not just by the fact that they are usually well off, but also by the numerous works of all kinds in wood, metal, and stone that they make each day; in the reputation they have made for themselves in large cities; in the remarkably large number of them who,

despite serious obstacles, have amassed a considerable nest egg. (Chandonnet, p. 140)

Intellectuals as different from one another as Honoré Beaugrand and Father Édouard Hamon joined in this campaign of counter-propaganda. It is true that in his novel, *Jeanne la fileuse*, Beaugrand tended to extol especially the material success of the immigrants—albeit without entirely neglecting the religious dimension—whereas Father Hamon, denouncing "the malevolence of some Canadian newspapers," developed a defense based on the messianic dimension of departure from the homeland. Only an unusual situation such as this one could have brought the anticlerical Beaugrand and the Jesuit Hamon to be on the same side of an argument. And in fact, the situation created by emigration was indeed exceptional in many respects.

The immigrants were confronted with a unique moral dilemma by the very fact of their having settled in a foreign country and having to adhere to the demands their leaders made on them which, more often than not, were contrary to the values of the Anglo-Saxon milieu. The result was a protracted conflict on two levels: between *la survivance* and assimilation on one level, and between constraint and instinct on another.

Misunderstood by their Canadian countrymen and scorned by the dominant group in their adopted country, the first immigrants naturally turned to their faith, language, and traditions, the very essence of their cultural background, just as their ancestors had done after the Conquest. They were of invaluable help and comfort to them during the difficult period of adjustment in their new country.

But their leaders were now attempting to transform what at first had been only an instinctive reaction into a permanent institutional framework. These leaders—priests and journalists in the vanguard—more profoundly attached to their native land than were the masses, began to preach to them about their duty to remain loyal to the faith, language, and customs of their ancestors. What had originally been a comfort to them became in time—perhaps even before the start of the twentieth century—a burden and a source of guilt, especially when they were told they had to maintain their faith, language, and traditions to avoid "lapsing into insignificance."

The shrewdest maneuver in this strategy on behalf of *la survivance* was probably the linking of religion to the French language, since it allowed the notion of *la survivance* to endure well into the 1950s, after which the awareness grew that one could exist without the other. The slogan—*"Qui perd sa langue, perd sa foi."* ("He who loses his language, loses his faith.")— lost its power over the people.

Coined as early as the 1850s, this slogan was widely disseminated and believed to be true. In retrospect, it may seem to members of the younger generation that to link eternal salvation with preservation of the French language was too convenient an argument for the clergy, since loss of faith necessarily entailed consignment to hell's eternal fire. Although avoiding damnation while "earning one's heaven" was already life's goal for the vast majority of Canadian immigrants, they now had an additional burden to bear since eternal salvation could only be attained in a language which went counter to that of the Anglo-Saxon environment.

The idea of *la survivance* endured, nonetheless, as various cities vied for leadership of the movement: Lewiston, Maine, proclaimed itself "the Athens of French-speaking America," Manchester, New Hampshire, called itself "the most French of American cities in the United States," whereas Woonsocket, Rhode Island, was known as "the Québec of New England," and Fall River "the third-ranking French city in America" after Montréal and Québec. Until about 1950, *la survivance* served both to isolate the group and to create solidarity within it. Living in a new country, surrounded by others of the same nationality, and continually being urged to pray together in the language which their forebears had struggled to protect—all the while preserving their customs—led to the creation of group solidarity—an "us against them" mentality. At the same time, such a situation isolated the group by creating a cultural ghetto which annoyed and confused other Americans. In their eyes, Canadian immigrants, in pursuing the goal of *la survivance*, seemed to be rejecting Yankee culture. Having themselves endured the scorn of Europe's aristocracy and intelligentsia, Anglo-Americans were very critical of this attitude on the part of the immigrants. They were also very sensitive to anything that might impede their efforts to confer a powerful identity on the United States by transforming a young and rapidly developing country into a great power, one that would be recognized and respected by the community of nations.

This being the case, Anglo-Americans were quick to adopt an air of superiority, of contempt even, vis-à-vis minority groups in the United States. Now, contempt is not easily borne, especially when it emanates from those in the majority, the lords and masters of the country in which one has come to settle. As much as one would wish to be loyal to one's ancestors, it is not easy to resist the constant social pressures to conform to the majority view, to speak English like everyone else, to adopt American ways, and to pursue the socioeconomic advancement of the country.

There were assimilationist pressures at work within the immigrant community from the outset. When, for example, leaders urged immigrants to become naturalized and play a more active role in the political life of the United States, they were, albeit only implicitly, encouraging assimilation. And when those same immigrants were able to provide their children with an education, sometimes up to an advanced level, this guaranteed that their children would be even more involved in the life of the adopted country than the parents had been. And for those children born in the United States, the adopted country had become the native land so that, in the end, assimilation appears to have been inevitable.

The road to assimilation, however, usually passed through the "Little Canadas." Almost every city and town that received a fair number of immigrants had neighborhoods called Irishtown, Little Italy, *Kleindeutschland,* or Little Canada. It is not easy for us to judge the quality of life in the Little Canadas, the drawbacks *vs.* the "warmth" of these neighborhoods having been variously interpreted by commentators according to the depth of their filial piety or the strength of their biases.

Current research suggests that Little Canadas evolved considerably from the nineteenth to the twentieth century. In its annual report for 1880, the description of Lowell's Little Canada by the Massachussets Board of Health hardly inspires nostalgia. According to this report, the space between the buildings was so narrow that a person could barely get through. It was dark after 3:00 p.m. inside the tenement "blocks," and to open a window was to risk a shower from a bucketful of the upstairs neighbor's dirty water. According to some observers, housing conditions in certain Little Canadas were worse than those experienced by black slaves; but there is no evidence to support this generalization.

The early years were difficult ones from the standpoint of health since the immigrants did not practice preventive medicine; perhaps this was a luxury that only a few could afford. Unsanitary conditions appear to have been more the rule than the exception, at least for a time, and in at least some Little Canadas, there was a high rate of infant mortality.

In conditions like these, the most constructive aspect that emerged was human solidarity. It was the family, considered as the foundation of the social organization and the unit of economic production, that sustained the individual. And, since the spirit of mutual assistance often extended beyond the nuclear family, cousins and friends could also enjoy its benefits. True, poverty was always to be reckoned with—some people felt its oppressive presence for many long years—but it could be alleviated to some degree by sending children to work in the mills even before they had reached the State's legal minimum age. Family solidarity, perseverance, resigning oneself to hard work in the mills, confidence that one could improve one's situation with time, all of these factors made life bearable for the majority of immigrants.

The self-sufficient nature of the Little Canada was an added benefit. Their location near the mills made it easier for those who lived there to walk to work and, along the way, they could pass by their church and their parochial school, as well as stores and shops, many of which belonged to "Canadians." They could read the familiar posters in French, about a club, a newspaper, or perhaps that of a charitable organization. A few Canadian physicians and dentists had their offices in the neighborhood, and there was often one building on the street more solid-looking than the others: the funeral home, bearing the name Archambault, Héroux, or Carrier. Since everyone spoke French, one could comfortably remain in the neighborhood, seldom having to leave it.

In short, the Little Canada of the nineteenth century seems to have been as reassuring as it was confining, both a source of solidarity as well as an isolating factor; and in this respect it functioned much like the notion of *la survivance*.

At the end of the nineteenth century, there were about 400 mill towns in New England whose economy was dominated by various industries, especially textiles, but also boots and shoes. The ever-increasing use of machinery in these factories significantly reduced the level of technical training needed to obtain work in them. A few days were usually enough to acquire the necessary know-how. A great number of nonskilled workers were hired, and in no time, the Québec farmer, lumberjack, day laborer, or craftsman was transformed into a mill hand.

Submissive, undemanding with respect to working conditions, and willing to accept the most menial jobs, French-Canadian immigrants were well thought of by their employers; for they did not cost a great deal, especially the women and the children—a great advantage in a highly competitive industry.

What most impressed those who have described these immigrant workers was their great docility. Too docile, at least in the minds of union leaders, since they were opposed to strikes and were not interested in joining the labor movement. It has been argued, but never demonstrated, that their attitude led to lower wages in the New England textile industry, though some foremen did find them to be willing collaborators in their struggles against the unions.

It is true that in some cases—Fall River was one—good relations existed between the local Canadian élite and the mill owners; they were both equally distrustful of union reformers, regarded as "revolutionaries" and "troublemakers." The educated class assured the people that they had a right to work and that sometimes patriotism, understood as both loyalty to the group and to the new country, demanded that they play a passive role. This is how Canadian workers were persuaded to break the Fall River strike in 1879.

Perhaps these immigrants were too passive, but one may also attribute their tendency to obey blindly, where strikes were concerned, to their dire poverty. Happy to have found steady employment, they were not inclined to make demands, not wanting to appear ungrateful when "manna was falling from heaven." This is why they were so reliable and hardworking, turning into "excellent hands" as their leaders called them.

They succeeded in adapting themselves to debilitating and monotonous factory work. While it is true that agricultural labor was also monotonous, mill work was very different from farm work. In the factory system, work was broken down into discrete tasks, each worker being responsible for a single operation. A worker could thus find his job to be alienating—he got to see only a tiny part of the manufacturing process, and his personal involvement was limited to a few mechanical operations that never allowed for any creativity on his part.

Despite the dehumanizing monotony and the unhealthy working conditions, the *Canadiens*, nonetheless, threw themselves into their work. Neither the speed of the operations, nor the risk of accidents, not even the long twelve-hour days in overheated, poorly ventilated, and extremely humid workrooms, or even a ridiculously low salary, could demoralize Canadian workers. They were realistic about accepting their lot, as is shown by this remark of an old Canadian: "We're making money, but we're paying for it!"

One aspect of the group's behavior that is still poorly understood is the involvement of children in factory work. Without suggesting that the Canadians were never guilty of abuses in this area, it can be said in their favor that the wages paid by textile companies in the nineteenth century were not sufficient for a father to support his family without the help of his children and often that of his wife. Moreover, this was a time when the family's welfare took precedence over that of the individual. What had been true in Québec, where children began to work at an early age, sacrificing their education and their future to the needs of the family, would also be true in the United States and would remain so for quite a few years after emigration.

With time, a number of immigrants improved their lot by learning a trade or opening a small business. These gains did not always occur in a single generation—it took much longer to "get out of the mill" than it had taken to get in. But the nearly universal hope was that succeeding generations would enjoy a better life than that of their parents, and this hope was largely realized.

This behavior on the part of the immigrants—making the most of a bad situation—can be explained largely by their faith. Around 1900, they had about one hundred parishes they could call their own, and the Church in Canada continued to send priests and religious to New England, considering it to be missionary territory. These priests and religious were the living links between the immigrants and their native country, and they continued to play this role until about 1960—in some cases, even beyond. The congregations of religious women devoted themselves primarily to teaching, but they also cared for orphans, the sick, the elderly, and other people in need. At this time, the largest communities in New England were those of the Sisters of the Presentation of Mary, the Sisters of Saint Anne, the Sisters of the Holy Cross, and the Gray Nuns.

In nineteenth-century Québec, Catholicism had enjoyed a renaissance, revitalizing itself as the century advanced. In New England, it constituted one of the basic components of the immigrants' identity. Religion also provided them with a sense of belonging to a community, both earthly and heavenly. It offered a goal—eternal salvation—and raised people's hopes well above the humdrum of daily life. Finally, it represented something the immigrants could be sure of—it was a secure bulwark in what, to the immigrants, must have seemed a confusing world.

Although Catholicism was a source of courage in the often difficult lives of the people, it was also one of the principal causes of their submissiveness. The Church incessantly preached that submission needed to be practiced in church, at work, and just about everywhere else. Notions of obedience, duty, and respect for the established order were instilled in children even before they had reached the age of reason.

In exchange, the Church offered enough solace to explain why the people unhesitatingly gave it their trust, assistance, and support. On the whole, these immigrants were a deeply pious people and religious practice was a high priority for them. Father Hamon cites two examples from around 1890: the High Mass on Sunday, at which a large congregation reveled in the pomp and plain chant; and the "major mission" or annual retreat, faithfully attended even by the men, as Hamon was quick to emphasize. A preacher of parish retreats in New England, Father Hamon was one of the rare eyewitnesses to have left us a description of the religious practices of the immigrants. This is how he described "a major mission":

> There is no need to worry here about scheduling sermons for men only; the church will be packed every night for two weeks. These workers are not only profoundly religious, they also have a very keen desire to hear someone speak. They will listen most attentively for an hour, even two, provided you speak simply, stay down-to-earth, and as the popular expression goes, you don't "raise the feed rack above their heads."
>
> Once the sermon is over, confessions begin and they can last until ten or eleven o'clock. The next morning, as early as 4:30, these good folks will be back in church to hear mass and receive holy communion.
>
> We often witness some truly heroic deeds during these missions. Every night, in the middle of winter and over rough roads, some workers will walk five to seven kilometers to "come to prayer," as they say.
> (Hamon, *Les Canadiens-français de la Nouvelle-Angleterre,* pp. 96-97)

The immigrants expressed their faith through a host of pious observances—retreats, processions, novenas, triduums, and special devotions.

The century ended, nonetheless, on a discordant note where religion was concerned since the immigrants continued to insist on the absolute necessity of separate parishes similar to those being sought by Germans and Poles. Here is how an old Canadian, forced by circumstances to attend an Irish church, explained this insistence to Father Hamon: "Father, I'm poor, I often don't have the ten cents I need to get into church; then I don't understand the sermon: I don't know any English; their music doesn't appeal to me; I don't know much more when I come out of there than I did before I went in. . . . You realize, don't you, that *you really have to make an effort* to go to those kinds of masses." (Hamon, p. 61). Fearing apostasy, schism, or the widespread abandonment of religious practice, the episcopate made some halfhearted concessions.

The outlook and lifestyle of the immigrants remained very Canadian, even if their new name, "Franco-Americans"—used more often by the élite than by the people—denoted an evolving identity. Faith, language, traditions, family spirit, a small-town mentality, ethnic solidarity, within the confines of a strongly hierarchical structure, these were the signs of continuity during this transitional period.

They were living in a hostile atmosphere, attacked by Yankees, Irish-Americans, and their own compatriots who had stayed in Canada. The immigrants, who also had to resolve the conflict between the forces of *la survivance* and those of assimilation, were understandably confused and unsure of themselves. They felt helpless and, above all, isolated, and they reacted by withdrawing into themselves within the Little Canadas which reminded them of the *real* Canada in the most reassuring way possible. Meanwhile, on the intellectual level, the leaders were busy fine-tuning the doctrine of *la survivance* and responding to its critics.

This conflict between two schools of thought, with all of its cultural and psychological dimensions, would be experienced with greater or lesser intensity well into the twentieth century, and would subside only with the passing years. On one side were the supporters of assimilation, some of whom were called "extremists," but who, for the most part, now appear to have been moderates. On the opposing side were the die-hards of *la survivance*, those whose "Canadian" patriotism became more entrenched with every defeat. They sought to strengthen the bonds with Canada and promote the Canadian concept of the parish. These men were the directors of important ethnic organizations and the leaders of the religious struggles; the last of this breed would only pass away between 1970 and 1980.

And so it was that Franco-Americans had two selves: a private one which tended to be Canadian in essence and was visible mostly at home, in church, and at school; and a public self, true-blue American, that could be seen at work, perhaps, or at Fourth of July celebrations. This was the case even for the old-timers, those first immigrants who had to cope with the economic and political realities of their new environment; it would be even truer, however, for their children, and this for quite some time as well.

To understand just how divided was the Franco-American psyche, one must recall another duality: that constituted by the contrast between élite and popular culture. The "official" culture of the élite was dominated by a clerical-nationalistic ideology; it was expressed in unmistakably "patriotic" terms as interpreted by the ethnic societies and the French-language newspapers. Popular culture, only recently the object of some study, was made up of songs, traditional music, dances, and other components of a folkloric nature. It was in the areas of religion and language that the popular culture and that of the élite came together.

Seen from the vantage point of a century later, the Canadians, much like the immigrants who came from Europe and elsewhere, appear to have been isolated. Excluded from the Québec and Acadian societies from which they had exiled themselves, the immigrants from Canada were definitely marginalized in the Anglo-Saxon society of their adopted country. But, even within these confines, genuine pride was felt and often expressed although solely within the group since these manifestations were designed primarily to inspire pride in the Franco-American immigrants themselves. This can be seen in the preface written by Charles Daoust to his *Histoire des Canadiens-français du Rhode Island*, published in 1895:

> Faithful to our sacred traditions, and filled with the enthusiasm of those noble souls who preceded us in this land of true liberty, we will inscribe our deeds on the bronze tablets of history so that in centuries to come, our children will see there the realization of that ancient dictum whose truth is now acknowledged by everyone: *Gesta Dei per Francos!*

With criticism coming from all sides, it is hardly surprising to find orators and journalists constantly resorting to trumpeting pride in their origins.

French-Canadian immigrants had other reasons to be proud, not the least of which was their self-sufficiency. Whether out of distrust of a new, and therefore strange country, or out of an instinctive desire to pass unnoticed, or from their concern with not "disturbing "others, the immigrants created an entire network of schools, hospitals, and charitable institutions. To achieve this, they even accepted a system of dual taxation, making regular contributions to support their institutions while paying the taxes imposed by the government, thereby asserting a certain independence vis-à-vis the Anglo-American majority.

Such a marked preference for self-sufficiency reveals a deep sense of solidarity at both the family as well as the parish level. Individuals felt responsible for the needy and found a way to assist them, rejecting the notion of asking for help from "strangers, that is, from a public assistance agency.

But this solidarity had its limits. On the political level, one might have expected the group to form a cohesive block so as to present a solid, united front, but such was not the case. The two major parties, Democrats and Republicans, shared the votes of the naturalized immigrants.

The ever-increasing level of participation in the political life of the United States was yet another sign that, in point of fact, the community was evolving towards permanent settlement. At the same time, adaptation to urban life was taking place, accompanied no doubt by some sadness at the loss of the warm relationships that had once been experienced in rural Québec or Acadia. In an urban setting, particularly in factories, more often than not, these relationships tended to be impersonal. Emigration meant adaptation.

Obviously the young adapted more quickly. Having little or no knowledge of Canada, they were more inclined psychologically to distance themselves from it. They naturally felt more American than did their parents. Moreover, mostly as a result of economic prosperity, they sought to Americanize themselves. And if they married a non-Canadian, the process of Americanization increased all the more quickly since English would be the language spoken at home.

It should also be noted that at the turn of the century the presence of Acadians in New England became ever more noticeable. They sought to federate their organizations, following the realization in

Acadia that the Acadians of the diaspora were becoming too numerous in New England to be ignored.

Around 1900, the migratory flow had become irreversible and the majority of the immigrants were in the process of settling permanently in their adopted country. Constantly replenished and reinforced by newcomers, the group would reach its maturity, if not its golden age, two or so decades later. It would demonstrate its vitality by the very struggles it would undertake in later years.

Estimated French-Canadian population of New England by regions and selected communities, 1900

Region & Community	Number	Region & Community	Number
1. Blackstone	120,000	6. Quinebaug	35,000
Woonsocket, RI	17,000	Southbridge, MA	6,027
Worcester, MA	15,300	Webster-Dudley, MA	3,650
Providence, RI	8,000	Putnam, CT	2,800
Warwick, RI	7,700	Plainfield, CT	2,800
Fitchburg, MA	7,200	Thompson, CT	2,500
Central Falls, RI	6,000	Willimantic, CT	2,400
Pawtucket, RI	5,200	Taftville, CT	2,000
Marlborough, MA	4,000	Danielsonville, CT	1,800
Spencer, MA	4,000	7. Boston	35,000
Gardner, MA	2,400	Salem, MA	6,900
Leominster, MA	2,000	Boston, MA	5,800
Warren, RI	2,000	Cambridge, MA	3,200
2. Merrimack Valley	87,000	Lynn, MA	2,700
Lowell, MA	24,000	Newton, MA	1,450
Manchester, NH	23,000	8. Western Vermont	30,000
Lawrence, MA	11,500	Burlington, VT	5,000
Nashua, NH	8,200	Winooski,VT	2,600
Haverhill, MA	5,500	St. Albans, VT	2,000
Suncook, NH	2,200	Brandon, VT	1,600
Laconia, NH	2,000	Swanton, VT	1,550
Concord, NH	2,000	Rutland, VT	1,500
3.Maine & Southeastern NH	60,000	9. Aroostook County, ME	20,000
Biddeford-Saco, ME	16,500	10. Central & Southwestern Connecticut	16,000
Lewiston-Auburn, ME	13,300	Waterbury, CT	4,000
Waterville, ME	4,300	Meriden, CT	1,700
Old Town, ME	3,000	Hartford, CT	1,650
Somersworth, NH	2,840	New Haven, CT	1,200
Brunswick, ME	2,800	Bridgeport, CT	1,000
Westbrook, ME	2,400	11. Berkshire County	13,000
Augusta, ME	1,900	North Adams, MA	5,000
4. Southeastern MA	57,000	Adams, MA	3,000
Fall River, MA	33,000	Pittsfield, MA	1,700
New Bedford, MA	15,000	12. All other areas	55,000
Taunton, MA	4,200	Berlin, NH	3,000
Brockton, MA	1,600	St. Johnsbury, VT	2,100
5. Central Massachusetts	45,000	Claremont, NH	2,000
Holyoke, MA	15,500		
Springfield, MA	6,500		
Chicopee, MA	4,200		
Ware, MA	3,200		
Northampton, MA	2,800	**Total New England**	**573,000**
Palmer, MA	2,100		

This table, taken from Ralph D. Vicero's "Immigration of French Canadians to New England 1840-1900: A Geographical Analysis" allows us to see at a glance where French Canadians had settled in New England by 1900. Most of these cities and towns are located on a river, the mills' source of power.

II

GROWTH AND CONFLICTS
1900-1935

The French Canadians who immigrated to the United States between 1900 and 1930 formed part of the last major wave of immigration. While immigrants from Northern Europe—English, Germans, Scandinavians—had been the most numerous between 1860 and 1890, the greatest number from 1890 to 1914 were Southern Europeans and Slavs.

Some Americans were distressed over this immigration from southern and eastern Europe. They denounced the invasion of the country by this "human debris" that was transforming it into a "cesspool." In 1894 the Immigration Restriction League spearheaded a movement that, for racial reasons, sought to deny entry to all but members of the Nordic race, a vague term that seemed to exclude French Canadians. This was the period when a developing racist ideology was furthered by those who sought at all costs to maintain American racial "purity" and avoid the degeneracy that mixed marriages would inevitably entail. This racism reached its zenith during and after the First World War, and such was the turmoil it created in the United States that it was sometimes difficult to distinguish between authentic patriotism and fanaticism.

During the 1920s, the distrust of "hyphenated Americans" led to attempts, legislative especially, to "Americanize" the country as quickly as possible and to ban any further immigration. But, in the century before 1930, more than thirty million immigrants had settled in the United States, including nearly a million French Canadians.

From 1900 to 1930, religious and civil authorities in Québec and Acadia continued to denounce emigration. Seeking to maintain a population level high enough to meet the demands of the nation's future, they, like their predecessors, were ready to characterize emigrants as "traitors," "deserters," or even "vile mercenaries," and again, just as in the past, with no apparent success at stemming the tide of departures. For some of these leaders, persons seeking to leave their homeland had to be deviants. As late as 1926, for example, Rev. Georges-Marie Bilodeau could write:

> The true cause of the exodus from here is a flawed mentality which banishes thrift from homes along with parental authority and love of the land. Pleasure becomes life's primary goal. This mental deficiency has not been sufficiently countered by our preaching, our teaching, our newspapers, or our power of example. (Bilodeau, *Pour rester au pays*, p. 27)

Meanwhile the comings and goings across the Canadian-American border continued as Canadians repatriated themselves either temporarily or permanently, depending on the job market. New means of transportation meant greater mobility, and this made emigration less traumatic than it had been in the nineteenth century. In fact, it was said that people were leaving on the slightest pretext: "A man loses a rooster and he leaves for the States."

The Immigrant as a Proletarian

From 1900 to 1930, immigrants coming from Québec and Acadia to take part in New England's industrialization were drawn especially to medium-sized cities stretching from Lewiston, Maine, to Waterbury, Connecticut, with population levels between 50,000 and 75,000 people, or to cities, like Fall River and Lowell, both of them in Massachusetts, with populations reaching 100,000 persons, or even to larger cities like

Worcester and Springfield, Massachusetts. These cities were usually located on waterways powerful enough to supply the energy needed for factories employing several thousand people. In fact, many Franco-American population centers can be found on a map just by following the course of major rivers like the Androscoggin in New Hampshire and Maine, the Merrimack in New Hampshire and northeastern Massachusetts, and the Connecticut which runs north-south through New England.

By the end of the 1900 to 1930 period, newcomers and their predecessors had found their way into almost all of the industrial and commercial sectors in the region. They made political inroads while the country continued to attract a certain number of professionals: physicians, men and women of the teaching orders, nursing sisters, journalists, and clergymen. Research reveals both a diversity of employment along with a heavy concentration in the textile industry.

Diverse factors help explain the attraction that this industry held for French-Canadian immigrants. First, they were drawn by its prodigious expansion in the second half of the nineteenth century, as seen by the many factories built during this period in New England and New York State. Moreover, jobs in these factories did not require a lengthy apprenticeship, although this varied with the type of operation, and the large number of nonspecialized factory jobs provided work for entire families, including relatively young children. Because wages were low, a family often had to sacrifice the children's education in order to survive. Finally, by 1900 and even earlier, their reputation for combining docility with competence made it easy for French-Canadian immigrants to find work in the textile mills.

Contrary to all appearances—jobs aplenty and the opportunity for a great many immigrants to achieve a standard of living higher than they could have enjoyed in Québec—the textile industry was in fact going through a difficult period. The Quebecers and Acadians who came to work in the spinning mills between 1900 and 1930 arrived at a time when this industry, the most important one in the region, was on the verge of failing and plunging the New England economy into an abyss from which some cities, even today, have yet to emerge. Since this calamity affected hundreds of thousands of French-Canadian immigrants, it deserves careful consideration.

Anyone reflecting for a moment on this troubled period in the region's history soon realizes that it is riddled with controversy. Rather than risk widening the areas of disagreement, it seems preferable to describe here, as objectively as possible, the circumstances that led to the collapse of the textile industry in the North. Two of the principal factors were the industrial development of the South and the rise of the labor movement in the North.

At the conclusion of the catastrophic Civil War (1861-1865), the South was forced to rebuild its economy under very difficult conditions. The success of industrialization in the North encouraged several State governments, including North and South Carolina and Georgia, to begin industrializing the region on a vast scale.

To attract capital investment, these States began by exploiting the advantages they already enjoyed and adding some whenever they could. Some twenty years later, the transformation of the South was well under way, due in particular to the easy access it had to natural resources. This included some types of cotton that the North had been selling at a good profit for the last half century despite the high cost of transportation. Moreover, these States were located nearer than the northern States to the rich Appalachian coal deposits, thus helping to reduce their energy costs. Energy, especially electricity, was already cheaper in the South than in the North. The South also offered investors a large and manageable work force badly in need of jobs. The prospects of industrialists were further enhanced by the passage of legislation favoring them over workers in such areas as taxes, property evaluations, working conditions, and wages. This explains why, by 1880, one-fifth of the textile industry in the United States was already located in the South. But this was just the beginning of the South's market penetration; its dynamic competitiveness would make it so dominant that a half-century later, around 1930-1940, northern industrialists would have to admit defeat.

All of these advantages would continue to favor the South which, throughout its period of expansion, was able to forestall demands for labor unions and wage increases. The absence of even minimal conditions that might have protected workers from abuse—not to say exploitation—gave the South a decisive edge in its economic competition with the North. Since the cost of living was lower in the South, workers could get by on salaries that would have seemed absurdly low in New England. In addition, southern industrialists were more willing than their competitors in the Northeast to take advantage of technological advances. While factories and equipment were becoming increasingly obsolete in the North, the South was constantly modernizing with the building of each new plant.

This industrial growth of the South also coincided with the development of labor unions in the Northeast. Already hampered by laws that, since the end of the nineteenth century, protected workers against certain abuses (including night work for women and children and the hiring of children under the age of thirteen) and struggling to respond to market fluctuations, management in the Northeast cast a grudging eye on this new power which the unions represented.

For textile workers—the lowest paid in American industry—it was more a question of stabilizing their situation than improving it. At the turn of the century their working conditions were already too closely tied to an uncertain, seemingly capricious market. If there was a downturn, management—as it was wont to do—could lower wages and increase working hours; or it could reduce the number of working hours and thereby lower wages. If workers resorted to a strike, management needed only to close the mills, as it did in Fall River in 1904. The shutdown which lasted six months put 30,000 workers out of work. This marked the beginning of the era of labor disputes.

It is difficult to document in any detail the attitudes and behavior of Franco-Americans during this tumultuous period in their history. In certain specific cases—Fall River in 1879 and Barre, Vermont, in 1922—French-Canadian immigrants served as strikebreakers, whereas in other situations, many "Canadians" went out on strike. While the current state of research reveals certain facts, which need to be carefully interpreted, it does not allow for any kind of generalization.

While it might be unfair to characterize all French-Canadian immigrants of the nineteenth century as strikebreakers, historians leave no doubt that they were viewed as such by their fellow workers of other ethnic groups. And we know that early leaders, like Rev. Pierre-J.-B. Bédard in Fall River, urged the immigrants to submit to the demands of their employers. Leaders like *Curé* Bédard, who wanted the newcomers to be accepted by the Anglo-American majority, could appeal to the well-known docility of the *Canadiens* as well as to their ingrained sense of family solidarity. It is also hard to imagine how these immigrants, just down from their farms in Canada, could immediately have grasped what was at stake in the unrest or the complexity of an economic system in the process of transition. It is scarcely conceivable that their sense of solidarity would readily extend to co-workers who were "strangers" to them, while everything served to remind them of their responsibilities: their centuries-old family-oriented tradition, their Church's conservative teachings, and their own very recent decision to emigrate to the United States for the express purpose of improving the lives of their families.

Moreover, unions soon acquired a bad reputation. They threatened not only the managerial *status quo* but, in the eyes of some, the social order itself. Trade unionists were perceived as troublemakers, even as hardened revolutionaries capable of spreading the "gangrene" of European socialism in the United States. In such an atmosphere, Canadian leaders were well advised to extol the long tradition of French-Canadian antirevolutionary sentiment both to the immigrants themselves and to the Yankees who controlled the job market.

In time, Canadian workers came to realize that unions were not necessarily revolutionary, that there was no inherent conflict between union membership and family duty, indeed that a union could combat the injustices of the industrial system. A significant number of French-Canadian immigrants joined unions, although there was never a consensus in the immigrant community on this issue. In varying degrees and depending upon local circumstances, these immigrant union members took part in the series of strikes which, from 1900 to the late 1930s, had a direct impact on the majority of *Canadiens* and contributed to the disruption of the New England economy.

It would be impossible to examine in detail each of the many strikes—sadly, there were far too many—whose effects were felt in most of the French-Canadian working communities throughout New England. Besides, they resembled one another insofar as they all constituted a reaction on the part of the unionized workers to the announcement by management of a reduction in wages and, often enough, a lengthening of the work week.

The 1912 strike in Lawrence, Massachusetts, marked a turning point in what would become a war between labor and capital. It lasted two months and was led by the union called the Industrial Workers of the World (IWW), decried by some for its leftist tendencies. The capitulation by management resulted in higher wages throughout the New England textile industry and provided a new impetus to the worker movement.

Without minimizing the importance of other strikes that took place from 1912 to 1922—for example, the clashes occurring in Lowell in 1912 and 1918—the 1922 strike against the Amoskeag Company in Manchester was one of the most catastrophic. The founding of the Amoskeag Manufacturing Company in 1838 also marked the establishment of the city of Manchester, New Hampshire, which the company dominated for almost one hundred years. At the beginning of the twentieth century, out of a population of 55,000, some 17,000 people—one-third of them Franco-Americans—were employed in one or the other of the company's thirty mills. It was the largest textile company in the world, and its decline, due to Southern competition, only began around 1910-1915.

Once the boom arising from the First World War had come to an end, the Amoskeag again faced the same economic uncertainty it had experienced before the war. In fact, the entire New England textile industry declined after 1920. At the Amoskeag as in other mills, management abolished jobs and increased its demands on workers. On February 2, 1922, the Amoskeag directors announced that wages would be cut by 20 percent and the work week increased from 48 to 54 hours. The general strike that began on February 13 lasted nine months and marked the beginning of the end of one of the industrial giants of the North. Although management agreed to salary demands, the issue of the work week was left unresolved. Workers viewed the strike as a failure because it had destroyed the good relationship that had existed between them and management for three quarters of a century. The settlement left in its wake nine months of accumulated hatred and bitterness directed against both management and the unions, and even against family members, some of whom had been strikebreakers. In addition to the hardships they had endured for nine months, workers now had to cope with worsening working conditions, a carefully maintained company "blacklist," and the feeling that they had been duped by both management and the union; hence their growing and well-justified sense of insecurity about the future. After more clashes in 1935, the Amoskeag closed its doors.

Also in 1922, wage cuts provoked a veritable epidemic of strikes from Rhode Island to Maine. The twenty percent cut in wages announced in January of 1922 showed just how severe a crisis had resulted from southern competition since some companies had already reduced salaries by twenty and even twenty-two percent in 1921. In Rhode Island, Franco-American strikers felt betrayed when Governor Emery J. Sansouci, a Franco-American like themselves, mobilized the National Guard to maintain order. While unions would still win an occasional victory here and there, the end of the struggle was at hand. Sensing the futility of this wage war, manufacturers resorted to radical solutions, all at the expense of the New England economy; some liquidated their companies whereas others moved to the South.

Historians offer differing interpretations of the events that led to the failure of the New England textile industry even before the Crash of 1929 and the Great Depression of the 1930s. But they appear to be unanimous on one point: competition from the South. Permissive laws and a work force that accepted salaries and working conditions that would not have been tolerated elsewhere allowed industry in the South to keep its production costs well below those in the North. This proved to be such an advantage that the South would continue to increase production even in the darkest hours of the Depression.

Experts differ in their appraisal of the attitude that management adopted in the northern factories. What is clear is that, in response to competition from the South, management in the New England mills always resorted to the same solution: lower wages. On the other hand, what is not so clear is why they refrained from using the technology that was then available to modernize their equipment. Did they lack the needed interest or dynamism? Did they for too long harbor the illusion that, since their products were of better quality than those made in the

South, this would assure their success? Or did they simply underestimate the challenge from the South? Finally, did they do all that they might have done to avoid the depression in the New England textile industry that preceded the worldwide Depression by several years? If the answer to the last question is negative, one must still ask why they did not, and to this there is no satisfactory answer. To be sure, the generation of owners that was in charge between 1910 and 1930 was different from the preceding one. In part, it was made up of the heirs of the mill founders, and they might have lost interest in an enterprise for which they had no real liking.

One thing is certain: the coming of vast numbers of French-Canadian immigrants into the factories of New England remains an event of primary importance in the history of the region. Without them and other immigrants from Europe, it is unlikely that the textile industry could have generated the fabulous profits that marked its golden age (1900-1910). Does this mean that these immigrants had fallen into a trap? No, not if one remembers the miserable prospects they faced in their native land. Moreover, while the majority of these immigrants remained confined to the mills for life, some were able to escape them, while others avoided them entirely by either practicing a trade or establishing a business.

In this light, the admittedly bleak picture of French-Canadian immigrants being exploited in New England mills appears a little less gloomy. Some of them, called *"coureurs de facteries,"* ("factory hoppers") traveled from city to city in search of a better life. We know very little about this group of immigrants (seasonal workers perhaps) who managed to prolong the tradition of the *coureurs des bois* well into the twentieth century. It would seem that in their own way these people were able to turn the industrial system to their advantage. They too serve to brighten the otherwise dark picture that the collective memory seems to have preserved of the early generations of immigrants. In the final analysis, it is clear that prior to its collapse, the textile industry provided hundreds of thousands of people with jobs they desperately needed. This is doubtless the most positive aspect of any assessment of the situation.

Institutional framework

After providing for their economic needs, the immigrants turned to other priorities, such as those arising from religious and social obligations. This led them to establish a multiplicity of institutions, organizations, and groups of all kinds, their number varying from one "Canadian" center to the next depending on the availability of human resources and more or less diverse according to the distinctive nature of each of these centers.

The most important of these, indeed the most influential one in the daily lives of the greatest number of people, was the parish along with, in most cases, its elementary school. At the municipal level, the immigrants began building secondary schools that could serve a citywide Franco-American population, along with hospitals, old folks' homes, and orphanages. All of this was done at considerable expense by poor immigrants who insisted on caring for their own needy. These institutions were staffed by competent and devoted members of religious orders of both men and women drawn for the most part from Québec, but also from France.

At either the city or neighborhood level, there were theater groups, literary and social clubs, music and marching groups, financial institutions (credit unions, for example), along with various coordinating agencies for all these organizations. At the regional level, New England and New York, there were fraternal benefit societies—the so-called "nationals"—like the Association Canado-Américaine and the Union Saint-Jean-Baptiste d'Amérique that offered life insurance and did their utmost on behalf of *la survivance*. The Cercles Lacordaire, founded in Fall River in 1911 to promote temperance, were also active throughout the region and in Canada.

Individuals made use of these diverse institutions and organizations as they saw fit. Some used them to isolate themselves in an almost self-sustaining Franco-American community, whereas others joined in the hope of connecting with the Franco-American population of the entire city or region. The vast number of these groups—thousands of them, from parishes to region-wide societies—has puzzled more than one observer. This apparent plethora was in fact the result of both a gregarious spirit and an individualism straight out of the old Gallic folk heritage still present in the Franco-Americans of that period.

The reasons that had prompted the early French-Canadian immigrants to demand parishes of their very own—French language, Gregorian chant, elaborate ritual, familiar liturgy—had lost none of their validity at the turn of the century since immigration continued unabated. The natural growth of families that had arrived before 1900 also increased the need for new parishes. Moreover, if there was one notion, after that of the family, which was firmly implanted in the minds of all French Canadians, immigrants or not, it was that of the parish. It was a mindset that dated back to the first years of New France, and it constituted an integral part of the immigrants' cultural inheritance, whether they had arrived in 1900 or in 1870.

Canadian immigrants expended an enormous amount of energy to obtain "Canadian" parishes. As has been stated earlier, Irish-American bishops did not look favorably upon requests from minority groups for separate parishes, fearing they would delay acceptance of Catholicism by Anglo-Americans and complicate Church governance because of the variety of "foreign" customs that separate parishes would bring into the Church. Sometimes a bishop was trapped between two pressure groups. On one side were the Irish, founders of the first parishes, those who had accomplished the difficult and thankless task of pioneers, the very ones who, willy-nilly, had accepted the "Frenchies" when they were too poor to found their own parishes. On the other side were these unilingual Francophones, reluctant to learn English and integrate themselves into their adopted country, who were abandoning their religion, so disconcerted were they by the absence of priests and parishes of their own nationality.

All the same, not wanting to aid and abet religious indifference or schism, bishops continued to allow the founding of Franco-American parishes whenever the immigrants were sufficiently numerous and their financial status sound enough to justify such an undertaking. But the *Canadiens* had to fight tooth and nail before obtaining these parishes, and at times they had to endure reprimands even from the pulpit, especially during the period of rampant xenophobia around the time of the First World War.

In spite of these obstacles, the trend towards the founding of so-called "national" parishes continued. Often a new parish was established by the division—"dismemberment" was the forceful expression used—of a predominantly Irish or even a Canadian "mother" parish. As a result of these "dismemberments," by the end of the period under examination some large population centers like Manchester, Woonsocket, and Fall River had six Canadian parishes; New Bedford had seven.

From an institutional standpoint, this period was characterized by the practice of dividing older parishes in order to create new ones. It was also marked by the number and the quality of parish buildings that sprang up in the major Canadian immigrant centers. In many cases, the modest wooden church dating back to the beginning of the settlement was replaced by an impressive stone temple. This was the start of what might be called "the age of the cathedral-like churches," given the size and majesty of some of these edifices.

Such was the case in Fall River, for example, when in 1906 the Franco-American community twice had reason to celebrate solemn church dedications in two "Canadian" neighborhoods. On July 4, the bishop of the diocese blessed the new Saint Anne Church, the last masterpiece of Napoleon Bourassa, one of Québec's great architects. This parish, administered by the Dominicans, was to exert an exceptional influence through its sanctuary which continues to attract the faithful to this day. On November 6, the new Notre Dame de Lourdes Church was dedicated. This parish was already well-known in the nineteenth century for having been that of *Père* Pierre Bédard, the pastor whose generosity toward the immigrants was legendary, and because it was the site of *l'Affaire de la Flint,* discussed in Chapter One. The new Notre Dame Church was as beautiful as Saint Anne's, even more so, according to some. The romanesque cathedral-like church was the work of Louis-G. Destremps, an architect born in Berthierville, Québec, who had immigrated to Fall River. Its steeples, nearly 300 feet high, could be seen for miles around. The interior, built without columns, was especially impressive, featuring the works of two Italian masters: the sculptures of Joseph Castagnoli and the paintings of Ludovico Cremonini. The most remarkable of these paintings, *The Last Judgment*, covered almost the entire vaulted ceiling, stretching from the nave to the rear of the church. Measuring fifty-five by seventy-seven feet, this religious masterpiece was lost in a fire on May 11, 1982, which destroyed the church.

During this period, the Canadian immigrants built other spectacular churches in New England. In New Bedford, Saint Antoine, dedicated in 1912, was designed in the French Renaissance style by the Montréal architect, Joseph Venne. Its uniqueness is due in part to its red stone exterior and the profusion of baroque elements on the inside. Above the main altar, the sculptor Castagnoli created an unusual statuary ensemble depicting the vision of Saint Anthony. Of monumental proportions, this work of art fills a half-rotunda measuring seventy feet high. It is said to have been sculpted according to a fourteenth-century tradition.

Joseph Venne, the architect, also left a splendid church in Southbridge, Massachusetts. Notre Dame, completed in 1916, is romanesque in style. Its brick construction has a marble façade, and its interior is a synthesis of gothic, renaissance, baroque, and rococo elements; its bronze doors are magnificently adorned with bas-reliefs depicting the life of Christ.

Rhode Island's Franco-American architectural masterpiece, Saint Anne in Woonsocket, completed in 1918, was built under the direction of Walter Fontaine, a native of Woonsocket and one of New England's great architects. The exterior is inspired by the French Renaissance while the interior is Roman, with Corinthian style columns. The frescoes, added during the 1940s, as well as the grandiose aspect of the ensemble continue to delight art lovers.

Each one of these churches was built at a cost of over a quarter of a million dollars. When added to the cost of the other parish buildings—schools for girls, schools for boys, high schools, convents, residences for the teaching brothers, rectories, annexes, and sometimes even an orphanage or an old people's home—the total often surpassed a million dollars. Not all Franco-American parishes counted as many buildings as did the large ones, but in most cases the church was surrounded by a school, a convent, and a rectory, generally built prior to 1935.

This period of building vast new churches coincided with the anniversaries of the older parishes. This concurrence of events—the new evolving from the old—reveals how firmly the Canadian immigrants had taken root in American soil. It is during these years that the celebration of parish anniversaries became a part of Franco-American tradition. These festive occasions featured a range of activities designed to attract as many participants and as wide an audience as possible.

To be sure, a parish jubilee might not have all the glitter of a church dedication which was enhanced by the presence of bishops, sometimes even archbishops, from Canada. But even a parish jubilee was not without its pomp. The basic formula varied depending upon available resources, circumstances, and the pastor's good will, but usually included a pontifical high mass celebrated by the bishop of the diocese, with selections by the parish choir to embellish the event, and an appropriate homily, which could sometimes be a masterpiece of sacred eloquence. Mention would be made of the special decorations that adorned the church, the occupants of the reserved pews would be recognized: religious of the teaching orders, representatives of parish organizations, and sometimes an honor guard. Solemn vespers and veneration of the Blessed Sacrament would be held in the afternoon. Often there would be a special children's mass as well as one for the deceased members of the parish.

Later, either at the banquet or during the play or the recital, which took place at these celebrations, speakers would invoke the heroism of the parish pioneers and insist upon the importance, especially in an adopted land, of remaining faithful to one's Catholic and French origins. Sometimes the featured speaker came from Canada, and his presentation would cause a stir, as in 1919 when Henri Bourassa spoke to the parishioners of Saint Anne in Fall River and, again in 1920, to those of Notre Dame in Worcester. At Saint Anne, the audience cheered as the respected Canadian orator aroused their faith and patriotism: "How is it that the French Canadians who are today Franco-Americans were able to assimilate so readily into the new republic? It is because you were Americans long before nine-tenths of those who claim to be the only Americans." He further added: "In the past twenty years, I have never spoken to a Franco-American audience without offering this friendly advice: become naturalized citizens, all of you;

take full advantage of your rights as Franco-Americans. You will be twice as effective in demonstrating to Americans, so busy pursuing wealth, how much they need your participation as both a French and a Catholic people."

As a rule it was the diocesan clergy that served in Franco-American parishes, but a few religious orders—Oblates, Marists, Dominicans, the LaSalette Fathers, and the Fathers of the Sacred Hearts—were also in charge of a certain number of parishes. The presence of these communities was sometimes marked by controversy. At times the problem was an internal one, as with the Dominicans in Fall River and Lewiston who had belonged originally to the mother house in France (the first Fathers having been French) and who finally joined Québec's Dominican Province. Of greater concern to the Franco-American laity was the quarrel surrounding the decision by the Marist Fathers to focus on the spiritual, even if that meant sacrificing the concept of *la survivance*. The Oblates were more flexible; they sought instead to reconcile spiritual and ethnic interests. Disagreements aside, these religious communities were an integral part of Franco-American parish life. They also had a regional influence through their campaigns for vocations, their preaching, and their shrines which they established as pilgrimage sites.

Even the most summary discussion of the Franco-American parish as an institution cannot overlook the great number of organizations, activities, and projects of all sorts integral to its mission. Specialists in the sociology of religion will have to determine why there were more initiatives of this kind in Franco-American parishes than in many others. Were the immigrants, consciously or not, striving to imitate their Québec and Acadian models? Or was this profusion of activities, like so many other Franco-American phenomena, the result of the meeting of two cultures? These questions remain to be answered.

The pastor of a newly created parish had to devote his energies to three tasks: building a church, founding a parochial school, and establishing religious organizations for all the parishioners. The latter accomplished a dual purpose: nurturing religious fervor, so that each member would be ever mindful of his or her personal sanctification, and creating a cadre of pious souls ready to exert themselves on behalf of the parish. From the end of the nineteenth century up to about 1960, the most widespread religious organizations were the Sacred Heart League for men, both young and old, the Guild of Saint Anne for married women, and the Children of Mary for young women. Around 1930, there might be some ten to fifteen of these organizations in a flourishing parish.

Groups of this kind, like the Children of Mary of Saint Anne in Fall River, typically performed several functions. Over and above their regular special devotional practices either in church or at home, these zealous souls were in charge of the parish library, and in 1906 they sponsored theatrical and musical evenings as part of their Silver Anniversary celebration. They were also involved in fund-raising activities to help finance the many building projects of an ever expanding parish. Organizations like this embodied an approach that was probably as much Canadian as it was American: that of an active faith, a faith that expressed itself in charitable works.

Some groups and activities were influential beyond the confines of their parish of origin. This is true of the Cercles Lacordaire, founded in 1911 in Fall River's Saint Anne parish, and of the Lourdes Grotto at the Franco-American Orphanage in Lowell. The latter was originally conceived by the Oblates as a place of worship for Saint Joseph parish, and it was subsequently immortalized by Jack Kerouac in his novel, *Doctor Sax*.

Indicative of the piety of the time, the dedication of this grotto on September 4, 1911, was marked by an array of impressive ceremonies.

A long parade that included floats, delegates from regional and religious organizations, orphans dressed as pages, honor guard units from everywhere—"an array of rifles and drawn swords above which the flags unfurled"—preceded the float carrying the statue destined for the grotto:

> At long last, flanked by four guards and drawn by six white horses with their six riders in medieval garb, came the float of the statue of Notre Dame de Lourdes. Hats are doffed respectfully as the statue passes by. She is so beautiful that the mere sight of her brings a prayer to the lips. She truly resembles a queen enthroned on this float which she graces with her alabaster beauty.

This parade, followed by public ceremonies before a large crowd on the orphanage grounds, represents the triumphal era of the French-Canadian Church. Celebrations of this kind were held in several major Franco-American communities. On May 29, 1910, for example, the first Corpus Christi procession through the streets of a city was held in Lowell. It was undoubtedly a very tolerant city, one which in time would became accustomed to seeing tertiaries, both men and women, processing in their religious garb, temporary outdoor altars set up here and there throughout the Little Canada, besides the annual Saint-Jean-Baptiste parade. There were also Corpus Christi processions held in the streets of other communities, like that in Putnam, Connecticut. All of these public demonstrations of faith and ethnic solidarity evoked the Québec or Acadian models which they imitated.

After 1900, major parishes like Saint Joseph of Lowell and Saint Anne of Fall River were able to add newspapers to their network of parish activities. *La Semaine Paroissiale*, founded by the pastor of Saint Anne in 1911, soon rose to a sizeable circulation when this eight-to ten-page magazine became the voice for all the Franco-American parishes of the city. The editors were able to combine news with religious topics so that even today it makes for interesting reading. In

Lowell, the Oblates also published their *Bulletin*, a magazine whose documentary value continues to grow with each passing year.

Another undertaking worth mentioning was that of the "Canadian" cemetery located in each of the centers. Usually established by the "mother parish," the oldest of the local Franco-American parishes, it would subsequently be made available to all Franco-Americans in the area. The "Canadian" cemetery was an integral part of the parish and was often the site of an annual pilgrimage with hundreds and sometimes thousands of faithful participating. Prayers recited for the souls of the departed were followed by a sermon on the union through prayer that must exist between the living and the deceased.

Finally, it should be noted that from 1900 to 1935 the Franco-American parish continued to nurture its ties with Canada. These were institutional links since various parish organizations often formed part of a Québec confraternity. Many Franco-American priests having been trained in the *collèges classiques* and seminaries of Canada, the bonds were also personal, based on informal contacts within the network of clergy, a better knowledge of which would be of great interest. Preachers like Édouard Hamon and Louis Lalande, Jesuits from Québec, were well-known in New England; other French-Canadian clerics spent time in New England, some of them sojourning in immigrant communities for many years: Henri Beaudé, whose pen name was Henri d'Arles, and the historian and poet Denis-M.-A. Magnan are among the better known. All of these ties ensured Canada's continued presence in New England, a presence reinforced by the religious personnel in schools and hospitals as well as by the activities of the mutual benefit societies.

The Franco-American institutional framework can be viewed as a pyramid. At its base were the parishes along with their array of devotional groups. At an intermediate level, specifically that of a city, there were the branches of the major fraternal benefit societies, known as "nationals," along with a number of local groups: older charitable associations, credit unions, coordinating and liaison organizations, clubs, social circles, music groups (chorales, orchestras, bands), military and marching guard groups.

At the regional level, some thirty-five religious communities of men and women served the group in various ways: education, care of the sick and the needy, and domestic service to the clergy. At the apex of the pyramid were the "national" societies: the Association Canado-Américaine, the Union Saint-Jean-Baptiste d'Amérique, the Artisans, and the Société l'Assomption, actively engaged in promoting the advancement of Franco-Americans and ensuring the preservation of their cultural heritage. The role played by these "national" societies from 1900 to 1935 and beyond, a role second only to that of the parishes, must be highlighted in any study of the Franco-American institutional framework. They were multipurpose organizations that exerted a major influence on Franco-American life in New England and, to a lesser extent, in New York State.

At the turn of the century, the leaders of the "national movement" in the United States were able to achieve in part what they had long dreamed of and discussed at length in the nineteenth century: the federation of small, local organizations based upon the principle of "in union there is strength." But "unity" does not mean "unanimity"; the result achieved was not one, as many had hoped, but three major "national" societies that would inevitably compete against each other. They were the Association Canado-Américaine (ACA), founded in 1896, the Union Saint-Jean-Baptiste d'Amérique (USJB), founded in 1900, and the Société Mutuelle l'Assomption, founded in 1903 for Acadian Americans.

To complete the picture (or almost), one needs to add three facts. In 1906 some 30,000 Canadian immigrants, members of the Catholic Order of Foresters, left their national organization because they had been forbidden the use of French; they founded the Ordre des Forestiers Franco-Américains. In addition, a significant number of Canadians had joined Montréal's Société des Artisans before immigrating: they remained members of this organization, enabling it to establish branches in the United States and even recruit new members. Finally, some older charitable associations, jealous of their autonomy, refused to be subsumed under a larger organization and opted to go their own way with no outside interference. Such was the case of the Société Jacques-Cartier in Rhode Island, having its home office in Central Falls, and for the Ligue des Patriotes in Fall River, both of which celebrated their silver anniversary in 1910.

This movement toward federation, however, did not deter a great many immigrants from joining mutual benefit societies like the Irish-American Knights of Columbus, or even the non-denominational Order of Foresters. They were attracted by lower insurance premiums or perhaps even the chance to leave, at least symbolically, the Canadian cultural ghetto. This tendency of providing financial support to organizations that did not promote the advancement of Franco-Americans was viewed as a sign of assimilation, even as a "cowardly betrayal" in the eyes of some *patriotes*, and it would be denounced as such and vigorously opposed for another fifty years or so.

Some might say that the campaigns conducted by the Franco-American national societies were nothing more than lengthy, self-serving appeals. Though we need not go so far as to state that these societies were acting simply out of pure altruism, we must, nonetheless, recognize that many of their spokesmen were motivated by something other than mere self-interest. For Franco-American mutualists—the *patriotes* of the early twentieth century—as for some of their successors, joining a non-sectarian or Irish society signified a break with the group which resulted in weakening community solidarity. In a speech at the 1901 general convention held in Springfield, Massachusetts, the journalist Charles Edouard Boivin offered a penetrating and balanced analysis of the immigrants' tendency to become members of so-called "foreign" societies:

> In all of our endeavors, we have relied too often and too much on sentiment, believing that patriotism would always be sufficient to provide our societies with the strength and vigor they need to compete with English-speaking associations that are constantly improving. We have been wrong in this assumption.
>
> If most "foreign" societies are more advanced than ours and more advantageous from the viewpoint of mutual assistance, death benefits, as well as other programs, the fault lies with us for not having known how to give our own societies the impetus required to remain competitive.
>
> We lack confidence in ourselves; this is almost a national fault. We are too easily attracted by all that comes from elsewhere, and I know more than one "good Canadian" who swoons with joy and grows taller by a full six inches, English measure, whenever a fellow member of any pan-saxonist society calls him "brother." We must admit also that it is no small matter to hear yourself called "brother" by a member of the superior race, someone who has the undisputed and inalienable right, both divine and human, to walk all over us, if he wishes to satisfy this "harmless" whim. (*Historique des conventions générales*, p. 391)

This speech is not just a moving endorsement of Franco-American organizations. The author raises a set of issues that will be debated throughout the first half of the twentieth century: the future of "national" societies in a highly competitive environment, the type of relationship that could exist between immigrants and the members of a majority group, and beyond this problem of group psychology, that of individual identity in a new and changing social environment.

The Association Canado-Américaine (ACA) and the Union Saint-Jean-Baptiste d'Amérique (USJB) resembled one another inasmuch as they were both economic and fraternal associations. The sale of life insurance to Catholics of French or French-Canadian descent allowed them to pursue their mission through a variety of so-called " patriotic" activities. Both of these societies were active at many levels. To their members, they advocated the preservation of their faith and their French language and participation in the civic and political life of the United States; to the general public, they made known France's historic role in the development of the North American continent; they lobbied both civic and religious authorities for the right of the Franco-American people to preserve their faith, language, and traditions. During the stormy period which followed World War I, the leaders of these societies worked together to organize a systematic defense of Franco-American parochial schools whose freedom had come under attack.

Additionally, the ACA and the USJB were both involved in many similar philanthropic endeavors that included financial aid for students. They both reached thousands of people on a regular basis through their quarterly magazines that still exist today, *Le Canado-Américain* and *L'Union*, and through a host of cultural and social activities, not just in Manchester and Woonsocket where their home offices are still located, but throughout New England. Since these two "sister societies" (albeit competitors) had branches in almost all the Franco-American centers, they had easy access to local populations. Moreover, both societies possess remarkable collections of Canadiana and Franco-Americana which together constitute the bulk of the group's archives in New England.

Where they differed was in their understanding of the attitude to be adopted toward Canada and France. More Canadian than French, the ACA, in 1930, had one-third of its 15,000 membership in Canada. Without repudiating France, it sought through the years to strengthen the bonds which linked it to the mother country. In contrast, the USJB, which numbered 50,000 members in 1930, looked to France rather than Canada, arguing that it was French culture that should be emphasized and not ties to a motherland one had just left behind. The USJB did not recruit in Canada, but although focusing its efforts on New England

and New York State, it succeeded also in founding *conseils* (branches) among Franco-Americans in the Midwest.

From 1916 to 1934, the Fédération Catholique Franco-Américaine sought to unite some twenty organizations in New England, including the "national" societies, so that Franco-Americans could present a united front whenever their religious or language interests were threatened. This organization sought to transcend local issues, and despite its brief existence, it succeeded in mounting a successful fund-raising campaign on behalf of Assumption College in Worcester. It was also successful in organizing opposition to a movement which sought to ban so-called "foreign" language newspapers and make English the only language that could be taught in the elementary schools.

In the first third of the century, its leaders attempted to unite Franco-Americans from all spheres of life everywhere in the region. They hoped to avoid the dispersal and dissipation of energies which, if combined, could create a force with which Irish or American leaders would have to reckon. It would be tedious, if not impossible, to draw up an inventory of these various attempts at consolidation, so numerous were they. However, a few more examples will reveal the scope of this dream of region-wide Franco-American solidarity.

In 1908, the Association de la Jeunesse (Youth) Catholique Franco-Américaine was founded; it was active primarily in Manchester, N.H., and Central Falls, R.I. Since guard units known as *gardes* were popular throughout the region—there were about one hundred of them around 1910—an umbrella organization, the Brigade des Volontaires Franco-Américains de la Nouvelle-Angleterre was formed in 1906. This group succeeded in affiliating some forty of these independent *gardes* who were encouraged to fraternize and, predictably, to "preserve their language, faith, and 'national' *esprit de corps.*"

At the local level, efforts were made to attract young people by enrolling them in all kinds of groups: sports teams, music ensembles, drama clubs, devotional and collegiate societies. At one point in Manchester's Saint Mary parish and Woonsocket's Precious Bloood, there were groups modeled on the Catholic Worker Youth Movement (Jeunesse Ouvrière Catholique—JOC), founded in Belgium. Many parishes had their Boy Scout and Girl Scout troops.

For women, the Cercle Jeanne-Mance was founded in Worcester in 1913 in the wake of the first Congress of the French Language, held in Québec in 1912; this led to the formation of similar groups in other areas of the region, notably in Lowell and Springfield. According to its constitution, the Cercle Jeanne-Mance sought "to promote the advancement of its members through the study of the French language, religion, the sciences, and literature, and to encourage philanthropic and charitable works." In addition to its French classes, the program of regular activities included lectures and soirées featuring music or the theater and folklore. In 1915 the Cercle Jeanne-Mance of Worcester presented the première of Corinne Rocheleau's *Françaises d'Amérique*, a series of living tableaux based on the history of New France. On February 13, 1915, *L'Opinion publique*, Worcester's Franco-American newspaper, comparing the Cercle Jeanne-Mance to a famous seventeenth-century French *salon,* offered the following assessment of the evening:

> We declare that this group has been of great service to our people, but it has done even more: it has been largely responsible for discrediting that myth that more and more Americans have come to accept: that there are two French languages, the Canadian and the Parisian. Today, Americans in Worcester know that the French spoken by a Canadian is the same as that spoken by a Frenchman from France. It is to the credit of the *Cercle Jeanne-Mance* that it has fought so competently and so successfully in overcoming such a deeply entrenched prejudice.

The attempt to set up an economic infrastructure for Franco-Americans, begun in the nineteenth century, increased in scale between 1900 and 1935. The leaders sought to encourage thrift in a people whose financial situation was improving as a result of persistent hard work and because a growing number of them had gone into business for themselves. It was during this period that credit unions were established in Franco-American centers. It is worth noting, however, that as early as 1889, a group of Franco-American citizens from western Massachusetts had already founded the City Cooperative Bank in Holyoke whose first priority was service to the immigrant community. They had chosen as their motto: *"Faire fructifier l'épargne"* which can be loosely translated as "Make Savings Grow."

In 1908, Rev. Pierre Hévey, pastor of Sainte Marie in Manchester, invited Alphonse Desjardins, the founder of Québec's Caisses Populaires, called Credit Unions in the United States, to speak to his parishioners. So successful was his visit that the first credit union in the United States, Sainte Marie, was founded forthwith. Due to the continuing efforts of Desjardins and some Franco-Americans who were convinced of the need for such banks, the idea spread. For example, Rev. Joseph Béland, the pastor of Notre Dame in Central Falls, unhappy over the discrimination apparently being practiced against Canadian immigrants by local banks, solved the problem by founding a credit union which became one of the most prosperous of all the Franco-American cooperative banks.

Another example of the successful implantation of an economic infrastrucure and the financial success that characterized this period was the establishment of local Chambers of Commerce dedicated to the advancement of Franco-Americans. Whereas membership in the Woonsocket Chamber, founded in 1914, was restricted to Franco-American businessmen, the New Bedford Chamber was more open: according to its 1925 charter, it sought to "promote the fraternal, social, and educational well-being of its members in particular and that of all the citizens of New Bedford in general." During the same period, in 1922, the businessmen of Augusta, Maine, founded the Club Calumet, and those of Worcester, Massachusetts, founded the Harmony Club in 1925. Their goals were similar to those of the Chambers of Commerce, but the founders restricted membership to white-collar Franco-Americans.

So numerous were the organizations that liaison groups based on a system of proportional representation were established to ensure at least some communication among them. In 1919 the Ligue des Présidents which brought together the presidents of Franco-American societies, associations, circles, or clubs of New Bedford was established, and the Ligue des sociétés de langue française (League of French-Language Societies) was established in Lewiston in 1923.

It would be impossible to formulate an in-depth evaluation of the work of all these groups or even to comment on their profusion without a detailed analysis of their records. We know for a fact that they shared the same ideology, and that all of them were based on the three universal values of the Franco-American group: faith, language, and traditions. In other words, these groups, in varying degrees of course, were the expression of the attitude and determination which, in the United States, was known as *la survivance*.

Ethnic Education

All of the organizations that have just been examined—from parishes to so-called "national" societies—were involved in the ethnic education of Franco-Americans, since the élite took advantage of every opportunity to remind the people of the pressing need to preserve the cultural heritage. Parishes, organizations, and newspapers practiced a form of continuing education through their incessant calls for self-improvement, personal discipline, and ethnic pride. Their efforts were a continuation of the educational effort that began in the parochial schools.

The Franco-American elementary school, the building block of ethnic education, was not born overnight, far from it. In more than one respect, its origins lay in the Middle Ages. The religious spirit that permeated it—its almost Manichean vision of reality, its simplicity, its crusading spirit—was closer to the faith of the twelfth century than to that of modern times. And the rule of some of the teaching orders that sponsored these schools, like that of the Sisters of Saint-Joseph-du-Puy from France, for example, can be traced back to Saint Augustine.

In a more recent past, those who devised the program of Franco-American elementary education were greatly influenced by the Counter-Reformation, by the English Conquest of Canada, and by the religious renewal in Québec in the second half of the nineteenth century. Two of the religious communities that came out of the Counter-Reformation, the Ursulines in the sixteenth century and the Congrégation Notre-Dame in the seventeenth, were responsible not only for the staffing of some Franco-American parochial schools but also for the pedagogical principles and ideas that were adopted by the religious orders founded after them. And it was the British Conquest of French Canada in 1760 that gave birth to the ideology of *la survivance*.

Although his name is not usually associated with Franco-Americans, Bishop Ignace Bourget, Bishop of Montréal from 1840 to 1876, contributed in important ways to the development of the Franco-American community. Among the several religious congregations he recruited from France, two in particular played a leading role in New England: the Sisters of the Holy Cross and the Religious of Jesus and Mary. And among the Canadian congregations whose founding he encouraged, the Sisters of Saint Anne expanded in a remarkable fashion in northeastern United States. Because of his decisive influence on Québec Catholicism, Bishop Bourget also played a major role in shaping, for a long time to come, the religious conscience of even the Franco-Americans, its leaders as well as its people.

The traditional Catholicism practiced in Québec, as well as in Franco-American circles, permeated the public lives of the faithful through its control of key sectors: the parish, the school, and charitable organizations. Moreover, it regimented the *entire* private life of the individual, insisting that every thought and deed be oriented to life's ultimate goal: eternal salvation. This none-too-subtle way of dividing reality into two categories, good and evil, recalls Manichaeism and gave rise to a moral rigor that, at least in theory, was supposed to permeate the life of every individual.

In all things, both great and small, the Church demanded total and strict obedience to the rules prescribed by an ultraconservative episcopate. Little encouragement was given to individual initiative, and one's personal fulfillment could be pursued only in imitation of approved models like Jesus Christ, the Blessed Virgin, Saint Joseph, and a number of other saints. The faithful were urged to action, for the Church clearly preferred an active faith to a purely contemplative one.

Another characteristic of Franco-American parochial school education was the idealism that sprang from the traditional Catholicism of Québec. Like the clergy in nineteenth-century Québec, the teaching sisters were constantly reminding young people of the goal of life—perfection—to which, though unattainable, one constantly had to aspire.

There were also triumphal tendencies in the Franco-American Catholic Church. Since its accomplishments were more modest, these tendencies were less pronounced than in the Church of Québec, but an obvious messianic character is evident in both of them. The "mission" varied: sometimes prayers were said for the conversion of the Anglo-

Saxons in the United States, sometimes for Russia or for the pagan lands—China or Japan. But the point to be made is that Franco-American schools, much like the people of French Canada, were deeply influenced by the messianic spirit, and Franco-American students lived in a Catholic environment which had originated in nineteenth-century Québec. But how does the Franco-American parochial school fit into the overall context of immigration?

From the outset, a Canadian colony in a New England manufacturing center was a beehive of activity. This level of activity would be sustained for three decades—from 1900 to 1930 some sixty Franco-American parishes were founded. About ninety existed before 1900, and in the majority of these parishes, a school was built.

The impetus for the founding of parochial schools in the United States came from the meeting of American bishops at the Baltimore Council in 1884. In ordering the establishment of a school in each parish, the bishops were bowing to the wishes of the Holy See which had condemned public school attendance in 1875. Like all American Catholics, Franco-Americans subjected themselves to dual taxation since the government banned the use of public funds for the financing of private schools.

But even in a country where the episcopate required that parochial schools be built and frequented, the Franco-American parochial school was not a given. First, came the battle with the bishop of the diocese over the authorization to establish a so-called "national" parish. If there was already a Franco-American parish nearby, this battle would be fought by zealous and dynamic immigrants assisted by the local Franco-American clergy. If no parish existed, the petitioners had to face the bishop on their own, and he, like his episcopal colleagues, barely tolerated the existence of non-territorial parishes. Or, as was the case for Rev. Joseph Augustin Chevalier, New Hampshire's first Franco-American *curé*, the pastor had to act alone in a hostile environment to defend the right of the immigrants to have their "Canadian" school.

Sometimes the opposition arose from within the parish in the form of a group of apathetic parishioners whom the pastor needed to persuade. At the turn of the century, Louis-O. Triganne, pastor of Notre Dame des Sept Douleurs (Our Lady of the Seven Sorrows) in Adams, Massachusetts, developed the following persuasive and humorous argument in one of his sermons. After postulating that his parishioners would surely not want their children to become "turncoats," "foreigners," or "degenerates," he summarized their own thought process in the following manner:

> On the contrary, what you really want is that your children be proud of you, just as you are proud of your ancestors; you want them formed in your image and likeness, with your outlook on life, your ways of thinking and acting. You want to live on in them, and you want them to be an extension of your life.

After having praised this noble ambition, the pastor concluded by asking a question to which there could be but one answer:

> But how will your children turn out the way you want them to be, with souls as Canadian as your own? How will they bring respect to your name which brings honor to them? How will you realize such a noble ambition? How? There is only one way: the Canadian school. It alone is capable of forming your children in your image and likeness; it alone is able to make them love what you love and worship what you worship.

In order to maintain parochial schools for over a century the clergy had to wage a virulent propaganda campaign against American public schools. Though condemned as dens of iniquity, these schools continued to attract immigrant children for a multitude of reasons that pastors seldom found valid: living at a distance from the parochial school; a misunderstanding between the family and one of the teaching sisters; parental apathy toward religion; a bias against the rigor of parochial school discipline, etc. From the clergy's point of view, nothing could justify attending public schools. They were perceived as being either hostile to the teachings of the Catholic Church or as neutral with regard to religion. But even neutral public schools were still unacceptable, since the primary goal of the school was the formation of good Catholics.

So the Franco-American school, as unassuming and as quiet as it might appear at first glance, was not a haven of peace. It soon became a weapon in that incessant counter-propaganda campaign mentioned earlier, a campaign that extended even beyond 1930. To Quebecers, Franco-American schools were proof of Franco-American loyalty to *la survivance*; they were also meant to demonstrate to Anglo-Americans the importance that Franco-Americans attached to education.

* * * * * * * * *

In the United States, the First World War gave rise to a wave of patriotism not exempt from racism. This racism was directed at first against Americans of German descent; and then—after the Russian Revolution—against those suspected of socialism; and finally it turned against Jews, Blacks, and Catholics. In short, anyone who was not a white Anglo-Saxon Protestant was suspect, and what was demanded was nothing less than "one hundred percent Americanism."

At the same time, at the level of the federal government as well as in many States, there was a marked trend toward centralization, and in fact the country's history is marked by pendulum swings between centralization and decentralization. When the country is in danger, as in wartime, people feel more secure with a strongly centralized government. And it is undoubtedly to be expected that some political leaders take advantage of such situations, seeking to centralize powers that could remain decentralized, such as the control of private schools.

This was the atmosphere in which the supporters of Franco-American parochial schools had to struggle to preserve an autonomy and an identity that they had wrested only with enormous difficulty from both the State and the Irish-American hierarchy. From 1914 to 1925, they had to defend their schools against a long series of threats to their existence that took the form of legal measures proposed by several of the New England States.

In 1914, for example, a bill giving the State the right to monitor parochial schools closely was introduced in Massachusetts. Ever on the alert, Élie Vézina, secretary-general of the USJB, wired his colleagues on the board of directors: "Parochial schools in danger." The USJB organized delegations that attended the public hearings on the bill in Boston. Franco-Americans joined with other groups to constitute a common front—Irish, Italians, Austrians, and Poles—whose schools were also targeted. The bill was tabled.

Although the participation of other minority groups in this kind of struggle was reassuring, it also raised the question of multi-ethnic solidarity, an issue that over the years had often been debated by Franco-Americans. Fearing that the Irish might seek to take advantage of this kind of collaboration to gain control of Franco-American organizations in order to Americanize them, the leaders kept their distance without burning their bridges with other groups.

During the war, and even afterward, hostility toward parochial schools increased in intensity. The federal government launched an Americanization program, and twenty-two States passed legislation aimed at abolishing parochial schools, especially those in which a foreign language was being taught. There was a debate in Congress over a bill to establish a Department of Public Education to control and Americanize the subject matter being taught. Ottawa's newspaper, *Le Droit*, pointed to the similarity of all these measures to Ontario's highly controversial Bill 17 which threatened the existence of separate French-language schools.

In 1919 two new threats suddenly came to the surface in the Massachusetts Legislature. One bill sought to limit foreign language instruction to one hour per day. Élie Vézina retorted: "One hour per day, that's enough to lose your language." And once again he set about organizing the opposition. No sooner was this bill suppressed than a similar one was introduced, and the give-and-take began all over again: Franco-Americans met and signed petitions, journalists wrote articles, and pastors denounced this latest attack from their pulpits. Public officials were reminded that during the war the United States was fortunate enough to have Franco-American soldiers capable of serving as interpreters in France, soldiers who had come out of the very same parochial schools they now threatened to eliminate. The arguments brought forth were convincing, and Massachusetts parochial schools were spared.

Mention should also be made of the Peck Educational Bill which created a political tempest in Rhode Island and aggravated tensions between Franco-Americans and State officials. For it was in this tense atmosphere laden with conflict that the Sentinelle Affair was about to explode.

During the 1922 legislative session, a representative from Providence, Frederick Peck, succeeded in having a bill passed that shifted control of private schools from the municipalities to the State. Faced with this new assault on the parochial school, members of the Rhode Island legislative assembly, led by Representatives Henri Nesbitt of Pawtucket and Édouard Belhumeur of Woonsocket, both Franco-Americans, were able to have an amendment passed in 1925 which repealed the Peck Bill. Meanwhile, the United States Supreme Court had ruled that no State could prohibit the teaching of foreign languages in private schools, and again, in 1925, it declared an Oregon law requiring attendance at public schools to be unconstitutional. In addition to the protection provided by these Supreme Court decisions, the efforts of the defenders of Franco-American parochial schools were bolstered by the provisions of the new Nesbitt-Belhumeur law; by this act, the State had officially sanctioned the right to teach academic subjects in a language other than English.

The atmosphere remained strained as Anglo-Americans accused Francos of being "un-American," which was tantamount to being "unpatriotic." With the passage of measures like the Nesbitt-Belhumeur Bill, Anglo-Americans feared the spread of papism in the United States. Then, in 1921, a new threat to Franco-American parochial schools reared its head with the appointment of a known proponent of centralization, Bishop William Hickey, to the episcopal See of Providence.

Despite these problems, the Franco-American school system was booming during the years 1900 to 1935. From the start of the twentieth century, its doctrinal foundations were solidly established, and since the school-age population continued to increase, there were barely enough teachers to meet the needs of the pastors in staffing them. As with the churches, the modest wooden structures that had served provisionally as schools were often replaced with modern, impressive brick buildings, like Saint Anne School in Fall River, completed in 1925 at a cost of $700,000. In short, schools remained a parish's priority, and their upkeep was assured by the generosity of parishioners who seldom complained about the dual taxation imposed on all the groups who sought to maintain separate schools in the United States.

This period was also marked by the development of Franco-American secondary and post-secondary education. Prestigious institutions were founded by religious orders of men and women. Boarding schools like Saint Anne Academy, which the Sisters of St Anne established as early as 1888 in Marlborough, Massachusetts, the

Villa Augustina, established in 1918 by the Religious of Jesus and Mary in Goffstown, a Manchester suburb, or the one founded in 1926 in Hudson, New Hampshire, by the Sisters of the Presentation of Mary come to mind. As early as 1909, the Brothers of the Sacred Heart had opened an academy in Central Falls; in 1920, the Marist Brothers established a secondary school for boys in Lowell's Saint Joseph parish, and in 1924, Mount Saint Charles, also under the direction of the Brothers of the Sacred Heart, opened its doors in Woonsocket.

But the institution that was the pride and joy of the Franco-Americans of that time was Assumption College and its preparatory school, founded in 1904 in Worcester by the Augustinians of the Assumption, an order of French origin. The eight-year program, similar to that of the Canadian *collèges classiques*, required that most subjects be taught in French. As the Franco-American population became more anglicized, the college had little choice but to go along or close its doors; however, French culture remained a priority.

Intellectual and Cultural Life

The period from 1900 to 1935 was one of historical assessments and writings on various aspects of the "ethnic question." Polemics and propaganda were omnipresent since all the authors, with but few exceptions, were writing to support *la survivance*; hence the utilitarian and didactic nature of this literature. Since many of these texts were published for special events like a church dedication, the blessing of a school, a congress, an anniversary, or a June 24th celebration, they fall into the category of occasional papers known in French as *littérature de circonstance*. There was also a great deal of devotional literature distributed in books and periodicals published by religious communities.

History was the most practiced literary genre, and two names deserve to be mentioned in this regard: Rev. Denis-M.-A. Magnan and

Alexandre Belisle. Rev. Magnan, a Quebecer who knew the Franco-Americans very well as a result of his ministry among them, published his *Histoire de la race française aux États-Unis* in Paris in 1912. It is the only study of its kind to date. (Ronald Creagh's *Our American Cousins: The History of the French in America*, published in 1988, does not include the French Canadians or the Franco-Americans.) The entire story—the Huguenots in Florida, the explorers in the Midwest, the Ursulines in Louisiana, the Canadians in the Far West after the American Revolution, and on to the Great Migration—is told with obvious pride, in a spirited style, and for the avowed purpose of fulfilling a patriotic duty. The author sought not only to inform his readers but to present them with models. Rev. Magnan also wrote an important historical monograph, *Notre-Dame-de-Lourdes de Fall River, Massachusetts* (1925).

Like Rev. Magnan, Alexandre Belisle (1856-1923) wrote both local and national history. An endearing figure, Belisle was a son of emigration, his family having left its native village of Sainte-Victoire, Québec, for Worcester around 1860. A self-educated man, he learned his trade as a journalist at *Le Travailleur* where he remained as a member of the staff until the death of Ferdinand Gagnon in 1886. In 1893 he founded his own newspaper, *L'Opinion publique*, which he directed until his death in 1923.

By publishing, in 1911, his monumental *Histoire de la presse franco-américaine,* Belisle has bequeathed a treasure to posterity. It is all-encompassing in its scope, covering all of French-Canadian journalistic endeavors—from 1817 to 1911—throughout the United States, from New England to California. The work is also impressive for the detailed manner in which Belisle describes the most significant undertakings. The author's ability to synthesize is in no way hindered by his attention to detail.

Although he is also remembered for his *Livre d'or des Franco-Américains de Worcester, Massachusetts* (1920), Alexandre Belisle is less known for his participation in the Anglo-American cultural life of Worcester. In 1907, for example, he presented a well-documented lecture on "The French-Canadians in the Development of our Country" before the august Worcester Society of Antiquity. It was so well received that the Society published it in its *Proceedings*.

Though not a literary work, the *Guide Franco-Américain des États de la Nouvelle-Angleterre*, published in 1916 by Albert Bélanger, constitutes an excellent survey of Franco-American life. It contains well-documented historical monographs on several Franco-American centers—Lowell, Fall River, New Bedford, etc.—and some useful biographical sketches, including those of Rev. Pierre Bédard and Hugo Dubuque. At times the author raises the bar, and his *Guide* then becomes polemical, more argumentative, making it all the more interesting. Its value is enhanced by the iconographic material it contains as well as several rare texts, like the "Chant officiel de la Ligue des Patriotes"—lyrics by Rémi Tremblay and music by Calixa Lavallée. In short, its 800 pages are replete with information, ideas, and insights on the Franco-American life of the period.

Some centers were fortunate enough to have individuals who, though not professional writers, decided to record what they knew about the local Canadian colony. Félix Gatineau's *Histoire des Franco-Américains de Southbridge, Massachusetts* (1919), could almost serve even today as a model for this type of work. As a general rule, these local histories: Alexandre Belisle's *Livre d'or* for Worcester or Marie-Louise Bonier's *Débuts de la Colonie Franco-Américaine de Woonsocket, Rhode Island*, contain a wealth of detail on the early immigrants and their progress over the years. After having outlined the lives of the first *curés,* the authors took pride in identifying local Franco-American businessmen and professionals. Over and above the lists of cultural organizations and activities, which they contain, these studies are noteworthy in several respects: first, for their efforts to anchor the immigrants in their adopted city by showing how they had become integrated into it; then for their attempts to situate their local colony within the wider community of French and Catholic North Americans; and finally, for their authors' attention to stylistic detail.

Similarly, historians should not overlook what might be called "parish literature" for it reveals a great deal about the life of the period, and its interest extends beyond the parish boundaries. For example, the *Album-Souvenir,* published in 1925 to commemorate the benediction of the new Saint Anne School in Fall River, has some surprises in store for the reader. This remarkable large format work contains a number of anonymous polemical and propaganda articles written, most probably, by the Dominicans of the parish. The authors take aim at Protestant clergymen and at the Canadians in Canada who underestimated the loyalty of the immigrant to Catholicism. One can also find in it valuable comments on the Franco-American lifestyle in 1925. Anglomania is denounced—the anglicizing of family names being but one of its most "tragic" manifestations. There is also an attempt to warn readers about the danger that Protestant friends represent. A lengthy essay on American public school education reveals the presence within the Franco-American community of a "vein" of scholarly literature which researchers would find worthy of exploration. Several passages prove that in 1925 the French-Canadian messianic theme was still very much alive in New England. At first glance, one would hardly have expected to discover texts like these in a souvenir-album.

Saint-Antoine de New Bedford, published anonymously in 1913, but attributed to the Jesuit Louis Lalande, represents yet another interesting "slice" of cultural history. In this publication, the most mundane observations are intermingled with the loftiest rhetoric, in uneven proportion. After his brief overview of the parish's early years, the author devotes ten pages to a legal action brought against the parish. This is followed by a few pages on various topics like the church basement and its heating and lighting systems. Finally, the author moves on to what seems to be his real intention in writing this book and to which he devotes almost two-thirds of his compendium: the solemn celebrations held by the parish between 1910 and 1912. In fact, the book, illustrated with photographs of dignitaries, is really a collection of speeches and homilies given by Canadian bishops and by Father Louis Lalande himself at the inaugural ceremonies of the Casavant organ in September 1912 and at the church's dedication on November 20 of the same year. This volume has retained all of its value because of the precious documentation it provides on that period; it is also a primary source for the sacred oratory inspired by the Franco-American experience of that era.

The cause of *la survivance* was also well served by the publication in 1927 of the most important extant compilation we possess on Franco-American nineteenth-century congresses. Entitled *Historique des conventions générales des Canadiens français aux États-Unis*, it was compiled by Félix Gatineau, a past president of the USJB whose substantial grant for this five-hundred-page volume made possible its publication. Portions of Franco-American cultural heritage would otherwise have perished, undeservedly so, and would thus have been unavailable to succeeding generations.

In this limited space, it would be impossible to attempt a complete or even a systematic study of the essays that were published during the years 1900-1935 for the very good reason that most of them appeared in newspapers and periodicals which have yet to be inventoried. Some examples of essays published in volume form will serve to illustrate the diversity of this genre.

Henri d'Arles, pen name of Rev. Henri Beaudé (1870-1930), wrote in many genres. He published several collections of essays on art, literature, history, and religion—his 1909 book, *Essais et conférences*,

constitutes an example of his varied production. He also championed
the cause of the French language which was under attack by Anglo-
American super-patriots at the time of the First World War. But it was
in his more personal writings that this polemicist revealed his literary
gifts: accounts of his travels, meditations, a personal journal, in all of
which he developed his "artistic" style of working. He was equally at
home in the prose-poem (*Laudes*, 1925) as he was in his 1908
sociological essay, "Le collège sur la colline," on Brown University.

In 1922, G.-L. Desaulniers published his *Précieux pêle-mêle
franco-américain*. Attractively illustrated, it could easily serve as a
manual for anyone interested in *la survivance*. It is a collection of
articles selected from French-language Catholic periodical
literature—what was then called "*la bonne presse*" (morally sound
journalism). In addition to the articles one would expect to find in a
volume of this kind—on Christian marriage, the dangers of alcohol, the
heroic figures in the history of France and Canada—there are some
surprises—"Saint Thomas and the Franco-Americans" for
example—and even some previously unpublished material. The
volume attempts to reach out to the average reader by placing at his or
her disposal the main points of Franco-American thought and beliefs
as propounded by its leaders; this accounts for the preface, a letter by
Monsignor Charles Dauray, dean of the region's Franco-American
clergy.

By contrast, *The Chinese of the Eastern States*, published in 1924
under the auspices of the Société Historique Franco-Américaine,
aimed to reach an educated Anglo-American readership. In his reply to
an article in an American journal in which the author had repeated the
"Chinese of the East" insult, J. Arthur Favreau, writing on behalf of the
Franco-American Historical Society, brought together a collection of
quotations praising the Franco-American immigrants. These comments,
all of them in English, had been culled from speeches or taken from

works and periodicals published in English by American public figures since 1881.

A very different kind of work, *Lettres à mon ami sur la patrie, la langue et la question franco-américaine*, was published in 1930. The author was Rev. Hormisdas Hamelin (1865-1949) who enjoyed a solid reputation for his previous quite orthodox essays on marriage and the priesthood. In his *Lettres à mon ami*, Rev. Hamelin, however, departs radically from accepted opinion on *la survivance*—which he denounces, and on assimilation—which he views as a normal development for immigrants and the sign of a natural evolution. In doing so, he is repeating the gist of the argument made by Colonel Caroll D. Wright, "One is either Canadian or American, and not a mixture of the two." Rev. Hamelin's colleagues did not appreciate this stand on a topic so dear to their hearts, coming as it did from their very midst, a Franco-American pastor of Québec descent, especially one who had written an important work, *Notre-Dame-des-Sept-Douleurs ou une paroisse franco-américaine*. They appreciated even less his decision to dedicate his book—ironically it seemed—to "his dear Franco-American compatriots." For some, Rev. Hamelin's repudiation of *la survivance* made him a traitor to the cause.

As for other literary genres—poetry, the novel, the theater—the period extending from 1900 to 1935 appears rather barren despite the presence in Boston of the Québec critic Louis Dantin [pen name of Eugène Seers] (1865-1945), who encouraged Franco-American writers. The few poems written during these decades were heavily influenced by French romanticism. The catchall novel, *Mirbah*, by Emma Port-Joli—pen name of Emma Dumas (1857-1926)—recounts the early days of the Canadian colony in Holyoke, Massachusetts. In his work *Under Canadian Skies* (1922), Joseph Choquet evokes the 1837 Rebellion in Québec against British domination and attempts to paint a favorable picture of French Canada. As for the theater, though many plays were performed, only one was written and published in volume form by a Franco-American playwright: *Françaises d'Amérique*, by Corinne Rocheleau (1881-1963); it is an ensemble of historical tableaux in which the author's love of New France is given a dramatic representation.

Given the questions that arise in Franco-American historiography regarding the relationship between the élite and the people, one might very well ask whether or not the works mentioned above constitute a literature for the élite. There is no easy answer. While most of the extant works were written by an élite—priests, physicians, or other professionals—they often reveal a marked desire to educate and proselytize. Pending a more complete inventory of magazines and newspapers, it can be argued, at least provisionally, that these writings were intended as much for the people as for the élite. It was hoped that the latter would keep the sacred torch of *la survivance* burning brightly. The writers hoped also to reach the people, either to rekindle in them a dying flame or raise their cultural level, rightly deemed to be inadequate. The issue of the relationship between the élite and the people is not one that arises simply in discussing literary questions; it is important for all of twentieth-century Franco-American history, and it will resurface many times in the course of this history.

French-language journalism was undeniably one of the most widespread cultural undertakings of the period. Notwithstanding complaints by journalists that Franco-Americans did not support them, there were seven dailies and twenty weeklies or biweeklies in 1911. Moreover, from 1900 to 1935, about ninety newspapers were founded in New England, not counting those in the Midwest or in New York State, though most of them enjoyed an admittedly brief existence. From Connecticut to Maine, these were primarily local papers, although the editors—a fraternity of interesting characters who deserve to be better known—freely exchanged material so that here and there one finds articles of a more general import.

Out of this very large group of newspapers, some names deserve a special mention. When Alexandre Belisle founded *L'Opinion publique* in Worcester in 1893, he succeeded Ferdinand Gagnon as the editor of a serious newspaper having a regional influence. In fact, Belisle would spend thirty years defending the interests of the Franco-Americans in their efforts to obtain a clergy of their own. He was quick to denounce the assimilationist policies of the bishops, especially when one of them sought a new solution to an old problem by assigning Belgian or French priests to Franco-American parishes. *L'Opinion publique* disappeared in 1931 and was quickly replaced by Wilfred Beaulieu's *Le Travailleur*.

Equally noteworthy was the sojourn in New England of the Québec journalist Jean-Léon-Kemner Laflamme (1872-1944). From 1901 to 1907, he was the editor *La Tribune* in Woonsocket where another *patriote*, Olivar Asselin, just as spirited as Laflamme, had previously been employed. After his jousts in New England, Laflamme returned to Québec where in 1908 he founded *La Revue franco-américaine* in which he sought to arouse the public's interest over the fate of their emigrant compatriots.

La Semaine paroissiale (1911-1930), founded by the Dominican Fathers for their parishioners at Saint Anne in Fall River, had an impressive circulation prior to its sudden disappearance in 1930. By 1913, this newspaper had become the official voice of all the Franco-American parishes of the city, and in 1920 special editions began to be published for Rhode Island and Maine. Along with pious narratives and moralizing stories, lengthy articles on the First World War as well as pieces by the Québec authors: Emile Nelligan, Albert Lozeau, Blanche Lamontagne, and Lionel Groulx, among others, were to be found in this publication. It is amazing, nonetheless, that a modest parish newspaper could have contributed in this way to promoting Canadian literature in the United States.

* * * * * * * * * *

The fraternal benefit or mutual aid societies played a major role in Franco-American cultural life in the first half of the twentieth century. The history of these organizations reveals two distinct features that were sometimes combined: on the one hand, their corporate ethos; on the other, their role as cultural catalysts at the local and regional levels.

The Union Saint-Jean-Baptiste d'Amérique, for example, was marked by a veritable cult of hierarchical structure based on a quasi-military or ecclesiastical model. The apex could be found in the home office located in Woonsocket, Rhode Island, the meeting place of the general officers and the board of directors. The base consisted of the network of branches situated throughout the Franco-American centers of New England, New York State, and the Midwest. The exact duties of each member, from the president down to the lowliest steward, were defined with the greatest precision. This hierarchy functioned according to a protocol and ritual prescribed in a *Cérémonial* (its fifth edition was published in 1931) which was used in all of the branches. Everything was organized in the most rigorous fashion, and step-by-step instructions for establishing branches, initiating members, installing officers—in short, for the entire official life of the society—were set forth in meticulous detail.

With only minor variations, this was also the case for the other fraternal benefit societies which numbered about 100,000 members in 1930. After the ritual ceremonies had been concluded with great solemnity, the meetings of these societies became festive occasions to which all the local Franco-American membership was invited, and these celebrations, with their banquets, their patriotic speeches, and their music drew large audiences. Clearly, this was a cultural phenomenon solidly rooted in Franco-American life.

These societies also contributed to the diversity of cultural life at the local level. The branches ("courts" for men and "villas" for women) of the Association Canado-Américaine presented a great number of theatrical productions to audiences fond of comedies and operettas. The ACA also invited French-Canadian lecturers to New England. In 1918, for example, Father Louis Lalande lectured in Manchester on Count Albert de Mun before an audience of 1200 people; Henri Bourassa and Rev. Lionel Groulx, the historian, also drew large crowds. L'Orphéon Canado-Américain, a forty-voice male chorale, founded in 1920, delighted the music lovers of the region. In 1927, the ACA inaugurated a series of excursions to Québec which members enjoyed and, in keeping with the official policy of the society, served to keep alive the bonds with the mother country. A memorable account of the 1930 excursion to Gaspé was written by Edmond Turcotte (1898-1960), a Lowell journalist who was later named an ambassador by Canada.

During this period, Franco-American culture was often on display at public events, and contemporary observers extolled the "splendor" and "brilliance" of these occasions at which faith and patriotism were combined. One example from among hundreds: the Franco-American Rally in Manchester from September 4 through 6 in 1910. It featured the congresses of three organizations: that of the Association de la Jeunesse Catholique Franco-Américaine (AJCFA), the Société du Denier de Saint-Pierre (Peter's Pence Society) and also that of the Union Saint-Jean-Baptiste d'Amérique. The program for the Catholic Youth Congress was typical of many Franco-American congresses: solemn High Mass with general communion, "resounding resolutions," and a "brilliant public session" during which the guest speaker held forth for more than an hour.

The 1910 rally's "feature event" began at Sainte Marie Church with the performance of the *Messe Royale* in four parts by a one-hundred-voice chorale and was followed by the Blessing of the "Roses of the Sacred Heart." The parade, featuring the Brigade of Franco-

American Volunteers, included over 1500 military personnel and thousands of delegates representing various societies. The event concluded with a Grand Tournament, a competition among the drill teams, and thousands of compatriots were on hand to applaud the winners.

"Success" and "hopes for the advancement of our group"—that is what these public demonstrations represented for one chronicler who remained anonymous. And he concluded: "Citizens of all faiths admired and applauded the noble sentiments that inspire our people in their inviolable attachment to Church, to Homeland, and to the soul of our ethnic group."

So it was that even Franco-American celebrations took on the pragmatic aspect so characteristic of Franco-American literature; everything was designed to *prove*, to *demonstrate*. Other minority groups also manifested this tendency to make a public show of their devotion to their adopted country; and the country expected it. Such was the case at the "grandiose celebration" in Manchester of Saint John the Baptist Day in June 1926. Two of its components clearly reveal the attachment to two countries and two cultures. First, during the "gigantic" parade consisting of about 5,000 people, some floats depicted subjects which can now seem somewhat surprising: in addition to the usual representations of historical figures from Canada's seventeenth century, there was also a "Roadside Cross," an "Angelus," a "Ploughman," and a "Country Schoolhouse." As these themes indicate, even in 1926 Manchester's Franco-Americans had not left Canada completely. But this nostalgic evocation of Canada was counterbalanced that same evening when, after two band concerts, the fireworks display ended with "the roar of 150 explosives in commemoration of the 150th anniversary of the American Declaration of Independence."

The leaders of the group seemed to be constantly on the lookout for any excuse to rally their followers in a public expression of collective fervor. For example, one might think that the 25th anniversary of a parish group would be observed by, at most, a commemorative mass of thanksgiving. But in 1905 the Children of Mary of Saint Anne parish in Fall River marked the occasion by organizing a "Silver Jubilee" that extended over a period of six days and featured a host of concerts and plays.

The theater, although a very popular activity, remains one of the least known aspects of Franco-American culture. Certain centers, lucky enough to have a professional actor in residence, at least for a year or two, took advantage of this by establishing a theater group. Such was the case in Worcester where Paul Cazeneuve, the artistic director of France's National Theater, founded the Cercle Sans-Gêne in 1914. The group's repertoire included plays by Victorien Sardou, Adolphe d'Ennery, and Émile Fabre; and the group gave performances as far away as Lowell and Manchester. Sometimes also a parish group would put on a play "for the benefit of the parish."

Franco-Americans also loved music, as can be seen from their many musical organizations of various kinds. A center would often have its own band, several music teachers, and as many choirs as there were Franco-American parishes. As early as 1924, the Franco-American Chorale of Manchester was recognized for its concerts of sacred music, particularly for its rendition of "The Seven Last Words of Christ," an oratorio by Théodore Dubois. Starting in 1913, the songbooks published by E.-L. Turcot of Lowell helped assure the popularity of "songs old and new, patriotic, comic, classical, and popular."

During these same years Adélard Lambert (1867-1946), a Manchester merchant, built such an impressive collection of Canadiana that in 1918 it was purchased by the ACA so that it could remain available to researchers. Added to over the years, this "Lambert Collection" remains one of the most impressive of its kind in the United States; and it is still available to researchers at the home office of the ACA which is justly proud of it. Lambert was also an ethnologist, and with the help of Marius Barbeau, the Canadian folklore specialist, Gustave Lanctôt, and others, he preserved for posterity thousands of folklore items, especially stories and songs. His "Canadian Folk Tales" were published on several occasions in the prestigious *Journal of American Folklore*. He also published polemical essays, autobiographical sketches, and fictional accounts. These are amazing achievements for an immigrant, a man of humble background whose formal education never extended beyond elementary school.

The photographer Ulric Bourgeois (1874-1963), whose work was rediscovered in the 1980s, was also active during a part of this 1900-1935 period. Born in Fulford, Québec, he settled in Manchester around 1900 and became a highly respected professional photographer, one of the few Canadian immigrants to do so. He is remembered primarily for his extensive documentation of both the Manchester region and his native countryside which he often revisited.

The Sentinellist Conflict

To understand the Sentinelle Affair, the context in which it occurred must be recalled. In the United States, the First World War had aroused a fear of anything "foreign." Anglo-Americans, aware that tens of millions of immigrants and their descendants were now living in their midst, were deeply concerned about the future of their culture and national identity. Having endured seventy-five years or so of successive waves of Catholic immigrants who had become well organized into parishes and dioceses, Protestant Anglo-Americans now feared an eventual takeover of the country by the Pope. This explains why parochial schools and so-called "foreign" languages were under attack everywhere. This nativist mood was accurately reflected in a popular slogan of the time: "One country, one flag, one language!"

Meanwhile, the episcopacy, dominated by Irish Catholics who had no "foreign" language to protect and wanting to save what, from their viewpoint, was the essential element—religion—reaffirmed its goal of anglicizing immigrants by making English the only language of instruction in Catholic schools. Anticipating immigrant resistance, the bishops resorted to the same tactics the State had used: the centralization of power, but in this case at the diocesan level and at the expense of the parishes.

The polarization created by these sociopolitical forces was particularly ominous in Rhode Island where the Legislature had adopted the Peck Education Bill. Confronted by the overbearing powers of both the State and the Church, whose widespread control could hamper the preservation of the cultural heritage of ethnic groups, Franco-Americans devoted to *la survivance* reacted vigorously. Perhaps no one in 1922 could have foreseen just how extensive and bitter that reaction would become.

As simplistic and erroneous as it might seem today, the French-Canadian adage, "To lose one's language is to lose one's faith," nonetheless expresses a belief which French-Canadian immigrants shared with other groups that had settled in the United States. It was this same belief that led German immigrants at the end of the nineteenth century to demand a clergy of their own kind; and at the beginning of the twentieth century, this same mentality was prevalent enough to induce Polish immigrants to establish this country's first schismatic Church, the Polish National Catholic Church.

Those who would become the leaders of the Sentinellist Movement were well aware of this situation. The better informed among them were equally familiar with Gallicanism, a French doctrine which considered the local Catholic Church as being somewhat independent of the papacy, and they had followed the development of the arch-conservative, anti-democratic *Action française* in France and Québec. They had also kept abreast of the struggles in Ontario to maintain French-language schools. They were also in contact with the Franco-Ontarian leaders whom they looked upon as heroes in a battle pitting a French-speaking David against the Goliath of Protestant Orangemen and the Irish-Canadian hierarchy. Moreover, the Sentinellists were imbued with the French-Canadian nationalistic spirit prevalent in Québec since the Conquest. And, most of all, they were well aware of the religious struggles of their predecessors and neighbors in other New England States.

These conflicts did not involve issues of dogma or morality, but arose over the establishment and administration of "Canadian"—that is to say, Franco-American—parishes. These struggles against an openly assimilationist episcopacy challenged that authority in only one clearly circumscribed area: the rights of the immigrants as parishioners. Did the immigrants have the right to be served by clergy of their own ethnic background, in their native language, and in parishes designated as "national" rather than in the anglophone "territorial" parishes that served all the Catholics of a town or neighborhood? This was the basic issue.

The *patriote* leaders involved in these conflicts are often criticized, not just by their adversaries but even by outside observers who fail to grasp their point of view: that of an immigrant in transition between the milieu of his native country, to which he naturally remains attached, and the environment of his new country. What both neutral and hostile observers fail to understand is that the French-Canadian immigrant had a dual loyalty to maintain—to nationality as well as to religion—and that this duality was being undermined by an episcopacy bent on assimilation.

Nor did these same observers understand that this dual loyalty could provoke a crisis if an individual were forced to choose between his faith and his people. Yet a crisis of conscience did arise because, for most immigrants, "nationality" meant "identity," and faith was inseparable from this identity. To force French-Canadian immigrants to attend mass in a "territorial" parish, where they understood neither the language nor the customs, was to demand, in fact, their immediate assimilation—and thereby ensure their "alienation," in the modern sense of the term. Hence the insistence of both the élite and the people on having "national" parishes and priests of French-Canadian origin.

If the struggles for "national" parishes made such enormous demands on the group's collective energies, this was because the *patriote* leaders believed so firmly in the permanence of the French as a people in North America. It was inconceivable to them that it might die out or that, even in New England, its needs might evolve over time. Outsiders, however, tended to view racial ties as temporary, reactionary, based on nostalgia, and in the long run harmful to the sociocultural development of the country.

The North Brookfield Affair (1897-1904), named after the central Massachusetts village in which it occurred, is representative of these struggles. When Thomas Beaven, Bishop of the Springfield diocese, refused to create the separate parish that the French-Canadian immigrants had long desired, they appealed to the Pope. Shortly thereafter, Bishop Beaven informed the *ad hoc* committee that the Prefect for the Propagation of the Faith had denied their request. The protesters argued that a letter addressed to the bishop did not constitute a direct reply. There was lingering uncertainty, punctuated by occasional feverish outbursts. Exasperated by the situation, some parishioners invited Jean Berger, a French priest of questionable juridical status, to minister to the Franco-Americans of North Brookfield, although the bishop forbade him to do so. *Abbé* Berger's supporters formed the Association Religieuse Canadienne Française, elected trustees, and built a chapel.

This controversy was the subject of numerous lengthy articles in Franco-American newspapers. Sometimes the editors themselves held forth on the rights of minorities, at other times they published unsigned articles written by *patriote* correspondents. The role played by newspapers in these religious conflicts reveals a great deal about the mentality of the period when, for example, a Connecticut *patriote* comments on the struggle in North Brookfield in a Fall River newspaper. In 1900 when the issue was "national" parishes, the entire Franco-American élite closed ranks:

> It has often been demonstrated and proven that in order to serve his parish, a pastor must not only speak the language of his flock, he must also be of the same extraction if he wishes his work to be succesful in obtaining good results. A priest of another nationality may command respect, but since he does not know the ways and customs of his parishioners, nor their fundamental character traits, he cannot inspire them with the boundless confidence he needs to fulfill his delicate mission. *(L'Indépendant*, Fall River, January 6, 1900)

> To deprive a people of this right [to serve God in the language which suits it] is to act unjustly. To invoke spiritual authority in requiring that a people virtually abandon their language for fear of not being able to practice their religion would be a sacrilegious abuse of power, and anyone guilty of such an abominable tyranny incurs an appalling responsibility before God and humanity. (*Ibid.*, January 19, 1900)

The excommunication of the recalcitrant parishioners in September 1900 served only to aggravate the situation. *Abbé* Berger continued to say mass until the situation got out of hand: padlocks on the doors of the chapel, trials, judicial hearings, threats to establish a French-speaking Protestant church, all of this filled the pages of Anglo-American newspapers and reflected poorly on Canadian immigrants. Out of this sound and fury arose a note of pathos when, at one meeting, an old Canadian declared: "We've been asking for a Canadian pastor for the past twenty-eight years."

Eventually the Affair was almost forgotten, its issues unresolved, leaving the Franco-Americans without a parish of their own. Most remembered was the depth of conviction demonstrated by some immigrants who were prepared to brave the Church's wrath in order to achieve their goal. Also remembered was the divisiveness that, in the minds of outside observers, weakened the Franco-American community. Finally, although conflicts of this kind may have served as "noble precedents" for the Sentinellists, it is not unreasonable to surmise that they did little to persuade authorities in Rome to look favorably upon an ethnic group so recalcitrant to ecclesiastical discipline.

The Sentinelle Affair involved three contending forces: the Bishop of the Diocese of Providence, Rhode Island, William Hickey; one group of Franco-Americans, the Sentinellists, who rebelled against the bishop's demands; and another group of Franco-Americans, the anti-Sentinellists, who accepted the bishop's authority. But even before the conflict erupted, an internal struggle had already divided Rhode Island's Franco-American population.

Around 1920, some Woonsocket Franco-Americans began planning for a technical-commercial high school despite the fact that one already existed in Central Falls, about ten miles from Woonsocket. The project was given the highest priority by Monsignor Charles Dauray, pastor of Precious Blood parish in Woonsocket and dean of the Franco-American clergy of southern New England. Thanks to his considerable prestige, he was able to rally a good number of supporters to his cause. There was a great deal at stake here for Rev. Joseph H. Béland, pastor of Notre Dame in Central Falls and founder of Sacred Heart Academy: the local population could not afford two schools of the same kind, and it was expected that the Central Falls Academy would have to close if another were built in Woonsocket.

It was at this time that a small group of Franco-Americans formed a secret society called *les Croisés* (the Crusaders). The group may have been founded in response to a wish formulated by Québec's Cardinal Bégin during a visit to Woonsocket. What is certain is that the Cardinal Archbishop of Québec and a leading Québec canonist, Canon Gignac, approved the new group's constitution and ceremonial which were modeled on those of the Knights of Columbus. The *Croisés* were committed to action, and they sided with Rev. Béland against Monsignor Dauray, convinced that the technical school planned for Woonsocket would be a diocesan institution under the control of an assimilationist bishop and that French would thus be neglected. Subsequent events would prove them right.

Between 1920 and 1922, the project progressed to the point where the new school was now viewed as a monument to Monsignor Dauray, the venerable prelate who had devoted over fifty years of his life to the French-Canadian immigrants of the Providence diocese. In 1922 Bishop Hickey announced a subscription campaign for diocesan schools that would include the proposed Mount Saint Charles in Woonsocket. The goal was a million dollars, and the campaign would run for three years, from 1923 to 1925.

The year 1922 also marked the appearance of the *Catechism of Catholic Education*, published by the National Catholic Welfare Conference, the official assembly of the American bishops. The text clearly asserted that control of the nation's Catholic schools rested with the bishops, this despite the teachings of Leo XIII who, in his encyclical *Sapientiae Christianae*, had proclaimed the exclusive authority of parents over their children's education. Moreover, the *Catechism of Catholic Education* reminded its readers that the goal being pursued was that all subjects would eventually be taught in English in the nation's Catholic schools.

Consequently, the *Croisés* decided that they would oppose the concept of diocesan secondary schools, first because they would be under the bishop's control and second, they would assimilate the very youth on which these leaders were relying to ensure *la survivance*. They resolved to thwart the subscription campaign by challenging the bishop's right to require the Franco-Americans to contribute.

For the *Croisés*, the doctrine formulated in the *Catechism of Catholic Education* and Bishop Hickey's fund-raising campaign raised two questions: does a bishop have the right to impose a tax on Franco-American parishes, and can he then use the proceeds from this tax for projects that Franco-American parents deem inadmissible? The *Croisés* saw this as an abuse of power; they rejected a tax which they characterized as arbitrary, capricious, and designed to anglicize young Franco-Americans, and they refused to accept the passive role which decreed that parishioners had only "to pay and obey."

Bishop Hickey's tax, disguised as a "subscription campaign," raised yet another problem for the *Croisés* because, according to Rhode Island's Parish Corporation Law, it was illegal. Under the leadership of Woonsocket's Elphège Daignault, president of the Association Canado-Américaine and a fiery lawyer, they consulted French-Canadian canonists who shared their point of view and who assisted them in drafting a petition which was presented to the Pope in January 1923. This petition informed Pius XI that Catholics in the Providence diocese could not afford to pay the "exorbitant" tax that Bishop Hickey had levied without endangering existing parish programs, including their schools and churches, and asked the Holy Father for his protection against this tax.

In May 1923, still hoping for a favorable response from Rome, the *Croisés* submitted a formal petition to the Apostolic Delegate in Washington. Specifically, they asked him to require that Bishop Hickey declare his subscription campaign to be a voluntary one and that he be enjoined from dipping into parish funds to meet his goals. They also asked him to protect them from the bishop's wrath:

> Grant the petitioners your protection. Your Excellency will doubtlessly be surprised to learn that in this land of all freedoms, there is one freedom which is often impeded: that of Catholics to present their grievances to the Sovereign Pontiff or to his Representative. The complaint they lodged last autumn has led to their being denounced as rebels against authority; the petition they now place before Your Excellency will expose them to new denunciations which will cause them suffering.

Despite these measures, the construction of Mount Saint Charles went forward. The subscription campaign was launched, with the bishop resorting to all of the public relations techniques at his command: parishes were encouraged to compete against each other, press releases drummed up interest, and prizes were offered to the most successful teams. The bishop personally admonished recalcitrants, stating: "Learn to think in terms of the diocese."

Some thought the *Croisés* were "tilting at windmills" in their struggle against so powerful a figure as the bishop of the diocese. Today, three-quarters of a century later, what is particularly striking is the arbitrary nature of the bishop's decisions and the relativism that characterized some of the Church's administrative procedures. During the course of the nineteenth century, the hierarchy of the Catholic Church in the United States had succeeded in dramatically curtailing the power of parish trustees. In fact, parish corporations were largely controlled by the bishop.

Another factor may have influenced the judgment of some people during this period. The idea that parish finances should be controlled by the pastor and his parishioners was not invented by the *Croisés*. On the contrary, the custom dated back to the time of Bishop François de Laval, the first Archbishop of Québec (1659-1708), and it was based on a democratic principle, to wit: those who contribute money to a cause should be able to determine how it will be used. This notion failed to take root in the United States, where democracy reigns supreme, because the administration of parishes had long been viewed as the prerogative of the bishops.

The *Croisés*, both then and since, have fared rather badly in all this; nevertheless, they were the only ones who raised the fairness issue, though many others, clergy and laymen, had similar misgivings over the bishop's tactics. At the time, however, episcopal authority was as unyielding as it was intimidating, and the system did not provide any method for appealing possible abuses. Most of those who had doubts kept them to themselves.

The first stage of the campaign (1923) was a huge success; only two parishes failed to meet their goal. It was widely known that Rev. W. Achille Prince, pastor of Saint Louis in Woonsocket, did not support the bishop. In Central Falls, especially at Notre Dame, Rev. Béland's parish, the issue was further complicated by a plan to build a Franco-American hospital (would it be under local or diocesan control?) and by the presence there of the boarding school run by the Brothers of the Sacred Heart, whose prestige the parish would have to sacrifice to Mount Saint Charles.

In order to provide a more detailed explanation of their position to a greater number of people, the *Croisés* decided to found a newspaper similar to Québec's *L'Action catholique* and Ottawa's *Le Droit,* both polemical in nature. They were encouraged to do so by both laymen and priests throughout New England as well as in Canada, where Elphège Daignault had the support of a few bishops. Montréal's Société Saint-Jean-Baptiste endorsed the idea even before the publication of the first issue and urged its members to subscribe. The *Croisés* decided that the paper would be a militant one and, as editor-in-chief, they appointed J. Albert Foisy, a journalist who had learned his trade at both *Le Droit* and *L'Action catholique*. But, very quickly, a cloud appeared on the horizon: at Bishop Hickey's request, the National Catholic Welfare Conference refused to provide the newspaper with access to its news service.

In spite of this refusal, *La Sentinelle* began publishing on April 4, 1924. A daily at first, it became a weekly at the end of 1924. The first issues included letters of support signed by Canadian bishops, beginning with Cardinal Bégin:

> You tell me that the new paper will be above all Catholic and completely devoted to the religious and national interests of the French as a people; that its goal is to provide families with good literature, to proclaim the truth, combat error, and in a word to accomplish in the United States what *L'Action catholique* and *Le Droit* do in Canada. . . .

> Needless to say, I warmly applaud this worthy initiative, one that responds so well to the wishes of the Sovereign Pontiff and that beautifully demonstrates the spirit of faith and the genuine patriotism of its zealous promoters.

The *Croisés*—now called Sentinellists because of the name of their newspaper—succeeded in winning many new friends in Canada. Rev. Édouard Lavergne, editor of *L'Action catholique*, came to preach the Lenten retreat in Pawtucket, Rhode Island, and attended some of the meetings of the *Croisés*. He became an enthusiastic supporter of the movement and sang its praises in his newspaper. Subsequently, the *Croisés* promoted his book, *Sur les remparts*, in which he defended Catholic journalism and condemned "the apathetic." *La Tribune*, Woonsocket's other Franco-American paper, criticized the attitude of *La Sentinelle*. This was the first clash between these two newspapers.

Some of the other main characters in this ethnoreligious drama now began to play a more active role. Élie Vézina, secretary-general of the USJB, reaffirmed his confidence in Monsignor Dauray on the question of the French character of Mount Saint Charles. But the Sentinellists remained convinced that events would again prove them right, just as they had been about the boarding school in Central Falls that, in August 1924, was converted into an ordinary parochial school. To explain this change, the Brothers of the Sacred Heart cited the shortage of personnel needed to staff two schools of the same kind along with the lack of space at the Central Falls school.

The stance adopted by the Union Saint-Jean-Baptiste d'Amérique and by Élie Vézina, one of its leading spokesmen throughout the conflict, together with the closing of Rev. Béland's boarding school in Central Falls, roused the ire of the Sentinellists. They sensed the bishop's meddling hand in every important decision, and they were increasingly baffled by what they perceived as the overly zealous eagerness of the USJB to please the bishop and Monsignor Dauray.

La Sentinelle reaffirmed the principle that the Sentinellists would uphold to the end: according to natural law as interpreted by the Church, parents are responsible for their children's education. More menacingly, it declared: to use the funds contributed by Franco-Americans to assimilate their own children constituted embezzlement. Though it has never been verified, tradition has it that articles of this kind were inspired by members of the clergy who opposed the bishop's attempts to control education.

At the end of 1924, Albert Foisy resigned as editor of *La Sentinelle*. He was replaced by the team of Elphège Daignault, Phydime Hémond—formerly with *L'Union,* the USJB's newsletter—and Henri Perdriau, a Frenchman with a solid background in theology. A break with an imposing wing of the Franco-American establishment appeared imminent: the Sentinellists had taken on the

Union Saint-Jean-Baptiste d'Amérique with its 52,000 members, as well as Mount Saint Charles—the large, handsome commercial school which had opened its doors in September 1924 and was the pride of Woonsocket's Franco-Americans. For Monsignor Dauray, Mount Saint Charles, located in his parish, Precious Blood, was a dream come true as well as the crowning glory of a long career.

Faced with such adversaries and all the resources they had at their disposal, irresolute persons might have given up. But the struggle continued, with no trace of discouragement, weariness, or doubt on the part of the Sentinellists, despite the inaugural ceremonies at Mount Saint Charles in the fall of 1924. On hand for the celebrations was the Apostolic Delegate, who the Sentinellists had hoped would intervene to resolve the crisis; there were also several French-Canadian bishops and about a hundred priests representing Franco-American parishes throughout New England. During the ceremonies, Monsignor Dauray was awarded the French Legion of Honor, and Bishop Hickey congratulated Franco-Americans for being, on the whole, a highly esteemed group of people.

La Tribune considered Bishop Hickey to be "the friend, the protector" of Franco-Americans, and reiterated its confidence that at Mount Saint Charles, French would be given a special place in the curriculum. But the Sentinellists pointed out something they considered to be symbolic: at the main entrance to Mount Saint Charles, the coat of arms of the Brothers of the Sacred Heart had been replaced by that of Bishop Hickey, indicating that this high school, the pride and joy of Woonsocket's Franco-Americans, was to be—just as predicted—a diocesan and assimilationist institution, one in which Latin and catechism were taught in English and where students were encouraged to confess their sins in English. *La Sentinelle* noted ironically: "This school was built with our money. True, the money is no longer ours since, after we turned it over to the bishop of the diocese, he lent it to us, and we are now obliged to pay back the loan."

From the very outset of the conflict, there was a growing involvement on the part of the two major fraternal benefit societies, the ACA and the USJB. The ACA, backing its president Elphège Daignault, supported the Sentinellists, whereas the USJB sided with the bishop. This alignment reflected each society's general orientation. The ACA recruited in both Canada and New England and sought in this manner to strengthen its ties with the homeland. But the USJB, with its stateside focus, recruited only in the United States and was seeking to eradicate from the collective psyche an "exile mentality" which it deemed pointless if not unseemly. In light of their repeated lobbying on behalf of "national" parishes, it was logical that both these societies would play leading roles in a conflict of this nature. A spirit of fraternalism, infused no doubt with a degree of self-interest, led these societies to identify with the people at both the local and regional levels. Indeed, to some extent it was because they both had branches throughout New England that interest in the "Rhode Island Affair" grew as it did from 1924 to 1929.

The congresses of the Fédération Catholique Franco-Américaine served to make people even more aware of the conflict. Representatives of some twenty-five organizations met each year, just as they had done at the general conventions held in the nineteenth century, to discuss matters of common concern. At the congress held in Willimantic, Connecticut, on December 15, 1924, the Sentinellist crisis erupted with a vengeance. In a resounding speech, Eugène Jalbert, FCFA president and legal counsel to the Union Saint-Jean-Baptiste d'Amérique, defended the bishop of Providence and attacked Elphège Daignault:

Nor am I insensitive to the attacks coming of late from a certain newspaper and from certain people, "more zealous than intelligent," to borrow an expression from a bishop friend, attacks directed against His Excellency the Bishop of Providence and against the venerable old man in charge of Precious Blood Parish in Woonsocket. . . . If we have complaints, Rome is there to hear us. We do not have the right to parade our grievances, real or imagined, before the bar of public opinion. . . .

When all is said and done, courting public support under the pretext of alerting readers is to ignore the rights of Rome; it drags respect for authority through the mud and sows the kind of disdain and hate that leads to schism.

This speech and the bitter discussion that ensued between and among spokesmen for both sides marked the true beginning of the war of ideas between the ACA and the USJB; Daignault would later call it the "Willimantic stab in the back."

In January 1925, the Sentinellists submitted a second appeal to Rome in which they cited the obligatory nature of Bishop Hickey's subscription campaign. According to the Sentinellists—and they were so advised by Québec canonists—a bishop had no right to impose taxes of this kind. This was greeted with silence from Rome.

A new complication arose in the diocese of Manchester where the ACA had its home office. Sentinellists assumed that Bishop Guertin, a Franco-American who had been named bishop in 1907, would be supportive. But Bishop Guertin called the ACA's attitude in the Rhode Island Affair "completely reprehensible," judging that it showed a "total disrespect of ecclesiastical authority," and he ordered the Association to disavow its position, formally and publicly. On January 17, 1925, no retraction having been published, Bishop Guertin removed the ACA's chaplains, thereby raising a crucial question: could the Association continue to be a Catholic organization without its chaplains? Some people—maliciously or not—doubted it.

Elphège Daignault and the team at *La Sentinelle* nonetheless continued their criticism of episcopal abuses, singling out the bishop of Hartford, Connecticut, and Bishop Guertin in Manchester, calling them "mitered assimilationists." By thus extending the conflict into other dioceses, the Sentinellists indicated the scope of the Franco-American problem and widened the discussion to include all of New

England. Bishop Guertin, from whom so much had previously been expected, was a bitter disappointment to the *patriotes*. This is why they denounced him with such vehemence, especially since he refused to establish any Franco-American parishes, which prompted Daignault to write: "The bishop of Manchester is seeking to 'denationalize' us." *La Tribune* accused *La Sentinelle* of "bishop-bashing," and the war of words escalated.

Despite the protests and petitions of the Sentinellists, the subscription campaign entered its third phase. Members of the Franco-American clergy remained divided over the campaign's fairness and over the answers to the questions raised by the Sentinellists: Which comes first, the diocese or the parish? What role should the faithful play in decisions involving money or the education of their children? Some pastors condemned "the rebels" from the pulpit; others discreetly encouraged them.

During the course of 1925, denunciations flew back and forth at the expense of both fairness and truth. The Sentinellists decried the anglicizing atmosphere at Mount Saint Charles while Élie Vézina and his supporters professed their delight at the privileged status that French enjoyed there. Father Antoine Rabel, provincial superior of the Marists, rebuked Daignault and his colleagues: "Whoever, with his pen or with his tongue, attacks the bishop or the clergy and then claims that he is still a devoted son of the Church and serving a cause that is dear to it, that man is lying to himself." One should not lose sight of the fact that these condemnations were sparked by a dispute over the management of the Church's temporal goods; it was not a question of dogma or morals. But, in their public statements, the clergy of the period did not, for the most part, distinguish between the two. The essential point, the one that needed to be underscored, was the audacity of the Sentinellist attack on ecclesiastical authority. For any "right-thinking person," this was all but sacrilegious.

Some members of the French-Canadian clergy saw the conflict in a different light, and the Sentinellists could count on precious support from the Seminary in Québec City, the bishopric of Saint Hyacinthe, and Montréal's Jesuit-run Immaculée-Conception parish. Even the city of Nicolet was perceived to be a "hotbed of Sentinellism."

At the end of 1925, the bishop's faction appeared to have won. The projected one million dollars had been raised although several Franco-American parishes of the diocese had been forced to dip into parish funds to meet their goal. There is no good explanation for this aspect of the conflict, as important as it obviously is. Pastors had always resisted spending funds that had been accumulated, slowly and painfully, over the years. Why had the faithful forced some pastors to resort to this radical measure to meet the bishop's goal? Did they no longer care? Were they worn out by the increasing number of collections? Or had the Sentinellist movement had a real impact on them? Finally, in December of 1925, the Vatican Council's Sacred Congregation rejected the Sentinellists' petition submitted the previous January. But there were still some unanswered questions: Had Rome really understood the actions of the Sentinellists or, "briefed" by the Irish-American episcopacy, did Rome view the entire matter simply as a revolt that needed to be suppressed?

At the beginning of 1926, the Sentinellists sent the Pope a final petition on the Franco-American "national question." In it, they took pains to specify that they were not motivated by "that excessive nationalism which Your Holiness so justly condemns." The various aspects of the question were reviewed, especially the "illegal system" by which the bishop had raised funds, along with the need for a "national" clergy and the rights of parents regarding their children's education. The petitioners asked the Holy See for an in-depth investigation into the situation that Franco-Americans were facing in the Diocese of Providence.

During 1926, while everyone awaited Rome's reply, the crisis worsened. But in spite of everything, the Sentinellists still had reason to hope. To replenish their often empty campaign coffers, they launched the "Patriot's Dollar Campaign," and contributions were received from priests and laymen throughout New England. Meanwhile, the "offertory strike" recommended by the Sentinellists was having some success. A few Canadian newspapers, *Le Courrier de Saint-Hyacinthe, Le Droit*, and *Le Patriote de l'Ouest*, endorsed the movement. There were also financial contributions from Canada and letters of support signed: "X—priest." Prior to becoming archbishop of Québec, Bishop Raymond Rouleau had also indicated his support. Leaders in the Franco-Ontarian struggle, like Samuel Genest, felt an affinity for the Sentinellists, and Genest urged Daignault to continue his "admirable struggle."

French-Canadian canonists furnished Daignault with arguments drawn from official Church doctrine. The names of Canon Gignac and Monsignor L.-A. Pâquet are often mentioned in the correspondence of the leaders of the movement. And when Monsignor Pâquet published an article on "The Church and National Clergies" in the October 1926 issue of *Le Canada français*, the Sentinellists viewed this as public encouragement, since in his article the cleric developed theses he had previously formulated in his secret consultations with them.

Pro-Sentinellist meetings also helped maintain the zeal of the combatants. The mass meeting held in Manchester in October of 1926 in honor of the thirtieth anniversary of the founding of the ACA had all the earmarks of a Sentinellist demonstration. As guests from Québec looked on, Daignault was given a hero's welcome. On December 12, 1926, a Sentinellist banquet in Woonsocket drew 1500 people, and some of the speakers who voiced their support were from French Canada. In particular, Rev. Édouard Lavergne attacked the Irish episcopate: "There is scandal here, that's true, but it comes from the National Catholic Welfare Conference; it stems from bishops who gather there to mislead Rome and conspire against any race that does not want to follow the Irish model." Samuel Genest added that the fight that was being fought in New England was the same as that in Ontario.

But clouds were gathering on the horizon. Rome's condemnation of the Paris-based *Action française* movement created considerable turmoil both within the ranks of Montréal's *Action française* and among the Sentinellists; several of them, including Henri Perdriau, were partisans of the Paris group. The blow was especially painful in French-speaking North America where, from New England to western Canada, every effort had been made to link "nationalism" with submission to religious authority. What would happen now to the concept of "language as the guardian of faith?" Whither "nationalism" itself? Henri Bourassa was given his answer in person by Pius XI who, at a one-hour private audience, on November 18, 1926, set forth his opposition to "nationalism." This meeting would later have repercussions on the Sentinellist movement.

The struggle became more intense during the year 1927. In February, the Sentinellists brought suit against twelve parish corporations—of which the bishop was an *ex officio* member—for misappropriation of funds. A preliminary hearing was scheduled for October. For such a provocative step—"dragging the bishop into court," opponents said—Daignault was subjected to another hailstorm of insults and abuses by *The Providence Visitor*, the bishop's official paper, and *La Tribune*. In its reporting, the latter attempted to minimize the influence of the Sentinellist movement, claiming that it represented the views of only a small number of "fanatics" doing "the devil's work" on the road to schism. The verbal violence on both sides indicated that an ideological struggle had degenerated into personality conflicts. From that time on, the exchanges were all too often marked by rancor, spite, self-importance, and an accusatory tone. Was this not a sign that the crisis had already lasted too long?

But popular interest was still on the rise, as Sentinellists could observe during their speaking tours and at events held here and there throughout New England. From the anti-Sentinellist viewpoint, what was at least as disturbing as this popular interest—if not more so—was the support of priests. Some have claimed that in 1927, of the fifty-five Franco-American clergymen in the Boston archdiocese, fifty-two were Sentinellists. *La Tribune* denounced these priests who "mount the rostrum to inflame the faithful against their bishops."

Even within the USJB, whose secretary-general Vézina was leading the fight, there was no consensus regarding Sentinellism. Some branches objected to the stance taken by the home office, and some members resigned—membership fell from 52,000 in October of 1925 to 50,000 in 1927. The Artisans and the Forestiers were divided too, as were the journalists. Only the editors of *L'Étoile* in Lowell and *L'Opinion publique* in Worcester supported *La Sentinelle*.

Rallies in favor of Sentinellism continued unabated. Before an audience of 2500 people in Worcester on April 3, 1927, Rev. Georges Duplessis of the Boston archdiocese listed the main tenets of Sentinellism: inviolability of parish funds; establishment of national parishes; opening of bilingual schools that would respect the rights of parents in educational matters; opposition to Americanization as envisaged by the National Catholic Welfare Conference.

The Sentinellists lived through some painful moments during the summer of 1927. For their role in the "Sentinellist agitation," Rev. Joseph Béland, pastor of Notre Dame du Sacré Coeur in Central Falls, and Rev. W. Achille Prince, pastor of Saint Louis de Gonzague in Woonsocket, were suspended by Bishop Hickey. Because of the high esteem in which these priests were held by Franco-Americans, they were viewed as martyrs. When he did not recant, Rev. Prince was dismissed from his pastorate despite his tenured status. A protest meeting drew several thousand supporters, and in the fall, *Abbé* Prince left for Rome to plead his case. His many friends would long remember his farewell in which he declared: "I especially commend myself to the prayers of your little children so that my exile will not last for too long a time."

In July of the same year 1927, the dedication of the USJB's new home office building turned into a counter-demonstration against the Sentinellists. The parade, the pontifical High Mass sung by Bishop Alphonse Deschamps, auxiliary bishop of Montréal, with Bishops Hickey and Guertin of Manchester in attendance, the impressive banquet and display of pomp throughout the ceremonies seemed to confirm the establishment's triumph. During these solemn celebrations, as if to underscore the reasons for this victory, the president-general of the USJB, Henri Ledoux, reaffirmed the gratitude and submission of the Franco-Americans to religious authority.

On July 18, 1927, *La Sentinelle* published the "Manifeste catholique franco-américain." Despite its endorsement by thousands of Franco-Americans at a meeting in Woonsocket on July 28, this manifesto managed to provide opponents with additional ammunition. The document's most controversial provision was doubtless the recommendation to abstain completely from "making contributions to parish funds." The Sentinellists also renewed their demands for "national" parishes and schools, for "priest-patriots," and for the right of Franco-Americans to administer parish property. Now legitimized by the "Manifesto," the offertory strike spread, and when Daignault's pastor, Rev. Camille Villiard of Saint Anne in Woonsocket, voiced his objection, the Sentinellist leader reminded him that he owed his own pastorate to the 1914 "rebels" who had defeated the bishop precisely by means of an offertory strike. Naturally, this "Manifesto" was deemed unacceptable by Bishop Hickey for, if its major provisions were applied, the bishop would lose all financial control over the parishes and lay parishioners.

In October, and despite the threat of excommunication—a prospect that delighted the anti-Sentinellists—Daignault argued the civil suit in Rhode Island's Superior Court against the twelve parish corporations (and thus against Bishop Hickey). The Court's three-part decision prompted a great deal of discussion. It began by affirming the Court's own jurisdiction in ecclesiastical matters; it then granted the Sentinellists legal standing, asserting that those who contribute to parish funds have a right to an accounting; but it ruled against Daignault in asserting that the legal use of parish funds is not restricted to individual parishes and that this property is at the disposal of the Church in general.

The anti-Sentinellists made much of the ruling's negative aspects: the Church had been subjected to civil jurisdiction, and the decision seemed to allow any group of rebels to "drag" ecclesiastical authorities into court. In the minds of the anti-Sentinellists, the infamy of having "degraded" the Church in such a manner was directly attributable to the leader of the rebels, Elphège Daignault himself who, again with the encouragement of French-Canadian canonists, announced that he would appeal the ruling to the Rhode Island Supreme Court.

On November 16, 1927, Daignault left for Rome. He hoped to present the Vatican authorities with an overall picture of Franco-American religious life and show just how much religion depended upon *la survivance* among Franco-Americans. Daignault, who had been warned by a Québec priest that "the Knights of Columbus had vowed to break him," met with a cool reception at the Vatican, in part because of the Church's recent condemnation of *L'Action française*. The Vatican was wary of anything that in any way smacked of the "nationalist heresy." It seems clear also that Daignault's opponents had exaggerated the separatist aspect of his movement and its numerical weakness while stressing the dangerous precedent that the Sentinellists had created by appealing to an American civil tribunal that had now asserted its jurisdiction in ecclesiastical matters.

What Daignault learned from all this was that he needed to impress the cardinals with the number of his supporters. He also learned, and this was a decisive point in this controversy, that in 1925 Rome had sent Bishop Hickey a *monitum* (secret communiqué) forbidding him to levy taxes on parishioners. This *monitum,* which vindicated the Sentinellist position as early as 1925, allows us to view the conflict from an entirely different perspective than that adopted by traditional historiography.

The drama's final act was played out during the painful years of 1928 and 1929. Between January and March of 1928, Daignault's supporters collected the signatures he needed to show Rome just how widespread the movement was and bolster his request for a papal inquiry. Daignault remained confident: "Let me repeat: when Rome learns the whole story, we will obtain justice." Meanwhile, the Sentinellists continued the offertory strike which Bishop Hickey denounced as a "conspiracy against the very existence of the Church and its essential institutions." His words went unheeded. During the collection, strikers would display a card bearing a single word: "Justice."

On Holy Thursday, April 5, 1928, Daignault arrived in Rome armed with 15,000 signatures. In its Easter Sunday edition, *L'Osservatore Romano* announced the excommunication of sixty-two Sentinellists—the signers of the civil suit against the parish corporations—and the interdiction of the newspaper, *La Sentinelle.* The news reverberated throughout New England and Canada. The Sentinellists reacted by reaffirming their confidence in the belief that justice would be done as soon as the Holy See was better informed.

Despite the ban decreeing that anyone reading *La Sentinelle* was guilty of mortal sin, the newspaper lost few subscribers. True, as of May 31, 1928, *La Sentinelle* was replaced by *La Vérité*; but only the name had changed. One could still find in this "new" paper articles by

Henri Perdriau along the lines of: "Abandon Our Just Claims? Never." Perdriau and some other partisans were approached by Casimir Durand, bishop of a schismatic sect, who sought to convert them to his Orthodox Latin Church, also known as the American Catholic Church. One concrete result of these contacts was the publication, in the spring of 1928, of a brochure entitled *Fiat Lux! Le bon sens et la logique* (Common Sense and Logic). Although it appeared without the author's name, it was attributed to Perdriau and bore an *imprimatur* from *Casimir, episcopus*. Despite the inscription on the title page which read, "by a Catholic who wishes to become even more so," the brief work, with its 10,000 copies, was viewed as a call to schism.

Upon his return from Rome, Daignault learned that the Supreme Court of Rhode Island had upheld the Superior Court's decision: the appeal to the civil courts had resulted in victory for the bishop's supporters. Then, reacting to the schismatic tendency of the brochure attributed to Perdriau, Daignault ordered the burning of all but a few copies.

As 1928 unfolded, the tide of events turned increasingly against the Sentinellists. Élie Vézina, the establishment's lay strategist, decided that despite the excommunications and the rulings of the civil courts the movement still had too many supporters. He thought of a way to deliver a staggering—and probably fatal—blow to the movement he so abhorred: he would seek the intervention of Henri Bourassa, a man who was admired by every francophone "nationalist" on the continent. Bourassa promised to write a series of articles for *Le Devoir,* Montréal's intellectual newspaper, in which he would denounce Sentinellism.

While this plot was being hatched, the bishop suspended Perdriau and Antonio Prince for their Sentinellist activities. Nevertheless, there was a large crowd for the 1928 celebration of Saint John the Baptist Day, organized by *La Vérité* in Bellingham, Massachusetts. This village, located on the very edge of Woonsocket, is part of the Boston archdiocese whose archbishop, Cardinal O'Connell, was thought to tolerate the Sentinellists out of dislike for his colleague in Providence.

The Bellingham celebration of June 24 had all the trappings of a Sentinellist rally, as did the 14th Congress of the ACA, held in Québec on July 31. Although the excommunication of president Elphège Daignault and many delegates was still in force, several organizations cooperated in preparing the warmest welcome imaginable for their brethren from across the border. The provincial government, the city of Québec, the Société Saint-Jean-Baptiste of Québec, the parish of Notre-Dame-de-Grâce, whose pastor, Édouard Lavergne, had not forgotten his old friends, the press, including *L'Action catholique*, all joined in extending to the "Canados" what the latter called "the golden hours of French-Canadian hospitality." But anti-Sentinellists were hard pressed to understand how an organization that called itself Catholic could reelect a president, Elphège Daignault, after he had been excommunicated.

At the end of 1928, the Sentinellist newspaper, *La Vérité,* was condemned, and it was replaced by *La Bataille*, of which there was but one issue on November 8, 1928. On December 13, Daignault and his colleagues began publishing *La Défense*. Since they had "sacrificed" Perdriau, this, they claimed, made it "a new venture." *La Défense* continued to be published until February 14, 1929.

From 15 to 19 January of 1929, Henri Bourassa published five articles in *Le Devoir* in which he blasted Daignault and the Sentinellist Movement. In his preliminary remarks, he condemned "the blind animosity" that too many French Canadians and Franco-Americans displayed towards the Irish. He then traced the movement's history, but in such a cursory and biased manner that he weakened his position. For example, when he claimed that the movement was just "a repetition, in an abridged form, of the story of *L'Action française*," this was an obvious oversimplification.

In his third article, "Schisme gallican orthodoxe," Bourassa created the impression that the brochure, *Fiat Lux*, attributed to Perdriau and destroyed by Daignault (except for a few copies), accurately summarized the Sentinellist position. He then devoted a major part of his article to "demolishing" *Fiat Lux*, riddling with sarcasm the brochure's author along with the schismatic bishop, Casimir Durand, a disciple of the Patriarch of Antioch. Here again Bourassa distorted Sentinellist doctrine.

In a fourth article, "Haine (hatred) de l'autorité," Bourassa accused the dissidents of misunderstanding the principle of authority embodied in "that perfect society" which is the Church. Their "crucial error," he believed, was "the campaign of attacks, insults, and slander" waged against the bishop. In his final article, "Démocratisme et nationalisme outrancier (excessive)," the author quoted first from his conversation with Pius XI during his private audience of November 18, 1926, and then offered his wishes of Christian peace to the rebels.

This series of articles, reprinted as a booklet entitled *L'affaire de Providence et la crise religieuse en Nouvelle-Angleterre* (The Providence Affair and the Religious Crisis in New England), was widely distributed by the Union Saint Jean-Baptiste-d'Amérique. Even today, one is stunned and shocked by the pamphlet's excessive and violent language, all the more so since Bourassa knew that the excommunicated were about to submit. These articles created a considerable stir at the time, particularly in the ecclesiastical circles of Québec and Franco-American New England. A few voices rose to challenge the great Canadian orator. For some, like Philippe Armand Lajoie of Fall River's *L'Indépendant* and Edmond Turcotte of Lowell's *L'Étoile,* it was clear that Bourassa had printed only a caricature of the Sentinellist Movement. According to Lajoie, Bourassa had simply failed to understand that the movement was an expression of "national conscience" and an authentic cry for help.

After publishing his articles, Bourassa continued to correspond with Élie Vézina. It is strange to see him adopt one of the principal Sentinellist themes: "Now that the rights of authority have been clearly established and recognized, it will still be necessary for the powers that be to understand that the Irish must stop seeing themselves as the designated leaders of the Catholic Church in America." In reply, Vézina expressed another idea that Sentinellists had espoused:

> The parish needs to be allowed more latitude regarding the administration of funds contributed for the Catholic cause; but especially those earmarked for the development of parish activities. Of course the bishop of the diocese must find ways to provide the various parishes with the institutions they need, but it should be done without undermining the generosity of the faithful who prefer that, as much as possible, the monies they give to the pastor remain in the parish.

Encouraged by priests friendly to them, the Sentinellists completed the formalities for their submission to ecclesiastical authority. The clergy, for the most part, were pleased with this submission which, they said, made the dissidents "grow in stature." But it was difficult for the former rebels to discern any charity—or justice, for that matter—in the rewards and punishments that the bishop of Providence was busily distributing. They were particularly appalled that Bishop Hickey had either dismissed or expelled from the diocese *Abbés* Achille Prince, J.-Alfred Fauteux, and J.-Albert Forcier and forced the resignation of *Abbé* Joseph Béland. And it was perhaps not just coincidental that at the congress of the Union Saint-Jean-Baptiste d'Amérique held in Burlington, Vermont, in October of 1929, President Henri Ledoux and Secretary-General Élie Vézina were decorated by the French Ambassador in Washington, Paul Claudel, "in the name of the President of the Republic."

It is hard to imagine that, in such an atmosphere, peace reigned in the hearts of the faithful. Still, Daignault claimed to be satisfied with his third trip to Rome in the spring of 1929 during which he was able to make a comprehensive presentation of the views that he and his comrades-in-arms had been defending since the early twenties.

In the meantime, Perdriau began the publication, in Central Falls, of a bilingual weekly, *Cahier des communiqués de la vérité*, perfectly orthodox in tone and similar to *La Sentinelle*. Renamed *L'Intransigeant*, it appeared only in April-May of 1929. In New Hampshire, some members of the board of directors of the ACA, known to all as "notorious Sentinellists," revived *Le Progrès*, a Nashua weekly which they relocated to Manchester, inviting that veteran of the "nationalist" campaigns, J.-L.-K. Laflamme, to serve as editor. This paper, which received some funding from the Société Saint-Jean-Baptiste in Montréal, was eventually absorbed in the early thirties by Wilfrid Beaulieu's *Le Travailleur*.

Thus ended the known history of the Sentinellist Movement. Despite the official submission by Daignault and his partisans, many people continued to espouse the viewpoint they had defended, so much so that to this day one can still find here and there octogenarians who proudly call themselves "Sentinellists."

These days, Sentinellism continues to elicit conflicting appraisals. Locked archives and a wall of silence serve only to increase curiosity by leaving Franco-Americans in the dark over this most highly publicized episode of their history, an important chapter in the collective past of Québec and the Franco-Americans of New England.

Since the archives remain closed, anyone reading the extant documents and reflecting on the passionate intensity which the conflict unleashed, can only wonder about all that remains to be known and desirous of knowing more. What really motivated the contending parties? How much popular interest was there both in Canada and New England? What exactly was the role of some of the players, including Cardinals Bégin and Rouleau, Bishop Georges Courchesne of Rimouski, Monsignor Louis-Adolphe Pâquet, Canon Gignac and Rev. Édouard Lavergne, to name but a few? In fact, one would like to know more about the whole matter, including the validity of the excommunication which some called unjustified, since those who had recourse to the courts were apparently not liable to such punishment.

Any attempt to determine just how influential the movement was is fraught with uncertainty. In his report published in 1936, *Le vrai mouvement sentinelliste en Nouvelle-Angleterre (1923-1929) et l'Affaire du Rhode Island*, Elphège Daignault did not hesitate to call it "a redemptive drama," claiming that anything bad that might have come from the crisis was more than offset by the reforms it produced. For him, the movement ended in victory because the policy of arbitrary taxation was subsequently abolished in the Providence Diocese, and it was never adopted by other bishops.

Robert Rumilly, who cannot be accused of being a Sentinellist since he wrote his history of the Franco-Americans for the USJB, agreed with Daignault to some extent: "The great Sentinellist Affair was perhaps the near-fatal crisis of a period of consolidation. Its consequences, fortunate and unfortunate, were hardly felt in 1930. The Sentinellist crisis revealed the strength of the Franco-Americans. It gave the assimilationists pause. But it led some bishops to stop recruiting clergy in Canada for Franco-American parishes."

There was a further evaluation, favorable to Sentinellism, attributed to a contemporary figure, anonymous like so many other actors in this drama. He reportedly told the leaders of the movement, "You have won everything, except for the appearance of having won." This declaration, apocryphal perhaps, may contain a grain of truth, but this cannot be confirmed so long as the archives remain sealed.

The influence of Sentinellism on *la survivance*, however, seems to have been generally negative. The recourse to extreme measures, civil courts, "anticlerical" meetings, the public criticism of the bishop, followed by the excommunication and the placing of *La Sentinelle* on the Index, this whole scenario was hardly conducive to converting the passive or the uncommitted to the cause of *la survivance*. Already in the 1920s, as the Americanization of minds and customs was gaining ground, especially among the young, there were some who castigated "the exile mentality" of the *patriotes*. To have made the question of *la survivance* even more complicated and the object of controversy, at a time when it was increasingly seen to be uninteresting and old-fashioned, could hardly have increased support for it. On this point, Wilfrid Beaulieu, one of the excommunicated, argued that the clergy's abdication—that is to say their abandonment of *la survivance*—could be traced to the Sentinellist period:

> It is especially at this time. . . that our clergy's abdication became more pronounced. Seeing such great injustices committed and how, in high places, the utmost was done to mollify, to "cover up" rather than condemn, the clergy adopted a "what's the use" attitude; this was also true of a great number of intellectuals, professional people, and businessmen throughout Franco-American New England.
> (*Le Travailleur*, February 4, 1954)

Notwithstanding its negative aspects, Sentinellism appears to have been a positive—even a legitimate—movement in more ways than one, even if most commentators have accentuated the negative. In *Le vrai mouvement sentinelliste. . .,* for example, Daignault quotes a letter of January 22, 1926, from his Roman procurator asserting that Rome viewed Bishop Hickey's request for contributions not as a tax or a command, but rather as "a pressing request." Could there have been some misunderstanding between the Holy See and the Bishop of Providence? What is certain is that those who have written on the Sentinelle Affair all agree that in the communications between Bishop Hickey and his pastors, the issue was always taxes and not "pressing requests." The contents of the Roman procurator's letter raise a crucial question regarding the information given Rome by Bishop Hickey, an issue that documents now locked away in the archives could no doubt help to clarify.

Another fundamental question left unanswered is a bishop's right to tax parishes. According to Daignault, the Vatican Council's Sacred Congregation did not decide the issue on its merits but merely "rejected" the Sentinellist petition. For Daignault, this rejection did not constitute an answer to the question brought up in the petition. And finally, the *monitum* which Rome sent to Bishop Hickey in 1925 proved that the Sentinellists were justified in protesting since it enjoined the bishop not to tax the members of his diocese.

In a wider context, the Sentinellists surely had doctrine and tradition on their side in their assertion of parents' rights in educational matters, since these rights had been affirmed repeatedly by the Pope and the bishops. What had apparently been left to the discretion of the bishops of each country was the method by which immigrants would be integrated into the Church in their adopted countries. In addition, there does not appear to have been any established procedure for resolving disputes between a bishop and a minority group.

But what constituted the core of the Sentinellist doctrine was a certain conception of the parish along with a refusal of the secondary role assigned to it by the American hierarchy. Underlying this refusal was an awareness of the relativism of Church practice in this regard: in Canada the parish enjoyed considerable importance, but in the United States it was clearly subordinated to the diocese. The anti-Sentinellists, on the other hand, supported the principle of authority which, in their view, required total obedience to the Church over and above any question of nationality.

Working against the Sentinellists was the official policy of the bishops of the United States who were just barely willing to allow the founding of so-called national parishes for immigrants from various countries, only on a temporary basis, and solely as a means of facilitating their transition into unilingual English-speaking parishes. But for Franco-Americans, and especially for the Sentinellists, Franco-American parishes had two characteristics which the episcopate never accepted: they were permanent, and they had to be administered at the local rather than at the diocesan level.

There were other aspects to this conception of the parish that would seriously aggravate the crisis. For the Sentinellists and those who supported them—both overtly and covertly—the parish was not only the principal link between the individual and the Church Universal, but it was also an extension of the home. There is a passage in Daignault's account of the Sentinellist Movement that is most revealing in this regard. While urging his reader to judge the behavior of the Sentinellists, he makes several major points that have been largely ignored to date:

> But, before judging us, let him [the reader] think about how these sincere Catholics must have felt when they awoke one morning to the fact that what had been their dream for more than a half-century was now over: the fortress of their faith, their language, and their ancestral traditions—their parish—had become the property of another. It was no longer theirs. An enormous change had taken place in the understanding of parish rights.

> They believed themselves to be dispossessed of their most precious earthly possession as a result of this new policy regarding parish administration, one that sacrificed the parish to diocesan requirements and to the many charitable works of the Church Universal. Their church and their parochial school, along with the monies they had so generously contributed to the parish, were no longer theirs. This centuries-old understanding of the parish concept had collapsed!

This text clearly reveals the depth of the sense of parish ownership and the outrage that was caused by this unanticipated dispossession. These paragraphs also indicate that, for Daignault and his supporters, the conflict ended with the usurpation and the destruction of what was perceived by them as their patrimony. It was because they had foreseen this possibility as early as 1923 that the Sentinellists had revolted.

The Sentinelle Affair was the ultimate and extreme expression of a feeling shared by Franco-Americans in general, that is, the malaise they had experienced over the years when others interfered in one of the most intimate and sacred dimensions of their lives. Franco-Americans had always felt a deep distrust of those outside their group. When some of them meddled in their religious life, there was always a Franco-American minority ready to protest—a minority that alas knew that its protests could not count on the unanimous support of its own people.

To fully understand Sentinellism, one needs to recall the disdain in which Franco-Americans were held by the Irish-American clergy. In the minds of some Irish pastors, they were considered to be second-class Catholics. In several cities, Irish priests boasted that *theirs* was *the* "Catholic" church, whereas the Franco-American one was "only French." It is hardly surprising that the Irishman became the "natural enemy" and that his well-known disdain added fuel to the Sentinellist fire.

None of the writers on Sentinellism has ever pointed out that at the heart of this conflict was a clash of two conservative viewpoints, two loyalties, even if the dissidents appeared to be radicals or revolutionaries. In fact, while the Sentinellists sought to remain loyal to the French-Canadian conception of the parish, the anti-Sentinellists chose to conform to their adopted country's then current system. It appears highly significant to us that the defining moment in Franco-

American history, the most explosive conflict of all, was marked by an appeal by both sides to loyalty—that typically French-Canadian virtue.

It is especially regrettable that neither those who were indifferent to the Sentinellists nor those who opposed them understood this dual loyalty. Nor was either of these groups able to understand that this loyalty might provoke a crisis if an individual were forced—or thought he was being forced—to choose between his faith and his race. Opponents then and since have had an easy time pointing out the errors and excesses of the Sentinellists. Having been excommunicated, the latter had to endure the scorn that the "establishment" and all "right-minded people"—those on the side of law and order—reserved for rebels who have been found guilty, denounced as "fanatics," punished, and abandoned to their own devices.

No one, however, should attempt to hide or minimize the errors and excesses of the Sentinellists, especially the deplorable violence with which they conducted their campaign, their lack of tact, diplomacy, or good taste. But all of these characteristics, along with an undeniable intransigence, can be ascribed to both contending parties.

In an attempt to place this conflict within the context of French-Canadian and Franco-American history, what comes to mind is the insight of the journalist, Philippe-Armand Lajoie regarding the Sentinellist Movement which this lucid observer of Franco-American life viewed as "an expression of the national conscience." This remains valid, granting all the while the role that bias may have played among the Sentinellists. Historians have tended to minimize the movement's positive aspects; they have not seen it as an "expression of the national conscience," nor have they granted it the kind of probity that this statement suggests. True, the Franco-American milieu, largely under the influence of an anti-sentinellist clerical élite did not encourage such a viewpoint. Still, once the crisis had ended, several well-known Sentinellists demonstrated an integrity above reproach throughout their long, post-Sentinellist careers. Among the better-known were the journalists, Wilfrid Beaulieu and Philippe-Armand Lajoie himself.

But why, it might be asked, did Sentinellism fail to gain the unanimous or near-unanimous support of Franco-Americans? First, it must be conceded that no one will ever know exactly how many people may have supported the movement in their hearts while prudently behaving as though they supported the bishop. But both responses to what for the immigrants was a novel situation were expressions of the two contradictory aspects of the French-Canadian and Franco-American soul or, if one prefers, of the "nationalist conscience." On the one hand, there was passivity, resignation, a tendency to submit to authority even when one is loath to submit and there is much to be lost by doing so; on the other, there was the contrary instinct of the rebel, the one which led some French Canadians to support the American Revolution, inspired the insurgents of 1837-1838 and motivated the supporters of Louis Riel, the metis leader executed in 1885 for having led uprisings against the Canadian government.

During the course of French-Canadian and Franco-American history, the majority found submission—real or feigned—to be easier, more natural perhaps, than revolt. For the anti-Sentinellists, submitting to the authority of the Catholic Church was one of the duties of a practicing Catholic, much like believing in only one God. Moreover, as Daignault points out in his account of the movement, Franco-Americans seldom moved beyond words to deeds. Even after ten or so known ethno-religious conflicts, it was more characteristic of the population to go along, to conform after having denounced the deed or formulated a few resolutions during a convention.

But in this case, we believe that the Sentinellists were at least to some extent motivated by a typically French mindset—an ancestral Gallicanism—and, to a lesser degree, by a certain admiration for *l'Action française*. The Sentinellist mind could and did make allowances; it could and did distinguish, for instance, between what was human and what was divine in matters of religion. For such a mind, a sincere faith does not necessarily entail blind obedience to religious authority. That point of view means that an individual retains the right to discuss, to argue, to criticize, to disagree with the representatives of Church, especially when the issue is such an obviously human, relativistic and arbitrary one like the administration of parish property.

The foregoing discussion has focused deliberately on the ideas and principles that lend themselves more readily to critical reflection rather than on the rivalries that existed between persons or organizations, all the more so because of the gray areas that remain due to the ban on access to the archives. It may seem to the reader that this discussion favored the Sentinellists over the bishop. Granted, a conscious effort was made on our part to highlight the good points of the Sentinellist Movement, for these have been neglected by traditional historiography, more inclined to blame and criticize than to recognize the positive aspects of a movement condemned by the Holy See. Furthermore, the Church's position has been explained and defended at length by most historians. Theirs was an approach that sought above all to safeguard the principle of authority, and it would seem that, from start to finish of the movement, this is the principle that prevailed. As a result, it did not appear to require any further elaboration on our part.

Sentinellism is admittedly controversial: one need only turn for proof to the works of two academics, Hélène Forget and Richard Sorrell, and this despite their belonging to a post-Sentinellist generation. There has been an attempt here to balance more than a half-century of bad publicity which the movement has received so that it can be appraised in a more equitable manner. But this controversial episode is likely to remain a fertile research area for scholars for quite some time to come.

Thus ends the period of the major ethno-religious conflicts. Admittedly, the last word has not been said on this issue. Far from it! No mention has been made of the so-called Corporation Sole controversy that sowed such dissension in Maine (and elsewhere) at the beginning of the twentieth century. The limitations of space, the desire to avoid repetition necessitated this abbreviated version of the facts.

The urban landscape that became the new home of French-Canadian immigrants to New England was dominated by textile mills. An early mill building (above) in Lewiston, Maine, clings to the falls of the Androscoggin River, its source of water power. A later and much larger mill complex (below) in New Bedford, Massachusetts, was built away from the river as steam-generated power replaced water power. New mills and new neighborhoods attracted an even larger number of French-Canadian workers.

Women and children found employment in the textile mills, and, although probably more grueling than work on the farms in Québec, work in the mills of New England was not foreign to French Canadians who understood that everyone had to contribute to the survival of the family unit. These photos by Lewis Hine were used at the turn of the century to document working conditions in the mills of Manchester, New Hampshire. (MHA Library)

(Left) Thanks to the steadfastness of Msgr. Louis de Goësbriand, a Frenchman and the first Catholic bishop of Burlington, Vermont, French-speaking priests from Québec became available to serve the growing French-Canadian congregations in New England.

(Right) Laymen like journalist Ferdinand Gagnon played a major role in forming public opinion. His newspaper *Le Travailleur* of Worcester, Massachusetts, was the most influential of the many French-language newspapers in the United States in the latter part of the 19th century. (Portrait by L. de Nevers at ACA Archives)

Not all French Canadians found employment in the textile mills; many worked in brickyards or for the railroads. Men from Québec and New Brunswick often found employment in the lumbering operations of the Northern States. These lumberjacks are from the Old Town area of Maine. (NMDC Files at ACA Archives)

(Left) Major Edmond Mallet, Civil War hero and civil servant in Washington, D.C., was an ardent supporter of the *survivance* mentality. Upon his death, his personal papers and library formed the nucleus of the Mallet Library in Woonsocket, Rhode Island, a research center operated by the Union Saint-Jean-Baptiste, now a division of Catholic Family Life. (ACA Archives)

(Right) In 1868, Rev. André-Marie Garin,O.M.I., founded Saint Joseph Parish in Lowell, Massachusetts, the first Franco-American parish in the Diocese of Boston. (Monument at Saint-Jean-Baptiste Church in Lowell, from A. Chartier Collection)

Calixa Lavallée, one of Canada's most famous musicians and the composer of the Canadian national anthem, spent many years in the United States. His song *Restons français*, published in 1891, was one of many efforts to bolster the *survivance* philosophy of the élite. (Bust by A. Laliberté at ACA Archives, music from the A. Chartier Collection)

The magnificent interior decoration (above) of Saint-Antoine-de-Padoue Church in New Bedford, Massachusetts, has been the pride of many generations of parishioners (A. Chartier Collection). Saint-Jean-Baptiste Church in Lowell, Massachusetts, offered an appropriate setting for the pontifical mass held in 1951 to commemorate the 2000th anniversary of Paris, France.

By the turn of the century, members of many Franco-American parishes had built a complex of structures to include a church, a rectory, a convent, schools and, as in the case of Sainte-Marie Parish in Manchester, New Hampshire, a hospital and an orphanage. (ACA Archives)

Inspired by the *Caisse populaire* movement in Québec, the increasingly stable Franco-American community in Manchester, New Hampshire, formed Saint Mary's Bank in 1908 as the first credit union in the United States. The first bank office (below), located in the home of a local attorney on Notre Dame Street, was purchased in 1995 by a non-profit group to be developed as a historical site. (ACA Archives)

The 1890s saw the birth of many small Franco-American businesses similar to the Gagné Millinery store run by these women in Lewiston, Maine. (NMDC Files at ACA Archives)

Théophile G. Biron, the first French-Canadian overseer in the giant Amoskeag Textile Mills of Manchester, New Hampshire, convinced a group of friends in 1896 to found Association Canado-Américaine, the first Franco-American fraternal benefit society. At its centennial, the organization changed its name to ACA ASSURANCE while maintaining its cultural and philanthropic goals. (Portrait by L. de Nevers at ACA Archives)

The first Franco-American to be elected governor of any State in the United States, Aram Pothier of Woonsocket served seven two-year terms as governor of Rhode Island from 1908 to 1914 and again from 1924 to 1928.

This Laliberté family portrait was taken in 1907 in Manchester, New Hampshire, when the sculptor Alfred Laliberté (upper left) returned from his art studies in Paris, France. Laliberté became the most prolific Franco-American sculptor of his period. (ACA Archives)

Franco-Americans in smaller cities also achieved financial success with their businesses. Joseph Bergeron, the son of Julius Bergeron, founder of the Ashuelot Valley Farm, is shown with his milk wagon in 1910 in Keene, New Hampshire. (M. Langford Collection)

Prominent Franco-American families sent their sons to Assumption College in Worcester, Massachusetts, founded by the French-based Assumptionist Fathers in 1904. Many Franco-American boys were also sent to classical colleges in Québec for their education. Those who went to Québec schools often joined the hockey teams while the Assumption students were more inclined to play baseball. (1915 photo from Verrette Family Files at ACA Archives)

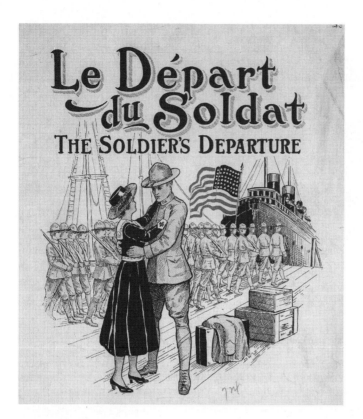

The Champagne brothers of Lowell, Massachusetts, were prolific composers of popular music in the 1910s and 1920s. Their publishing house turned out thousands of copies of this and other popular songs written by themselves and other Franco-American and French-Canadian lyricists and musicians. (ACA Archives)

This monument honoring the members of Notre-Dame Parish in Fall River, Massachusetts, who died in World War I, is among the most impressive memorials to the Franco-American war heroes of the era. The work of Alfred Laliberté, it was erected in 1920. (A. Chartier Collection)

Parish organizations were formed to cover every facet of community and family life, including women's groups such as *les Dames de Sainte-Anne* of Sacré-Coeur Parish in Laconia, New Hampshire, seen ready here to participate in a Saint-Jean-Baptiste parade. (ACA Archives)

St. John the Baptist was designated the patron saint of both French Canadians and Franco-Americans and his feast day on June 24 was the occasion for parades in many New England cities and towns with a Franco-American community. The parades nearly always featured a local lad who personified the patron saint. Here is a 1926 photo of Roland Messier of Central Falls, Rhode Island. (Institut Français Collection)

The Saint-Jean-Baptiste parades gave local organizations the opportunity to make themselves known. Here, the Manchester, New Hampshire, chapters of *Les Artisans*, a fraternal benefit society based in Montréal, Québec, sponsored a float promoting the virtues of the rural life left behind in French Canada. (Photo: Durette Studios)

Started in the home of Paul A. Duchaine, the My Bread Baking Company of New Bedford, Massachusetts, became very successful. Today, the family business has diversified with products sold world-wide. (Photo: My Bread Baking Company)

Dramatic and musical stage productions in French proved very popular in every Franco-American community. These students at the Oblate Junior Seminary in Colebrook, New Hampshire, presented *Le Moulin du Chat qui Fume* (The Mill of the Smoking Cat) in 1927. (A. Chartier Collection)

By the 1920s and 1930s, Franco-American parishes were numerous, and many were prosperous enough to build brand new churches including (above) Saint Joseph in Old Town, Maine, and Assomption in Chicopee, Massachusetts, the latter designed by Georges Dion, an architect and parishioner.

(Above: NMDC Files at ACA Archives; right: A. Chartier Collection)

Started in 1906, Sainte-Anne Church in Waterbury, Connecticut, was completed only in 1922 due to delays caused by World War I. Since 1997, the church has been largely restored.

The famous French writer Paul Claudel, then ambassador of France to Washington, was invited to the celebrations marking the 25th anniversary of Assumption College in Worcester, Massachusetts, in 1929. Above is the cover of the program for the public banquet held in his honor. (Assumption College Archives)

Dinner *in honour of*

His Excellency

PAUL W. CLAUDEL

AMBASSADOR OF FRANCE

Many convent boarding schools for girls were founded by French and Canadian religious communities, including this one in Hudson, New Hampshire, opened in 1926 by the Sisters of the Presentation of Mary. Here and elsewhere the curriculum was bilingual, as was the school life. (Marcelle Fréchette Collection)

A biography of Rose Ferron, the stigmatist from Woonsocket, Rhode Island, was widely read and translated into many languages. Popular devotion to this frail, young woman, whom many considered to be a saint, continues to this day.

Une stigmatisée canadienne
résidente aux États-Unis
MARIE ROSE FERRON
1902-1936

Among the major protagonists in the *Sentinelle* Affair during the 1920s were (left) Elphège Daignault, an attorney from Woonsocket, Rhode Island, and Elie Vézina, the secretary general of Union Saint-Jean-Baptiste, also of Woonsocket. Daignault served as president general of Association Canado-Américaine of Manchester, New Hampshire, from 1922 to 1936. (ACA Archives)

The 1934 graduating class of the Commercial Course at Saint-Antoine High School in Manchester, New Hampshire, included Maurice Lemelin, Fernand Vallée, Léon Demers, Gérard Robitaille, Joseph Maltais standing, and seated, Irène Boisvert and Cécilia Ladieu. (ACA Archives)

Les Francs-Tireurs (the Sharpshooters) was one of the most popular organizations in the New Bedford, Massachusetts, area, lasting from 1891 to 1970 (A. Chartier Collection)

III

A 1935 ASSESSMENT: *SURVIVANCE* UNDER SIEGE

If such a phenomenon as a Golden Age ever existed for Franco-Americans, it can be said to have occurred in the years between the two World Wars. The great wave of the migratory tide having ended around 1930, most of the institutions had by then been established to serve the nearly one million immigrants, not counting the second American-born generation. Most of them had settled in the Little Canadas of the industrial cities where, in varying degrees, they had to contend with the warring forces of assimilation and *la survivance*.

The vast majority remained Catholic and continued to worship in a "Canadian" church where services were conducted in French. The continued presence of the "old-timers," those who had actually experienced immigration, was a powerful force for preserving a "Canadian" atmosphere, especially at home and in the parish. Most parishes had bilingual schools staffed by members of Canadian or French religious orders. The multiplicity of organizations is but one of the many indicators of the vitality of Franco-American life during this first third of the twentieth century.

By 1930, most of the sociocultural elements of Franco-American life were in place, and since the decade is one of relative calm prior to the storm of the Second World War, it readily lends itself to an overall assessment.

Americanization and Survivance

Immigration lasted until 1930 and the *patriote* leaders continued to advocate *la survivance* and promote groups dedicated to the preservation of the faith and the language. Meanwhile, other organizations sought to integrate the immigrants into the social and political life of the United States; naturalization clubs spearheaded this effort.

Founded at the end of the nineteenth century to help the immigrants secure and protect their rights, naturalization clubs had to overcome the indifference of the immigrants, their ignorance of the advantages that citizenship would confer, their dream of permanently resettling in Canada, and quite possibly their reluctance to assume new responsibilities, such as conscription. The club leaders, who sometimes had political aspirations themselves, were persistent in their efforts, and they finally succeeded in getting their message across. In this they were aided by the fact that the immigrants' children, born in the United States, were American citizens in their own right.

At the same time, enormous efforts were made to persuade the immigrants of the need not only to become citizens but to participate in the political life of the United States. At the last general convention held in Springfield, Massachusetts, in 1901, Godfroy Dupré, an attorney from Biddeford, Maine, exhorted his brethren in terms that would often be repeated:

Instead of exchanging compliments and invoking the memory of our ancestors, which seems to be the one and only theme our orators know, and instead of priding ourselves on a glorious past to which we ourselves have contributed nothing, it would be wiser and more patriotic for us to take a hard look at ourselves, get an education, and involve ourselves in civic affairs. (Gatineau, p. 421)

Again, in 1919, at the Congress of the Fédération Catholique Franco-Américaine, there was talk of the need to establish permanent naturalization committees in order to encourage citizens to take part in elections. Slowly, the advice was heeded, and after 1900 there was a steady increase in the number of naturalized citizens. But progress was slow, since the immigrants were inclined to distance themselves from American political life, even at the local level. It would take time for them to overcome their reluctance, their indifference towards public affairs, and the lingering anti-governmental bias that was part of their mentality.

Despite the slow pace, there were more and more successes in the political arena. At the turn of the century there were Franco-American legislators in all the New England States, and they represented a significant challenge for both the Anglo-Americans and the Irish. Between 1900 and 1930, Franco-Americans were elected as mayors in about ten or so cities, from Lewiston, Maine, to Danielson, Connecticut. Where they were sufficiently numerous, as in Southbridge, Massachusetts, they controlled the public sector jobs and almost all the important political positions.

Some *patriotes* were remarkably successful. Hugo Dubuque was the first Franco-American to be appointed as a judge to the Superior Court of Massachusetts in 1911. In 1916 Lowell Representative Henri Achin succeeded in having New Year's Day included in the list of legal holidays in Massachusetts. In time this Canadian tradition would become an integral part of American culture throughout the land.

It was in Rhode Island that Franco-Americans achieved their most resounding political successes during this period. In addition to several Franco-American mayors, the state elected a Franco-American governor, Aram-J. Pothier, in 1908. Born in 1854 at Saint-Jean-Chrysostome, Châteauguay County, in Québec, Aram Pothier had come with his family to settle in Woonsocket. Rising from modest beginnings, he became a banker and won several important elections; he was elected mayor in 1894 and 1895. In 1889 and again in 1900 he was Rhode Island's representative to the Universal Exposition in Paris. He served as governor from 1908 to 1914 and again from 1924 until his death in 1928. Without repudiating his origins, Aram Pothier succeeded in quickly adapting himself to "the American way of life," all the while insisting that Canadian immigrants not live in isolation from other groups. Another Franco-American, Emery J. Sansouci, was governor of Rhode Island from 1921 to 1923; Louis Monast was a congressional representative in Washington from 1927 to 1929; Félix Hébert of West Warwick was a United States Senator from Rhode Island from 1929 to 1935.

But it would be a mistake to think that Francos were a politically homogeneous group; they belonged to both major parties, and from the beginning the Franco-American vote was divided between Democrats and Republicans. Some observers decried this lack of cohesion, claiming that it was due to traditional Canadian failings: jealousy, a tendency to quibble, individualism, and a disdain for everything Canadian by those who chose to distance themselves from the group by Americanizing themselves. Others saw these divisions as a surefire method of getting a fair share of patronage, whatever party happened to be in office.

What is certain is that Franco-Irish hostility, spawned by job competition and by the decision of the Irish bishops to Americanize immigrants, often proved to be an advantage to the Republicans, since the Irish had taken control of the Democratic Party even before the arrival of the Canadians. Just how much of an advantage was this for Republicans? It is difficult to say. It would be risky to attempt to generalize in an area that has been studied so little, but the facts suggest that there was a growing demand on the part of Canadian immigrants that they be recognized, at least for their numbers, and that candidates to elective office had to reckon more and more with "the French vote."

At the time, "to be recognized" meant that candidates had to indicate their support for Franco-American interests in general and, after the election, prove their goodwill by the jobs they handed out.

The ever increasing number of shopkeepers, businessmen, bankers, and professionals was another sign of how well the immigrants were adapting to life in the United States and that they had grasped the meaning of the old saying: "The business of this country *is* business." They could be found in almost every sphere of business and industry as well as in the liberal professions.

It would be tedious to list all of the occupations in which Canadian immigrants rose from modest beginnings, learned a trade, and eventually demonstrated enough initiative to become the owners of a business. This was the case for a good number of grocers, bakers, carpenters, and pharmacists. An extensive study to determine which businesses attracted immigrants would be worth undertaking. Such a study, for example, might reveal the extent to which so many of them were involved in real estate. In one city (and perhaps in others also), a group of hard-nosed business and professional people formed an association locally known as "the forty thieves" and made what at that time was a fortune out of shrewd speculations in real estate.

Some particularly noteworthy careers were made during the years 1900-1935. As governor of Rhode Island, Aram Pothier succeeded in attracting several textile companies from northern France to Woonsocket. With their thousands of jobs, these companies played a major role in New England's industrial development. In Manchester, a descendant of native Quebecers, Frederic Dumaine (1865-1951), managed to rise to the prestigious position of treasurer of the Amoskeag Manufacturing Company, the mammoth industrial complex employing between fifteen and twenty thousand people. The immigrant William E. Aubuchon founded his first hardware store in Fitchburg, Massachusetts, in 1908; today, the Aubuchon Hardware Company has

147 stores and is the largest family-owned chain of its kind in the United States.

The Yankee establishment did not fail to recognize these achievements by Franco-American business and professional people. One telling sign of this recognition: Anglo-American authors of local histories included biographical sketches of these successful individuals in their works, an indication of their integration into "the American way of life" and their above-average economic status. Anyone reading these sketches today and knowing the hold that the philosophy of *la survivance* had over the majority of immigrants would probably be astonished at how many of these business and professional people joined non-denominational associations, for instance, the Benevolent and Protective Order of Elks or the Fraternal Order of Eagles, this despite all the efforts made by *survivance* leaders to dissuade them. But it is also a fact that some of them achieved integration by joining both non-sectarian and Franco-American organizations. These same biographical sketches also reveal that many of these individuals laid claim to an ancestor who had participated in the Rebellions of 1837-38. Frederic Dumaine's grandfather, for example, had seen action at Saint-Charles in 1837, and his grandson took obvious pride in recalling this exploit.

Finally, let us remember also that, with their several millions of dollars in assets, the credit unions and the life insurance programs of the fraternal benefit or mutual aid societies also contributed a great deal to the country's prosperity during this period.

In 1917-1918, a considerable number of Franco-Americans chose another way of becoming Americans: by enlisting in the armed forces. The mutual aid societies were also involved in the war effort as a result of their participation in programs established by the federal government to finance the war. In fact, the war affected everyone, either through the economic boom in various industries—munitions, textiles, shoes—or through the departure of a close relative who had volunteered or been drafted.

The war was an excellent opportunity for all immigrants to prove their loyalty to the adopted country, and, in truth, the climate of supercharged patriotism required such proof. Franco-American organizations sponsored many events of all sorts at which the people lavished support on the "doughboys," all the more so since they were fighting to liberate France—the ancestral land—in places like Soissons, Château-Thierry, Saint-Mihiel, and Verdun. Soon the bells began to toll for heroes who had "died on the field of honor," and after the fighting had ended, Franco-American parishes organized "homecoming celebrations" to welcome the combatants back from the war. With their flags and patriotic songs, their cheers and their tributes, these were celebrations that would long be remembered by onlookers and participants alike. There was reason for added pride in the Manchester area when the important national organization for veterans, the American Legion, authorized the designation of one of its affiliates as the William H. Jutras Post No. 43, immortalizing the memory of a son of Saint Augustine Parish who had died heroically in France.

The First World War also coincided with a loosening of the bonds between Québec and the Franco-Americans who were at a loss to understand the province's lack of support for the war. Notwithstanding its proximity and despite the continuing immigration, Canada's influence waned as the century advanced. An increasing number of children were now being born in the United States, and since this new generation was bilingual, it was necessarily more American than the preceding one and took very little interest in Canada which they viewed as a land of suffering from which their family had fled. But, especially among the élite, there remained a strong core who, opposing total Americanization, sought to strengthen the bonds with French Canada and who defended *la survivance*, often in an aggressive manner.

A substantial part of the population was living *la survivance* without having to make a conscious effort at so doing. For them, the French-Canadian cultural patrimony constituted a system of values, a philosophy of life, and a mental and spiritual universe, which, taken together, guided Canadian immigrants in their daily lives as they adapted to their new environment and waged their struggle for existence. But this was less true of the rising generations, and it was at them that the élite directed their innumerable patriotic speeches and newspaper articles, as well as their books, such as *L'Âme franco-américaine* (1935) of Josaphat Benoit and *Les Franco-Américains peints par eux-mêmes* (1936), a compilation of articles published by the Association Canado-Américaine.

For the élite, *la survivance* was above all a question of identity: the will to preserve both the individual and the collective identity of the Franco-Americans. This was because the notions of identity and cultural patrimony were virtually interchangeable, especially where faith, language, and traditions were concerned. For *la survivance* die-hards, this triad of faith-language-traditions constituted a sacred possession, one that must be preserved and transmitted. The élite's ongoing analyses of *la survivance* were occurring in a social context that was generally hostile to cultural pluralism, and this resulted in a clerical-nationalist ideology which, in many respects, resembled that of French Canada.

It was from Canada that the ideologues of *la survivance* imported the core of their doctrine. In French Canada—and the Franco-American élite never forgot this—the tradition whereby whatever is English is to be resisted had begun on the day after the Conquest. This tradition formed an integral part of the patrimony—the identity—of French-Canadian immigrants. Respect for this tradition of resistance, along with the cult of the entire French past on the North American continent, were the cornerstones of *survivance* ideology, rivaling in importance the Catholic religion and the French language. By 1935, however, these building blocks, much like religion and language, had become stumbling blocks in the relationships between the Franco-American élite and other ethnic groups in the United States.

To begin with, this attachment to the past did nothing to endear the supporters of *la survivance* to young Franco-Americans, especially in a country where the majority, indifferent at best to the past, looked only to the future. Nevertheless, partisans of *la survivance* persisted in their efforts at merging past and future, at projecting the past into the future, as if a break between a group's heritage and its destiny would be sacrilegious. This accounts for the aspect of unchanging inflexibility, that came to characterize *survivance* ideology and was the source of further conflict with an Anglo-American culture in which change was a fundamental principle. With time, and especially after 1940, young Franco-Americans repudiated this kind of entrenchment which they deemed paralyzing. In so doing, they also rejected the symbiosis which had existed between home, church, school, "national" society, and the Franco-American newspaper—the major existential components that taken together constituted the organic and harmonious entity required by *survivance* ideology which provided answers to all of life's problems; but they were answers fashioned in accord with a past and its moral rigor which came to be viewed as outdated by young people hungry for change and eager to adopt Anglo-American models.

For its supporters, with their profoundly conservative tendencies, *la survivance* was all but synonymous with order, and they viewed Americanization or assimilation as a form of disorder, a manifestation of chaos, an unnatural phenomenon—all the more so since, for some, *la survivance* had always implied a messianic role: was assimilation not the betrayal of the race's providential mission to remain Catholic and French so as to convert Protestant America? At the very least, it was a betrayal of the collective past, and this was enough of a lapse to enrage any true *patriote*. This accounts for the dogmatism that was also one of the main characteristics of this ideology.

The *patriote* élite continued incessantly to blame, reprove, accuse, and exhort the people. They denounced the American way of life, that seductive web of the radio, movies, sports, automobiles, English-language newspapers, and non-denominational organizations in which they perceived a conspiracy against faith, language, and traditions. *Survivance* ideologues condemned materialism—the worship of the golden calf that seemed to result in a lack of concern for the group. The élite did not seem to understand, or refused to accept, the fact that the immigrants, who were in the process of freeing themselves from abject poverty, did not all have the requisite energy to devote their leisure time to the cause of *la survivance*, institutionalized in its organizations, movements, and newspapers.

In the first third of the twentieth century, a fairly large group of these *patriotes* continued to analyze the popular trends on a regular basis, and their conclusions pointed almost inevitably in the same direction. What accounts for their hard-line approach, their intransigence, and to what extent was it justified? Much of it can be ascribed to the great value the élite attributed to the notions of uncompromising loyalty and entrenchment, which call to mind the words of the fictional Maria Chapdelaine. "To persist," and "not change"; to remain loyal to the past, this was the core belief that motivated an élite filled with a zeal and an idealism which, according to some, the people did not share. But their analyses tended to be subjective, and in retrospect, it appears that the people remained more loyal than one might conclude from the acerbic comments of the *patriotes*.

All in all, the people—that is to say, Franco-American adults in 1935—remained Catholic and *Canadien*, even if they continued to become anglicized; but the élite persisted in denouncing their love of all things American. These leaders claimed not to understand why all Franco-Americans did not teach their children French, why they did not all send their children to bilingual parochial schools, why they did not all speak French all of the time. Adolphe Robert, for instance, made the following observations in 1936 just after being elected president of the Association Canado-Américaine:

> How sad it is to have reached the point where we are obliged to mount campaigns to promote the use of our own mother tongue among our own people. This is an anomaly, the worrisome symptom of a weakness of character. And this is all the more anomalous because the French language is one that needs no defense, since its clear and supple genius imposes itself on any mind that thirsts for knowledge and truth. (*Les Franco-Américains peints par eux-mêmes*, p. 122)

In this same collection of articles, there are proposals to reintroduce French into the home and to "restore our French soul"; this strongly suggests that, as early as the 1930s, the situation had already "deteriorated" from the viewpoint of the *patriotes*. Statements of this kind would be repeated into the 1970s, indicating that the people and the non-*patriote* élite were no longer as deeply committed to their cultural heritage as were the *patriotes*.

Nevertheless, these men did their best to persuade the people to remain what their ancestors had been. But the people were evolving while the élite were clinging doggedly to a rigid and limited vision of reality. The tenacity of this outlook, one that was not universally shared even among the élite, can to some extent be attributed to the ties which certain Franco-American leaders maintained with Québec, where Henri Bourassa and his supporters viewed Franco-American New England and the provinces of Western Canada as outposts of a besieged "fortress Québec," under attack by Anglo-American influences. This explains the warm welcome extended to Franco-Americans who took part in the mass rallies of French-speaking North Americans, such as the Congresses of the French Language of 1912 and 1937.

Though this was the attitude that the Association Canado-Américaine had adopted, not all of the élite endorsed it—far from it.

During the Sentinellist conflict, for example, the Assumptionists at Assumption College in Worcester had kept their distance, invoking a distinction long considered valid between cultural and ethnic issues. This led them to adopt a policy that sought to transmit French culture while avoiding internecine conflicts. George Filteau, future secretary-general of the USJB, had published an article in 1924 that reflected the Assumptionist position; it would come to characterize the USJB's official stance:

> In pledging our allegiance to the stars and stripes, we did not swear to forget our language, our traditions, or our faith; nor did anyone ask us to do so. But we did make a solemn promise to abandon all ties with Canada, an English colony in which we no longer wanted to live. . . . Our *patriote* predecessors of 1880 bear a great responsibility for what is happening to us today. They more or less distorted our mentality and it is because of them that we are still, in our hearts, almost as Canadian as we are American. . . .
>
> The time has come to change our mentality, and we can only do this by breaking radically with Canada, from both a psychological as well as a practical point of view. This will not prevent us from cherishing the memory of the country of our ancestors or making a dutiful visit there every now and then. (Quoted by Rumilly, *Histoire des Franco-Américains*, p. 380)

In this defining text, George Filteau was impugning the exile mentality of some of his compatriots and expressing an idea that was gaining favor. In dismissing outright any designs of cultural imperialism toward Franco-Americans which Québec might have had, he formulated a notion that became increasingly popular over the years, to wit, that Franco-Americans constitute a separate sociocultural reality, distinct from that of French Canada. At the same time, he implicitly raised a crucial question regarding *la survivance* itself: did it lead to group solidarity or to isolation from the mainstream? In retrospect, *la survivance* does appear to have been more of an isolating factor than a source of solidarity, but even this assertion needs to be qualified.

There is little doubt that *la survivance* fostered solidarity among the early generations of immigrants and, in large measure, among the élite class through the 1930s. But it is obvious that, from the thirties on, it distanced the élite from the people as the two diverged along different paths. The documentation available to us regarding the period 1930-1940 also reveals, however, a sociocultural phenomenon that historians have tended to minimize, that all the while the Franco-American élite was decrying anglomania and reporting signs of assimilation everywhere, Yankee observers were denouncing the refusal of Franco-Americans to assimilate and their obsession with a type of cultural separatism harmful to American national unity.

Practical and human concerns, quite as much as ideological issues, were at the source of this Anglo-American appraisal of the situation. Franco-American parochial schools, for instance, could be the cause of eventual complications when public school administrators submitted their budgets to municipal governments. In the major centers, not only did Franco-Americans not support these requests: they voted against budgetary increases. From an American standpoint, an attitude such as this one hindered the progress of public education.

Other incompatibilities existed as well. When *patriote* leaders urged immigrants to pray for the conversion of the United States, calling it an "impious, barbaric, and degenerate" country, this hardly contributed to reconciling the two groups. Conversely, when the same leaders encouraged Franco-Americans to play a greater role in American civic life, all the while preserving their identity, Anglo-Americans tended not to hear the first part of the message, but they remembered the second and viewed it as contempt for themselves and the country. In general, what Anglo-Americans especially perceived in this ideology of *la survivance* was hostility toward the United States; for some, it was even considered to be blatantly unpatriotic.

It is clear that for Anglo-Americans in the 1930s, the ideological rhetoric surrounding *la survivance* carried an emotionally charged threat that is perhaps difficult for us to imagine today. Québec's waning influence on New England's Franco-Americans during these years, as well as the distancing from Québec that was occurring in some quarters, while true, would have been perceived as negligible by Anglo-Americans as they observed the daily shipment into New England of some 25,000 copies of Québec newspapers—especially *La Presse* and *La Patrie*. For Protestant Yankees, these newspapers seemed to represent Catholic propaganda which sought to extend the power of that most despised of figures: the Pope.

This was the heart of the problem. Anglo-Americans felt threatened in their New England fortress by this invasion of French-Canadian Catholics, several of whom actually boasted of having been papal Zouaves, i.e., men who had volunteered to defend the Papal States! For them, French-Canadian immigration was nothing less than an extension of Catholicism and popery. They needed no further proof than the refusal by a good number of immigrants to become Americans and the control which the Church exercised over the Franco-American population. Some works published in New England also fed these fears, as for example when they read in the *Guide français de Fall River* (1910) that marriage with "foreigners," that is to say, non-French-Canadians, constituted "a crime against God and a national abomination." Similarly, Church laws against birth control increased their hostility, for they saw this as another sign of a papal plot that encouraged large families so as to control, through population increase, at least half of the United States, that is the entire territory east of the Mississippi. In a word, what was feared was the fulfillment of an old dream that Father Édouard Hamon had expressed in *Les Canadiens français de la Nouvelle-Angleterre*: that of a single people united across the 45th parallel and in such numbers that someday the domination of the region, if not the continent, might become a possibility.

Today, fears of this sort appear either to have been ill-founded or to have been experienced by only a small minority—the more faint-hearted and francophobe wing of Anglo-American patriots. But let us not forget that a historian of the stature of Arnold Toynbee also thought that the French Canadians were conquering New England. As to the validity of Yankee fears and hostility, how could they have thought otherwise, given the fighting spirit of the leaders of *la survivance*? The mere fact of their reiterating *ad nauseam* the old saws about the French race's providential mission in North America and the French language as the expression of the world's greatest civilization, while denouncing non-denominational organizations, likening them to nothing better than "foreign" groups, was enough to preclude any understanding between the supporters of *la survivance* and the Anglo-American majority.

In time, new generations of Franco-Americans would come to view such official *survivance* pronouncements as insignificant, banal, and outdated. As for the Yankees of 1930, they could only find this kind of rhetoric gravely offensive. Without attempting to defend one point of view over the other, one can legitimately ask a question that is likely to remain unanswered. Why did Franco-American *patriote* leaders make these kinds of statements in their adopted country? Were they insensitive to the feelings of the Anglo-Americans, or did they simply not care what their reactions would be? Were they, either consciously or unconsciously, expressing their contempt or hatred for the traditional enemy of France and French Canada? Did they think that their statements would go unnoticed? Or conversely, were these oratorical excesses simply the result of their zealous pursuit of *la survivance*?

While Franco-American leaders continued to denounce the "assimilation pirates," the people themselves were quietly adapting to the new country and were poised somewhere between *survivance* and assimilation. Individuals, of course, made their own choices from among the various "Franco" and "American" cultural elements, deciding which to incorporate into their lives. While it cannot be claimed that they generally struck a perfect equilibrium between ethnic pressures and the pull of the American milieu—the many variables and nuances that influence the life of an individual preclude any generalization of this kind—it can be asserted that the phenomenon of a dual identity became more and more common from 1920 to 1940. Life was divided into two spheres of activity: a private one that was lived in French, at home or in church, and a public sphere lived in English, at the mill, in the market place, and in politics. There was also an intermediate zone which was bilingual, and it encompassed the neighborhood, the parochial school, and Franco-American business establishments.

Faced with this situation, *patriote* leaders remained committed to the cause of *la survivance*, and they functioned as a special interest group, bringing pressure to bear on the people to preserve the cultural heritage and on the politicians to recognize Franco-American interests. For them, assimilation was a constant cause for concern if not anguish. But these same *patriote* leaders also insisted that the people participate fully in American life, especially in politics. And these leaders reminded one and all that during the First World War, Franco-Americans had shed their blood for their adopted country. Hence, when reading the Yankee diatribes of the period about Franco-American "cultural separatism," this kind of global judgment also needs to be qualified, albeit without denying the militancy of the *patriotes*.

The advocates of *la survivance* continued the "good" fight, ignoring the critics who belittled it by pointing to the utopian nature of this compensatory struggle. We may choose to call this determination the expression of an exile mentality, an escape into a beautiful dream, an attempt to delay the inevitable, or a noble and heroic effort. Whatever the case may be, the doctrine formulated by Josaphat Benoit in 1935 would continue to inspire *patriotes* for a few more decades:

> The home, the parish, and the school are directly responsible for the development of the Franco-American psyche; they teach the language and the prayers of the forefathers; they instill the meaning of "national" identity allied to catholicism; they strengthen hearts and minds against the menacing flood tide of assimilation. When these three institutions have done their work thoroughly, Franco-Americans can confidently take up the struggle for *la survivance*, a battle whose outcome depends less on attack than on resistance, less on victory than on defense, less on resounding deeds than on quiet and humble loyalty to the heritage of the past.

Little Canadas

In his autobiographical novels, *Doctor Sax* and *Visions of Gerard*, Jack Kerouac has left some memorable descriptions of Lowell's Little Canada as he knew it in his youth—the twenties. Since a very high percentage of Franco-Americans grew up in similar surroundings, these two novels represent an invaluable account of important aspects of Franco-American life.

Around 1935, most Franco-Americans lived in a neighborhood often called "Little Canada"; this was where the first immigrants had settled in the years 1870-1880. In many cities, however, Canadian neighborhoods were known simply under the names of the local Canadian parishes. In any event, these neighborhoods played an important role in the history of the industrial cities since, in many instances, they remained intact for almost a century. It would appear also that these neighborhoods evolved over time, for in a speech at Saint Anne in Fall River in 1919 Henri Bourassa referred to those bygone days when "people spoke of a 'Little Canada' as if they were talking about an Indian reservation."

While the physical appearance of a Little Canada varied depending on whether it was located in a city or a town, its general characteristics can be described. Nearby stood the mills, often located on waterways which had provided the water power needed to run them in the early days. The housing stock was principally composed of dozens and sometimes hundreds of multistoried houses all in a row, in a network of streets whose symmetry formed a grid. Built in the era of "three-decker madness" that characterized New England residential architecture in the years 1900-1920, these three- and sometimes four-story houses contained one or two apartments per floor, called tenements. Some "blocks" of tenements, as in Lowell, had up to forty-eight apartments. A commercial street ran through the neighborhood, making it virtually self-sufficient; and above it all rose the steeple of the "Canadian" church.

Overpopulated until 1950, and far from luxurious, these neighborhoods were never known for their physical beauty. But they had a definite appeal for newcomers arriving from Canada because of the sense of security which a Little Canada offered them during the period from 1900 to 1935. Integration into the adopted country and social relationships were facilitated by the presence of immigrants like themselves. A feeling of solidarity and the availability of mutual assistance were the norm in a Little Canada. It was the antithesis of the impersonal world of the 1900s. Moreover, the neighborhood was lively and picturesque, and its diversity is captured in the following description from the pen of Lowell's Oblate Father Armand Morissette:

> Moody Street, with its network of streets running either across or at right angles to it, was Main Street for Lowell's Franco-Americans. It ran all the way from City Hall, called "la négresse," the Yorick Club, and the Public Library to the Marist Brothers' residence on top of the hill.

First came Dutton Street, then Worthen, Coburn, Tilden, and Tremont; Prince Street, where the offices of *L'Étoile* were located; then Hanover, Suffolk, Ford, Dodge, and Race Street where the future actress, Bette Davis, lived for a while, followed by Cabot, Austin, Aiken, Spaulding, and James. . . . You could find anything and everything on Moody and its adjoining streets. . . .

There were restaurants, bars, grocery stores, delicatessens, bakeries, variety stores, both large and small, garages, Bellerose's bicycle shop and Rousseau's doughnuts, Philias *"Garçon"* Rochette's poolroom, Rochette's autos, Mayor Beaudry's block and Monsieur Rocheville's monkey, Brownstein's shoeshop and those of Harvey Saucier, the old Greek shoeshine man who also cleaned men's hats, April, the friendly shoemaker, the Chinese laundry. During Prohibition, there were also those "dreadful brewers and merchants of moonshine" who ended up as rich big shots.

Then there was the smooth-talking photographer, Charlie Landry, a good guy and a fight promoter at C.M.A.C. (Corporation des Membres de l'Association Catholique, an athletic club for Franco-Americans). There was Lambert's Lounge too—the Cabot Lodge now—where you could often take in a "first-class" show; it was on the corner of Cabot and Moody in the building now known as the Club Passe-Temps (Pastime Club).

There were barbers, hairdressers, prostitutes, and midgets; drug stores, the branch post office; the inventor of potato chips, Baron's bookstore, the Champagne brothers at the corner of Spaulding, and, on the opposite corner, Bergeron the violin teacher, Miss Georgianna Desrosiers who taught piano, and farther on, Raymond Tremblay's pianos.

There was also *La Pipe* Geoffroy's little store near Saint Joseph's Convent and the home of the Grey Nuns.

There was a lot doing on Moody Street. Summer meant Fourth of July fireworks and big parades, the Dubois peddlers and the icemen. Fall brought Halloween and Thanksgiving; and then came snow banks and Christmas lights, New Year's gatherings,—where each wish was punctuated by *"et le Paradis à la fin de vos jours"* ("and Paradise at the end of your days")—sleighs and sleigh bells, then Lent and having to give

up candy and, at the end, visits on Holy Thursday to the Blessed
Sacrament on highly decorated altars and the great feast of Easter,
followed by lilacs for the month of Mary, awards at graduation
ceremonies, weddings, and vacation days. (*Le Journal de Lowell*, October
1977)

As can be seen from this detailed description, a Little Canada
could and did include all the key elements around which revolved the
lives of Franco-Americans: the family and its home, the mill, the
church, and the school.

Following a custom for which no clear explanation has emerged,
nineteenth-century Yankee industrialists gave their mills Native
American names. These captivating names—Androscoggin, Wamsutta,
Waumbec, and a host of others—became part of the Canadian
immigrant's everyday language since they designated places where for
several decades two or three generations of them earned a living.

It was a hard life, focused on the demands of faith and work, the
one helping to endure the other. Nineteenth-century Anglo-American
men and women who had preceded the immigrants in the mills had
viewed factory work as a form of prayer. While Franco-Americans did
not go that far, it would be wrong to state that their workday was
entirely divorced from their spiritual lives. It would be more accurate
to maintain that—at least among the more devout workers of the 1920s
and 30s—the spiritual was ever-present even during the daily routine
of the mill. The religious life of the Franco-American worker has yet
to be studied, but we know that religion, far from playing an
insignificant role, permeated their lives. The devotion to Saint Joseph
the Worker, proposed as a model to all family men, and the special
Workers' Mass celebrated at five in the morning on holy days of
obligation are two examples of this real-life religious experience. It
should also be pointed out that this was also a time when the obligation
of "doing one's duty" was taken seriously.

One really had to be in dire need of work in order to be able to put up with the dehumanizing atmosphere of the textile mills: the infernal din of the machines, so huge that floors, walls, and ceilings shook continually; the humidity, unhealthy but needed for the preparation of cotton fabric; the cotton dust one had to avoid inhaling by covering one's face; the suffocating heat that could exceed 100°F. In spite of all this, workers somehow managed to spend sixty and sometimes even seventy-two hours per week in this environment, spurred on by the fact that since there was no work on Sunday, the work week was, in fact, shorter in the mill than it had been on the farm.

In exchange for this debilitating labor, workers were paid what today would be considered wretched wages. It is true that salaries did rise from an average of $3 per week in 1900 to around $20 to $25, starting with the First World War. And it is also true that for a good many years these wages, combined with regular employment, provided these workers with a better life than that of the Québec farmer. They were nevertheless too low, so much so that it was often necessary for the entire family, including young children, to work in order to make ends meet.

Despite all that has been written about it, the controversy over sacrificing the education of the young in order to send them to work remains unresolved. That this was often an economic necessity seems beyond dispute. But to claim that greed was never a factor in the decision—all too frequent, alas—to send a ten- to twelve-year-old child to work would be to paint a picture of reality as idealized as it is erroneous. In *Canuck* (1936), a novel that chronicles immigration, Camille Lessard was able to provide useful corroboration on this issue.

Equally controversial was the employment of women in the textile mills. Some of them may have viewed factory work as a release from the chores and isolation of domesticity; others sorely needed the additional income. But the question deserves much closer study.

French-Canadian immigrants who started working in the textile industry after 1900 seemed to have arrived at just the right time; but it was to become increasingly clear that, in fact, the opposite was true since control of the textile market by the South was progressing rapidly. Efforts by unions to improve the lot of their members gave rise to a series of strikes in which the workers suffered most, according to at least one eyewitness to the 1922 Amoskeag Company strike in Manchester, N.H.:

> They (the workers) lost all their savings, went deep into debt and lived on baked beans while the hope of winning the battle was kept dangling before their eyes. They were told almost every day by the strike leaders to be patient and tighten their belts because victory was in sight. But there was no victory, only defeat for all concerned. (Philippe Lemay, in Doty, *The First Franco-Americans*, p. 24)

While some immigrants found work in other industries or in other cities, an undetermined number of them returned to Canada. After the First World War, the industry's decline in the North became irreversible, and the depression of the thirties led to the spread of dire poverty throughout the region. The country would recover only at the start of the Second World War.

Among the distinctive aspects of work in the textile mills, one was the close relationship which developed between the world of work and that of the family. The extended family, which operated as a reliable source of information on such things as job openings, the world of working conditions, bosses to avoid, etc., served as an intermediary between the individual and the workplace.

This spirit of mutual assistance also extended to the apprenticeship period that every new employee had to serve. A great many newly hired workers learned their trade alongside a member of their immediate or extended family. When there was a strike, relatives would try to meet the most pressing needs of an out-of-work family, and family members living in other industrial cities remained on the lookout for possible jobs.

It is more than likely that the decision to send a child under fourteen to work was also a family matter, but we know very little about this aspect of the Franco-American work experience. It is plausible, however, that the Canadian custom whereby the entire family worked on the farm was a key factor in pushing the young person toward a quick and definitive entry into the world of work. Wages in the New England mills were so appallingly low that the salary brought home at week's end by young people, who turned over their pay to their parents in return for a modest allowance, helped make ends meet. And no doubt some young people viewed their release from school as an opportunity for economic independence.

The state of current research barely allows for a few general conclusions on how workers between 1920 and 1935 viewed their jobs. The workers themselves tended to have both positive as well as negative reactions. For a minority, the prospect of returning to Canada may have lightened their burden and tempered their outlook on factory life. But the majority appear to have thrown themselves heart and soul into what they recognized as their economic salvation and their assurance of having their daily bread.

Many an immigrant thanked *le bon Dieu* (God) for having been hired and asked nothing more of Him than the health needed to do a full day's work. What these workers wanted most was to be able to do their best, and their desire to "do a good job" is reminiscent of the ideal of the medieval craftsman. Some were proud to be associated with a famous company and share, albeit at a distance, in its reflected glory. They took pride in showing family and friends the products they had helped make: sheets, blankets, dresses, and shirts.

Company loyalty went hand-in-hand with a perseverance captured in the saying, *"Petit train va loin"* (Slow and steady wins the race). This was so true that within a few years some immigrants were able to buy a home, and the cleverest (or luckiest) were able to purchase a second or third one to supplement their income. Conscientious, loyal, and persevering, the Franco-American worker was above all resigned, docile, devoted to a thankless—perhaps alienating—task and stoic in his acceptance of a situation that came close to resembling servitude. Spurred on in some mills by the system of "piecework" that gave the workers an opportunity to increase their base salary—the faster they worked, the more they made—perked up during brief work breaks which gave them the chance to exchange a word or two with their co-workers, supported by relatives in their exhausting labor, perhaps they felt less forsaken, "alienated," or as "outsiders" than one might think. And when they left the mill each day, they could at least be certain that they would find a lively social life at home, one in which solitude was highly unlikely, if not impossible.

Family and relatives played an essential role in emigration, the major event in the lives of so many. For nearly a century—1840 to 1930—the French-Canadian élite tried in vain to oppose emigration, denouncing it for all kinds of reasons. But people continued to emigrate, and they were encouraged to do so by those already settled in the United States—relatives who would help them find a job and a place to stay and guide them in their efforts to build new lives.

Most often it was entire families that came to seek their fortune in New England, and these families preserved their distinctive traits—solidarity, sociability, patriarchal character—for a period of years that varied depending on their individual propensity to Americanize themselves. Before long, the family's traditional character—its pursuit of economic self-sufficiency and its primacy over the individual—would present younger family members with difficult choices. Should they remain loyal to this mentality with its age-old practices, or should they yield to the spirit of personal enterprise and initiative so highly valued by American society?

While deciding one way or the other, the individual continued to participate in a fairly intense family life compared to that of today. Before television became common in the early fifties, relatives visited each other very often in Canadian neighborhoods throughout New England. For such large families, life's important events—weddings, christenings, funerals, as well as "the holidays"—served as just so many opportunities to visit throughout the year; and there were frequent *veillées* (evening gatherings) that would bring people together at the home of one family member or another. While there is nothing surprising in this for a gregarious people, it is important to note these moments of ethnic sociability so as to destroy the stereotype that would reduce the lives of these earlier generations to just "religion and work."

In summertime, family members spent quiet weeknights together on the porch, but get-togethers on Saturday and Sunday evenings were more lively. Popular culture was much in evidence at these parties, with their traditional music and dances along with the much appreciated art of storytelling and card games of either Canadian or American origin.

Traditional Franco-American culture reveals the centrality of the French language. Even while it was becoming Americanized, it persisted in its Québec or Acadian variants, and the people, just like the educated class, attributed paramount importance to it. Some immigrants refused to speak English, either out of negligence or because of their antipathy toward the language of their traditional enemy. But even they learned enough English to deal with English-speaking shopkeepers, and they were the first to encourage their children to become bilingual, echoing a commonly accepted thesis among Franco-American grandparents in New England: "A man—or a woman—who knows two languages is worth two persons."

In some centers like Biddeford, Maine, Franco-Americans made up such a high percentage of the population that immigrants had no need to learn English. In those communities, French was even the language spoken at work, and—much to the delight of *patriote* leaders—some employers even learned a few words of French so as to be able to communicate with their employees.

Before the Second World War, while Canadian immigrants adapted bit by bit to the American way of life, most people were still apt to express themselves in French. For the most part, they agreed with the élite in equating identity with language, as indicated by the expression, *"un Canadien manqué"* ("a 'failed' Canadian"), to designate a Canadian immigrant who refused to speak French. In fact, notwithstanding the fulminations of the élite, a great number of immigrants sided with them in defense of *la survivance*. For, even if the people failed to give monetary support to all the institutions, activities, and programs of *la survivance*, and even if they were adapting more and more to their adopted country, they nonetheless remained Catholic, spoke French, at least in the presence of their elders, and for the most part they attempted to transmit certain oral and musical traditions to the next generation.

The make-believe world of Franco-Americans in this first third of the twentieth century was still grounded for the most part in Québec or Acadia, witness the great number of bogeymen, will-o'-the-wisps, goblins, and ghosts found in the tales, legends, and scary stories told by the elders. No detailed study of the different versions of these tales and legends exists as of yet, but it is known that some of them were given new life in the cities. The exploits of Québec strongman, Jos Montferrand, for instance, were much appreciated by his co-workers at the giant Amoskeag textile plant in Manchester. In the Lowell area, the flying birch-bark canoe of the lumberjack's legend was magically transformed into a convertible bus. Telling tall tales was evidently still a popular pastime for Franco-Americans around 1935.

To the traditional repertoire of stories from Québec and Acadia were added yarns spun from family and local history, stories of emigration—the departure, the trek, the arrival—as well as adventures of "strongmen" like Lowell's Louis Cyr. Gossip, bawdy jokes, and off-color stories also formed part and parcel of this oral tradition.

A great number of beliefs, sometimes of a superstitious nature, were widespread. The following is one such example: if you want a child to walk at an early age, have him take his first steps during high mass. Sayings, proverbs, and expressions of all kinds abounded. For example, "*Ils étaient assez fâchés que les portes en faisaient du feu*" ("They were so angry it was setting the doors on fire") and, "*Il est fin comme un petit enfant Jésus de Prague*" ("He is as sweet (and charming) as the Infant Jesus of Prague"); or, "*Il a toujours des fours à benir*"("He always has some ovens to bless," i.e., business to take care of here and there).

These clever expressions reveal the creativity of the people. The fanciful exaggeration of the first saying, the abbreviated, almost telegraphic method of indicating that a child is as bright as he is cute, in the second, and in the third, the painting of someone's portrait in a single brushstroke, which transforms him into a character type, are examples of psychological perspicacity as well as inventive ability.

Singing, music, and dancing were also an integral part of Franco-American culture in the first half of the century. Love songs, ballads, patriotic songs, and lullabies were the favorites, and bawdy songs were sometimes allowed. Lowell was fortunate in being the hometown of the Champagne Brothers; with their orchestra and their publishing company, they were able to promote their own compositions as well as traditional music. The best gatherings featured either an accordion, a harmonica, or a piano player who could also lead the group in the traditional sing-alongs or get everyone's feet tapping and eager to dance a jig or a quadrille.

Franco-American folklore also includes folk medicine and traditional cooking. With but few exceptions—the wood sculptures of Adelard Côté and the paintings of Gilbert Roy, for example—cultural artifacts have yet to be studied.

A detailed analysis of popular Franco-American culture would reveal the continuing presence of Canada in the lives of the immigrants. Families stayed in touch with extended family members through the regular exchange of letters and visits. Both the automobile and vacation travel facilitated these family visits, and a great number of Franco-Americans were eager to make the trip round the Gaspé Peninsula or cruise up the Saguenay River. In addition, the seminaries, academies, and boarding schools of French Canada were still recruiting in the United States, and this increased the contacts on both sides of the border. Pilgrims visited sanctuaries like Saint-Anne-de-Beaupré and Saint Joseph's Oratory, and religious magazines published by these shrines reached a large number of readers in New England. Canada was also present through its major newspapers that competed with the Franco-American papers, as well as through theater troupes and music and dance groups that often toured the Northeast.

What conclusion can be drawn from all this? That Franco-American culture is richer in oral expression than in material artifacts? It would be unwise to answer such a question categorically until extensive research has been conducted. Judging from popular manifestations, the Franco-Americans of 1900-1935 were, like their ancestors, undeniably a people who loved words, who enjoyed listening to fine religious or patriotic orators, and who valued the art of storytelling. They handed down an oral tradition which reveals their simple faith, their "great big" common sense, their deep-seated honesty, their ready hospitality as evidenced by the saying, "*Soyez chez vous, chez nous,*" which can be translated as "Make yourselves at home," but which lacks the finesse of the original with the nice symmetry of the *Chez vous - chez nous* combination.

There was a nobility of spirit present in the collective soul as well as in the wisdom transmitted from generation to generation as evidenced by this entire tradition. Their detractors notwithstanding, these Canadian immigrants clearly did not neglect their imaginative and emotional needs. That this tradition lasted as long as it did proves both the influence of their faith and the persistence of rural habits in these new city dwellers.

The People's Religion

In 1935 almost all Franco-Americans continued to practice a Catholicism outwardly more French-Canadian than American. To a greater or lesser degree, depending on the individual, religion was one of the most important aspects of a person's life; and for a goodly number, it was even *the* most important aspect, since both their private and social lives were subordinate to it. Though not all were devout to the point of being scrupulous, religious practice was, nonetheless, an integral part of their way of life, and for many it was a daily source of strength throughout the long years of an arduous existence.

Springing more from the heart than from the mind, this simple faith—often naïve and verging on the superstitious—was centered on the parish. A sense of mutual belonging existed between these people, who still called themselves *Canadiens*, and their parish—the parish was theirs, and they in turn *belonged* to such and such a parish, as they so aptly put it. A myriad of pious associations recruited members from various groups in the parish population: men, young men, married women, single women, etc. To retain these members and attract new ones, parishes expanded their programs to include sports teams, marching bands, and drill units. They also organized pilgrimages to Québec or Franco-American shrines.

The parish placed the seal of religion on every phase of life and sought to develop the religious sense of the faithful so that each parishioner would constantly be guided by a concern for his or her eternal salvation. There was also a desire to protect the faithful from evil influences, like socialism or Protestantism, which were viewed as possible dangers. Pious associations and programs helped parishes nurture an active faith, one that promoted charitable works. Such a range of initiatives produced a cadre of highly dedicated people in every parish and, for a substantial part of the population, created a home-church-school symbiosis that remained intact until the Second Vatican Council in the 1960s.

The pastor and, to a lesser degree, the curates were the key people in the life of the parish. After the Sentinellist crisis, only a handful of clergymen made mention of the priest's "patriotic" role. French was still the language spoken in church, but most priests were no longer actively involved in the *survivance* movement. Clearly, ethnic considerations were pushed aside—spiritual concerns alone now mattered, and to avoid any return to Sentinellism, members of the clergy now restricted themselves to the purely religious aspects of their work.

The power and influence of the priest, especially the pastor, remained considerable at this time. Ever on the alert for anything that might affect the lives of his flock, the *curé* did not hesitate, for instance, to denounce from the pulpit a Franco-American newspaper that appeared to be straying from the right path. Pastors and curates were usually available for private consultations, and the parish visits they made once or twice each year strenghtened their ties with parishioners while allowing the pastor to gauge the family's level of devotion as well as its needs.

Pending more detailed studies, it would be unwise to venture beyond the evidence available from today's elders as well as that from other sources, like contemporary Franco-American newspapers, among other documents of the period, which make clear that evening family prayer, consisting of the rosary followed by the "Remember, O Lord, . . ." was a common practice up to the Second World War.

Sunday mass was the most important religious event of the week. The people attended in such large numbers that they filled the church several times over during the morning hours and various groups attended mass at different times, as noted by Rev. Denis Magnan:

> In the neighborhoods of American cities where a good number of our people reside, Sunday mornings are really quite interesting. With the dawning of day, the Canadian parish church becomes a focal point, drawing people from all around. The first to come are the pious souls who attend the so-called Communion mass. Next come the children: happy, lively, and boisterous but piously respectful once they have entered the Lord's House. They are followed at a later mass by radiant young people in the full bloom of their youth. Finally, it is high mass that summons the more mature parishioners: fathers and mothers, along with the leading figures of the Canadian colony. (Magnan, *Histoire de la race française aux États-Unis*, p. 343)

Because the people were fond of ceremonial pomp, clergy and sacristans, in keeping with the liturgical season, prepared services imbued with great solemnity which included every possible element needed to enhance the ceremony: a profusion of candles and flowers around the main altar, a myriad of lights throughout the church, magnificent vestments, a solemn and elegant liturgy, all embellished by well-known hymns that were greatly enjoyed by the congregation.

The cycle of the liturgical year differed but little from the one French Canadians had known for generations. After the quiet period that followed Christmas and New Year's Day, late winter brought the Lenten season and its four weeks of retreats reserved for men, youth, married women, and single women in succession. School children had their three-day retreat at the beginning of Holy Week. Retreats were obligatory at this time, and they were seen as a useful custom, since a "good retreat cleanses the conscience." So there would always be "a big turnout" to hear either a Redemptorist preacher, perhaps from the shrine of Saint-Anne-de-Beaupré, an Oblate, or a Dominican—either a "Canadian from Canada" or a "Canadian from New England." Crowds were so large in some churches that as many as eight or ten priests would hear confessions, either in the confessionals or behind the grilles that had temporarily been set up at the communion rail. Some of this zeal was probably due, at least in part, to the custom of "apologetic" retreats at which parishioners were encouraged to submit questions, anonymously and in writing, on any aspect of faith, dogma, or morals. Retreats, either open (in parishes) or closed (in retreat houses), were such a success that in 1937 the Association of Franco-American Retreatants was founded.

On Easter Sunday, early risers could see the sun dance, just as in Canada. And religious practices based on Québec or Acadian models continued: mass and communion on First Fridays of the month, (it was said and believed that nine of these in succession guaranteed the presence of a priest at one's deathbed); devotions every night during May, the month of Mary. Hymns like *"J'irai la voir un jour,"* *"O Jésus, doux et humble de coeur,"* or *"Nous vous invoquons tous,"* this last to the tune of *"My Country, 'Tis of Thee,"* were sung with great fervor at these ceremonies. Devotions of a similar nature were repeated in October, the month of the Holy Rosary. In the interim there were the three-day observances of the feast of the Sacred Heart in June, of Saint Anne in July, and of the Assumption in August. In November, prayers for the souls of the departed were recited, and once again the arrival of Advent heralded the coming of another Christmas.

In the meantime, individuals found time to practice their "special devotions," which deserve a further study. Some parishioners, for example, liked to complete the thirteen Tuesdays of Saint Anthony, especially if they were facing a major decision like marriage. Others recited twenty-four "Glory bes" every day, one for each of the twenty-four years that Saint Theresa of the Child Jesus spent on earth. Still others promoted devotion to Saint Joseph, conferring "St. Joseph's ring" on a sick person so as to invoke the saint's healing powers. These prayers, including the brief but fervent supplications that accompanied them, often granted a precise number of "days of indulgence," thereby reducing the time one would have to spend in purgatory.

On this subject of popular devotions of the period, two noteworthy figures exerted considerable influence: Rose Ferron (1902-1936), the Woonsocket stigmatic, and Brother André (1845-1937), the great Montréal miracle worker. As an immigrant herself—Rose Ferron was born in Saint-Germain-de-Grantham in Drummond County, Québec—the story of her life fired the imaginations and the hearts of her compatriots living in the United States. The tenth child in a family of fifteen children, Rose Ferron had lived first in Fall River and then in Woonsocket. Stricken at an early age with a mysterious illness which she accepted as her vocation, she remained bedridden for the last twenty years of her life. Her ecstasies, stigmata, and other sufferings, along with her acceptance of "martyrdom" for the love of Christ, attracted a great many visitors to her bedside and earned her a reputation that remains controversial to this day.

Some claimed to have seen blood flowing from her forehead, and they never for a moment doubted that they had been in the presence of one of God's truly elected ones. To a woman visitor around 1928, who told her that she looked radiant with joy, Rose is said to have replied: "When you understand your vocation, you are very happy, and it is the soul's beauty that is radiant." Her biographer, Rev. O. A. Boyer, reported that Bishop William Hickey visited Rose Ferron during the Sentinellist conflict and that Rose, unbidden, volunteered herself as "the official victim for the Providence diocese" so that the crisis might be resolved more quickly.

Generally speaking, there is no longer any talk of "little Rose's" eventual canonization, but those who believe in her virtues and her supernatural gifts continue to write and speak out on her behalf. In his *Manuel de la petite littérature du Québec*, Victor-Lévy Beaulieu numbers her among "the authentically religious," stressing the horror that her life inspires to a post-Quiet-Revolutionary writer like himself. What is certain is that, even now, sixty or so years after her death, the "case" of Rose Ferron remains a puzzle for anyone seeking to understand her strange destiny in an objective manner.

The cult of Brother André, more widespread than that of Rose Ferron, was already well-established among Franco-Americans many years before his death in 1937. Of humble origins himself, Brother André was liked by the people as much for his propagation of devotion to Saint Joseph as for his achievements as a healer and a builder. He had many personal contacts and relatives in New England where he had lived for a time as a young man. His visits were greeted with enthusiam both by the sick as well as by the Franco-American population at large. His type of active faith held a special appeal for a group of people who were in the process of becoming Americans and as such greatly appreciated efficiency and pragmatism. A humble, pious, and practical man, Brother André was, nonetheless, "a strong man" of the spiritual realm. Soon after his death, pictures along with statues of him and copies of his biography could be found in an increasing number of Franco-American homes where prayers were said either for his beatification or to obtain his intercession. These prayers were answered in 1982 when Brother André Bessette was beatified by the Pope during grandiose celebrations.

Rose Ferron and Brother André are only the best known among the "saintly" Franco-American figures in 1935. People were also beginning to recognize the sanctity of Father Zénon Décary (1870-1940), the Biddeford, Maine, faith healer, of Father Marie-Clément Staub, Augustinian of the Assumption (1876-1936), the founder of the Sisters of St. Joan of Arc, and of Dominican Father Vincent Marchildon (1876-1972), the dynamic director and driving force at Saint Anne's Shrine in Fall River. The task to which Father Marchildon devoted his life, the cult of "good Saint Anne," shows her importance in the Franco-American spiritual pantheon of the period beside the Blessed Virgin, Saint Joseph, and of course, Jesus Christ.

Since the orthodox Catholicism to which they adhered was Christocentric, it was natural for the most highly valued traits to be the known aspects characteristic of "God-made-man." Everyone was free to adopt the traits that most appealed to him or her, and the clergy of the time reminded these working-class people of the events most likely to stimulate their imagination and their feelings: Christ crucified, the risen Christ, the Sacred Heart of Jesus, and the Precious Blood. With young people, it was the Nativity and the Christ Child's obedience to his parents that were underscored.

As in French Canada, devotion to the Blessed Virgin became widespread due to the efforts of the clergy and the religious communities. Her cult was spread first by the women of those religious orders consecrated in a special way to Mary. The influence of these women religious in schools and hospitals was seconded by that of the men of the Franco-American religious orders which, for the most part, were also dedicated to the Virgin: the Oblates of Mary Immaculate, the Missionaries of La Salette, the Marist Fathers and Brothers, among others.

Franco-American Catholic iconography in the first half of the twentieth century also revealed special devotions to the Holy Family, to Saint Joseph as the ideal father figure for heads of families, and to Guardian Angels. For women and, in particular, young women, Saint Theresa of the Child Jesus was highly respected, and a statue or picture of her could be found in many Franco-American churches. Saint Anthony, who helps find lost objects, Saint Jude, the advocate of lost causes, and Saint Cecilia, the patron saint of musicians, also had many followers. A study of Franco-American parish names would confirm these claims.

An explanatory inventory of devotional aids used by Franco-Americans would tell us a great deal about their prayer life. For example, someone walking through a typical tenement around 1935 would have found a crucifix in every room and, in many homes, a holy water font in every bedroom. Wealthier people could afford statues, one of which would have been the Infant Jesus of Prague. This devotion spread during the period between the wars, no doubt because it was said that He brought good luck, but also because He could provide steady employment if his statue faced the front door of the apartment or if someone carried a small statue of the Infant with him at all times.

Medals were popular, as they were in Canada, and there was at least one to represent each of the aspects of the life of Jesus and the saints named above and especially one to the Blessed Virgin, known as "miraculous." The brown scapular, called the Scapular of Mount Carmel, was the most popular among those in use; it was given to children on the day of their first communion. The green scapular was worn by someone requesting a very special favor: the conversion of a hardened sinner, for instance, or recovery from an illness. The red scapular was worn by the members of an archconfraternity under the direction of the Sisters of the Precious Blood of Saint-Hyacinthe in Québec; they promoted the recitation of the devotional office of the Precious Blood, and their publications had long been in circulation among Franco-Americans. A multitude of missals and prayer books were also in use, and it would be worthwhile to inventory them.

In a word, the faith of Franco-Americans in 1935 was simple and robust, adapted to their status as workers and sustained in concrete ways on a regular basis through devotional aids or elaborate liturgical ceremonies. The clergy would make allowances for an individual's private devotional practices provided they were orthodox. In some homes, for instance, one might find a photograph of Father Jacquemet, the apostle of temperance, while for reasons of their own the people next door might have a special devotion to Mother d'Youville, foundress of the Sisters of Charity known as the Gray Nuns, from the color of their habit. Some immigrants and their descendants left the Church, but they were looked upon with disapproval by the vast majority. Generally, there was a desire to avoid being seen as a Catholic "*à gros grain*," i.e., "in name only" or even worse a "*rongeux de balustres*," literally "a gnawer of communion rails," i.e., a pious hypocrite.

For Francos, faith sought to express itself in deeds, and during the period from 1900 to 1940 social and hospital services were greatly expanded, especially in major centers, from Lewiston to Woonsocket and Fall River. Since most of these institutions—hospitals, old folks' homes, orphanages—have not published any histories, it is impossible to present an overall view of their accomplishments. What is certain, however, is that the founding of a charitable institution at a given place and time depended mostly on the local clergy, the will of the bishop, and the availability of personnel. One factor common to all of these initiatives, however, was the generosity of the faithful who were in general more inclined to contribute to the development of a "Canadian" hospital or old folks' home in their own city than to an "Irish" institution.

Still, even at the beginning of the century, some founders demonstrated an ecumenical spirit. When he founded Saint Anne's Hospital in Fall River, in 1906, the pastor of Saint Anne, the Dominican, Father Raymond Grolleau, specified that while it would be a Catholic and French-language institution, it would be open to all who needed it, without regard to nationality or religion. To insure that the hospital had a competent staff, Father Grolleau brought over the

Dominican Sisters of the Presentation from Tours, in France, to staff it. A zealous women's guild, called *dames patronnesses*,—whose volunteer counterparts could be found in most Franco-American centers—collaborated with Father Henri Beaudé in organizing raffles, carnivals, and fund drives for the benefit of the hospital. Thanks also to the devotion of the sisters, Saint Anne's Hospital was in full expansion in 1935, and as of 1927, it even had its own school of nursing.

As a matter of fact, a considerable number of Franco-American hospitals, old folks' homes, and orphanages had been founded throughout New England by 1935. Some were under the direction of lay persons, but most of them were sponsored by orders of women religious from Québec. The Sisters of Charity of Saint-Hyacinthe seem to have provided Franco-Americans with the greatest number of religious in the social service field. In Lewiston, they were in charge of institutions founded before 1900, including Saint Mary's General Hospital, Maine's first Catholic hospital, founded in 1889, and Healy Home, an orphanage dating from 1893. In 1908, they founded a school of nursing and in 1928 *l'hospice* Marcotte for the elderly. This same order was also present in other centers: Manchester, Berlin, and Rochester in New Hampshire, and Woonsocket in Rhode Island. Other religious orders active around 1935 included the Sisters of Charity of Québec, the Sisters of Charity of Montréal, and the Little Franciscan Sisters of Mary, the latter founded in Worcester in 1889. Mention should also be made of the Sisters of Saint Joan of Arc, a congregation founded in 1914 by an Assumptionist priest, Father Marie-Clément Staub (1876-1936), to care for the clergy. In 1918, its mother house was transferred to Bergerville, now Sillery, Québec. It is worth noting that most of the charitable institutions in existence around 1935 had been established on such a firm footing that they endured from fifty to seventy-five years. Some of them are still in existence, either on an autonomous basis or merged with a similar institution.

Equally worthy of note is the growth by 1935 of another kind of religious undertaking, that of the shrines founded and administered by religious orders of men. The most popular Franco-American shrine before 1940 appears to have been that of Saint Anne, located in the church of the same name in Fall River. Established in 1892, its reputation grew with each passing year, especially under the direction of a "holy" Dominican priest, Father Vincent Marchildon (1876-1972). A native of Batiscan in Québec, he devoted some sixty years of his life to this ministry. As its director, Father Marchildon not only kept up the numerous activities initiated at the shrine over the years, he added some others as well. Large numbers of pilgrims, alone or in groups which sometimes numbered more than a thousand at a time, flocked there to pray at the feet of the statue said to be miraculous. They were also drawn to the shrine by the perpetual novena to Saint Anne which took place on Tuesdays, the Sunday afternoon special devotions, or the solemn novena which concluded with the feast of Saint Anne on July 26. During his lifetime, Father Marchildon was reputed to be a faith healer. He spent his entire life serving the poor and the afflicted and contributed mightily to the reputation of this shrine which has attracted faithful from all over the United States for over one hundred years.

Retreats, one of the least studied among Franco-American religious endeavors, truly deserve special notice—for example, all the efforts made over the decades by the Oblates. In 1921, they were granted their own Franco-American province centered in Lowell. They also had their own houses of formation—juniorate, novitiate, and scholasticate—in New Hampshire and Massachusetts. In their recruitment campaigns for vocations, the Oblates resorted to such powerful slogans as: "Save your soul—become an Oblate." They were knowledgeable public relations practitioners who utilized numerous approaches to awaken the faithful to the urgent needs of the missions. *L'Apostolat des Oblats de Marie-Immaculée,* a "monthly magazine published by the Saint John the Baptist Province in Lowell," exhorted the members of the Missionary Association of Mary Immaculate to recruit new members and support missionaries through prayers, sacrifices, and charitable donations. The magazine brought news from distant lands for its readers in Lowell's Little Canada: from Laos, Ceylon, the Canadian Far North, the then Belgian Congo, Bolivia, Australia, in short, from every country in which the Oblates had missions. The "little missionary's page" was aimed at the young, and to pique the curiosity of readers of all ages, a quiz on the contents of the various articles was included in every issue.

Lowell's Oblates also organized major campaigns to publicize the exhibits they mounted during the thirties. Thousands of people visited these kiosks to view reproductions of altars then in use in missionary lands as well as exotic miniatures of African, Eskimo, or Amerindian villages. Eager to take advantage of every promotional opportunity, the Oblates sold picture postcards of these kiosks, which was, of course, another way of helping the missions.

These Oblate undertakings represent but a single aspect of the Church's involvement in missionary activities. Sensitizing children to the missions was part of the school curriculum, and they were the recurring subject of homilies throughout the year. The clergy, and sometimes a priest belonging to one of the missionary congregations, exhorted the faithful to become "apostles" themselves by praying for the conversion of the pagans and contributing generously to the missions. This served to develop a sense of spiritual solidarity, for by helping the missionaries with prayers and donations, the faithful were rewarded in turn by the prayers and masses of these same missionaries who now became a source of grace for those who supported them.

Among other religious endeavors, the Cercles Lacordaire for men and Sainte-Jeanne-d'Arc for women were soon in the forefront of the campaign against alcoholism in both Franco-American New England and Canada. Father Joseph-Amédée Jacquemet (1867-1942), a French Dominican, was the founder of these Cercles, federated in 1912. In the course of his parish ministry, he had witnessed firsthand the problems stemming from alcoholism. He became a zealous advocate of total abstinence which he saw as the only effective solution to the problem. The movement spread quite rapidly throughout the six New England States and Canada. In 1939 the Canadian *Cercles*, with their 3000 members, became administratively independent of the headquarters in Fall River. Father Jacquemet devoted over thirty years of his life to this apostolate and its many activities: lectures, meetings, private counseling, and various publications, including a magazine, *Le Réveil* (The Awakening). He was greatly assisted by Victor Vekeman (1867-1947), whose numerous plays against alcoholism were well received both in Canada and New England.

The Formation of the Young

While not everyone in 1935 thought there were enough Franco-American schools—this despite the fact that there were over 200 of them—the infrastructure for the parochial school system was well established, and secondary education was being developed. There was no consensus, however, on the direction that primary school education should take.

Government officials, reflecting the Anglo-American outlook, urged attendance at public schools, theoretically neutral in matters of religion. After their unsuccessful efforts to control—if not abolish—Catholic schools, departments of education and school committees kept a watchful eye on the curriculum to insure that students were being taught the basics—reading, writing, arithmetic, geography, history of the United States, etc.—along with some training in civics designed to make them good American citizens. Public school supporters and those who backed the Catholic schools accused each other of intolerance and dogmatism, and some American scandalmongers returned again and again to the old saw that the teaching Sisters were not professionally trained; worse yet, since they themselves were immigrants, they were simply not competent to teach students English and prepare them to participate in American civil society. The most malicious critics opined that the hours these students spent in church were stolen from a school day already hobbled by the teaching of religion and French. It should also be remembered that public schools offered an attractive option. Discipline was less strict and the atmosphere more relaxed than in Catholic schools, making them all the more appealing to young people thirsting for freedom.

On the other side, diocesan authorities, wanting Catholic schools to be recognized by the civic authorities, fought tooth and nail to insure that neither their teachers nor the programs for which they were responsible, would in any way be inferior to those of the public schools; anything less would have threatened the very existence of denominational schools. It goes without saying that pastors, both Franco-Americans as well as those of other ethnic groups, argued for the parochial school approach. In conjunction with the teaching orders, they made sure that both teachers and students met public school standards. In their sermons and in the articles they wrote for Franco-American newspapers, pastors defended the teaching of both religion and French, the two most contentious issues in this debate. As a result they found themselves having to argue that this additional work, far from harming young Franco-Americans, actually resulted in a much better education than that provided by their rivals, be they Irish or American. To this already complicated situation must be added the influence of the parents, that of the *survivance* ideologues, called *les patriotes*, as well as that of the religious orders.

The question of the influence of parents on education is a delicate one. Was their only right—and one that pastors contested—that of withdrawing their children from a parochial school and sending them to a public institution? Provisionally at least, it can be affirmed that in 1935, the rights of parents seem to have been minimal at best compared to those of the State and the Church.

The role that *survivance* ideologues played in education is no easier to determine than that of parents. Journalists like Wilfrid Beaulieu and Philippe Armand Lajoie, essayists including Josaphat Benoit and Alexandre Goulet, and priests, the Reverends Adrien Verrette and Georges Duplessis, for example, wielded their pens as weapons in their calls to order, in their exhortations, and their commentaries—so much so that the influence they may have had on education cannot be overlooked. These guardians of the cultural heritage were unanimous in their conviction that without the help of the schools, the forces of assimilation would make short work of *la survivance*. Because their point of view was so misunderstood, it must again be emphasized that they were not cultural separatists in any sense of the term. They agreed with the majority that education had to be bicultural, but the issue of what balance needed to be maintained between the Canadian and the American aspects of this education was an ongoing bone of contention.

For the most ardent *patriotes* of the thirties, a vanishing minority even then, the ideal school would be *un coin du Canada* [a little bit of Canada] set in a Franco-American parish. Dominican Father Jean-Dominique Brosseau, for example, the presumed author of the history of Fall River's Saint Anne parish that was published around 1919, stated there that the primary purpose of a Catholic parish is to insure the Catholic education of children. He also added: "Here [i.e., in the United States], the Catholic school also has the mission of protecting nationality, family customs, and the household virtues." In the pre-Sentinellist era, it was still possible for a priest to argue for such a close link between religion and nationality in his reflections on education. Declarations of this kind, however, would become rare with the passage of time.

In his book on *la survivance,* entitled *L'Âme franco-américaine* (1935), Josaphat Benoit defended the Franco-American school and indicted the American school system which he viewed as being in essence a tool of protestantism. In warning his compatriots against the supposed neutrality of American public schools, Josaphat Benoit was echoing the conviction expressed by Rev. Édouard Hamon in *Les Canadiens français de la Nouvelle-Angleterre* (1891).

After asserting that dispensing "religious and moral education" was "the parochial school's primary reason for being," Benoit added that there was another urgent reason why it was necessary to continue founding Franco-American schools: to teach children "the French language and their national history, rightly considered to be the cornerstone of their ethnic survival and the necessary condition for their total development." For the ideologues of 1935, the concepts of *la survivance* and identity were inextricably linked. Josaphat Benoit's work reflects the persistence and continuity of the ideology propounded by the élite from 1860 to about 1940. If one looks for the intellectual and spiritual roots of Franco-American education, they can be found in the clerical-nationalistic ideology of French Canada which was the dominant influence from start to finish of the immigration period.

But this ideology was not universally adopted. Again in the thirties, some observers, like Rev. Georges Duplessis of the Boston archdiocese, were of the opinion that "national" education was lacking in this or that Franco-American school. Duplessis supported the viewpoint of Québec's Cardinal Bégin who argued that education in a Franco-American milieu had both "a patriotic as well as a religious mission." According to *Abbé* Duplessis, such an education had to include the teaching of the history of Canada as well as that of the United States, so as to inculcate pride in young people in order to ensure "the formation of the Franco-American soul."

After the condemnation of the "nationalist heresy" by Pius XI and in the wake of the Sentinellist crisis, it should not come as a surprise that "nationalist" oriented education was lacking in some schools, especially if one takes into account the conservative attitude of most pastors and members of the forty-odd religious orders who taught in Franco-American schools. Committed, first and foremost, to winning acceptance for Catholic education in a Protestant country, and also obligated to teach French, since they were serving French-speaking immigrants, pastors and religious orders were hard-pressed to find room, in an already overloaded academic program, to inculcate notions of "patriotism" or "nationalism." In fact, they did manage this feat quite often but in varying degrees.

As for the religious orders, not enough has been said about the essential role they played in the development of the network of Franco-American schools. Without their vow of poverty and their spirit of sacrifice, renewed each day for a hundred years or so, an educational system of this kind could never have been established, let alone maintained for such a long time. The economic condition of the immigrants could never have furnished the means necessary to hire an adequate number of lay teachers to provide for the educational needs of those thousands of children. By 1935, religious orders of both Canadian and French origin had already influenced two generations of Franco-Americans since the first religious had come to New England at the end of the 1860s.

The influence of these religious orders varied, of course, but it is not an exaggeration to state that the total dedication to the life of the spirit shown by these men and women religious cannot but have made a profound impression on all Franco-Americans, a large percentage of whom were educated by these brothers or sisters. The student reaction to this all-encompassing spirituality ranged anywhere from indifference to a desire to emulate, and, indeed, a number of young people did choose to become nuns, teaching brothers, or priests. There is no doubt that the religious orders were largely successful in fulfilling their primary objective: the formation of Catholic youth. Did they also meet their secondary goal, that of producing generations of bilingual and bicultural Franco-Americans? This would appear to have been the case, though as early as 1935 some observers were seeing a serious decline in this regard.

It should also be noted that in 1935 there was no standard curriculum common to all Franco-American parochial schools. Programs and textbooks varied, depending upon the pastor and the preference of the teaching community in that parish, but remained always within the boundaries prescribed by diocesan authorities. Still, the schools were more alike than different from one another. It is clear that teaching techniques used in these schools were influenced by the *Ratio studiorum* developed by the Jesuits in the sixteenth century; hence the firm discipline, the traditional emphasis on memorization, and the custom of encouraging students to compete with one another.

Teaching in the Franco-American schools of the period embodied a high degree of professional concern and demonstrated a determined pursuit of excellence on the part of the teachers in them, both men and women. Total education was their goal, one that addressed the will and the heart, as well as the mind. These schools sought to strike a careful balance between tradition and progress by updating curricula and selecting textbooks that reflected the most recent scientific and pedagogical discoveries.

In 1935 many schools still operated on the half-day schedule. Classes—numbering as many as sixty or seventy students in the larger parishes—were divided into two groups: one would be taught in French in the morning and in English in the afternoon, and the other vice versa. The school day was about five and one-half hours long and the school year lasted forty weeks. Religion, the French language, the history of Canada, and sometimes art and music were taught in French; in addition to the English language, pupils learned arithmetic, history, geography, and hygiene during the English portion of the day. Civics was also part of the English program of studies.

Religion was at the core of this program, not simply as a subject matter to be taught in the classroom, but also as an atmosphere to be created and fostered. The goal, captured in Mother Marie Rivier's incisive saying, was "to etch Christ in the heart of the child." In fact, students were exposed on a daily basis to living examples of this religious ideal: the sisters themselves, whose lives were a constant reminder that personal sanctification was the primary goal of existence and that it could be achieved only through repeated effort. Having taken vows which encompassed poverty, penance, self-denial, and obedience, these sisters preached through word and deed the virtues of faith, hope, and charity. They also sought to communicate something of their own spirituality, one that was centered on the life of Christ and the cult of the Blessed Virgin. They sought, finally, to do everything with fervor and zeal, since the superiors of these religious orders did not tolerate half-hearted individuals.

The school day began with a morning prayer, recited out loud, generally followed by religious instruction which, over the eight-year period of elementary education, included in turn the catechism, Bible history, liturgy, and sometimes a smattering of Church history. The most widely used textbook appears to have been the so-called "Baltimore" Catechism prescribed by the Third Plenary Council of Bishops held in Baltimore. The *Catéchisme préparatoire à la première communion*, by Rev. J.-A. Charlebois, a Cleric of St. Viator, and the *Abrégé du Catéchisme de persévérance*, by Bishop Gaume, were also in widespread use at the time.

The "Baltimore" catechism contained the prayers deemed to be essential along with the basic teachings of the Church—all of it dutifully memorized by several generations of Franco-Americans. If today the very concept of a catechism seems too rigid, at the time no one doubted its effectiveness. Those who studied the terse answers it gave to life's thorniest questions were likely to remember many of them throughout their lives. While this catechism has been praised for its clarity, its succinctness, and its unambiguous presentation of the essentials of Catholic doctrine, some have deplored the fact that it hardly lent itself to dialogue or discussion.

Depending on which texts were being used in a given school, there may have been some cross-referencing between the catechism and what was then called *l'histoire sainte,* i.e., sacred or Bible history. Around 1935 the *Abrégé d'histoire sainte,* first published in 1888 by the Sisters of the Congrégation Notre-Dame of Montréal, was still being used. Though it too was written in the question-and-answer format, the presentation seems less boring since it included a collection of stories, sometimes terrifying (Cain and Abel, the Flood), sometimes reassuring (Moses rescued from the Nile). Often the illustrations accompanying these disconcerting stories imprinted images on those young, impressionable minds: the engraving of young David grasping Goliath's severed head or the representation of the flagellation of Jesus.

It should come as no surprise then that a child reflecting on the doctrine presented in his catechism or on the biblical stories might find it a worrisome, even troubling experience, such was the insistence on God's power and wrath. Forced to accept the reality of an often angry God and the uncertainty of eternal salvation—the very goal of one's existence, lest the reader forget—we can see how a child might turn with hopeful optimism to the study of liturgy, the third facet of the religious studies curriculum in the elementary schools of 1935.

In fact, liturgy could capture the child's attention for it taught him what he could do on his own to progress along the path of salvation, all the while providing him with specific information on the diverse forms of worship: the mass, the holy seasons, and the sacraments. Moreover, the study of the sacred vestments, the protocols for candle lighting and processions allowed the student to escape from the humdrum of everyday life into a realm rich in symbolism, aesthetic values, and mystery. More opportunities for escape were provided by the quality illustrations to be found in a manual like the *Précis de liturgie* that featured photographs of the cathedrals of France, engravings of liturgical objects used during the Middle Ages, and the prints and reproductions of great religious painters.

French was both a subject matter and a language of instruction. During half of each school day, students were taught in French and were expected to use it. It was this approach, beginning with kindergarten, in which students enrolled at the age of five, and continuing up to and including the eighth grade, that produced bilingual students. And the proof of the effectiveness of this teaching method is that the majority of those who completed their elementary education at this time could remain bilingual for the rest of their lives.

To our eyes, the approach may seem to have been austere, with its heavy emphasis on grammar studied from the very early years, along with spelling. Students were required to master the complete conjugations of the verbs, in all tenses and moods, including the subjunctive pluperfect, along with the myriad rules for the agreement of the past participle and the sequence of tenses.

A variety of teaching techniques was used to help students assimilate these numerous precepts. Detested by most of the students, the daily *dictée* (dictation) was always corrected, often in class, and mistakes were identified and explained. For homework, students were assigned an *analyse grammaticale* which required a description of every aspect and grammatical function of each word. In the higher elementary grades, the *analyse logique* was employed to good effect; this consisted of the detailed study of a complex sentence, with emphasis on the interrelationships among the various phrases within the sentence. The *composition*, in a format that followed the teacher's detailed instructions, was also regularly assigned. Finally, an active approach to reading was fostered by means of the *cueillette*, the culling and copying into a notebook of thoughts, expressions, and stylistic devices for future use in a composition.

How children were taught to read in French reveals the extent to which the teaching of this subject, like that of every other, was imbued with religious moralism. The textbooks utilized in parochial schools were generally ones that had been edited in Canada by religious communities. The *Série de livres de lecture à l'usage des Écoles chrétiennes*, first published at the turn of the century, and often reprinted thereafter, enjoyed a certain popularity before the Second World War. The reading selections also served a practical purpose since the authors wrote on matters of general knowledge and offered their readers good advice. In Book III of the series *Lectures graduées*—intended for sixth-year students who were about eleven or twelve years old—there is a brief selection entitled "Autumn" which is typical of the genre. It is replete with useful information about an autumn that one might experience in rural Canada. The selections are also highly diverse; there are some on the classification of animals and plants, others on one's duties: to parents, to country, and to God. Texts on agriculture are to be found along with poems written by French-Canadian poets Napoléon Legendre and Octave Crémazie, La Fontaine, the French writer of *Fables,* and Adolphe-Basile Routhier who wrote the words of "O Canada," the country's national anthem.

The history of Canada, taught as late as the 1950s, underscored the religious aspect of French Canada and highlighted the "heroic precedence" of the French in North America. One of the texts in use was the *Histoire du Canada*, by C. S. Viator [*sic*]. Published in 1917 by the Clercs de Saint-Viateur, it was devoted primarily to political and military history. Teachers inevitably proposed as models certain historical figures like Madeleine de Verchères and Dollard des Ormeaux, both of whom saved a fledgling 17th-century French-Canadian community from obliteration at the hands of the Iroquois. While the "Frenchness" of these names "from France" was impressive, some students, with or without malice, wondered how they might imitate the exploits of these heroes and heroines while living within the confines of a Little Canada which offered little opportunity for military prowess.

The French component of the curriculum just described reflected the transitional nature of the period which Franco-Americans were experiencing in 1935. The teaching of religion, French, and the history of Canada was reinforced by the singing of French-Canadian songs and the presence in the classroom of crucifixes, pictures, and statues that reminded students of the importance of religion and the history of Canada. Strict rules, most probably originating in the Québec mother houses of the teaching orders, governed the behavior of the students at every moment and on each occasion. The spirit of competition, of Canadian rather than American origin, was strongly encouraged through the publication of student rankings in the monthly report card and by means of a system of rewards and punishments.

Graduation ceremonies were also more reflective of a Canadian mentality and served as the crowning point of the young person's education. At the solemn awarding of prizes and in the presence of the pastor, family, and friends, students would receive either devotional objects—statues or missals—or large, red, richly bound volumes with gold embossing, imported from France, whose contents can be classified in the category of "edifying literature." A prize for excellence was given in every subject, and even those at the bottom of the class received a prize, often a tiny booklet called "galette" (denoting something thin and insubstantial), in recognition of a second-rate performance—either a disheartening or a consoling experience, depending upon one's point of view. These year-end rituals were an integral part of the educational program, and they were yet another way of encouraging competition.

Presented to a large audience of parents and parishioners, the play, traditionally staged at the end of the year, was designed to help students develop a more rounded personality. In 1935, most of these plays were in French. Although we are uncertain as to their origin, we do know, however, that these plays were didactic in tone. We also know that the Sisters of the Holy Cross found some of the plays they staged in an anthology called *Les Fêtes de l'enfance*.

After 1935, the time devoted to English increased slowly but surely as Franco-Americans became more Americanized and removed from their Canadian origins. But, in 1935, the amount of time devoted to the teaching of religion, French, and the history of Canada pointed to the fact that the supporters of *la survivance* were still on the winning side in that battle. The victory would be short-lived, for time was running out. In general, pastors and religious communities agreed up to a point with *survivance* ideologues on the importance of preserving the faith, the language, and an awareness of the collective past; they were also in agreement on the importance of insuring that students receive an education that was both bilingual and bicultural. But ideologues and those responsible for the education of Franco-American youth disagreed over the specific direction that this biculturalism should take and over the "patriotic" training of the students. Pastors and educators took pains to avoid the kind of "national" education that the most militant ideologues had in mind. For example, Franco-American history as such was not taught, and students learned nothing about the founding of Franco-American parishes, organizations, and newspapers. If, perchance, the names of the outstanding journalist, Ferdinand Gagnon, the erudite Civil War hero, Edmond Mallet, or Rev. Louis Gagnier—the immigrant founder of some ten parishes—meant something to them, it was not because they had heard about them in school.

This deficiency was due to some extent to the Sentinellist crisis of the twenties. It had left in its wake a divided élite, one that was wary of any kind of "nationalism," however muted it might be, that could lead ecclesiastical authorities to associate it with the attitude condemned by the Holy See. It must be noted also that in 1935 it was still too soon for people to fully appreciate the heroism of the first generation of immigrants. The generation of 1935 was characterized by a reticence, a humility, and a diffidence which later generations would find excessive, given the achievements of their immediate predecessors. While the history of Canada was taught out of respect for the elders, and that of the United States to fulfill the requirements of the adopted country, Franco-American history was not deemed to be an object worthy of study, and for the most part, the ideologues were perceived as trouble-makers.

As a result, while pastors focused almost entirely on their parishes and educators on their teaching, schools were an object of controversy. *Patriote* ideologues like Professor Alexandre Goulet and the Fall River journalist Philippe Armand Lajoie insisted on the rights of parents in the education of their children, while denouncing what they saw as an abuse of power by diocesan authorities bent on centralization and what they perceived to be too quick an acceptance of this state of affairs by those pastors deemed to be assimilationists. At the Second Congress of the French Language held in Québec in 1937, even though the Franco-American participants praised the Franco-American school system, pointing out its phenomenal growth and its achievements, some, like Goulet, Lajoie, and Josaphat Benoit, were far from optimistic concerning its future. It was left to Wilfrid Beaulieu later on, when the bilingual parochial school was under siege, to summarize the outcome which had been unfolding since the early decades of the twentieth century:

> We realized, perhaps too late, that the authentically bilingual parochial school was our most precious possession. Others had understood this well, and they maneuvered to take control of the system. It was against the bilingual school, the mainspring of any properly conceived notion of *la*

survivance, that a materialistic and politically-inspired assimilationist policy was able to achieve its most subtle but most damaging results. (*Le Travailleur*, April 29, 1948)

A great deal more remains to be learned about the formation of young Franco-Americans. The most serious gap in our knowledge is probably the absence of any detailed study of curricula and textbooks. We do not know how Canadian and French teaching methods were adapted to the American milieu. It would also be useful to know how administrative responsibilities for the schools were shared between pastors and religious communities in such matters as changes in the curriculum, in rules and regulations, the choice of co-curricular activities—religious or otherwise—the creation of an atmosphere conducive to learning. Additionally, the customs, milieu, and folklore of these schools, including their physical appearance, have yet to be described and analyzed. Finally, it would be helpful to know more about France's influence on these schools: for example, how was France viewed by the Franco-American clergy and the members of the religious communities, and how much of this viewpoint did they communicate to the young in their care?

Intellectual Trends

An assessment of intellectual activity in the 1930s reveals the existence of a considerable number of publications. The most practiced genres were history and the essay—propagandistic or polemic in tone—and this would continue to be the case for a long time to come. Imaginative literature was almost non-existent. In 1935, as in 1900, the primary purpose of these French-language publications was either utilitarian—defending the Franco-Americans against their detractors—or didactic—supporting an undertaking, be it a parish, an organization, or a newspaper.

Hence, writing was practiced first and foremost to serve the cause of *la survivance,* and it remained both committed and combative. But this type of writing can be qualified as having been pragmatic also since *patriote* writers sought to bring the past to bear on both the present and the future. Historical writings, for example, usually had a dual purpose: to praise the great heroes of the past in order to persuade readers to enlist under the banner of *la survivance.*

During the 1930s, this ideological literature was enriched by several new titles, some of which were the result of a rapprochement between the *patriote* élite and their Québec counterparts. The lecture series on Franco-Americans, sponsored by Montréal's Société Saint-Jean-Baptiste, and the Second Congress of the French Language held in Québec in 1937, and attended by hundreds of Franco-Americans, resulted in the publication of some important works. Moreover, Franco-American and Québec newspapers were widely distributed on both sides of the border, the works of Franco-American authors like the poet Rosaire Dion-Lévesque were published and reviewed in Québec, while the writings of Louis Dantin, an exile from Québec, living in New England, promoted an interest in Québec literature.

For Franco-Americans of the 1930s, the dissemination of ideas was facilitated by the existence of cultural organizations, newspapers, magazines, and to a lesser extent, by books, all of which served the cause of *la survivance* and were dedicated to the cult of remembrance. Around 1935, the Société Historique Franco-Américaine, founded in 1899, was given a new lease on life by two Franco-Americans from Lowell: Judge Arthur L. Eno and the journalist-historian Antoine Clément. From the start, this society had sought, through its lecture series, to highlight the contributions of the French to the development of the North American continent. It also awarded its *Grand Prix* Medal to individuals and organizations who had contributed to the cause.

In 1935 this society once again began to publish a bulletin under the direction of Antoine Clément, who would later prepare a substantial compilation entitled *Les Quarante Ans de la Société Historique Franco-Américaine, 1899-1939*. This tome of almost 900 pages, which contains either a summary or the actual text of the lectures given since 1900, has never been appreciated at its true worth. It is invaluable since the lectures it reproduces or summarizes, often given by major figures, are full of substance. We find there articles, such as "Washington and Coulon de Villiers," by Major Edmond Mallet (1902); "Fort William Henry," by William Bennett Munro (1910); "The Sources of Local History," by Pierre-Georges Roy (1925), and other such riches.

The names of other well-known speakers—French-Canadian and French as well as Franco-American—like Adjutor Rivard, Lionel Groulx, and Gilbert Chinard, are to be found in the table of contents of this work. But none was more highly appreciated than Cardinal Jean-Marie-Rodrigue Villeneuve, Archbishop of Québec, whose lecture entitled "Le fait français en Amérique," delivered on May 4, 1938, was widely circulated. Evoking the "spiritual brotherhood" uniting French Canadians and Franco-Americans and their "mission" on the American continent, the speaker recalled the glorious past of the French Empire in America and praised the French language. He urged his listeners to speak French "out of a civilizing spirit" and also because it is "a duty imposed by charity and justice." Finally, he examined the relationships between religion and language. These themes, reaffirmed by such a revered figure, were exactly what was needed to revive the zeal of the élite and encourage them in their proselytizing efforts on behalf of *la survivance* among the halfhearted and the indifferent. The concluding lines of the speech were considered memorable: "The French language is a treasure. Make the most of it!" They quickly achieved the status of a watchword.

The activities of Lowell's Alliance Française were similar to those of the Franco-American Historical Society, except for the occasional play that was added to the annual lecture series. Directed by Antoine Clément, both the Alliance Française and the Société Historique invited internationally known French speakers like Marcel Braunschwig and André Morize in addition to well-known French-Canadian and Franco-American speakers. The influence of this cultural activity was further extended by Antoine Clément through his publication in volume form of *L'Alliance française de Lowell*, a compilation of the lectures given between 1929 and 1937.

During the thirties, ideas were also being disseminated throughout the group by means of some twenty-five French-language newspapers and magazines published in New England. Dedicated in part to news reporting and in part to "patriotic" activity, these periodicals faced an uphill battle, surrounded as they were by competitors. Montréal's *La Presse*, for instance, published a Franco-American edition for which it printed 13,000 copies. Meanwhile, major American newspapers remained popular through the constant reporting of sensational stories and the advertising of all the material goods that a hedonistic and capitalistic society could offer. As for the Franco-American newspapers, it appears that around 1935 their total number of subscribers did not exceed 50,000.

Some Franco-American journalists attempted to compete with the English-language press by publishing items of national and international interest. But since translating the news was long, wearisome, and ultimately not very profitable, most editors concentrated on issues of local interest, all the while disseminating the *survivance* doctrine. Still, nothing seemed to work, and without the massive popular support needed to achieve economic stability, these newpapers continued to founder. There was less and less interest in *la survivance*, and outside of the élite there was no widespread attachment to a patrimony, which was now viewed as having no immediate usefulness.

Despite the approaching collapse, which they must have sensed, *patriote* journalists persevered in their impossible effort to unite Franco-Americans and defend their faith, language, and traditions against the tidal wave of assimilation. While one might choose either to praise or to blame them for their tenacity in devoting themselves to this thankless apostolate, everyone would likely agree that journalism played a key role in the development and diffusion of Franco-American literature. In 1936, for example, *Le Messager* of Lewiston serialized *Canuck*, Camille Lessard's novel about immigration, and later published it in volume form. Most newspapers followed the custom of publishing poems, feature stories, and essays that contributed to Franco-American literature; many of the essays referred to subjects that had already found a place in history, like the retrospective studies marking an anniversary or the foundation of a parish. In fact, the best journalists, those whose work has endured because of its substantive nature, its interest, and its stylistic value, were historians or, at the very least, chroniclers at heart. Such was the case, especially for Josaphat Benoit, Wilfrid Beaulieu, and Antoine Clément, each of whom left many articles that deserve to be collected and anthologized.

Although these newspapers all resembled one another, each had its own distinctive features. One was known for its political leanings, another for its linguistic and stylistic concerns, a third for its lively woman's page. But during this period, one newspaper stood above the rest and has earned the gratitude of future historians. Specializing in analysis and commentary, it was founded in Worcester in 1931 by Wilfrid Beaulieu (1900-1979) and named *Le Travailleur* to indicate its continuity with Ferdinand Gagnon's original *Travailleur*, also published in Worcester from 1874 until the death of its founder in 1886 although it limped along until 1892. In spite of innumerable difficulties, Wilfrid Beaulieu found a way to publish this newspaper until 1978, a few short months before his death.

The first issue of the new *Travailleur* appeared on Thursday, September 10, 1931. In a signed editorial, Wilfrid Beaulieu published his policy statement and guiding philosophy from which he would not deviate for forty-seven years:

> *Le Travailleur* will be a militant newspaper, whether some like it or not. To us, the word militant means that we are armed for battle and ready to fight in defense of our rights without, however, having constant recourse to war cries. As some of our colleagues and correspondents have already stated in other columns, *Le Travailleur* is, first and foremost, a newspaper where ideas can be set forth and commented upon. The paper will, of course, contain some news regarding Franco-Americans, but only inasmuch as this lends itself to favorable or unfavorable observations.

From the very start, Wilfrid Beaulieu was able to assemble an impressive team of correspondents, including Elphège Daignault, a choice which might, at first glance, seem surprising unless one recalls that Wilfrid Beaulieu had himself been one of the excommunicated Sentinellists. Two of his early collaborators deserve a special mention. Hermance Morin was that "visiting" Franco-American who signed her articles with aliases like *"Grain de Sel"* (Grain of Salt), *"J'en Assure"* (I Maintain). She was one of the mainstays of the paper, someone without whom, according to the editor himself, it would have folded. She wrote on any and all topics, ranging from history to current events. She was as adept at evoking the centennial of the execution of the *Patriotes* of 1837-38 (March 2, 1939) as she was in defending Franco-American interests against the assimilationist maneuvers of diocesan authorities (March 16, 1939). In a word, she is one of those writers whose reputation should be rescued from neglect. Dr. Gabriel Nadeau, for his part, was the author of bibliographical monographs of remarkable erudition all of which deserve to be reprinted.

Le *Travailleur* of the thirties contained other writings that have become essential documents for Franco-American archives: articles signed by Doctors Antoine Dumouchel, Paul Dufault, and Clément

Fréchette, by attorney Ernest D'Amours, and by Philippe Armand Lajoie, "the intrepid editor of *L'Indépendant*," in whom Wilfrid Beaulieu had discovered a kindred spirit. In an article entitled "The Cowardly Surrender of the Franco-American Élite" (June 25, 1936), Rodolphe Pépin develops the viewpoint espoused by the *patriotes*. In short, the *Travailleur* of the thirties had already become the voice of *la survivance* in New England. Since it was also interested in French Canada and France, *Le Travailleur* was anything but a local newspaper.

During this decade, two historians added several major works to the body of Franco-American literature. In 1931, as a sequel to his biographies of New Hampshire's first "Canadian" pastors, Manchester's *Abbé* Adrien Verrette (1897-1993) published a voluminous history of his native city's Saint Mary parish, *Paroisse Sainte Marie, Manchester, New Hampshire*; it remains a model of the genre. The book situates this parish in its sociohistorical context, which is to say at the very heart of the Franco-American colony, the local Church, and the city itself. In this work of nearly encyclopedic dimensions, the author provides biographical sketches of Saint Mary's pastors and traces the historical development of every parish organization. Such is his attention to detail that, for example, he includes the list of all the staff members, both physicians and religious, who had been associated with Notre Dame Hospital since its founding; he does as much for every institution within the parish. Similarly, he outlines the history of the foundation and development of the two religious orders of French origin—the Sisters of the Presentation of Mary and the Marist Brothers—who taught respectively at the school for girls and the one for boys. The author also devotes lengthy chapters to parish life, to Franco-American activities in Manchester's "Canadian" neighborhood, and to the parish's golden jubilee celebration.

Having stated that this voluminous work ranks as a model of the genre, its merits deserve further elaboration as do its weaknesses. Its wealth of detail and documentation, its desire not to overlook anyone, especially the most humble of the parish workers, its obvious wish to pay homage to those who had come before, are offset by a glossing over of controversy and a tendency to idealize the clergy. *Paroisse Sainte Marie* suffers from the typical defects of clerical-patriotic historiography. These writings also tend to leave out the anecdotal aspect, as though the past's strictly human dimension has no place in such a work. History is subordinated to what is perceived as a higher goal: that of promoting *survivance* ideology. Although these reservations about the work should be kept in mind, would that there were a work of this scope and caliber for every Franco-American parish!

During the thirties, Josaphat Benoit wrote two works which have become classics of *survivance* literature. In *L'Âme franco-américaine* (1935), a synthesis of the main characteristics of the group, the author paints in broad strokes a historical picture of the French presence on the North American continent before examining the causes of *la survivance* along with the obstacles that it was encountering. It is a work which combines social psychology and history. The author, himself a member of the élite, attempts to analyze various expressions of the collective psyche as he perceives them. It is a subjective work in which Benoit by turns judges, exhorts, and condemns, all the while seeking to convince the reader to share his enthusiasm for the "unforgettable past which is the foundation of future *survivance*." In his *Catéchisme d'histoire franco-américaine* (1939), the author presents similar material in a question-and-answer format that tends to stifle all discussion: "What has happened to Franco-Americans who have abandoned their language and changed their name? Most of them have become nobodies."

The Franco-Americans of 1935 were living in the twilight of the golden age of relationships between French Canadians in the mother country and those of the diaspora—in the Northeast and the

Midwest—represented by a small but dynamic group of intellectuals and men of action on both sides of the border who were united by the idea of a "French America." Together they constituted a community of minds pledged to the promotion of *"le fait français en Amérique"* (the presence and achievements of the French in America).

Two noteworthy events need to be singled out here. The first was a series of lectures on Franco-Americans that aired over station CKAC in Montréal from 1933 to 1936 under the joint sponsorship of the Société Saint-Jean-Baptiste of Montréal and the Association Canado-Américaine of Manchester. The other was the Second Congress of the French Language held in Québec from June 27 to July 1, 1937. *Les Franco-Américains peints par eux-mêmes*, published by the ACA, contains the texts of some twenty-five of the lectures broadcast by CKAC. This anthology is significant for us today because it contains a contemporary overview of the status of Franco-Americans from the viewpoint of *survivance* militants of the period. The group's strengths and weaknesses are listed, as well as indications on how the French language could be preserved and how some "stumbling blocks" might be avoided. In addition to the wealth of detail it provides on the Franco-American situation in 1935, the work contains many persuasive insights. Some of its statements, however, have remained controversial to this day: for instance, regarding the specific role played by the religious congregations in *la survivance* and on the need for assistance from Québec in order to ensure the survival of Franco-Americans as an ethnic group. On this latter topic, Elphège Daignault, for example, sought from Québec the kind of support and inspiration "whereby Franco-Americans can preserve the spiritual patrimony inherited from their forebears." Even today, the issue regarding Québec's role in the preservation of the Franco-American patrimony is far from settled.

In 1936 the *Société du parler français au Canada* provided a major incentive to the Franco-American élite with its announcement that the Second Congress of the French Language would be held in

June 1937 on the theme of the preservation and development of the French *esprit*. Both the Congress itself and the planning that led up to it provided a host of opportunities for manifestations of French cultural life. Franco-Americans answered the call sent forth by Monsignor Camille Roy, who presided at the Congress, by forming regional committees throughout New England so as to ensure that the project would receive maximum publicity and widespread participation.

The planning and publicity for the proposed Congress led to a close and sustained collaboration between the Québec and Franco-American élites, witness the brochure published by the Rhode Island Regional Committee which was written by Alexandre Dugré, a Jesuit from Québec. The author demonstrates an unusually accurate understanding of the Franco-American phenomenon, beginning with emigration itself, in which he sees a serious loss for Canada. He goes on to argue that *la survivance* could not be taken for granted in the United States. He rightly sees that the dilemma facing the group was how to ensure that the young would take up the cause. He suggests that this can happen "Only if we present it as an advantage and not as a routine thing: to remain French in one's soul must be a conscious decision . . . a person should remain French *by choice*, as a natural outcome of the blood flowing in his veins according to the will of God the Creator."

Father Dugré also understood that in the United States careers, schools, and neighborhoods, in fact "everything steers a person toward English and materialism." For these reasons, the decision to remain French is a difficult one, based as it is on "spiritual reasons, on imponderables." In a sense, the author revealed himself to be more Franco-American than the Franco-Americans themselves, calling for a parochial school curriculum that would include not only the history of Canada but that of immigration as well, so that men of the caliber of the journalist Ferdinand Gagnon, the founders of parishes such as Monsignors Pierre Hévey and Charles Dauray could be proposed as models. But when he declared that the only two choices were *"tenir ou trahir"* (to hold fast or to betray), Father Dugré did not differ in outlook from his *survivance* colleagues. Still, he deserves credit for at least alerting them to the dangers they faced and warning them of the need to find new ways of appealing to the young if they hoped to ensure their loyalty and thereby save the day for *la survivance*.

In light of the interest that the upcoming Congress was generating, the Québec central committee established a sub-committee for the United States in Manchester. Its chairman, Rev. Adrien Verrette, served as liaison officer with the Québec committee. One of his duties was to co-ordinate the publicity tour that took Monsignor Camille Roy into over twenty-five Franco-American centers in three weeks, a visit variously described as "a triumphal journey" and "an historic pilgrimage." Among the many other collaborative efforts, one in particular should be singled out, for it captures the spirit of solidarity that the Congress created. Omer Héroux published in *Le Devoir*, Montréal's leading intellectual newspaper, some twenty articles on the Franco-Americans that were reprinted in New England's French-language newpapers. During the months leading up to the Congress, these papers mounted an extensive publicity campaign, and in its wake, they published a great number of reports and commentaries.

An estimated 4000 Franco-Americans attended this Congress, described as "the meeting of an entire race." It brought together delegations from every francophone region in North America. Among them were over 300 young people from 114 New England parochial schools who came either as contest winners or who traveled at their own expense. During a five-day period, three hundred studies, reports, or documents were presented, some thirty of them, including four major addresses, by Franco-Americans.

Most of the Franco-American studies, along with press reviews and other documents relating to the Franco-American participation, were published by Rev. Verrette in a collection entitled *La Croisade franco-américaine*. These Congress-related studies—on the parish, the family, and professional life, on activities for the young, on the legal status of the French language in New England, on everyday language, etc.—have two themes in common: the need for loyalty to the ancestral country and the fear that the patrimony was threatened with extinction. Each study presented an appraisal of a given issue, and the collection of these essays constitutes a useful complement to the earlier *Les Franco-Américains peints par eux-mêmes*. While it would be an overstatement to speak of even a latent fatalism in these texts, an unmistakable note of distress surfaces in spite of the many expressions of confidence about the future of *la survivance*. This hint of concern is, nonetheless, accompanied by overblown expressions of patriotism and the desire to emphasize the positive aspects of the situation. Without questioning the good faith of the speakers, one cannot ignore the hyperbole in statements like the following: "The crusade of friendship among the French has been launched, and its challenge has been accepted here at home as it is in Canada; we are going to relearn our devotion to the past and teach it to our children." The latter part of this statement was doubtless wishful thinking.

Today, some sixty years later, how should the Franco-American participation at this Congress be evaluated? To see it as nothing but high-flown rhetoric would leave us well short of reality. And merely to criticize the stubborn attachment to the past reaffirmed *ad nauseam* throughout the Congress would be simplistic. An objective rereading of the texts can convince the reader that the appeal behind gatherings of this kind—there would be others of the same sort among Franco-Americans during the 1940s and 1950s—was as much a matter of the heart as one of the mind. The Franco-American élite of 1935 really did experience what Rev. Verrette described as "an irresistible attraction . . . for this land of our common origin." The Franco-American élite was united with that of Québec in the same fraternal spirit that

Monsignor Camille Roy termed "a spiritual bond that spans the border."

The *patriote* élite of 1935 had a much greater understanding of the obligations that this "spiritual bond" entailed than did the people, just as it could more readily recognize and appreciate the "feeling of family friendship" that existed between Franco-Americans and French Canadians.

The élite thus participated in the Congress partly out of filial devotion, and it took to heart the reminder expressed by *Abbé* Lionel Groulx, one of Québec's foremost historians: "Six or seven generations of your ancestors lie sleeping in the cemeteries of Québec." This was the moral dimension of *la survivance*, reflecting a strict interpretation of the fourth commandment: "Honor thy father and thy mother." This attitude was certainly not free of a sentimentality that often accompanied the interrelated themes of remembrance, loyalty in spite of absence, affection felt for one's "brothers" still living in the ancestral land, and even moral indignation at "traitors" who had surrendered to assimilation. Such sentimentality supports an interpretation of *la survivance* as not merely an ideology, but also as a form of romanticism.

One concrete achievement to come out of the Québec Congress was the creation of a permanent committee, called the Comité permanent des congrès de la langue française en Amérique, to follow up on the recommendations voted at this great gathering of 1937. Subsequently renamed the Comité permanent de la survivance française en Amérique and, finally, the Conseil de la vie française en Amérique—the name it bears to this day—this committee, which has always included a Franco-American representation, arranged for the publication of the Proceedings of the Congress. *La Croisade franco-américaine* was one of these volumes, and beginning in 1938, it provided financial support for the annual publication of *La Vie franco-*

américaine (1937-1952), compiled by Rev. Adrien Verrette. The work of this committee, including the publications that it underwrote, thus guaranteed that for some time to come there would be an exchange of ideas between the élites of Québec and those of New England.

What must also be underscored is the growing role of historicism among the Franco-American intelligentsia in 1935. Influenced by Québec, the writings of those for whom history played a preponderant role—clergymen, journalists, and members of the liberal professions—were characterized by a love of the mother country, a fervor, and an oft-repeated determination to perform "pious deeds" worthy of one's ancestors as well as the Church. This is why three-quarters of a century later, the story of the Sentinelle, which is *not* perceived as a "pious deed," remains taboo, resulting in a gap that may never be filled.

On the whole, these writings were basically concerned with the various aspects of but a single subject: the French presence in North America. Little attention was paid to non-French America, except for Marie-Louise Bonier who, in her *Débuts de la colonie franco-américaine de Woonsocket, Rhode Island*, enriched the Franco-American literary patrimony with a few precious pages in which she recounts in French the Native American legends of the Woonsocket region, stories that she had most likely first heard in English. Alas, what might have been the start of a tradition was not continued. Fortunately, however, the Bonier volume has recently been translated, updated, and profusely annotated by Assumption College's Institut français. This English-language version is entitled *The Beginnings of the Franco-American Colony in Woonsocket, Rhode Island*.

To complete this assessment—which excludes works of fiction for the time being—two research works were written as theses for French universities: Josaphat Benoit's previously mentioned *L'Âme franco-américaine* and Maximilienne Tétrault's *Le rôle de la presse dans l'évolution du peuple franco-américain de la Nouvelle-Angleterre.* Finally, an Anglo-American academic, Edward B. Ham, published in highly respected journals like *Le Canada français* and *The New England Quarterly* some serious studies in which objectivity does not exclude understanding. He was one of those rare Americans who asserted that Franco-American biculturalism, far from impeding the development of the nation, was an asset that the United States should seek to encourage.

The Arts

The arts represent yet another neglected field in need of research. This is true for all the arts, but most especially perhaps for the visual arts since there does not appear to be any study devoted to Franco-American painting or sculpture. At most, there are only a few essays on some of the traditional or popular artists. The goal here is not to propose any definitive classification or offer an exhaustive list, but only to cite a few names that ought not be forgotten.

A native of Woonsocket and the son of Jean-Baptiste Fontaine who was himself an architect, Walter Francis Fontaine (1871-1938) was trained in Europe. During his first stay in 1892, he spent several months in England, Belgium, and France, and his special interest in the cathedrals of the Middle Ages would later manifest itself in his work. On his second visit in 1907, he made a careful study of the Tiberghien factories in Tourcoing, France. [The Tiberghiens had opened textile factories in Woonsocket.] In 1911 he was elected to the prestigious American Institute of Architects. His sons Oliver and Paul were his associates in the Woonsocket firm of W. F. Fontaine and Sons.

Walter Fontaine has left us many works of several different kinds as can be seen in the number of public and private buildings located throughout New England, but particularly in Rhode Island. Though there does not appear to be any comprehensive inventory of his work, he was responsible for many churches, schools, convents, private homes, and other buildings. Without a doubt, his masterpiece is Saint Anne Church in Woonsocket. In the period from 1920 to 1930, he was responsible for the design of several buildings of particular interest to Franco-Americans, including the spacious boarding school of the Religious of Jesus and Mary, Mount Saint-Charles Academy, and the home office of Union Saint-Jean-Baptiste d'Amérique, all in Woonsocket. However, it is his churches that deserve special attention.

Of the twenty-five or so churches for which he drew up the plans, about half are in Franco-American parishes, and some of them are of particular interest. One of his first was for Saint Mary in Willimantic, Connecticut, designed in 1903. Its form is that of a Roman basilica but it contains Gothic elements like its rose window and quatrefoil; its portals and stained-glass windows are in the Romanesque tradition. The plans for Holy Family Church in Woonsocket date from 1908, and it, too, reflects a multiplicity of styles, predominantly Romanesque and Gothic. The same is true for Saint Charles Borromée (1915) in Providence and Sainte Cecile (*circa* 1925) in Pawtucket, whereas Saint Mathieu (1929) in Central Falls reveals an English neo-gothic influence.

Taken as a whole, the churches built according to plans drawn by Walter Fontaine reflect his enormous erudition in the history of architecture and his ability to integrate his knowledge in original works of masterful quality. A gifted ornamentalist, he was fortunate in exercising his talent during a period that was not hobbled by functionalism. At the national level, he participated in the renewal of interest in Gothic art in the United States, and in so doing, he endowed New England with monuments which, after a period of indifference, are now receiving the appreciation they deserve. There is no doubt that among the Franco-American architects of the period, his work is the most extensive and ranks as one of the most aesthetically rewarding.

Other families of architects include the Naults of Worcester and the Destremps family. Louis G. Destremps (1851-1930), who was born in Berthierville, Québec, immigrated to Fall River. He was responsible for a great many of the region's public and private buildings, including the courthouse, the armory, the local prison, several convents, and especially, his masterpiece, the church of Notre Dame de Lourdes in Fall River, tragically destroyed by fire on May 11, 1982. His son, Louis-E. Destremps (1875-1919), who was born in Montréal, also became an architect and had already completed several projects before settling in New Bedford in 1905. He was responsible for a number of the city's buildings, including the Third District Court, the famous Star Store building, and several schools. His contemporaries appreciated not only his architectural skills, but also his ability to integrate buildings harmoniously into their proposed surroundings.

"The head of a lion on the body of a young man"—this is how the poet Rosaire Dion-Lévesque described the painter Lorenzo de Nevers (1877-1967) whom he knew in his maturity. Born in Baie-du-Febvre, Québec, Lorenzo de Nevers began to paint and draw at an early age. To his mother's consternation, he would amuse himself by redecorating the walls of the family home. Misunderstood in school, he managed to survive his elementary education in Drummondville, Québec. Luckily for him, his older brother Edmond, a well-known essayist, was able to persuade his parents to send Lorenzo to Europe to study art.

De Nevers spent ten years (1902-1912) studying at the École des Beaux-Arts in Paris before returning to Canada around 1917, having placed ninth among the four hundred candidates for the Grand Prix de Rome, a prize which entitles the winner to spend a year in Rome studying and practicing his art. He had submitted one of his first important paintings, *The Flight into Egypt,* for this prestigious contest. Back in his homeland where he was misunderstood by his social circle, he responded by furiously painting one picture after another, less in pursuit of money than of his own aesthetic ideal. Throughout his long and productive career, he was often on the move, now in Montréal, now in New York or Woonsocket or in his studio in Central Falls where his family had settled after leaving Canada. He has left a large and varied output which has never been systematically studied, including many landscapes along with a great number of religious paintings: the *Sainte Face*, of which there were thousands of reproductions, an *Assomption de la Vierge*, an *Immaculée Conception*, and *La Mort de Saint Joseph*. He himself preferred *Le Christ de la Réconciliation*; it hangs in the Vatican museum, and it won him the praises of Pius XII. It is said that the model for this Christ was a wounded war veteran whom the painter had encountered, quite by accident, sitting on a bench in Jenks Park in Central Falls near the painter's studio.

There is another aspect of his work for which he is perhaps even better known than for his religious paintings—his series of portraits of "great men," beginning with King Albert I of Belgium. Some of his other subjects were King Alphonse XIII of Spain, who had been his classmate at the Beaux-Arts, and presidents Franklin Roosevelt and Dwight Eisenhower. Some of his paintings were reportedly sold and resold at fabulous prices, with little profit to the painter who always disdained money. Following his death in Woonsocket on March 29, 1967, Lorenzo de Nevers was honored in a very special way by U. S. Senator Claiborne Pell, who published his funeral oration in the prestigious *Congressional Record*. The following is an extract: "On March 29th, the State of Rhode Island lost one of its most distinguished residents and the United States one of its great artists. . . . The art of Lorenzo de Nevers will endure as an eternal homage to this painter. We mourn his passing."

Gilbert Octave Roy (1877-1947), a northern Maine painter in the naïve tradition, was born in Saint-Gervais-de-Bellechasse, Québec. After completing his elementary education in his native village, he became a decorative painter, and he would practice this craft for the rest of his life. In 1903 he emigrated to the United States, and in 1905 he settled with his wife in Fort Kent, Maine. For Gilbert Roy, the grand natural scenery of the St. John Valley would be the subject of over half of his known paintings. He appears to have been drawn to nature at its most peaceful, as in *Clair de lune, Nuit d'hiver,* and *Ruisseau.* Even the wild horses in *Chevaux* are captured at their halting place near a spring. This same serenity characterizes the murals he painted for homes in the St. John Valley. Gilbert Roy's portraits also hold some interest for art lovers. Although most of his subjects have been identified, the identity of several nudes remains a mystery. They are striking, as much for their subject matter—Gilbert Roy was living in a very Catholic milieu—as for their elegance and harmonious composition. The 1930s were his most productive period, after which he devoted the last eight or ten years of his life to religious art, especially paintings and the ornamentation of churches. He "redid" a number of church columns, by marbleizing them, and, in some cases, he amused himself by painting human and animal forms on them. Some of these can be seen at the Baker Brook church in New Brunswick. If this humble man's work is somewhat better known to us today, it is in part due to the excellent study of him done in 1979 by the Franco-American ethnologist, Roger Paradis.

A complete study of Franco-American painting would also include the work of Rev. Omer Chevrette. Born in Fall River in 1889, he was for many years pastor of Immaculate Conception parish in Fitchburg, Massachusetts. In addition to his hundreds of religiously-inspired paintings, Rev. Chevrette invented a method of "saturation painting" which he patented in 1942. This allowed him to paint on all kinds of dry surfaces: wood, metal, stone, canvas, and cloth. Immaculate Conception Church contains many of his paintings and frescoes.

The most highly reputed Franco-American sculptor is without a doubt Lucien Gosselin (1883-1940). Born in Whitefield, New Hampshire, he was a nephew of the Québec sculptor, Louis-Philippe

Hébert. Lucien Gosselin completed his elementary and secondary education in the parochial schools of Saint Augustine parish in Manchester. He then spent five years (1911-1916) studying sculpture in France, in particular at the Académie Julian. Having received many accolades in Paris, he established his studio in Manchester where he completed a great number of works. From 1920 until his death in 1940, he was a professor of sculpture at the Manchester Institute of Arts and Sciences.

Working in bronze, stone, marble, and plaster, Lucien Gosselin created works of every dimension, from medallions to large monuments; these can be found today throughout the Northeast. His abundant and diverse output reflects his patriotic love of the United States and his attachment to his Franco-American roots, evidence of which can be found in the numerous monuments he created for various parks, public places, and Franco-American cemeteries. Among his many works, his most noteworthy are the monument to the veterans of World War I and the equestrian statue of General Pulaski, the Polish hero of the American Revolution, both in Manchester, and the Sacred Heart monument in Fall River. He also sculpted busts of several Franco-American notables, including a bronze of historian, fraternalist, and politician Félix Gatineau for a monument dedicated to him in Southbridge, Massachusetts, and a plaster bust of Adolphe Robert, president of the Association Canado-Américaine, whose Manchester headquarters houses a large number of works by Gosselin.

There were no doubt other Franco-American sculptors before 1940, but they remain unknown, at least for the time being. Mention should be made, however, of Jean-Baptiste Boudreau. Born around 1869, he emigrated to Worcester, where he became an engineer and inventor. He also sculpted small statues in wood, of religious and rustic inspiration.

The art that was most practiced by Franco-Americans was music. The names of hundreds of Franco-American musicians can be found in cultural accounts at the local, regional, and even at the national level. These include professionals as well as serious amateurs who achieved a remarkable level of competence, either in instrumental or vocal music. Succeeding Emma Lajeunesse, the nineteenth-century star, the two best-known performers were Éva Tanguay and Rudy Vallée.

Éva Tanguay (1878-1947), actress, singer, and millionairess, was born in Marbleton, Québec. She emigrated with her family to Holyoke, Massachusetts, which she then left for New York at the early age of sixteen. At the turn of the century, she achieved some success in operettas and burlesque, but it was especially in vaudeville that she made her reputation. In 1909, she won a leading role in the famous Ziegfeld Follies, and a few years later, her salary was $35,008 per week, a dazzling sum at the time. While critics extolled her many talents—especially her "vivacious energy"—she would later bemoan her immense popularity which, as would subsequently be the case with Jack Kerouac, she was unable to integrate harmoniously into her life. She died in Hollywood, an impoverished and forgotten woman.

The singer and band leader Rudy Vallée was baptized Hubert Prior Vallée in Island Pond, Vermont, where he was born in 1901. After the family had moved to Westbrook, Maine, Hubert studied at Saint Hyacinthe parochial school and Westbrook High School. A self-taught musician, he learned to play several instruments—drums, the clarinet, and the saxophone—while pursuing his studies at the University of Maine and then at Yale where he was awarded a doctorate.

In 1927 he organized his own orchestra in New York—naming it "The Connecticut Yankees." It was a huge success. From then on, he was invited to play in all of the best music halls, and his concerts were aired over radio networks throughout the country. His fame increased throughout the thirties and forties for, in addition to his career as a band leader, he became a movie star, winning praise especially for his performance in *The Vagabond Lover* (1939). His other claims to fame include the founding of the United States Coast Guard Band, around 1940, his work as a music publisher, and an autobiography, *Vagabond Dreams Come True* (1929). Later still, he enjoyed success in television.

Quite early on during the immigration period, it was common practice, just as in the homeland, for Franco-American parishes to retain the services of a professional organist to meet their many liturgical needs: daily masses, weddings, funerals, not to mention Sunday vespers and the service surrounding the exposition of the Blessed Sacrament. This long and rich tradition of Franco-American organists and choirmasters deserves further study.

One of the most respected of these organists was J.-Ernest Philie (1874-1955) who was born in Saint-Dominique, Magog, Québec. He emigrated to Manchester at an early age and completed several lengthy assignments in various Franco-American parishes in New England—Woonsocket, Fall River, Springfield—before returning to his native country. During his long career, he served as the director of several choral groups whose concerts attracted appreciative audiences throughout the region. The music lovers of that period also praised his compositions of both sacred music and patriotic songs, as well as his collection of *Mélodies grégoriennes* (1924).

Born in Suncook, New Hampshire, in 1892, Rodolphe Pépin became the organist and choirmaster at Saint Louis de Gonzague in Nashua before assuming the same functions at Saint John the Baptist in Lowell for over twenty years. He composed and published masses as well as an *Ave Maria* which were much appreciated in Canada as well as the United States. He was also a theater director, a professor of music, a lecturer, and a concert organist in the Northeast. He succeeded in organizing performances of French music in Boston's Mission Church, an English-language parish administered by the Redemptorist

Fathers, and remained an active participant for many years in several Franco-American cultural groups.

René Viau, who was born in Pawtucket, Rhode Island, in 1903, began his career as a child prodigy in 1913, at the age of ten. He served as organist and choirmaster in several cities, and in 1935 he settled permanently at Notre Dame Church in Central Falls. A professor of music, René Viau also gave hundreds of concerts in the eastern United States and Canada; many of his concerts were also broadcast on radio. He founded several music groups, including the Woonsocket Symphonic Orchestra and the Vocal Arts Society of Central Falls.

One of the rare Franco-American violinists to win fame before 1940, Chambord Giguère (1877-1954), was born in Woonsocket. For four years, he had the rare privilege of studying with the great masters at the Royal Conservatory of Music in Brussels. As a professor of violin and an acclaimed violinist for over a half-century, he was highly praised by music critics in the United States and Canada. The *Chicago Musical Leader* wrote about him:

> Chambord Giguère, the Franco-American violinist, has an artistic temperament that is both flamboyant and well under control, and which yields excellent results. His phrasing is elegant; the fire, intelligence, and rhythm that he brings to his playing recalls without any doubt whatsoever that of his master, Ysaye. His own genius is revealed just as easily in a dreamlike *berceuse* as in a fiery concerto. His talent places him among the greatest artists of his day. His exquisite technique is subtly woven into the fire and delicacy of his playing. He creates an atmosphere . . . and his technique is forgotten. Giguère gave his last series of concerts during the 1931-1932 musical season.

In vocal music, the fine careers of several artists had either reached their peak or were just being launched during the 1920-1930 period. Émile Côté, born in Amesbury, Massachusetts, in 1898, became a star of the National Broadcasting Company network. He made a number of recordings for major companies, including RCA Victor and became increasingly famous during the 1940s and 1950s.

Other artists were building solid reputations in their respective corners of New England. Baritone Clovis Fecteau gave several live concerts as well as radio broadcasts in the New Bedford region: he was also heard over radio stations in Boston and Montréal. In 1933, choirmaster Hervé Lemieux (1903-1969) and Albert Vandal succeeded in forming a chorale, Les Gais chanteurs, a Pawtucket, Rhode Island, based chorale whose members were all Franco-Americans. For a great many years, this group, which still exists, sang only in French. Among the numerous professors of music, many members of religious congregations should be added to the list. The career of Sister Cécile-des-Anges, P.M. (1890-1955), born Bertha Wehr in Stanbridge, Québec, is noteworthy. We include her in this rapid overview because her career would have justified her being named an honorary Franco-American and because, having undergone ethnic influences in a French-American religious community, she formed several generations of young Franco-American musical talents. She chaired the music department at Rivier College in Nashua, New Hampshire, and was in charge of musical studies in all the educational institutions of the Sisters of the Presentation of Mary in the United States. Her influence on Franco-American students in the field of music was enormous. Sister Madeleine of the Savior (Jeannette Payer), of the Sisters of Saint Anne, born in New England in 1907, followed a similar path at Anna Maria College in Paxton, Massachusetts. She also composed vocal music.

* * * * * * *

In retrospect, the 1930s appear to have been a high-water mark if not a golden age in the evolution of the Franco-Americans as an ethnic group. True, the bitterness of the Sentinellist controversy was already showing signs of permanence, but this was offset by the plethora of achievements summarized in this chapter. In fact, the numerous signs of vitality and viability could have duped an observer into thinking that the Franco-American community would go on thriving indefinitely. This impression, which proved to be erroneous in the long run, will be dealt with in the remaining chapters of this book.

IV

TOWARD ASSIMILATION
1935-1960

In the thirties and forties, the Sentinellist crisis abated sufficiently, at least on the surface, to the point where the two mutual benefit societies, the Association Canado-Américaine and the Union Saint-Jean-Baptiste d'Amérique, who had been on opposite sides in this affair, were able to join forces in the struggle against assimilation. But this renewed solidarity could not offset losses in the ranks. The clergy, for instance, ceased to identify with the *patriotes*, very likely because of the Sentinellist crisis; while most clergymen remained French-speaking, they carefully distanced themselves from Franco-American nationalistic thought and endeavors. Unable to compete with the English-language press, the newspapers disappeared one after another. Meanwhile, with the end of immigration in 1930 because of the new government policies and the Depression, there were no longer any reinforcements arriving from the mother country.

The process of assimilation was gaining ground throughout this period. It was a multidimensional phenomenon, and it had already been described as such as early as 1903 in *L'Écho de l'Ouest*, a Franco-American newspaper in Minneapolis:

> It is a day-by-day absorption that unfolds over the years; in politics, customs, literature, geography, business, society, in specialized and local institutions, etc. Only someone who has personally left his country for a new one can understand the transformation, continual and unconscious, that occurs in the heart and mind of the newly-arrived immigrant who all the while must earn his daily bread.

This description is as valid for the period stretching from 1935 to 1960 as it had been in 1903, all the more so since new factors were now at work, in particular a more rapidly changing social environment. Having just begun to adapt to an urban environment, French-Canadian immigrants and their children found themselves participating in the nation-wide prosperity and social mobility that followed the economic upturn caused by World War II. And, during the 1950s, Franco-Americans also took part in that other postwar phenomenon—the exodus from the city to the suburbs.

Thus, within a few short years, Franco-Americans lived through two important social junctures: first, the personalized relationships of their traditional rural environment, modified by their life in the Little Canadas of the industrial cities, had been successively replaced by the impersonal setting of the city and then that of the suburbs. Added to this was the intermingling of different nationalities which tended to diminish both the need for, and the meaning of, belonging to an ethnic group—especially in an American sociocultural environment. This situation inevitably led to mixed marriages, a further source of indifference with regard to the cultural heritage. Moreover, as society evolved at breakneck speed during the 1940s and 1950s, the interests of the individual increasingly came to be seen as more important than those of the family.

If we add to this the various components of a materialistic and hedonistic society—movies, radio, television, newspapers, magazines, sports, automobiles, along with the omnipresence of advertising—it must be granted that there was hardly anything in an environment of this sort to encourage an ideal like that of *la survivance* or even of spiritual values in general.

Faced with this type of rapid social evolution, how did the *patriote* élite react? For the most part by a toughening of their stance combined with the establishment of New England-wide organizations, such as the

Comité de Vie Franco-Américaine and the Fédération Féminine Franco-Américaine. There was also an increase in the number of "patriotic" and historical observances. It was a time for commemorations—the 350th anniversary of Champlain's mapping of the New England coast, the bicentennial of the deportation of the Acadians, the bicentennial of the Marquis de La Fayette, and that of the battle at Fort Carillon (renamed Ticonderoga), the scene of a resounding French victory, not to mention the anniversaries of Franco-American "mother" parishes. So, despite the rapid progress of assimilation, the period was nonetheless marked by a proliferation of activities too numerous to be listed here.

Franco-Americans and the War

More than 100,000 Franco-Americans served in the armed forces of the United States during World War II, but a complete honor roll of those who died for their country has never been compiled. Franco-American newspapers published lists of those who had been killed or who were reported missing, and they singled out families which had three or more children in the armed services. In this latter category, the record in New England seems to have been held by the ten Frédette brothers of East Braintree, Massachusetts, and, nationwide, by the sixteen Gauthier brothers of Fort Worth, Texas. Under these circumstances, people no longer scoffed at the Franco-American propensity for having large families.

Franco-American newspapers of the period published lists of all those who achieved some distinction or other: officers, chaplains, physicians, nurses, young women volunteers, the decorated, the wounded. Churches reserved a special place for the Honor Roll on which the names of the servicemen were inscribed, and in some parishes there was an "altar of sacrifice" where these names were listed. Many cities commemorated the death of a hero by unveiling a plaque and renaming a public place—for example, Boudreau Square in

Concord, New Hampshire, Gagné Square in Lynn, Massachusetts, and Saulnier Square in New Bedford, Massachusetts. Sometimes a warship was named to honor the memory of a Franco-American who had died for his country, like the *U.S.S. Cabana* and the *U.S.S. Dionne*; the airfield in Nashua, New Hampshire, was named Boire Field, in memory of Ensign Paul Boire, an airman who had died in combat. But of all those Franco-Americans who made extraordinary contributions to their country, two deserve a special mention.

Jean Garand (1888-1974), a native of Saint-Rémi, Québec, emigrated as an infant to Springfield, Massachusetts, with his family. By the age of twelve, having had to leave school to help his family, he became an apprentice-mechanic and, before long, a master of his trade. While employed by a well-known munitions firm, he made improvements to the Springfield Rifle, the American Army's standard issue, and he was so successful that the Springfield was replaced by the Garand. This semiautomatic rifle, better known as the M1, was capable of firing from 50 to 100 rounds per minute, and it became the weapon of choice for the American armed forces. Thanks to the ingenuity of this French-Canadian immigrant, the effectiveness of the American fighting man was considerably improved. Jean Garand, who had changed his first name to John, also invented other firearms along with the parts needed to manufacture them.

René Arthur Gagnon (1924-1979) of Manchester, New Hampshire, participated in one of the war's most well-known exploits. A member of the 28th Regiment of the United States Marine Corps, he was one of the marines who on February 19, 1945, landed on Iwo Jima, some seven hundred miles from Japan. His company was ordered to take Mount Suribachi, and a bloody battle ensued. On the morning of February 23, René Gagnon and five of his fellow marines succeeded in raising the Stars and Stripes over Mount Suribachi. Thanks to the skillful eye of Joe Rosenthal, an Associated Press photographer who was on the scene, the image of the six men raising the American flag became one of the most famous photographs of the war and the symbol of the Allied victory over Japan. Three of these heroes died in the battle's waning moments. René Gagnon and the two other survivors were brought back to this country on orders of the President of the United States who personally received them at the White House. Joe Rosenthal's photo was distributed throughout the world, and the United States Postal Service issued a commemorative stamp of this feat. Today, in Washington, there stands a monument honoring the courage of these fighting men. It has become the nation's official monument to the U.S. Marine Corps.

It would be impossible to account for all the wartime efforts of Franco-Americans; like the rest of the American population, they took part in the general mobilization of human resources to ensure victory against the forces of oppression. They assisted the Red Cross and participated in the various drives for the recovery of war-related materials (clothing, paper, fat, and tin) in support of ground and naval forces. At the forefront of this collective effort that spanned four years were the clergy, the "national" societies, and the newspapers, thereby ensuring the widest possible publicity and the participation of most people.

The "Liberty Ship" program was one of the most successful civilian projects in the American government's nationwide campaign to raise the billions of dollars required by the war effort. From the outset of the war, Franco-American leaders had continually urged their compatriots to invest in War Bonds and to support other financial programs promoted by the federal government. In 1943, the government proposed a plan whereby Franco-Americans would subscribe $2,000,000, the cost of one Liberty Ship. In recognition of this, they would be allowed to choose the ship's name.

Leaders of the "national" societies rose to the occasion, and, after consulting among themselves, they decided to raise the goal to

$6,000,000, the cost of three Liberty Ships. The clergy, the societies, and the newspapers did not let up in their campaign to reach this goal. Innumerable speeches and articles, alleging that the group's "honor" was at stake in this effort, were given much publicity, since this gave Franco-Americans the opportunity to prove their loyalty to the United States. They also reminded people that these contributions would be reimbursed, with interest, by the government.

At the end of the campaign, which lasted from June 24 to September 6, 1943, Franco-American leaders proudly announced that subscriptions from Franco-Americans amounted to $12,600,000, more than double the amount they had hoped to raise. A spate of articles praising the generosity and patriotism of Franco-Americans appeared. Some analysts even viewed this success as a sign of the group's "social power" and new-found solidarity. *L'Union,* the publication of the largest Franco-American mutual benefit society at that time, went so far as to claim:

> We have finally given the lie to the charge against our race that characterized us as a group in which individual interests took precedence over the common good. We have understood that the interests of the individual are best served in cooperating harmoniously with others! (Quoted in *La vie franco-américaine* [1943], p. 117)

In *Le Canado-Américain,* house organ of the Association Canado-Américaine, Adolphe Robert praised all the "little" people whose modest savings had yielded such great results:

> Today there is perhaps no home, from the richest to the poorest, that does not have at least one war bond. The exhortation to "Buy Bonds Until It Hurts" was no empty slogan for our people. It was quite a sight after Sunday masses to see the people go to the rectory, the church basement, or the parish hall to buy their bond, as they had been encouraged to do so from the pulpit. And think about the rallies, the parades, and the door-to-door solicitations, all designed to promote the sale of bonds. In truth,

American public-spiritedness is not a meaningless expression for our people. (*La Vie franco-américaine* [1943], p.126)

The most delicate part of the campaign would prove to be the choice of the ships' names from the list that the general committee had been asked to submit to the government. As agreed, thirty names were proposed from among those Franco-Americans who had contributed the most to the advancement of their people in the United States. Their biographies were published in *Le Travailleur*. This provided an excellent opportunity to render a service to both the country and to Franco-American history. For the most part, the honorees were men who had founded the major parishes and the national societies. Because the Union Saint-Jean-Baptiste had extended its campaign and was thus able to raise additional funds, it was authorized to submit two additional names to the government. The names finally selected were: Monsignor Charles Dauray, Joseph Augustin Chevalier, Aram Pothier, Ferdinand Gagnon, Major Edmond Mallet, Hugo Dubuque, Jean-Baptiste Couture, and Bishop Albert Guertin. The choice of the latter, an anti-Sentinellist bishop, provoked a predictable protest from the veterans of this crisis of the twenties.

Meanwhile, Franco-Americans were divided in the conflict between Marshal Pétain and General De Gaulle. The majority, following in this the official position of the American government, sided with Pétain's Vichy government. During a propaganda visit organized by the USJB in December 1940, the French ambassador was warmly received in Franco-American centers like Woonsocket, where Eugène Jalbert, spokesperson for the USJB, proclaimed the admiration felt by Franco-Americans for Pétain "greater still at Vichy than at Verdun."

However, as early as 1941, Wilfrid Beaulieu defied this generally accepted opinion and announced the support of his newspaper, *Le Travailleur*, for the Gaullist cause. Whenever he could do so, Beaulieu

printed the general's speeches along with news of the Resistance to
Nazi occupation and the Vichy government. He published articles
signed by some of the great French writers of the period. One of these,
"La Mère humiliée" (The Humiliated Mother) by François Mauriac,
appeared in *Le Travailleur* on July 31, 1941, accompanied by the
following notice: "The newspaper that first ran this article was
suspended a few days later by the German authorities." Beaulieu was
also one of the first Franco-Americans to become active in France
Forever, an American group organized to come to the aid of Free
France. On another level, with the ACA supporting the Gaullist
movement and the USJB opposing it, there was a revival of the same
old tensions which had surfaced during the Sentinellist conflict.

To all intents and purposes, the war erased any doubts that might
have lingered about Franco-American loyalty to the United States. The
Common Council for American Unity, a government watchdog and
propaganda agency, issued a clean bill of health to the newspapers, the
"national" societies, and other Franco-American institutions, all of
whom were supporting the war effort. Loyalty towards the United
States had in fact become an almost integral part of the American
version of *survivance* ideology; the *Manifeste Franco-Américain,*
adopted in 1947 by the Comité de Vie Franco-Américaine, did little
more than grant official status to an attitude that had been prevalent
ever since the First World War.

In a word, the war quickened the pace of Franco-American
implantation in the United States. Specifically, the group supported in
every possible way the heroic efforts of the men and women in the
military. Given the fascination that history held for the Franco-
American leaders of the time, it is hardly surprising that Dollard des
Ormeaux was the model they proposed to those who served:

> At a time when the honor of the United States, our great country, is at
> stake, is it not a duty for us, Franco-Americans, to recall what is perhaps

the greatest military action of our history: the voluntary sacrifice made by Dollard des Ormeaux and his sixteen companions who unhesitatingly gave their lives for their beloved homeland which they realized was threatened with complete destruction? (*L'Union*, quoted in *La Vie franco-américaine* [1943], p. 93)

In a more practical vein, Edouard Fecteau, writing in Lowell's *L'Étoile,* spoke to his compatriots of "The Soldier's Nostalgia." He described the feeling with penetrating comprehension and obvious sympathy, calling for a serious and abiding moral support of the soldiers:

One of the principal duties of each individual should be to write to a serviceman—to a relative, a friend, or a young neighbor you hardly know but who is serving his country—write often and about everything, without expecting an answer. (*La Vie franco-américaine* [1943], p. 88)

Edouard Fecteau also hoped that civilians would write to the soldiers in French, even if they answered in English.

As can be seen from the above newspaper quotations, so typical of the unchanging mentality of the Franco-American leadership, the war did not lead to a neglect of *la survivance.* After the war was over, one of their first assessments of the situation deplored the losses which had befallen the group, not only because many had died on the battlefield but those who returned had succumbed to the lures of assimilation which the *patriotes* loathed almost as much as they did the Third Reich. These leaders were quick to gauge the upheaval caused by the war on an ethnic lifestyle already threatened by the traditional forces of assimilation. Generally speaking, returning veterans no longer saw any need to preserve their cultural heritage except for the faith and perhaps the language.

This heritage now appeared to offer only a truncated and outmoded view of reality for these men who had lived through unspeakable atrocities and had found themselves in situations where ethnicity played no role. For when it came to military preparation in the American army—training, discipline, formation of combat units—an individual's ethnic origin meant very little either to those in charge or to the army itself.

Moreover, since most soldiers underwent training at a great distance from Franco-American centers, there was nothing Franco-American in what little social life they did enjoy during those years. Conversely, because many Franco-American centers were located near New England's military installations and naval bases, young Franco-American women dated soldiers from every ethnic group in the nation. This gave rise to a considerable number of "mixed" marriages: a Franco-American soldier returning to Fall River with his young wife, an American born in Nebraska, or a young Franco-American girl leaving after the war to rejoin the Italian-American husband she had met at a social event held at Fort Devens, Massachusetts. In either case, this spelled the end for the cohesiveness of the group, its cultural heritage, and *la survivance*, because in the United States, these types of marriages have always resulted in families speaking only English.

Franco-Americans were nevertheless overjoyed to welcome their soldiers home from Europe or Asia. Through newspapers and personal contacts, the leaders encouraged these young people to take advantage of the free education being offered by the federal government. They also encouraged them to join the Franco-American Legion, hoping to avert the new threat to *la survivance* which non-denominational veterans' organizations represented. Did these organizations recruit more members than did the Franco-American Legion? Quite likely, but, renamed the Franco-American War Veterans, the group was increasingly visible after 1945 in regional patriotic observances and was still taking part in these military ceremonies in the 1980s although less so, given the advanced age of its members.

Among the many tributes honoring veterans, the statement by Senator Henry Cabot Lodge Jr. of Massachusetts was particularly well received by both the élite and the people:

> I believe that I am safe in saying that in all parts of the world wherever battles were waged during the second global conflict—whether on land, at sea, or in the air, be it against Japan or against Germany—there were always a few young Franco-Americans among the combatants. And I daresay that they demonstrated the same heroism in
> *La Vie franco-américaine* [1951], p. 411)

Attempts at Renewal

The most important attempt at reviving a dying cause took place in 1947 with the founding, at the University Club of Boston, of the Comité d'Orientation Franco-Américaine (later renamed the Comité de Vie Franco-Américaine). The founding of this organization by some thirty influential Franco-Americans was a direct result of the 1937 Second Congress of the French Language.

In 1946 the Comité Permanent des Congrès de la Langue Française en Amérique, itself an offshoot of the Second Congress, had held its annual meeting in Manchester so as to better inform itself on the current Franco-American situation and strengthen the ties between French Canadians and Franco-Americans. Manchester's *L'Avenir National* reprinted the article by Omer Héroux, editor-in-chief of Montréal's *Le Devoir*, which describes the optimistic spirit of this meeting:

> We hope that this visit to New England by the Comité Permanent will mark the beginning of closer and more extensive relations between Franco-Americans and French Canadians. We would all be the better for it. We do not know enough about the great things you have accomplished in the past seventy-five years. And perhaps you are not aware of what has occurred in Canada since your fathers left the country. Perhaps we are both too ignorant of the mutual support we could provide each other in the

struggle for the preservation of our French heritage. (*La Vie franco-américaine* [1946], p. 100)

At this meeting, the committee heard a report entitled "The Current Status of the Franco-Americans of New England" prepared by Rev. Thomas-M. Landry, a Dominican. Pastor of Saint Anne in Fall River, he would be called upon to play a leading role in the renewal. In his report, Father Landry described the state of affairs for Franco-Americans and recommended certain steps that he deemed essential in order to remedy a worrisome situation. He insisted particularly on the need for "moral, spiritual, and cultural support from France and especially from French Canada"; on the necessity of forming "a true lay, Catholic, and Franco-American élite"; and on the obligation to formulate a "concrete historical ideal that Franco-Americans must collectively seek to realize." He also underscored the need "for an organization that could rise above all our differences and at times all our rifts," and to create a Franco-American commission to study the situation and be responsible for implementing the recommendations he had just submitted. This commission was to be the forerunner of the Comité d'Orientation Franco-Américaine.

Under the leadership of persons like Adolphe Robert, president-general of the Association Canado-Américaine, Father Landry himself, and Rev. Adrien Verrette, then pastor of Saint Mathieu in Plymouth, New Hampshire, this committee constituted itself as the Franco-American "high command" and attempted to study and resolve the problems facing the Franco-American community throughout New England. Modeled on Québec's Comité Permanent and operating almost like a branch organization, the Comité d'Orientation Franco-Américaine relied heavily on the large fraternal benefit societies, "*les grandes mutuelles*"—the Association Canado-Américaine, the Union Saint-Jean-Baptiste d'Amérique, the Société des Artisans, and the Société l'Assomption. It also included journalists, representatives from some of the male religious orders, and various institutions, along with a few well-known leaders from within the group. In keeping with the practice of the time, women were excluded, but this would be partially offset by the founding of the Fédération Féminine Franco-Américaine in 1951, which proved to be one of the most enduring initiatives of the Comité d'Orientation.

Early on, the Comité d'Orientation began drafting a manifesto to determine "the broad outline of our Franco-American destiny and the common ideal all of us should adopt and pursue with unswerving purpose." This manifesto, *Notre vie franco-américaine*, would be the last policy statement formulated by the *patriote* élite.

In the first part, the anonymous author—no doubt Father Landry himself—defines the Franco-American group, underscoring both its uniqueness and its integration into the society around it. As was typical for this generation of intellectuals, a special place was reserved for history in the definition of collective identity: "The Franco-American group has the right, conferred by history, to a privileged position at the heart of the American nation because, in the continental sense of the word, the group was American even before it poured out of Canada into the United States." Additionally, the essential components of the group are identified as being its Catholic faith, its American citizenship, and its French character.

The second part of the manifesto summarizes the diversity of reactions of people both within the group and outside it. The responses to a public opinion poll on Franco-Americans ranged all the way from sympathy to antipathy and even included indifference. And yet, the manifesto asserted that it was the wish of "a very large majority" to preserve and transmit their French heritage to their descendants. This last statement now seems overly optimistic.

The third part of the document provides an answer to the question, "How should a Franco-American respond to this situation?" This section makes the case for a French-English biculturalism based on natural law, the Constitution of the United States, international law as it applies to minorities, historical rights, and the Church's social doctrine. It emphasizes the need to maintain "certain institutions": the parish, the school, the home, societies, and booster organizations. Finally, it states that Franco-Americans see themselves as "agents of an authentic peace based on the particular requirements of justice and Christ's love." Isolationism is rejected, and there is a reaffirmation of the collective will to integrate "our French experience into our lives as Catholics and as Americans."

The major flaw in this manifesto is the claim, based on historical right, that Franco-Americans have an "aristocratic" pedigree. Anglo-Americans would never grant such a status to any immigrant group. To prop up his claim, the author reminds his readers that the French had been present throughout every phase of the development of thc United States. By linking this French presence with the immigration of French Canadians to the United States, the author affirms an early presence akin to that of the descendants of the Pilgrims: "If there were a hierarchy in American citizenship, Franco-Americans would rank among the leading aristocrats: those of the land and of the blood." This was a magnanimous thought, to be sure, and a laudable effort to replace a minority complex with a sense of noble lineage, but it did little to enhance the day-to-day routine in the lives of ordinary people.

The fourth and final section of the manifesto outlines the requirements for the preservation of *le fait français,* i.e., all things French. Home, school, parish, and social relationships are all examined so as to underscore the urgent need either to preserve their French character or, if lost, to restore it. The fourth Commandment—"Honor thy father and mother"—is invoked as a reason for this effort since the retention of one's culture could serve to "enhance the total flowering of a child's personality." Some would see this as an improper interpretation of the fourth Commandment, as unwarranted and unjustified on a cultural or purely human level as on a supernatural one; others would view it as a highly questionable attempt to provide a religious foundation for something which, in fact, has no such basis; still others would reject this authoritarian approach which dictates what should be the optimal development of a young person's personality, seeing in it a kind of determinism that the Church itself rejects as a general rule.

Preserving a "French aura" in the home, infusing schools with a "French atmosphere," encouraging young people to attend Franco-American secondary schools and colleges so as to form a Franco-American élite, belonging to a Franco-American parish and helping it preserve its French spirit, all of these "duties" reiterated in the manifesto had been repeated over and over again for a century. But the "why" offered by the manifesto would, in time, come to be seen as somehow inadequate, insufficient: "Too many sacrifices were made in the past to build and preserve these parishes for a Franco-American to forget them. Honor and gratitude require that he remain in them." The next generation would see things differently; specifically, some were not convinced that the sacrifices made by their predecessors obligated them particularly. In an attempt to create a pact between the generations, the manifesto's author imputed a sense of honor and gratitude to the young that most of them did not possess.

Similarly, the conclusion states that this doctrine was "in every respect compatible with the requirements of the most unalloyed American civic responsibility" and reasserted the belief that the preservation of one's French heritage was "the most intelligent, the noblest, and the most powerful support" that the group could offer the country "in pursuit of its true destiny." Here again, the author was much too magnanimous, for at no time did the United States attempt, much less want, to take advantage—in the positive sense of this term—of the cultural richness that its various ethnic groups had to offer. Signed by twenty-five members of the Comité d'Orientation, the manifesto was accompanied by a brief report on French-speaking American Catholics in New England, in fact a census of Franco-Americans and their institutions.

Taken by itself, the manifesto provided a solid intellectual foundation for the philosophy of life that it presented. Curiously enough, however, it hardly mentions Canada, insisting instead on the French aspect of the Franco-American tradition, spirit, and heritage. Still, having been developed in response to a request from the Comité Permanent de la Survivance Française en Amérique, whose headquarters were in Québec, this omission no doubt reflects an attempt to win support from all *patriote* leaders, both from those who advocated a cautious distancing from Canada as well as from those who viewed French Canada as an indispensable ally. Does it also reflect a desire to renew contact with the original Franco-American motherland, one with greater international prestige than French Canada? This is a plausible hypothesis. Let us also note that the name of the organization that had called for the establishment of the Comité d'Orientation Franco-Américaine was in fact the Comité Permanent de la Survivance *française* and not *canadienne-française*.

Having outlined a guiding philosophy, the Comité d'Orientation took the next logical step and sought to have it endorsed by the people. This was the motivating force behind the idea of a mass convention to celebrate the "centennial" of the Franco-Americans as an organized group in New England. The rally was held on May 28 and 29, 1949, and its organizers deemed it to have been a great success:

> The celebration of the Franco-American centennial in Worcester was undeniably for us the most important event of our history in the past fifty years. Because of the problems it addressed and the resolutions approved by the delegates, it can be stated that this gathering was supremely and truly historic in nature.

Organized by the Comité d'Orientation, with the assistance of the Federation of Franco-American Organizations of Worcester County, the centennial involved painstaking preparations which included a publicity campaign skillfully developed by a young *patriote* living in Southbridge, Massachusetts. Gabriel Crevier, who often signed his articles "Desormeaux," the family name of that first and foremost 17th century *patriote,* Dollard Desormeaux, saw in the centennial an opportunity for renewal which also contained the possibility of charting the future course of the Franco-Americans as a group into its second century of existence. This perception was shared by newspaper and magazine editors across Canada, from Moncton, New Brunswick's *Evangéline* to Edmonton, Alberta's *La Survivance*, as well as by *Le Devoir* and *La Presse* in Montréal and *Le Droit* in Ottawa. Encouragements of this kind were greatly appreciated by the organizers of the convention.

Delegates from several hundred Franco-American organizations participated in the convention and especially in the study session at which the manifesto prepared by the Comité d'Orientation was discussed and approved. The delegates expressed their confidence in the determination of Franco-Americans to support the committee's leadership on behalf of the group in New England. Among the many speeches and presentations given by participants and their guests, including those by the French and Canadian consuls, the address given by Rev. Thomas M. Landry needs to be singled out, for it contains a warning which surpasses by far the customary expressions of patriotism heard normally on such occasions.

Father Landry first insisted on the absolute need for unity without which it would be illusory to think that Franco-American life could have a future. "This means that beyond our own personal view of things, we must be united with regard to certain essential matters, we must all learn to think alike, to want the same things, to act in concert with one another. This is a life or death question from which there is no escape for Franco-Americans." The concluding lines of the speech are even more explicit and are indicative of the gravity of the situation:

> Gentlemen, let us not attempt to hide the fact that, at the conclusion of this Centennial, everything needs to be thought through once again, to be done all over again, or at the very least, consolidated in our Franco-American edifice, especially at its base. A hundred years from now, we will be more Catholic, more American, and more French than ever if today and tomorrow we keep faith with the promise we carry within us. Let my last words serve to summon you all to this grand destiny. It is up to you to show the greatness of soul, the healthy ambition, and sufficient faith in God and in yourselves to make this happen.
> (*La Vie franco-américaine* [1949], pp. 65-66)

Because of this statement, in which confidence and idealism were mitigated by realism, Father Landry came to be known as the "austere prophet." He and his colleagues were quite aware that *la survivance* was far from assured, but they believed in it enough to remain committed and to devote their lives to it. With hindsight, it is easy for us to discern an excess of idealism in their attitude—ordinary people do not soar at such rarified strata of ideas or feelings. Yet, it hardly seems right to condemn them for having presented the people with an ideal born directly out of their past. Some say that the *patriote* leaders should have been more attuned to the social evolution that all the ethnic groups needed to undergo in the United States. But, by invoking the philosophy of cultural pluralism and providing for the discharge of American civic responsibilities in this "new guiding philosophy," the author of the manifesto and the organizers of the centennial truly believed that they had sufficiently taken the evolution of the Franco-American group into account. Not enough, we might say. But that "not enough" would not deter the leaders themselves from their pursuit of *la survivance* which, for them, was a matter of conscience.

Among the many laudatory newspaper articles which the centennial elicited in the French-language press, one in particular

The photo above, taken around 1940, shows the Franco-American neighborhood surrounding the buildings of Notre-Dame Parish in Fall River, Massachusetts. An equally extensive and cohesive Franco-American neighborhood existed at the same time in the southern part of Fall River in Sainte-Anne Parish (below). This landscape was replicated in dozens of New England cities. (A. Chartier Collection)

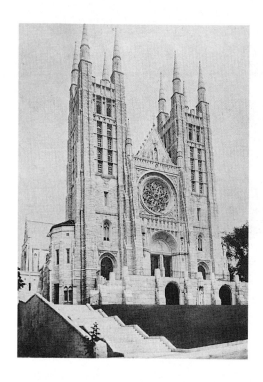

Completed in 1936, Saints-Pierre-et-Paul Church dominates the skyline of Lewiston, Maine. The cathedral-like structure is the second church on this site. This parish and that of Sainte-Anne in Fall River, Massachusetts, were operated for many decades by the Dominican Friars of Québec. Today, both parishes have returned to a diocesan administration and neither serves an exclusively Franco-American congregation.

The first Franco-American hospital was founded in 1888 in Lewiston, Maine, by the Sisters of Charity (Gray Nuns) of Saint-Hyacinthe, Québec. A new hospital built in 1900 and renamed Hôpital Général Sainte-Marie provided many community services including this "baby show" in the 1930s. A dozen similar institutions dotted the Franco-American landscape up into the 1960s. (NMDC Files at ACA Archives)

Elaborate bulletins were published by the larger Franco-American parishes. Like the local French-language newspapers, the Bulletin paroissial provides many important details to today's researchers. This one, published by the Oblate Fathers who operated Saint-Jean-Baptiste Parish in Lowell, Massachusetts, is devoted to the ordination of Bishop Louis Collignon, a Franco-American of Belgian ancestry. (A. Chartier Collection)

(Above) The founder in 1922 of a lay mission society known *as Les Rosiers Missionnaires de Sainte-Thérèse* (Misssionary Rosebushes of Saint Theresa), Irène Farley of Manchester, New Hampshire, collected hundreds of thousands of dollars from throughout the United States and Canada to foster native vocations in mission countries. (Photo by Ulric Bourgeois at ACA Archives)

Lorenzo de Nevers (1877-1967) was a popular artist who spent most of his life in Central Falls, Rhode Island. He painted formal portraits of many religious and lay members of the Franco-American élite as well as some landscapes during a lengthy career. (ACA archives)

Pfc. René Gagnon of Manchester, New Hampshire, achieved instant fame when he participated in the raising of the United States flag at Iwo Jima on February 23, 1945. He was one of a group of five Marines and one Navy Corpsman whose action was captured by war photographers, thus becoming the most potent image of American bravery in World War II. Relatively unknown, Gagnon died in 1979. (ACA Archives)

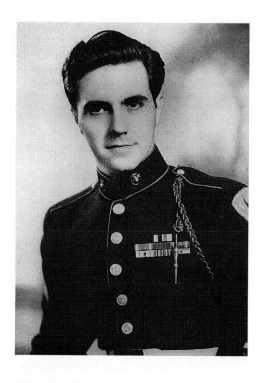

Two literary giants, Louis Dantin (left) and Rosaire Dion-Lévesque spent time together at Lévesque's summer cottage on the outskirts of Nashua, New Hampshire. A Québec writer, Dantin (1865-1945) was active in Franco-American literary circles and wrote at least one novel set in New England. Lévesque (1900-1974) was a popular poet whose works were acclaimed by *l'Académie Française* in Paris. (ACA Archives)

The junior choir of Sainte-Marie School in Manchester, New Hampshire, went to Québec City in 1947 where, accompanied by dignitaries of Association Canado-Américaine and the Société Saint-Jean-Baptiste of Québec, they laid a wreath at the foot of the monument to Samuel de Champlain, founder of Québec City. (ACA Archives)

Thousands of boys and girls were introduced to religious, classical, and traditional music thanks to the sisters who operated Franco-American parochial schools all over New England. Pictured here are the choirs of *l'École Franco-Américaine* in Lowell (above) operated by the Sisters of Charity (Gray Nuns) of Québec, and Immaculée-Conception School in Fitchburg, Massachusetts, operated by the Daughters of the Holy Spirit. The latter group won a contest among Franco-American parochial schools in 1949 and was rewarded with a trip to Canada.

A poet, Alice Lemieux-Lévesque was the first president of *La Fédération Féminine Franco-Américaine*, a federation of women's groups founded in Lewiston, Maine, in 1951. She was married to Rosaire Dion-Lévesque of Nashua, New Hampshire, and after his death in the 1970s, she returned to her native Québec where she continued to write.

Drill teams were a popular form of group activity in the 1940s. This group was part of the *Garde ACA* composed of members of Villa Royale in Dover, New Hampshire. Similar units existed throughout New Hampshire and often competed among each other. (ACA Archives)

The longest-lasting Franco-American newspaper, *Le Messager* (1880-1968) had its offices in the heart of downtown Lewiston, Maine. The long-time owners of the newspapers, members of the Couture family, also owned a number of radio stations which featured programming in French and English. (ACA Archives)

In the early 1950s, efforts were made to bring together Franco-American students attending various New England colleges. The *Comité de la Jeunesse Franco-Américaine* held one of its organizational meetings at Assumption College in Worcester, Massachusetts. Flanking Rev. Armand Desautels, A.A., president of Assumption College, were J. Henri Goguen, president of Union Saint-Jean-Baptiste (left), and Adolphe Robert, president of Association Canado-Américaine. (ACA archives)

The speaker at left, Rev. Thomas M. Landry, O.P., was involved in most movements in favor of the Franco-American *survivance* from the 1930s to the 1970s. A gifted orator and writer as well as a beloved pastor, he died in his native Fall River, Massachusetts, in 1996. Seated next to him is Dr. Robert Beaudoin of Manchester, New Hampshire, an equally ardent supporter of cultural survival for Franco-Americans. (ACA Archives)

The 50th anniversary of Sainte-Famille Parish in Woonsocket, Rhode Island, and the 50th anniversary of ordination of its pastor, Msgr. Stephen Grenier, drew a capacity crowd to a banquet held in 1952 at Mount Saint Charles Academy of Woonsocket. Thirty years before, a controversy around the funding of this high school operated by the Brothers of the Sacred Heart was one of the issues that fueled the *Sentinelle* Affair. (ACA Archives)

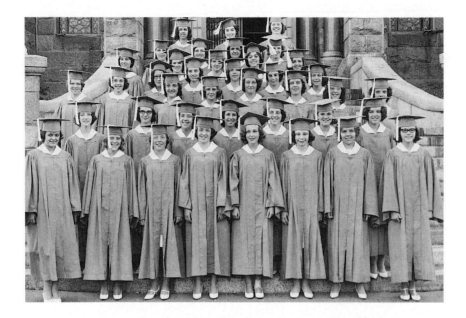

The 1964 graduating class of Notre-Dame de-Lourdes High School in Fall River, Massachusetts, showed remarkable ethnic cohesion with all but three of these twelfth graders having a French surname. By this time, a number of Franco-American parochial schools were about to close, and those that remained soon abandoned the standard bilingual French-English curriculum. (A. Chartier Collection)

The Board of Directors of the Franco-American Publishing Company of Manchester, New Hampshire, in 1968 was made up of of the traditional élite including Msgr Adrien Verrette (seated, left), one of the last and most ardent defenders of *la survivance*. The group published a weekly newspaper called *L'Action*. The last in a long line of French-language papers in Manchester, *L'Action* ceased to appear in 1971. (ACA Archives)

The opening ceremonies for the 1977 *Festival Franco-Américain* in Lewiston, Maine, featured state and natonal political figures. The festival was the result of a resurgence of Franco pride from the 1970s through the 1990s. Similar festivals appeared in Lowell, Holyoke, and Salem, Mass.; Madawaska, Old Town, Augusta, and Biddeford, Maine; Hardwick and Barre, Vermont, Berlin, N.H., and in Woonsocket, R.I. In many other communities, Franco-American groups began participating in multi-ethnic events. (NMDC Files at ACA Archives)

(Right) The most widely read Franco-American writer, Jack Kerouac (1922-1969), based much of his work on his youth in Lowell, Mass. World-wide fascination with his writings and his life continues to this day. Since the 1980s more and more Franco-Americans have claimed him as one of their own.

Since the 1970s, the Franco-American Center at the University of Maine (Orono) has worked for the inclusion of Franco-American content in the university's academic programs. It has also served as a focal point for a growing sense of ethnic awareness on campus and in the community. Looking over one of the early issues of the Center's bilingual publication, *Le Forum*, were Debbie Gagnon, Lisa Ouellette, and Yvon Labbé; in front, Denise Carrier and Paul Violette.

Franco-American writers from the Northeast started holding informal gatherings in the 1980s. This photo was taken in June of 1991 during an authors' day sponsored by the Franco-American Centre in Manchester, N.H. Standing, left to right: Denis Ledoux, Lisbon Falls, Maine; Armand Chartier, Kingston, R.I, author of this book; Claire Quintal, Worcester, Mass.; Gérard Robichaud, of New York City, whose novel *Papa Martel* broke ground in 1961; Richard Belair, Auburn, Mass.; Arthur L. Eno, Jr., Westford, Mass; and Annie Proulx, Vergennes, Vt., who would go on to win a Pulitzer Prize and a National Book Award. In front: Robert Perreault, Manchester, N.H.; Jacqueline Giasson Fuller, Gorham, Maine; Steven Riel, Amherst, Mass.; Susann Pelletier, Lewiston, Maine; Paul Marion, Dracut, Mass. (Photo: Franco-American Centre)

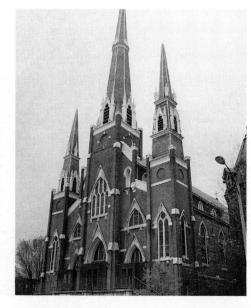

Changing demographics forced the closing of a number of ethnic or "national" Franco-American parishes in the 1980s including Précieux-Sang Parish in Holyoke, Massachusetts, where the gigantic church building was demolished. Elsewhere throughout the 1990s, Franco-American parishes were merged with other Franco-American parishes or with those of other ethnic groups. A few of them, including Sainte Anne in the inner-city of Lawrence, Massachusetts, were closed and re-opened to serve Spanish-speaking populations. (A. Chartier Collection)

Somewhat isolated from the Franco-American mainstream, Vermont's Franco-Americans created a musical movement inspired by the traditional music of rural Vermont and neighboring Québec. In the 1990s, this revival reached beyond Vermont thanks to *Jeter le Pont*, a group based in the Barre area composed of, left to right, Martha Pellerin Drury, Claude Methé and Dana Whittle.

In the early 1990s, the French Institute at Assumption College in Worcester, Massachusetts, worked with the U.S. government in the organization of seminars on American society for professors from French-speaking Africa. In 1991 there were fourteen history and geography professors in the program. Pictured with them are Claire Quintal, the founding director of the French Institute, and Gérald Pelletier from Hartford, Connecticut, of the Institute's Board of Directors. (Photo: Roger Trahan)

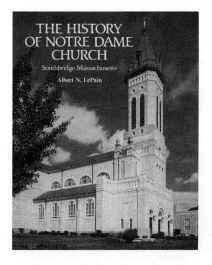

THE HISTORY
OF NOTRE DAME
CHURCH
Southbridge, Massachusetts
Albert N. LePain

Parish anniversaries lent themselves to historical research on the local level, leading to beautifully-illustrated publications like the 1991 History of Notre Dame Church of Southbridge, Massachusetts, by Albert N. LePain. For many Franco-Americans in the 1990s, ethnic pride often translates itself into a strong attachment to the parish of their youth.

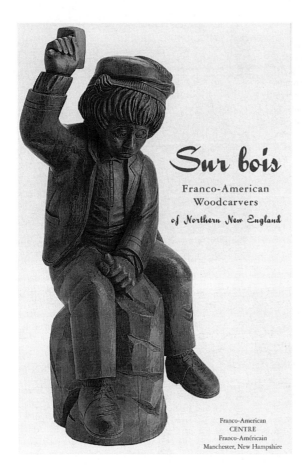

Sur bois

Franco-American
Woodcarvers

of Northern New England

Franco-American
CENTRE
Franco-Américain
Manchester, New Hampshire

Thanks to generous funding from private, state and federal sources, including the National Endowment for the Arts, a major exhibition of wood carvings by Franco-American artists was organized by the Franco-American Centre in Manchester, New Hampshire. After opening in Manchester in the spring of 1996, the show known as *Sur Bois* toured New Hampshire, Maine, Vermont, and Connecticut. This illustration is taken from the cover of the exhibition catalog. (Photo: Gary Samson)

Working from their home while holding other jobs, Albert and Barbara Côté of Lowell, Massachusetts, published a monthly French-language newspaper, *Le Journal de Lowell*, from 1972 to 1995. They were the most recent to follow the hundreds of journalists who worked in the Franco-American press for over 150 years.

Franco-American visual artists were featured in a series of exhibitions called *Migrant Within* in the early 1990s. Coordinated by the Franco-American Center at the University of Maine (Orono), the show traveled to venues in the Northeast and Québec. At the same time, a permanent art gallery for Franco artists was created by the Franco-American Centre in Manchester, New Hampshire. Above: the June 1997, opening of an exhibit featuring the paintings of Gisele Lamontagne (left) of California, and Louise Lamontagne of Montana. The two sisters, formerly of Manchester, are joined by their brother, Atty. Ovide Lamontagne, a one-time gubernatorial candidate in New Hampshire.

A special set for *Bonjour!*, the weekly French-language television show co-produced by ACA ASSSURANCE and MediaOne, was created in January of 1998 for the taping of the 500th program of the series. Started in 1987, the show has aired throughout New England, Louisiana, and the Maritimes, reaching a potential audience of 4.5 million. Pictured here are Paul M. Paré, producer, Douglas Pelczar, director, Josée Vachon and Carole Auger, the co-hosts.

The Museum of Work and Culture in Woonsocket, Rhode Island, includes a triple decker, one of the interactive components of *La Survivance*, a permanent exhibit illustrating Franco-American culture. A project of the Rhode Island Historical Society, the museum was opened in 1997 with funding from local, state and federal grants. It is part of the Blackstone River Valley National Heritage Corridor administered by the National Park Service. (Photo: Paul Darling, 1998)

Signing documents creating a *Partenariat pour la Francophonie Franco-Américaine* in June 1998, were Eugene A. Lemieux, president general of ACA ASSURANCE, and (seated) Maurice Portiche, the consul general of France in Boston at the time. Looking on was Elizabeth Dodge of Lewiston, Maine, representing the U.S. chapter of the *Forum Francophone des Affaires*. The partnership favors cultural projects involving Franco-Americans and the French.

The keynote speaker at the September 1998, New Hampshire International Trade Show was the Premier of Québec, Lucien Bouchard (right). Pictured with him are Atty. James Normand of the N.H. Governor's Council; N.H. Governor Jeanne Shaheen, and Adèle Boufford Baker of the Franco-American Centre in Manchester, New Hampshire. (Photo: A. Baker)

seems to have been appreciated more than the rest, in part because of the reputation of the author, Daniel-Rops, a popular French Catholic writer, and in part because his praise was founded on an accurate understanding of *la survivance*: "Franco-Americans, in a fine display of their loyalty, are teaching the world a lesson that needs to be emphasized." The centennial also gave rise to a number of articles that examined in detail the situation of the Franco-Americans and weighed their chances for survival as a group.

Thus, armed with a "mandate" from the group, the Comité d'Orientation moved quickly to its next projects, the first being the organization of its second convention, which it held in Lewiston from November 9 to 11, 1951. This was a noteworthy congress, since its principal goal was the founding of a federation that would be called upon to play a significant role in the work of *la survivance*: the Fédération Féminine Franco-Américaine, which still exists today.

The rationale for this new group was summarized in a speech given to the delegates assembled in Lewiston by Mrs. Gertrude Saint-Denis of Fall River, one of the founding members of the "Fédé." After having recalled the extent to which *la survivance* was threatened by a "painful illness," Mrs. Saint-Denis went on to suggest ways of countering the threat: insisting that French be used in the home, at school, and in church; opposing mixed marriages; providing maximum support for the entire network of *survivance* institutions. She also clarified the meaning to be given to the term Fédération: "We see it as an association of all our Franco-American women's organizations in New England: our religious organizations, our national societies, our alumni associations, our cultural organizations, and our clubs, be they social, political, or anything else in nature."

From the very start, "la Fédé" included 110 women's organizations representing a membership of 47,000. Franco-American and French-Canadian newspapers were quick to wish a long and successful life to this promising group. *Patriote* leaders showered it with encouragement and good advice. In her article, Yvonne Le Maître, a Lowell journalist, was her usual self—original, unpredictable, and realistic—going so far as to urge the women to begin by making money so as to ensure the future of their Fédération.

The Comité d'Orientation, in close collaboration with the Comité Permanent de la Survivance Française en Amérique, organized the Franco-American delegation to the Third Congress of the French Language held in Québec, Trois-Rivières, and Montréal from June 18 through 26, 1952. It was a Franco-American, Rev. Adrien Verrette, who, as president of both the Comité Permanent and the organizing committee, presided at the congress. After a year of promotional visits, *Abbé* Verrette had the honor of delivering the opening address to the congress that drew over 6,000 people, including several hundred Franco-Americans. He declared, "We have been granted this opportunity to revisit the sanctuary of our origins in total serenity and with confidence. We have come here to consult with one another as to how to embellish and enhance still further our Catholic and French conduct on this continent."

During these "historic days" and "splendid celebrations"given extensive coverage in Franco-American newspapers, the highlights included the unveiling of a plaque offered by the Franco-Americans in memory of Cardinal Villeneuve, held at the Laval Monument and the tribute to His Excellency Maurice Roy, archbishop of Québec, spoken by Henri Goguen, president of both the Union Saint-Jean-Baptiste and the Franco-American Congress Committee. Solemnities and festivities aside, the delegates were unknowingly attending the last of this kind of grandiose celebration which, from time to time, had summoned the members of the French family scattered throughout North America. There would not, in fact, be a major event of this kind until the series of "Fêtes du Retour aux Sources" (Festivities of the Return to Roots). Started in 1978, they were pale replicas of the 1952 Congress.

One has the impression that this Third Congress of the French Language was sounding the knell of Franco-American *survivance* in New England. Mrs. Gertrude Saint-Denis of Fall River, for example, candidly declared: "The French-American or French-Canadian branch of the French race has disappeared because a generation of our young people has decided to be something other than what God had made it to be." This Congress was really an opportunity for analysts to reflect on the state of mid-twentieth century Franco-American New England. Among them, Father Thomas M. Landry submitted an uncommonly lucid report that may have sounded pessimistic in 1952 but which now appears to have been farsighted.

Entitled "Y aura-t-il demain une vie franco-américaine en Nouvelle-Angleterre?" (Will There Be a Franco-American Life in New England Tomorrow?). Father Landry's text began by answering his own question in the negative. "Alas, at the rate things are going, it must be acknowledged that in the long run if among us, a life lived in French continues down the same path, it will, sooner or later, no longer exist. . . . Populations, just like individuals, pass away." The author concluded by declaring that a continued Franco-American experience would require a "gigantic effort" and left little hope that the requisite effort would be made.

A rapid survey of the group's most important human assets at that time explains the gloominess of his prediction. Estimating the number of mixed marriages by young Franco-Americans to be at about 50% of the total and observing that even traditional households were losing ground to assimilation, the author concluded that the Franco-American home was, generally speaking, no longer supportive of ethnic life. This was no less true of religious institutions since members of the clergy and the religious orders were no longer being educated in the French tradition. "Since 1937," he added, "our French way of life in New England has become increasingly atrophied. We are caught up in the whirlwind of assimilation, and we are driven along faster and faster. At this rate, we will sink to the bottom of the American abyss."

Father Landry went on to describe the three dominant trends in the intellectual life of Franco-Americans in the early fifties: first, the trend toward assimilation; second, the reactionary movement—a few diehards "swimming against the tide of our American life"—and third, the trend toward integration, the option which he endorsed and which consisted in integrating all three dimensions of Franco-American life: its Catholic, American, and French components.

Ernest D'Amours, a Manchester attorney who shared Father Landry's *patriote* views, was in full agreement. In an article published by *Le Travailleur* (November 6, 1952), Attorney D'Amours began by granting the possibility of *la survivance* but went on to list so many preconditions as to make it seem unlikely:

> Can it be done? Can we not only preserve but revive it as well? That will require commitment, will power, courage, studiousness, the awareness of an apostolic mission, total disinterestedness, in a word, a bit of heroism. This is perhaps too much to ask for in a century like ours . . . but in the end, our salvation—in both senses of the word—depends upon it.

The Comité d'Orientation Franco-Américaine, renamed the Comité de Vie Franco-Américaine, continued its work throughout the 1950s. Though autonomous, it nevertheless maintained close contacts with the Comité Permanent de la Survivance Française en Amérique. and, as a liaison agent, it endeavored to create and maintain a network among the many New England organizations. As stated in one of its press releases, "In keeping with its motto *Parate vias* (Prepare the Ways), it seeks to guide, direct, enrich, and serve the life we share in America."

The committee continued its study of the Franco-American issue and offered its solutions. When a more detailed history of this committee is written, it will be evident that it pursued a dual goal, namely both study and action, and that its activity was geared to a regional rather than a strictly local level. The committee did, nonetheless, retain its local connections insofar as its members came from every corner of New England, and its congresses were held in the major Franco-American centers: Lewiston, Maine, in 1951; Manchester, New Hampshire, in 1954; Woonsocket, Rhode Island, in 1957; and Fall River, Massachusetts, in 1959. Without attempting an in-depth study of these congresses, their core concerns need to be identified so as to better appreciate the contributions that the Comité de Vie made to the evolution of the Franco-American group.

Noting the absence of organizations for young people and concerned about the need to prepare for a changing of the guard, the committee organized its 1954 congress around the founding of the Association of Franco-American Youth. Due to a lack of members, this group failed to live up to expectations and lasted for only a few years. The 1954 congress was much more successful with the founding of Manchester's Richelieu Club, the first of its kind in New England. Started in Ottawa in 1945, the network of Richelieu Clubs, similar in nature to American service clubs like the Rotary, is now an international organization with 280 clubs located in ten French-speaking countries.

For its fourth congress, held in Woonsocket from October 18 to 20, 1957, the Comité de Vie adopted "Franco-American Solidarity" as its theme. This congress featured a series of study sessions and discussions on two documents prepared especially for this convention. In his report which he entitled "Synthesis," Father Thomas Landry spoke of the urgent need to build a new Franco-American solidarity, stating: "For any group or society, the solidarity of its members is a life-and-death issue." Referring to the reforms proposed in the Union Saint-Jean-Baptiste's survey on Catholic bilingual education, he declared them to be absolutely essential. This survey, which had given rise to the convention's two documents, included an essay by Monsignor Albert Bérubé, director of the USJB's scholarship program, on "The Practical Necessity of a Catholic Bilingual Education." In it the author argued that the old methods, valid at a time when students entering elementary school were bilingual, were now out of date:

> It is high time to revise the system, especially at the elementary level. It is no longer a question of teaching French to students who already know it, but rather to students who, with but few exceptions, are indistinguishable from English-language students, who live in an English-speaking environment, and never hear French spoken except in school or in Church.

The second document was presented to the congress by Théophile Martin, Director of Public Relations and Social Services at the USJB. The report revealed a wide diversity both in the number of hours reserved for the teaching of French—ranging from a half-hour to three hours each day, depending on local circumstances—as well as a great variety in the other "programs or subjects presented in French." Even where religion was still taught in French, teachers often had to resort to English to make themselves understood. Without actually using the word, the report all but admitted that the teaching of French was in a state of crisis.

Those in charge of the survey seem to have been more intent on apportioning blame than on recommending solutions. Once again, they decried the absence of French in the home, the "disastrous" consequence of mixed marriages, and the widespread indifference to the cultural heritage: "It seems then that the first guilty party is the family, and the first task will be to do everything possible to make Franco-American families aware of their responsibilities with respect to the preservation of the French language and culture." It is unfortunate that the solution recommended in the report was precisely the one that had already proved to be so ineffective: the constant reminder to the masses of how proud they should be of their origins!

It is not surprising, then, to hear the author of the report come to what was fast becoming the usual conclusion: "There is much uncertainty... the future remains bleak."

There was at least one piece of good news to come out of the congress. In response to the interest shown in the teaching of French in his diocese by John J. Wright, Bishop of Worcester, it was reported that in 1955 the diocese had adopted a new course for the study of French. Designed by Mother Raymond-de-Jésus, a Franco-American member of a French order, the Daughters of the Holy Spirit, it had already become popular even outside of New England.

As a result of the deliberations at this congress, the delegates expressed the wish that the Comité "create its own Association d'Éducation composed of lay members who, with the help of professional educators, would seek to develop a curriculum that would be most suitable for inculcating in the minds of our youth a knowledge of our mother tongue, our culture, and our history." Among the thirty or so resolutions and recommendations adopted by the congress, the call for the formation of an educational association—one of the most promising of its initiatives—produced no immediate results.

Judging from the evidence, the fifth congress of the Comité de Vie, held in Fall River from October 16 to 18, 1959, yielded even fewer concrete results than had the previous one. The theme, "The Importance of Bilingual Education for Franco-Americans," provoked some discussion but little action.

The committee's congresses had now become institutionalized and the formula would remain the same in subsequent years: there would be sessions devoted to the study of a pressing problem, a reception, a banquet, speeches, and a ball. Often, the Franco-American Order of Merit would be awarded to compatriots who, in the opinion of the Comité, deserved to be recognized for their work on behalf of the group. In 1959, the honorees were Philippe Armand Lajoie, long-time editor of *L'Indépendant* of Fall River, and Brother Wilfrid Garneau, a Brother of the Sacred Heart, founder and principal of Sacred Heart Academy in Central Falls, Rhode Island, and publisher of calendars highlighting the activities and the accomplishments of the French in North America. Each of them received this award in recognition of several decades of unremitting patriotic service. On the following day, Sunday, there would sometimes be a plenary session following a special mass celebrated in one of the major Franco-American parishes of the city where the congress was being held.

These congresses attracted mainly a *patriote* élite, united primarily in their commitment to *la survivance* and eager to give further thought to the future of the group. The meetings were often the only opportunity these scattered *patriotes* had to discuss these problems and to fraternize. Moreover, they resulted in publicity for the Franco-Americans and provided opportunities to meet with consular representatives from France and Canada who came to encourage the Franco-Americans to persist in their efforts and to praise them for having resisted assimilation for such a long time.

At the end of the 1950s, the Comité de Vie was an integral part of "official" Franco-American life. More prone to words than to deeds, according to some, the committee did, however, succeed in identifying problems and in making the public better aware of them. If that public was becoming smaller and smaller and paying less and less attention, this was, unfortunately, a sign of the times and not the fault of the committee, all the more so since the committee itself was unstinting in its study of all the major means of preserving the patrimony. Moreover, it was the only organization, along with the Fédération Féminine, to devote itself exclusively to *la survivance* and to do so throughout New England. Hence, to the extent that we can speak of a Franco-American self-awareness at a regional level, comparable to a Canadian self-awareness on a national scale, it was, for the most part, due to these two organizations: the Comité de Vie and the Fédération Féminine.

From its foundation in 1951, the Fédération Féminine—more affectionately known as the "Fédé"—made its presence felt throughout New England, especially by means of its congresses and its oral French contests. These were organized in pursuit of its goal of "grouping Catholic Franco-American women in order to strengthen through union their French activities in the family and society." The administration of the "Fédé" encouraged its affilitated groups to conduct their meetings in French—a thankless task at best during this period of rapid anglicization. Very early on, the "Fédé" began publication of its *Bulletin* so as to better communicate ideas and information to its wide audience. Under the leadership of its interim founding president, Pauline Moll Tougas of Manchester, as well as that of her successor and first elected president, Alice Lemieux-Lévesque, a Quebecer who had lived in Nashua, New Hampshire, since the thirties, the "Fédé" increased its contacts with French Canada. It was aided in this by personalities like the novelist Reine Malouin, the first woman member of the Conseil de la Vie Française en Amérique, who graciously accepted invitations to speak at meetings of the "Fédé."

Like those of the Comité de Vie, the congresses of the Fédération reflected the concerns of the élite. Thus, in choosing "Franco-American Education" as the theme for their 1956 Congress, the directors were attacking one of the root causes of what was perceived as the "evil" of assimilation. President Alice Lemieux-Lévesque summarized the thinking of her colleagues on this subject by stating, "If many of our young people no longer have the fervor of our forebears, is this not due precisely to a deficiency in their formation and in their education?" Following a format similar to that of the congresses of the Comité de Vie, these conventions demonstrated the importance that these women attached to meeting, discussing, and praying together in French, the only official language of the "Fédé." These congresses also displayed a concern for beauty and elegance that sought to raise the sociocultural aspirations of Franco-Americans.

The women of the "Fédé," at least the most active among them, came from the major Franco-American centers of New England, and their concerted action created a deep feeling of solidarity among them. It was distance alone that prevented them from meeting more often and working together in friendly harmony on a daily basis. From one congress to the next, board meetings were held on a regular basis, and the more dedicated members worked on committees formed to attend to high priority projects: the *Bulletin*, the oral contest, or the Fédération's participation in local Franco-American activities. The public speaking contest, held at regular intervals, required numerous planning sessions, and for a number of years, it was the Fédération's most public activity. These contests sought to instill a love of French and a spirit of emulation among the young of grade 8, high school, and college who came from throughout New England: Connecticut, Maine, Massachusetts, New Hampshire, Rhode Island, and Vermont. After assembling at Assumption College in centrally located Worcester, they appeared before a jury, which must have been an intimidating experience. After a brief prepared oral presentation on a topic specified in advance, each level being assigned a different topic, they would be asked to answer questions from the jury. In 1959 the topics for the contest were: "A French Pioneer in the United States," at the elementary level; "French-Canadian Folklore," at the secondary level; and "The Works of a French-Canadian Writer," at the college level.

The Comité de Vie and the "Fédé," two organizations founded in the same era (1947 and 1951), were attempts at stimulating popular interest in *la survivance* and in French culture. The most active members of these two groups demonstrated enormous dedication in their determination to stem the tide of assimilation and raise the cultural level of the people. Rising above merely parochial concerns, they succeeded in preserving regional solidarity, at least among an élite. Through their many sociocultural programs, they provided local organizations with invaluable support. The work of the *"Fédé"* continues to this day, though at a much reduced level of activity.

Institutions and Organizations

Among the Franco-American institutions and movements that one might think were never more numerous than in the years 1935-1960, the most important remain those that revolved around religion. At the end of the 1940s, for example, there were 178 Franco-American "national" parishes where liturgical services were conducted exclusively in French, 107 Franco-American "mixed" parishes where Franco-Americans formed the majority of the parishioners and where priests used either French or English at a given service, and 142 mixed parishes where there were a considerable number of Franco-Americans but, because they did not constitute a majority, English was the liturgical language in use. These parishes, both national and mixed, were served by about 1000 Franco-American priests, mainly secular, with some belonging to the regular orders: Oblates, Missionaries of La Salette, Marists, and Dominicans.

With very few exceptions, no new national parishes were founded after 1930; immigration had ended, and the American episcopate had always considered these types of parishes to be a temporary expedient.

Moreover, an important demographic shift occurred around 1950-1955, as many people who had previously belonged to large urban parishes (between five and ten thousand souls in the major Franco-American centers) moved to the suburbs. When a bishop saw the need to establish a new parish, it would be a territorial one, even if it included a very large number of Franco-Americans. Occasionally, in some localities, protests and petitions were circulated; but in the end, the protest leaders would give up, and calm would be restored.

Patriotes, however, along with a decreasing number of priests and lay persons, took a different view. For *Abbé* Adrien Verrette of Manchester who, along with Father Thomas M. Landry of Fall River, was one of the few priests to continue the struggle, the parish was still "the center and the hearth of religious life," as he declared in 1948. In fact, *Abbé* Verrette never changed his view of the parish, which he expressed as follows: "If we had to select the jewel from among our religious treasures, the parish would be the unanimous choice."

This opinion was shared by Adolphe Robert, president of the Association Canado-Américaine. In an article entitled "The Inviolability of the National Parish" (1948), he cited the new code of canon law in support of the preservation of the French atmosphere in Franco-American parishes, and he showed little sympathy for those who no longer understood French: they could go elsewhere. The losses sustained in more than one Franco-American parish due to members transferring to English-speaking parishes only served to aggravate the problem. According to Wilfrid Beaulieu, editor of *Le Travailleur*, the alarm had sounded well before 1948: "The eventual absorption of the Franco-American parish was, of course, the major goal in a standardization program whose vague justification was said to be based upon the administrative interests of the temporal affairs of the American Church, often in disregard of the rights and freedoms guaranteed by the Universal Church."

Finding themselves in the position of having to choose between the faith of a majority of parishioners and the language of a decreasing minority, American bishops, who had but grudgingly tolerated cultural pluralism, could only opt for the faith since it involved the Church's very survival. Well into the 1980s, this tension between faith and language would remain the sore spot that would continue to divide the clergy and a small number of the faithful in most of the Franco-American parishes of New England.

Those who for decades had supported their parochial institutions, following in the footsteps of their own parents who had contributed to the foundation of these institutions, felt betrayed by the Church or, more precisely, by the anglicization of the liturgy. Even today, there are parishioners who continue to believe that French should remain the liturgical language in parishes founded by Canadian immigrants. Just as in the forties and fifties, these people are still more committed to the notion of the parish as a permanent French-language institution, established as such by their parents' generation, than to the parish as an institution with economic needs which require that it have enough worshippers to ensure its future.

Resistance to the anglicization of the liturgy continued unabated throughout this period. In 1948, when the Marist Fathers announced that the homily would thenceforth be in English at two of the Sunday masses in their church of Our Lady of Pity in Cambridge, Massachusetts, they provoked an outcry in the militant press. There were enough articles, letters, and commentaries from journalists like Wilfrid Beaulieu, Antoine Clément, and Philippe Armand Lajoie to compile a several-hundred page dossier. The articles were as introspective as they were polemical, with the authors raising questions on all aspects of the situation. For these analysts inclined to historicism, the source of the problem was the people's ignorance of its own past. As Edouard Fecteau, a Lawrence, Massachusetts, journalist, was fond of repeating, "It is impossible to love and admire something which one does not know."

While continuing their campaign against the anglicizers, the *patriotes* took advantage of the celebration of parish anniversaries to teach the people—belatedly, perhaps—a lesson in Franco-American history. The oldest of the "mother" parishes, those founded in the years from 1868 to 1873 (and some even earlier), celebrated their seventy-fifth anniversaries, often with grandiose ceremonies. Such was the case in several major Franco-American centers like Lowell where the seventy-fifth anniversary of Saint Joseph parish in 1943 furnished the ideal occasion to honor the memory of its founder, Rev. André-Marie Garin, a French Oblate, whose achievements were all the more noteworthy since Saint Joseph, founded in 1868, was the first Franco-American parish in the Boston archdiocese. The parish of Saint Joseph, which was later renamed Saint John the Baptist when a new church was built elsewhere in the city, was also fortunate enough to have at its disposal a number of talented writers like Rev. Narcisse Cotnoir, another Oblate, and Yvonne Le Maître. For this reason, articles published in 1943, and in 1948 for the eightieth anniversary of the parish, can still be read with interest.

In 1946, the seventy-fifth anniversary of SS. Peter and Paul parish of Lewiston, Maine, provided an opportunity to point with pride to its many advantages: its "two high schools," the aesthetic merits of its church—a "monument of Gothic architecture"—and its population of over 15,000 souls which made it one of the largest Franco-American parishes in New England. The parishioners of Saint Joseph of Springfield, Massachusetts, whose seventy-fifth anniversary took place in 1948, were praised by *Abbé* Adrien Verrette for having successfully persevered in maintaining the parish, an undertaking made more difficult by the fact of their being scattered throughout a large city and isolated from the major centers of *la survivance*. The centennial in 1950 of Saint Joseph parish in Burlington, Vermont, the mother parish of all Franco-Americans that Bishop de Goësbriand had founded in 1850, was recorded in articles that remain of great interest to the present day.

The *patriotes* had a number of newspapers at their disposal, along with *La Vie franco-américaine*, the annual report of Franco-American activities prepared by *Abbé* Adrien Verrette. The latter was as quick to congratulate parishes celebrating their anniversaries as he was to castigate those who had "surrendered" and who were no longer committed to *la survivance*. When a *patriote* priest died, *Abbé* Verrette used the occasion to sing his praises, no doubt to edify the younger clergy and inspire them with patriotism. Here is how he described his last conversation with *Abbé* Stanislas Vermette (1876-1944), pastor of Saint Joseph parish of Salem, Massachusetts:

> . . . no one was more completely nor more resolutely devoted to our religious and cultural interests. With the simplicity and seriousness of one who senses that his end is near, he acknowledged that throughout his lifetime he had wanted to be the humble servant of his own people and the faithful defender of our special inheritance. With a touch of melancholy, he added that he could not conceive how any Franco-American, be he priest, religious, or lay person, could abandon so important a mission and still face eternity with equanimity.

Less respectful of the clergy, some *patriotes* were tempted to speak of betrayal by the clerics, but they referred instead to their "surrender" regarding *la survivance*, and even here distinctions need to be made. Like their pastors, who now restricted themselves to the exercise of their priestly functions, curates did not venture to join a nationalistic movement for fear of jeopardizing their own ecclesiastical advancement. Not to mention the fact that many young priests in the 1940s and 1950s, much like their lay contemporaries, felt less committed than their predecessors to the task of cultural preservation. Being bilingual, they knew enough French to minister to the needs of elderly parishioners who spoke no English. As for the seminarians of the period, the choice was made for them—this being said without any attempt at resolving the controversy over the major seminaries. Some bishops sent Irish-American candidates for the priesthood to study in the French-language seminaries of Europe and Canada. Was this an attempt to prepare future priests to better serve the parishes in which there were a large number of Franco-Americans? Or, as *patriotes* claimed, was it to better prepare them to assimilate the Franco-Americans?

While members of the secular or diocesan clergy were almost exclusively assigned to parish work, the regular clergy—except in the few parishes which they administered—served primarily as preachers for special occasions, such as the parish Lenten retreats or in the programs of so-called "closed" retreats. They were also in charge of the sanctuaries that drew more and more pilgrims as the automobile made travel easier. These priests also served as missionaries in foreign countries.

The Oblates of Mary Immaculate expanded rapidly after the canonical establishment of the Franco-American province in 1921. In 1943, at the time of its seventy-fifth anniversary, their "mother" parish in Lowell numbered 10,000 souls. That same year, one of them, Jean Louis Collignon, was enthroned as bishop of Les Cayes, in Haiti, where their missions were expanding. Their missions in the Philippines as well as in other countries were also growing rapidly. The monthly Oblate magazine, *L'Apostolat*, enjoyed continued popularity, and new centers for closed retreats, which attracted numerous retreatants, were opened in Maine and Rhode Island. Finally, soon after the dedication of Our Lady of Grace Shrine in Colebrook, New Hampshire, there was a notable increase in pilgrimages to what was reverently called the "Marian Valley."

The Missionaries of Our Lady of La Salette, active in New England since 1927, were also undergoing a period of expansion. In 1944 they numbered about 200 men—priests, brothers, and students—and, following their establishment as a Franco-American province in 1945, they purchased a mansion in Brewster, on Cape Cod, to serve as their headquarters and novitiate. At the same time, they welcomed the first group of pilgrims to their Attleboro, Massachusetts, sanctuary. Their house of study in Enfield, New Hampshire, inaugurated in 1950, was known for its statuary ensemble evoking the apparition of the Blessed Virgin at La Salette in France in 1846, as well as for its outdoor Way of the Cross. Their magazine, *Celle qui pleure*, had a circulation of over 30,000.

Another male religious order, the Assumptionists of Assumption College in Worcester, Massachusetts, assumed responsibility for directing the Sacred Heart Sanctuary in Beauvoir, near Sherbrooke, Québec, in 1948. The Assumptionists, who celebrated the centennial of their founding in 1950, often assisted in ministering to Franco-American parishes, and they promoted their college by means of several publications, including their periodical, *L'Assomption*.

During the same decades of the forties and fifties in New England, there were Franciscans from Montréal who had established their own Saint Francis College in Biddeford, Maine, as well as a center for closed retreats in Pittsfield, New Hampshire. There were also about one hundred Marist fathers of the Boston province assigned to various Franco-American parishes throughout New England while the Edmundites, founded in France in 1843, sponsored a college, Saint Michael's, in Winooski, Vermont. The Marists and Edmundite Fathers were often denounced as anglicizers in the *patriote* press which was much more supportive of the French atmosphere which the Dominicans maintained in their Lewiston and Fall River parishes.

Religious communities of women devoted themselves to charitable works and education. During this period, several of these congregations that had come from Canada—Sisters of the Presentation of Mary, of Saint Anne, of Jesus and Mary, of the Assumption, and of the Holy Cross—were granted autonomy and founded Franco-American provinces.

Around 1950, these communities of women, founded in France, Canada, and even New England—the Little Franciscans of Mary were founded in Worcester in 1889 where they still administer St. Francis Home for the elderly—were staffing some thirty hospitals and homes for the elderly in the six New England States. Far too little has been written about what these charitable endeavors represented in terms of selfless contributions to society. In discharging the most thankless of tasks, these women religious: Sisters of Providence, Gray Nuns, Dominicans, Daughters of the Holy Spirit, the Little Sisters of the Poor, who labored in obscurity and depended on benefactors for the success of their establishments—hospitals, old folks' homes, and orphanages—were often criticized for not doing more for the Franco-American cause. Their institutions were in fact monitored by the *patriotes* who denounced any anglicizing tendencies. These women had clearly been called to what was then known as a "special vocation" to have devoted themselves, sometimes for forty or fifty years, to a career so humble and so often marked by sacrifice and lack of appreciation. A number of these religious even held several positions concurrently since, with time, hospitals established schools of nursing in which they themselves provided the teaching.

Meanwhile, the teaching orders were also experiencing a period of growth. The Brothers of the Sacred Heart, for example, whose headquarters were located in Arthabaska, Québec, formed a Franco-American province situated in Sharon Heights, Massachusetts. Like them, other communities of men, especially the Christian Brothers, the Brothers of Christian Instruction, and the Marist Brothers, collaborated with the communities of women in the development of high schools while they continued to teach in the separate schools for boys of several Franco-American parishes. In 1949, the men and women of these religious orders constituted the teaching staffs of some 264 Franco-American educational institutions.

Other religious foundations include the Missionary Rosebushes of St. Therese, a society founded in 1922 by Miss Irène Farley (1893-1961) in Saint Anthony parish in Manchester. During a twenty-five-year period, this group donated over $300,000 to the training of an "indigenous clergy" in the missions.

When the Hospitalières de Saint Joseph from Montréal's Hôtel-Dieu agreed to direct the new Notre Dame Hospital in Biddeford, Maine, in 1948, they were one of the last French-Canadian orders to establish themselves in New England. This marked the end, not only of the implantation phase, but also of the growth period for religious institutions which came to an end in the late fifties and early sixties. From this perspective, the naming of Ernest Primeau to the episcopal see of Manchester in 1960 represents a culmination rather than a new beginning.

We turn now to the fraternal and cultural organizations. Had space permitted, it would have been enlightening to add material on other professional, economic, political, social, and even veterans' groups, for Franco-Americans were active in all of these areas, and they were often sufficiently well organized to form a federation or an alliance with like-minded groups at the regional level.

From the humblest social club to the most prestigious of the major mutual benefit societies, almost all Franco-American groups continued to celebrate—sometimes modestly and sometimes with great pomp—the feast of their patron saint, Saint John the Baptist, on June 24, or more likely the Sunday before, so that everyone would be free to attend. In some parishes, volunteers would be at the church doors distributing paper maple leaves at a penny each for Franco-Americans to wear as a sign of belonging. After mass, depending on local circumstances, there would often be a parade, a banquet, a soirée, or some other event, all of which featured flights of oratory, from the special homily to the patriotic speeches of the élite. Often a branch of one of the major mutuals was in charge of organizing the celebration.

During this 1935-1960 period, the major mutuals, also known as "fraternal benefit societies" or "national societies," included the Union Saint-Jean-Baptiste d'Amérique, headquartered in Woonsocket, and the Association Canado-Américaine, with its home office in Manchester;

to these must be added the Société des Artisans, a French-Canadian mutual with one-quarter of its membership in New England, and the Société l'Assomption of Moncton, New Brunswick, whose membership is almost exclusively Acadian.

Referred to as the "citadels" of *la survivance,* these multipurpose organizations were slowly beginning to downplay the fraternal spirit and charitable orientation that had characterized their early years in favor of economic expansion. In fact, the elders were constantly reminding the new general officers who were succeeding them that these organizations had been charitable *societies* prior to becoming federated mutuals. This was not a subtle distinction; it really pointed to a profound difference in mentality. For an older generation, a charitable society, by definition, had to embody fraternal and patriotic traits which seemed less important to their successors. More pragmatic than their predecessors, the new directors succeeded in transforming the mutual societies into insurance companies whose idealistic and cultural dimensions gradually diminished with time. The officers of the 1940-1950 period associated "mutualism" with "fraternalism" and "fraternity" while their successors were more intent on developing the economic vitality of these societies, albeit without completely eliminating their charitable and cultural characteristics.

Like the other mutuals, the Union Saint-Jean-Baptiste d'Amérique for example, with some 75,000 members, was enjoying a period of steady growth around 1960. It called itself the "national society of the Franco-Americans," since it was the only one of the "Big Four" that did not recruit in Canada. With its "councils" (branches) in Illinois and Michigan, as well as in the State of New York and the six New England States, the USJB was able to bring to its members in the East news of their "brothers" in the Midwest—all the more so because of the extensive coverage given to "council" activities in its bulletin.

The USJB's operational style was based upon that of a hierarchical organization. Its general officers would travel to preside over the solemn installation of local officers, a tradition maintained to this day. At these formal ceremonies, insignia of the Order of Merit and Honor would be awarded to those who had served lengthy terms as members of the council's executive committee, known as the *comité de régie*.

The USJB did not neglect the young. Each year, its *caisse de l'écolier* or Educational Foundation awarded scholarships to the brightest boys graduating from bilingual parochial schools who wished to pursue their studies either at Assumption College in Worcester or in one of Canada's *collèges classiques* known as seminaries. For about two decades, the USJB also hosted an annual drill team competition which brought together young girls, attired in military costumes, from all over New England. These contests entertained thousands of spectators and provided young people with an opportunity to develop a sense of personal discipline and team spirit. Finally, the USJB renewed its commitment to Franco-American higher education in 1955 by paying for the construction of La Maison Française on the new campus of Assumption College; it would become a center of French culture on American soil.

Only a detailed and objective comparative study would allow us to determine whether the differences between the USJB and the Association Canado-Américaine were either more numerous or more significant than their similarities. Calling itself "the Franco-American society par excellence" or "the eldest of our federated societies," the ACA numbered about 35,000 members in 1960, about one-third of whom resided in Canada. These virtually "organic" ties with Canada represent the most important difference between the ACA and the USJB. Moreover, the Archives Commision and the Institut Franco-Américain at the ACA, created to oversee the preservation and development of its collection of Canadiana and Franco-Americana, appear to have been more active than their counterparts at the USJB.

Like the USJB, the ACA also has had branches in the American Midwest (in Michigan), awards scholarships, but especially makes school loans to its young members. It also contributed to Assumption College, most notably to the building of its Chapel of the Holy Spirit. It publishes a periodical, *Le Canado-Américain,* which, like *L'Union*, is still of great value to researchers. Was the ACA more committed than the USJB to the cause of Franco-American history? The volume that it published in 1946, the *Mémorial des actes de l'Association canado-américaine*, compiled by its president, Adolphe Robert, would appear to indicate that it was. But, the USJB also demonstrated its commitment by underwriting Robert Rumilly's *Histoire des Franco-Américains* in 1958. In 1957, the ACA had also published Rosaire Dion-Lévesque's *Silhouettes franco-américaines*, some 900 pages of biographical sketches.

In any case, what is beyond doubt is the loyalty of the two mutuals to the Catholic Church and to the United States. All of their meetings, large or small, began with a prayer and the recitation of the pledge of allegiance to the American flag. From their very beginnings, both societies remained Catholic and American, even if the ACA enrolled members in Canada. Nor can there be any doubt regarding their sociocultural commitment to Franco-Americans. In addition to the many activities which they themselves initiated, these fraternal benefit societies were involved in every movement and every meeting of any importance, even at the local level. They were steadfast and dynamic in their support of all that was Catholic, French-speaking, and American in New England. Though they were Canadian-based, the Société des Artisans and the Société l'Assomption were nearly as visible and involved in Franco-American life as were the USJB and the ACA.

In the quarter-century from 1935 to 1960, even as the mutual benefit societies were expanding, the press was in decline. Although both were dedicated to *la survivance*, there was one important difference. If the mutuals were able to expand, it was because they offered Franco-Americans a service which they increasingly felt the need to purchase: life insurance, the sale of which provided the economic wherewithal to underwrite the fraternal, patriotic, and social activities we have described. The service provided by newspapers, even when they devoted more attention to the news, was not thought to be as essential as that of the fraternal societies. This was the case even after Agence France-Presse provided the newspapers (in 1950) with improved access to its news services, for they continued to function almost exclusively in support of *la survivance*, if only because they were written in French. From the point of view of the people, who were becoming increasingly anglicized during these decades, this use of French constituted a barrier not seen as worth overcoming. The people continued to belong to Franco-American parishes and, for the most part, send their children to parochial schools, while an important percentage—around 10%—supported the fraternal benefit societies. But this was because they viewed them much more as good insurance companies than as promoters of nationalistic or socio-cultural activities; meanwhile, out of indifference, they allowed the French-language newspapers to collapse.

The directors and editors, nevertheless, made repeated efforts to save their enterprises, and to the very end, they were able to retain the support of the Franco-American establishment who in oft-repeated expressions of loyalty to the religion and language of their forebears, as well as to their adopted country and to the major fraternal benefit societies, encouraged Franco-Americans to subscribe to their local French newspapers. But the unswerving commitment of these journalists to traditional values, considered remarkable by some, had little effect on the people. Mesmerized by their own socioeconomic progress and increasingly under the sway of society's materialistic values, they settled for the Sunday sermon as their only spiritual nourishment and, like the rest of the country, contented themselves with reading the news in English.

After the founding of the Franco-American Newspaper Alliance in 1937, journalists had continued to do their utmost to survive, recalling *ad nauseam* the precarious economic situation of the press, pointing to their record of past services, and reorganizing some newspapers so as to avoid bankruptcy. All of these efforts, however, served only to forestall for a few years the disappearance of the Franco-American press. It is conceivable that the value system that this "patriotic" press promoted, opposed as it was to that which permeated almost the entire Franco-American community at that time, made this demise inevitable.

In fact, the press could serve as a small-scale model of the wider drama that had undermined Franco-American continuity from the beginning. On the one hand, American civilization—founded as it is on the individual's socioeconomic mobility and on the continual change spawned by "future shock"—has generally been inimical to the preservation of cultural heritage of any ethnic group whatsoever; c. the other hand, by promoting the most alluring and captivating aspects of this civilization, English-language American newspapers could bring all of their moral, psychological, and economic weight to bear against foreign-language newspapers in the United States and make them appear anachronistic and pathetic in the eyes of the young.

In the end, this was but one aspect of the age-old struggle between two diametrically opposed mentalities: the idealistic and the pragmatic. We are tempted to add that it was also a struggle between self-sacrifice and self-indulgence: the most astute analysts seem to have already grasped this in the 1940s. Here, for example, is what Joseph Desaulniers, owner-editor of New Bedford's *Le Messager*, wrote in 1947: "In a few years, those who are now publishing French-language newspapers in New England will have disappeared, and the young people who will replace them will no doubt lack the zeal, the tenacity, and the patriotism of their elders."

In the 1950s, Franco-Americans could listen to some twenty French-language radio programs originating in as many cities, from Hartford, Connecticut, to Lewiston, Maine. In spite of the differences arising both from local conditions and the cultural background of those in charge of the broadcasts, these programs were alike in some respects: they all played French and French-Canadian songs (Tino Rossi was a long-time favorite), and they all carried advertising and announcements. Two of these programs deserve a special mention: in Manchester, Paul Gingras aired a "radio journal," conceived as a counterpart to the written press; in Holyoke in 1940, Léon Alarie inaugurated a series of broadcasts which spread to other communities and continued into the nineties.

But the organization which, alongside the press, made the most enduring contribution in the cultural domain was the Société Historique Franco-Américaine, founded in 1899. The more intellectually-inclined members of the press and the liberal professions, a few clergymen, and some francophile friends attended the biannual meetings. Following a reception and banquet—it would be unthinkable not to fraternize in this manner—there would be an authoritative lecture, worthy of publication. Sometimes the evening concluded with the awarding of a medal in recognition of an individual's contribution to French-American historiography.

The society had an enduring effect mainly through the publication of its *Bulletin*. In addition to the reports of its meetings, it contained the texts of the lectures—historical studies which included cultural and literary topics—as well as "documents and archival materials." The society also contributed to Franco-American archives by publishing documentary materials on the occasion of special anniversaries which, especially after 1950, it sought to observe in a special fashion. In 1955, for example, the society organized the celebration of the 350th anniversary of Samuel de Champlain's voyage of discovery along the New England coast. The festivities included a symphony concert, two exhibits, and the unveiling of a commemorative plaque. Located at Boston's Logan Airport, the plaque recalls Champlain's exploration and his naming of Boston Harbor as *Baye des Isles* (Bay of Islands). During the unveiling ceremony, mention was made of the fact that in 1605 Champlain had given the village of Plymouth, Massachusetts, site of the first permanent English settlement in North America, the name of Port Saint-Louis. In 1955, the society also took part in the observances surrounding the bicentennial of the deportation of the Acadian, by attending the ceremonies at Grand-Pré in present-day Nova Scotia and subsequently donating a bronze plaque to Saint Joseph parish in Waltham, Massachusetts, the city known as the "oldest" of the Acadian-American centers in New England.

In 1957, after having celebrated the bicentennial of the birth of the Marquis de La Fayette, hero of the American Revolution, the Société Historique, in conjunction with the Fort Ticonderoga Association, organized the impressive ceremonies which in 1958 marked the bicentennial of the Marquis de Montcalm's victory at Fort Carillon, the next-to-last French victory on the American continent. Renamed Ticonderoga by the British, this fort is located in northern New York State. On this occasion, the society also sponsored observances in some Franco-American schools; and thanks to its *Bulletin* of 1958, today's readers can relive not just the commemorative ceremonies but the battle itself, along with the pious legend surrounding "the Carillon Banner," a flag which, for decades, served as the "national" flag for French Canadians.

A complete study of the fraternal and cultural societies active during the period from 1935 to 1960 would also have to include credit unions, political groups, and the Richelieu Clubs since each of them, to some extent, was motivated by fraternal and cultural aspirations. Those who were then on their way to becoming "the old guard" were still present everywhere to ensure a minimum of solidarity, unity, and a sense of community; but these very words bespeak an era that was in the process of fading away.

The Presence of Canada and France

Throughout this period, Franco-Americans were establishing social and intellectual contacts with the French-speaking world. They turned first to French Canada, closer in both geographical and historical terms, and then toward France, the "first" of the two motherlands which Franco-Americans rediscovered during the Second World War. To a lesser degree, they would also be influenced by other French-speaking countries, like Belgium.

The explanation for this francophone influence can be found primarily in the admiration of Franco-Americans for all that was French—language, culture, *esprit*—or of French origin, as long as it was also Catholic. This attitude was also the result of institutions like Assumption College, a center of French culture since its founding in 1904, the presence in Boston of both the French consulate-general and the Canadian consulate, and the Alliance Française which had branches in certain Franco-American centers. It was due as well to *Le Travailleur* and the wealth of articles that editor Wilfrid Beaulieu published on Canada, France, French-speaking Belgium, and occasionally on the French-speaking populations of Switzerland and Africa; his articles on the mission activities of the Lowell Oblates made Haiti and its culture better known as well.

Except for the élite, French Canada of the 1935-1960 period was hardly a factor in the daily lives of ordinary Franco-Americans, this despite the membership of some 20,000 or 30,000 of them in the Société des Artisans of Montréal and the Société de l'Assomption of Moncton. Although several hundred young people took part in both the Second and Third Congresses of the French Language in Québec in

1937 and 1952, respectively, these events do not appear to have had a lasting influence, except on a very few.

Generally speaking, it appears on the contrary that during this quarter-century more links were broken with Québec than were forged. As religious orders of French-Canadian origin were granted autonomy from their former mother houses, some no longer maintained institutionalized contacts with Canada where most of them recruited few if any members. Moreover, towards the end of this period, around 1960, young Franco-American men and women no longer pursued their studies in the colleges and boarding schools of Canada as they had done since the beginning of immigration, another sign of both a loosening of the ties with Canada and a growing assimilation into American culture.

Not all *patriote* leaders in the 1935-1960 period regretted the waning of Canadian influence on the Franco-American scene. The Union Saint-Jean-Baptiste d'Amérique continued to encourage contacts and exchanges with France while the Association Canado-Américaine was attempting to extend its contacts in Canada, not just to sell more life insurance there but also because it viewed the support of Québec as essential to *la survivance*. Here is how *Abbé* Adrien Verrette, president of the ACA's Archives Commission, expressed it in 1950: "...we at the ACA are among those who have a profound belief in the importance of solidarity among all French groups in North America. Without this outlook, the French experience on this continent is an inexplicable phenomenon! And without it, that experience has almost no chance of continuing in a meaningful way!"

But there were fewer and fewer people who saw things this way. As the immigrants themselves passed away and their progeny reached adulthood on American soil, this sense of belonging to a Canadian community diminished as fewer people saw any need for it. During the Second World War, for example, there were very few Franco-

Americans who cared enough to even try to understand the conscription crisis in Québec caused by the reticence of French Quebecers to participate in yet another "British" war, much less explain it to their American counterparts. Here was another sign that Franco-Americans and Quebecers no longer shared the same identity, no longer lived in a symbiotic relationship—far from it—although here again some exceptions to this need to be singled out.

Since its founding in 1937, the Conseil de la Vie Française en Amérique (known at that time as the Comité Permanent de la Survivance Française en Amérique) had always included representatives from various francophone communities in North America. From the outset, three Franco-Americans—dubbed the "three musketeers"—represented their compatriots on the Conseil: Adolphe Robert, president-general of the ACA, Eugène Jalbert, legal counsel of the USJB, and *Abbé* Adrien Verrette of Manchester. After 1944, the number of Franco-American members serving on the Conseil was increased to five. Because of its sustained interest in Franco-American life, the Conseil succeeded in forging a close and fruitful collaboration with the Franco-Americans.

A tangible proof of this collaboration—and a very useful one as well—can be seen in the fifteen annual volumes of *La Vie franco-américaine* (1937-1952), edited by *Abbé* Adrien Verrette and published by the Conseil. The latter also awarded grants to Franco-American newspapers and the Alliance of radio broadcasters, and it encouraged the teaching of French with its gifts of prizes and books to Franco-American schools. In a word, from its founding the Conseil de la Vie Française en Amérique remained a constant source of inspiration, encouragement, and support for *survivance* activities in New England, promoting the very ideal that its name implied: a vital French America.

Other organizations, in particular, the fraternal benefit societies like the Société des Artisans and the Société l'Assomption, by being involved in Franco-American life, especially through the activities of their affiliates and by their tangible and ongoing support of *survivance* activities, extended Canada's presence among Franco-Americans. The Association Canado-Américaine, with a third of its members in Canada, exchanged ideas and information with Québec on a regular basis through its congresses, its bulletin, the welcome it extended to Canadian visitors, and its sponsorship of trips to Québec, including its annual pilgrimage to the Cap-de-la-Madeleine.

Relying on the love of music and theater that Franco-Americans shared with their Québec counterparts, various groups organized successful tours in the 1940s (fewer in the 1950s), and thereby forged new ties between the two peoples. The New England tours of the Jean Grimaldi Troupe and of "la Bolduc" brought fun and laughter while *Aurore, l'enfant martyre*, the play by Léon Petitjean and Henri Rollin, provoked consternation. Franco-American radio programs, by featuring Canadian and French music, made known the singers of popular music, notably "la Bolduc," whose great popularity among Franco-Americans was probably due to her masterful portrayal of the soul of the people. Some Franco-American music groups reversed the flow by giving concerts in Canada as guests of the Société du Parler Français or some other organizations.

During this same period, the Société Historique continued to remind its members of their origins by inviting guest speakers from Canada. For its fiftieth anniversary celebration in 1949, it was especially proud to have as its invited guest Canada's prime minister, Louis Saint-Laurent, whose lecture on the recent history of his country was much appreciated. Canada's presence, both official and symbolic, in the social and cultural life of Franco-Americans became institutionalized in 1949 with the establishment of the Canadian consulate in Boston. The first person to occupy the position, Paul-André Beaulieu, created a favorable precedent by attending all major Franco-American events and facilitating visits and exchanges between

Franco-Americans and Canadians. His successors, in particular Jean-Louis Delisle, became adept at using the position to develop friendly relationships between the two groups while working steadily at improving relations between Canada and the United States.

The contacts within the ecclesiastical network are much less well known. We know very little, for instance, about the influence that religious leaders of this period might have had on Franco-Americans beyond the fact that, until his death in 1947, Cardinal J.-M. Rodrigue Villeneuve, O.M.I., archbishop of Québec, was highly esteemed among Franco-Americans whom he visited on several occasions. As much can be said for Cardinal Paul-Emile Léger, Archbishop of Montréal. Whether it was Cardinal Villeneuve's famous speech before the Société Historique in 1938 or that of Cardinal Léger in 1954 at the Congress of the Union Saint-Jean-Baptiste d'Amérique, held in Springfield, *patriote* leaders believed that both men offered them "words to live by." The prophecy uttered by Cardinal Léger, destined to become famous in its own right, would often be quoted thereafter: "No longer can the French experience in America live off its past. It must turn to the present to find in itself its reason for being, or it will cease to exist." Aside from these ceremonial visits, we have no clear idea of what unofficial influence was exerted by these dignitaries or by other less famous religious figures.

Although Franco-Americans gave Québec pride of place in French Canada, Acadia, Ontario, and Western Canada were not entirely absent from their concerns. Of the three regions, the influence of Acadia was most pronounced due to the presence of several thousand Acadians in New England, with all that this entailed in cross-border visits by both "ordinary folks" and persons of note. Here again, it was the Société Historique, through its meetings and its *Bulletin*, that highlighted the links between New England and Acadia. In 1960, for example, Louis-J. Robichaud, Premier of New Brunswick, delivered an address on the "Acadian Resurgence" before the Societé, that was subsequently published in its *Bulletin.* And since French Canadians in Ontario and the West were also confronted by *survivance* problems in an English-speaking environment, they, too, captured the élite's attention in spite of their geographical distance.

French Canada was most certainly present in the intellectual life of Franco-Americans, for not only was it the source of *survivance* ideology, but it also served as the inspiration and model for those who sought to make this doctrine an authentic philosophy of life in New England. For example, disciples of Canon Lionel Groulx—the prominent historian and polemicist—were to be found among Franco-Americans; these would include not only historians, but also those who believed that a knowledge of history's influence constituted an integral part of every Franco-American's life. Moreover, the élite was interested in French Canada's intellectual life and kept the readers of Franco-American publications informed—witness the many reviews of Canadian books that appeared regularly. *Le Travailleur*, in particular, kept its readers abreast of the latest developments in Canadian literature, thanks to correspondents like Yvonne Le Maître, among others. For decades, one of *Le Travailleur*'s most faithful contributors was Harry Bernard, a novelist and journalist from Saint-Hyacinthe in Québec.

Conversely, the Québec press, although it stopped printing its so-called Franco-American editions, encouraged Franco-American writers by publishing their works. Such was the case when from 1952 through 1957, some three hundred biographical sketches by Rosaire Dion-Lévesque appeared in Montréal's *La Patrie* before being published in volume form.

From today's perspective, Canada's presence may appear to have been quite substantial, but at the time analysts did not think so, for they had seen better days. In 1950 for example, Father Gérard Saint-Denis, a Québec Dominican and a seasoned observer, wrote of the "ignorance

on both sides of the border that paralyzes fraternal relationships."
Writing in *La Revue dominicaine*, he made the following
recommendation:

> Let's both work at getting to know one another better in order to love one
> another. Then Franco-Americans would be less inclined to view
> Canadians as hopelessly behind the times, and Canadians would no longer
> see Franco-Americans as hybrid beings in whom they recognize no trace
> of their own flesh, blood, and spirit.

Their democratic inclinations notwithstanding, Franco-Americans
remained deeply attached to the France of the Ancien Régime, the
France known as the "Church's eldest daughter" and the land from
which their ancestors had come to build New France in the seventeenth
and eighteenth centuries. This explains why some parishes are called
Saint Martin, Saint Louis de France, or Sainte Jeanne d'Arc. Old
France remained as a presence because of the cult of the pioneers who
had built French America and the constant reminders by the élite of the
pride people could take in their origins. History was nearly as important
as the Catholic faith in the minds of those *survivance* leaders who, like
Josaphat Benoit, stated what they viewed as a truth worth repeating :
"It is the French and their descendants who discovered, explored,
colonized, and evangelized two-thirds of North America."

These same *survivance* leaders also liked to recall the role their
mother country had played in the American Revolution, particularly to
remind any Yankee who might have forgotten it. Here again it is
Josaphat Benoit who asks in his *Catéchisme d'histoire franco-
américaine*: "To whom does the American Republic most owe its
existence? To France. Without France's moral support, her money, and
her troops, the thirteen colonies could never have gained their
independence from 1776 to 1783."

And so the memory of Old France lived on in Franco-American
hearts in the period from 1935 to 1960. The names of its "heroes" were

often invoked: Jacques Cartier, Samuel de Champlain, *Monseigneur* de Montmorency Laval, Antoine de La Mothe, Sieur de Cadillac, or La Fayette, Rochambeau, de Grasse, and d'Estaing. The memory of their heroism was perpetuated in the historical calendars, known as "Sacred Heart Calendars," prepared and distributed by Wilfrid Garneau, a Brother of the Sacred Heart, who had spent a lifetime as a teacher and administrator in Central Falls, Rhode Island.

While France lived on through its past, its presence was also felt because Franco-Americans spoke its language, although the majority of them probably judged their French as being inferior to that spoken in France or Canada. *Patriote* leaders would have liked both to rid Franco-American speech of all English expressions and to establish its legitimacy in the eyes of Americans who, for the most part, considered it to be nothing more than a contemptible dialect. In any case, for both the élite and the people, nothing could match the prestige of "France French," and one often heard peremptory judgments expressed, such as: "He speaks *good* French, real French from France."

France was not only a source of inspiration for its history and its language, but also for its Catholic writers. Orators and journalists, both clerical and lay, readily quoted Corneille, Bossuet, Lacordaire, Veuillot, Bloy, and Péguy. Maurras, Gaxotte, Bernanos, Mauriac, and Daniel-Rops all found a warm welcome in the pages of Wilfrid Beaulieu's *Le Travailleur*. While readers may not always have shared the political views of these writers, they admired their Catholicism and their literary talents.

France was also present in word and deed. Eminent professors who taught in some of the region's major universities—René de Messières, André Morize, Jean Seznec—gave lectures to Franco-American audiences. Father Engelbert Devincq, a French-born Assumptionist and a professor at Assumption College, became a celebrity among Franco-

Americans as a teacher, preacher, lecturer, and writer. Such was his fame that upon his death in the Worcester tornado of June 9, 1953, Rosaire Dion-Lévesque wrote: "With this tragic death, Franco-America has lost one of its best known and most highly respected priests and academics, and Assumption College is deprived of its most justly acclaimed professor." Always eager to maintain personal contact with France, Franco-Americans thoroughly enjoyed the lectures sponsored by various academic, diplomatic, and ecclesiastical groups. Talks by writers like Vercors (Jean Buller) and Georges Duhamel and by famous preachers from Paris like Monsignor Georges Chevrot would leave a lasting impression and forge valuable links during the difficult postwar period.

This activity was encouraged by the French consulate, and its incumbent, Albert Chambon, won the hearts of Franco-Americans immediately upon his arrival at the end of 1945. A decorated soldier and a former prisoner in Nazi concentration camps, Albert Chambon was an appealing figure known for his piety and his eloquence. He knew how to strike the right chord with Franco-Americans, as can be seen in this passage from the *Bulletin paroissial franco-américain*, published by the Lowell Oblates: "The Consul-General created a sensation, especially when he argued with great feeling that France's cause deserves to be examined, encouraged, and safeguarded because it is—and insofar as it is—not only civilization's cause, but God's cause as well."

Through their organizations and newspapers, Franco-Americans were able to provide France with valuable assistance by making people in the United States aware of the urgent need for economic aid to that war-torn country. Franco-Americans joined their American compatriots in the creation of France Forever, a national organization that sought to assist a wounded France; thus did Franco-Americans play some small part, alongside Americans, in that country's massive reconstruction effort. Franco-Americans would remind their fellow citizens that "every man has two countries, his own and France." With the arrival in 1949 of the *Train de la reconnaissance* (Appreciation Train) that a grateful French nation had sent to the United States, there were public celebrations of joy and friendship. In Worcester, for example, 15,000 people turned out to listen to speeches by political figures and Franco-American representatives.

Though one consul succeeded the next in Boston, all of them sought—as had Albert Chambon—to strengthen the bonds between Franco-Americans and the land of their distant origins. Each consul took it upon himself, or sent his representative, to attend all the major activities of the Comité de Vie, the Fédération Féminine, and the Société Historique, among other events. The French government took advantage of these occasions to honor Franco-Americans who had contributed to extending the influence of French culture, awarding the Medal of Honor of the Ministry of Foreign Affairs, the Palmes Académiques (for achievements in the field of education) and, on rare occasions, the Legion of Honor. Wilfrid Beaulieu's *Le Travailleur* was honored several times. The awarding of these distinctions created opportunities for celebrations which became the object of well-orchestrated publicity campaigns, complete with photos and press releases in both the American as well as the Franco press.

For its part, the Alliance Française functioned as an active center of attraction for American francophiles, whatever their ethnic origins; nor was it simply by chance that branches sprang up in several Franco-American centers like Worcester, Lowell, Manchester, and New Bedford. In 1948, the Lowell journalist, Antoine Clément, published his second book. It was a compilation of actual texts or résumés of the lectures delivered at the Alliance Française de Lowell between 1937 and 1947. Clément, viewed at the time as a pessimist, argued that "these élite groups may prove to be the only elements of Franco-American life to survive after all our other achievements—parishes, schools, newspapers, and organizations—have been lost due to the greed of our enemies or the indifference of our own people."

France would also be present in New England for special commemorations like the two-thousandth anniversary of the city of Paris (1951) or the bicentennial of the Marquis de La Fayette (1957) which gave rise to several celebrations—some specifically Franco-American—and which were covered extensively at the time in the American as well as the Franco press. Other special celebrations included performances given by theater groups several times each year in Franco-American schools and colleges.

In the early fifties, when Agence France-Presse had made its wire services available to Franco-American newspapers—"a decision based as much on sentiment as on business," said the journalists of that period—francophiles could receive the very latest news from France. But the most memorable event of the period remains the triumphal visit to America by General Charles de Gaulle, elected President of the French Republic in 1958. Among the many commentaries inspired by this visit, that of Philippe Armand Lajoie summarized the feelings of the majority: Charles de Gaulle is "a Frenchman whom I do not hesitate to call a valiant knight in a land that has given birth to so many others. In my estimation, General de Gaulle embodies all that is best about France, all that is most lucid and life-giving, especially in those periods of acute distress and earth-shaking decisions."

Conversely, except for a handful of students studying in France or for an occasional article in the French press, the Franco-Americans hardly existed for the majority of French people. In 1953 Paul Mousset wrote an article in *France-Illustration* entitled "A Small Island of Old France in New England." The reporter and his readers were discovering Franco-America, "an oasis of good-naturedness in the heart of Puritan New England," as Mousset described it. He seemed to be astonished to learn that, in this center of French culture, an often anticlerical contemporary France was misunderstood. His conclusion: "the tenuous link between France and America must be revived."

Literature and Society

From the viewpoint of sheer quantity, there can be no doubt that most of the writings from this period belong to what can be labeled *survivance* or "patriotic" literature, for writing remained what it had always been from the start of immigration: a weapon which served an ideology. Repetitive though they may be, these texts remain of some interest to us, reflecting as they do the outlook of intellectuals and ideologues who are becoming increasingly aware that the battle over *la survivance* is one which they may not be able to win in the long run. If, in the words of Paul Valéry, civilizations are themselves mortal, what does this portend for the cultural heritage of a minority group that has neither armies nor laws to protect it? The titles of their articles are eloquent testimony to the growing anguish among militants: "The Grandeur and Woes of *la Survivance*," or "We Must Save Our Press!" Their distress also accounts for their endless analyses of a "deteriorating" situation and their numerous appeals to the conscience of the people to undertake the effort needed to reverse the trend.

Alongside this *survivance* literature there appear a number of other texts: poems, novels, biographies that describe an individual rather than a collective experience. Though these authors are not opposed to *la survivance*, they show no concern about it in their writings whose purpose is to tell their own story or to express admiration for their hero.

Notwithstanding these writings, nonfiction dominates the period, and in this category there are three works and three periodicals which top the list.

Though often denigrated—even repudiated—by the next generation, Robert Rumilly's *Histoire des Franco-Américains* (1958) remains to this day the basic work of reference, the one that must be consulted by anyone having the slightest interest in the subject. Published under the auspices of the Union Saint-Jean-Baptiste d'Amérique, this work is not as impartial as one might have wished. Moreover, with its focus on institutional development, Rumilly's book does not address the hidden forces at work in the evolution of Franco-Americans; nor does he discuss their intellectual and artistic achievements; hence, the image he presents of the Franco-Americans is incomplete. But the work is deservedly called "indispensable" because the author has included so much factual material which often suggests, at least implicitly, promising avenues for research.

Published in 1957 by the Association Canado-Américaine, the *Silhouettes franco-américaines*, by Rosaire Dion-Lévesque, is a collection of biographical sketches that the author had written for the Montréal newspaper, *La Patrie*, between 1952 and 1957. This compilation contains a wealth of information—some 300 biographies in 900 pages—on individuals who, from the mid-nineteenth century, had contributed to the development of French life in New England.

With her *La Littérature française de Nouvelle-Angleterre*, Sister Mary Carmel Therriault, a Sister of Mercy from Maine, was doing pioneer work since she was writing the first and, to date, the only history of Franco-American literature. One could easily fault this work, particularly its treatment of newspapers and the novel; and we can criticize the author's tendency to apply aesthetic criteria more appropriate to a literature like that of France though of questionable value when applied to the writings of a minority group. Nonetheless, this volume's invaluable spadework makes it the necessary starting point for anyone interested in Franco-American cultural history.

The three periodicals indispensable for the study of Franco-American history have already been referred to a number of times in this present study. They are: *Le Travailleur* (1931-1978), the *Bulletin de la Société historique franco-américaine* (1906 then 1935-1973; new series 1983-), and *La Vie franco-américaine* (1937-1952).

Le Travailleur closely mirrored Franco-American cultural life during the 1935-1960 period. No event of any importance escaped the attention of its editor, Wilfrid Beaulieu. He himself wrote many articles, especially those attacking anglicization, and he recruited talented collaborators like Corinne Rocheleau-Rouleau, the *grande dame* of Franco-American historiography, Yvonne Le Maître, one of the most endearing figures of Franco-American letters, and Adolphe Robert, whose writings are destined, in our opinion, to become classics of Franco-American literature.

Gabriel Nadeau, M.D., continued to furnish the columns of *Le Travailleur* with literary and historical studies that have lost none of their value. Dr. Nadeau first published the biography of his close friend, Louis Dantin—the noted Québec writer and critic—in *Le Travailleur,* thereby making its subscribers the first readers of this important work by an excellent scholar. Its publication began on April 12, 1945, and it continued to appear in each issue of *Le Travailleur* (a weekly) for almost two years. There is something of a paradox here: for nearly two years, Wilfrid Beaulieu, a practicing Catholic, devoted long columns in his newspaper to the biography of a defrocked non-believer who reportedly had just died unrepentant. Whether it be Dantin's atheism or Beaulieu's Catholicism that we find more to our liking, what in all fairness needs to be underscored here is the great service Beaulieu rendered to both Franco-American and Québec literature by allowing Dr. Nadeau to publish, in *Le Travailleur*, the biography of a writer whose reputation would continue to grow.

During the fifties, *Le Travailleur* served as the forum for a debate that remains unresolved. Under a headline that became famous, "*Vase clos . . . ou porte ouverte*," the subject was summarized in the February 10, 1955 issue by "Claire Fontaine," a writer whose anonymity has never been disclosed. For those who subscribed to the "*vase clos*," i.e., isolationist viewpoint, the principal argument could be stated as follows: "The entire Franco-American social structure rests on a single keystone: the French language." Their opponents believed that language was not the essential component of a group's cohesiveness. No less *patriote* than their adversaries, they argued, with Ernest D'Amours and Adolphe Robert among others, that it is primarily by blood that one is Franco-American: "It is the triple bond of blood, history, and community," claimed Adolphe Robert, "that will preserve us as a distinct people, so long as the language, even if it ceases to perform its usual function, is viewed as increasingly valuable for general culture, in politics, and at the national level." The debate would be carried on for quite some time in the pages of *Le Travailleur*.

As for the *Bulletin de la Société Historique Franco-Américaine*, over the years it published articles that appealed to the *patriote* intelligentsia. Whether lectures delivered at the Société's meetings or papers taken from the archives, these scholarly articles appear side by side with patriotic appeals. Members of the Société Historique are fond of reminding one another that though they are American citizens, they are also descended from the men and women who founded New France. To convey the extent of these heroic origins—both a source of inspiration and an object of veneration—the *Bulletin* published articles on Champlain, on Cavelier de La Salle, and on Carillon—whose very name evokes bittersweet memories.

The articles also recall the role that French Canadians played in the American Revolution and the Civil War. A hero of that war and a member of the Société until his death in 1907, Major Edmond Mallet was himself the subject of three lengthy articles for it was thought that the career of this "valiant warrior"—"one of us," as the members of the society were fond of repeating—was capable of instilling pride in young and old alike.

Alongside portraits of near-legendary figures, one can also find articles on social history in this publication. Corinne Rocheleau-Rouleau, for example, provided valuable details on the arrival of French-Canadian immigrants in Worcester. After the long train ride, they would get off at what was known to them as "Monsieur Lucier's depot," named after the friendly and resourceful railroad agent:

> After such a long trip, they were only too happy to get off and relax in the comfortable waiting room of this famous depot. The trains at that time were uncomfortable vehicles where you were either too warm or too cold, depending on the season, and passengers disembarked covered with soot after having been tossed about for hours on end amid an endless din of bells, alarm whistles, safety valves, and the horrible squealing of old brakes. The travelers arriving at "Monsieur Lucier's depot" were exhausted, but they were sure to find him perfectly calm and smiling, ready to solve any problem. . . .
>
> Sometimes Monsieur Lucier simply sent these newcomers, who were at a loss as to where to go, to stay with his own family and friends of his in different parts of New England. In those simpler and more hospitable times, everyone saw himself as more or less his brother's keeper, and our Franco-Americans needed no prodding to open their doors to French Canadians who, though strangers to them, had been reliably recommended. (1942, p. 61)

This is an example of one of the most important contributions that the *Bulletin de la Société Historique Franco-Américaine* made to French-American historiography—that is, this collection of texts dealing with the French-Canadian settlement in New England. Under the long-time direction of *Abbé* Adrien Verrette, the Société's president, the *Bulletin* also turned its attention to another chapter in the history of this implantation, that of the Acadians, those involuntary eighteenth-century immigrants. In two wide-ranging articles, which appeared in 1948-1949 and in 1950, Judge Arthur Eno of Lowell led his readers through a series of "Acadian documents taken from the Archives of the Commonwealth of Massachusetts." These included, for example, a list of names of Acadians according to the cities and towns to which they had been sent by the Massachusetts authorities. And in 1955, *Abbé* Verrette presented a comprehensive study of the "Acadians in the United States."

In addition to this scholarly literature, the *Bulletin* offered previously unpublished material that is still of interest. In 1954 for example, it published excerpts from the diary of Clara-M. Paquet, a Franco-American from Albany, New York, who had seen service in France with a corps of American women ambulance drivers in 1917 and 1918. Here is how Clara Paquet described the delirious joy with which news of the armistice was welcomed in the Beauvais region on November 11, 1918:

> The railroad platform at Beauvais resounds with noise and overflows with people. *Poilus* are everywhere. The terrible tension of years is broken at last, and these warworn men are half delirious with joy. At sight of us, they would engulf us and give each of us an accolade the while they acclaim us: "Vive les Américaines!" But smiling, we quickly slip through our compartment, and out the other side of the platform into a side street. The town seems topsy-turvy. The farther we advance, the more we find Beauvais in a turmoil of happiness and relief.

Another previously unpublished work, invaluable for both Québec and Franco-American literature, was a series of extracts taken from the diary of Henri d'Arles (1870-1930). This priest-aesthete composed a number of works during his two decades of ministry in the Manchester region. For the most part, these pages contain musings on the beauty of nature, on the duties of the priest, and on the delights of the life of the mind, seen as both a safe haven and a means of fulfillment. The following quotation captures the tone of these two hundred pages or so, written, according to the editor, on Japanese paper:

> I want to surround myself with books. I am so very conscious of the fact that I shall savor what is best about my life in this world of the mind. I am finding, as I grow older, that the company of my fellow human beings, which I never sought out, weighs upon me more and more. Books, these are the soul and spirit of an enclosed universe whose exhalations they give forth at our bidding to console our days.

The *Bulletin* introduces us to other personalities as well: *Abbé* Georges-Alfred de Jordy de Cabanac (1873-1936) about whom Oblate Father Léon Loranger, tells us in his funeral eulogy that he was "well bred," a descendant of "that old Languedoc nobility which gave Canada so many fine military men." *Abbé* de Jordy de Cabanac, "the aristocrat," arrived in the Manchester diocese in 1910. He became "a distinguished genealogist," exploring "the origins of the great Canadian families: the Beaudrys, the Casavants, the Choquettes, the Morins. . . ." In a word, this man who "passionately loved his country and his race" takes his place "among a long line of great churchmen who have honored science and French scholarship."

As can be seen from this brief look at the *Bulletin de la Société Historique*, the publication included nearly as many genres as it did topics. A more detailed study would encompass the texts of Luc Lacourcière, Antoine Clément, Canon Lionel Groulx, Marcel Trudel, and also those articles devoted to polemics and current events by the Dominican Father Thomas M. Landry, Burton LeDoux, and Monsignor Paul-Emile Gosselin, among others.

Much the same remarks can be applied to the books compiled each year by Rev. Adrien Verrette entitled *La Vie franco-américaine* and published under the auspices of the Conseil de la Vie Française. This collection of volumes, published from 1937 to 1952, containing as it does the detailed account of events and activities which took place during those years, constitutes an essential reference for anyone interested in the cultural history of Franco-Americans as well as for literary historians, since they contain sermons, speeches, essays, and personal accounts not found anywhere else.

To conclude this discussion of nonfiction published during the 1935-1960 period, it should be noted that many examples of the various sub-genres of historical writing can also be found and that not all of them were devoted to the polemical literature born of the struggle for *la survivance*. The histories of religious orders and the biographies that focus mainly on religious rather than on nationalistic themes fall into this category. Such is the case for *Un siècle d'histoire assomptionniste*, by the Assumptionist Father Polyeucte Guissard, and the autobiographical account entitled *Moscow Was My Parish*, by Father Georges Bissonnette, also an Assumptionist. Still, the fact is that most of the writings of the period belong to the campaigns waged on behalf of *la survivance* and against assimilation.

Imaginative literature written during the 1935-1960 period although not constituting as large an output as nonfiction, can be said to have laid the foundation of a literary tradition in the sense that some writers from the period between 1960 and 1985, though they were not directly influenced by these works, did become aware of the poetry and fiction of this previous generation. Additionally, there were more poets and novelists writing between 1935 and 1960 than there had been before. As for the theater, it remains the neglected stepchild of this literature.

If we view Louis Dantin as a Québec poet and critic living in exile in New England rather than as a Franco-American, then the poetry of this period was dominated by the works of Rosaire Dion-Lévesque (pseudonym of Léo Lévesque, 1900-1974), called the "national poet" of Franco-Americans by the establishment. This is a title that Dion-Lévesque earned not only because of the literary quality of his considerable body of work, but also because of his skillful utilization of French, Québec, and American cultures.

His first important volume of poetry, *Les Oasis*, dates from 1931. In it, the poet demonstrates his mastery of the sonnet form and expresses both his cult of the Blessed Virgin and his romantic predilection for abandoned churches. The poet's work then evolved in a surprising manner; in a collection called *Vita* (1939), he pays homage to the great nineteenth-century American poet and disciple of carnal love, Walt Whitman, going so far as to call him his "new Christ." Dion-Lévesque became the first Franco-American writer to profess a strong attachment for an American master and to choose him as his intellectual guide. In 1933 he had already produced a remarkable translation of what he considered to be his mentor's "finest pages," *Walt Whitman, ses meilleurs pages*. Astonishing though it may seem, Dion-Lévesque seems to have resolved for himself the conflict between the cult of sensuality advocated by Whitman and the teachings of his own Catholic faith. In a rather unusual "Magnificat," he argues that his Creator must accept the poet as he is, in the very essence of his nature, for he ". . . is just as You wanted me to be and just as You fashioned me. . . . Here is Your creature and it is as it is for your glory and your agony!"

Rosaire Dion-Lévesque was the only one of his generation of Franco-American writers to have so completely accepted his sensual passion and to have integrated it into works published during his lifetime. In *Solitudes* (1949), the poet recalls various friends and lovers with whom he had sought to overcome the solitude inherent in the human condition. Dion-Lévesque was twice decorated by the French government for "exceptional services to the cause of French culture in America," and in 1957 the Académie Française awarded him a prize for his poetry.

The poetry of Georges Boucher, M.D. (1865-1956), is dominated by his nostalgia for his native Québec. His *Chants du nouveau monde* (1946) show just how much the memories of a happy childhood in Québec's Rivière-Bois-Clair had nourished his imagination to the very end of his long lifetime. His "Ode to Québec," in which the poet sings the praises of "the old capital"—the city he loved most—is over six hundred lines long and remains one of his best poems:

Ô Québec! Ô cité dont toute âme est frappée!
Grandeur d'un autre monde, éclat d'un autre temps!
Ô terre qu'on dirait fraîchement échappée
De la plage hautaine ou régnaient les titans!
Laisse-moi te chanter, ville auguste et bénie,
Cité qui de mon peuple est l'âme et le soutien,
Ô roc où tant de gloire au sol même est unie
Et que doit à jamais chérir le Canadien.
O Québec! O city that strikes with awe the soul of every man!
Old world grandeur and sheen of yesteryear!
O land, seeming to have just escaped
From the heady heights where Titans reigned!
Let me sing of thee, majestic and blessed city,
Soul of my people, their strength and their sustenance,
O rock! Your glory is wed to the soil itself,
And every Canadian must cherish you forever.

A poetic work that should be rescued from oblivion is that of Rev. Joseph Eid, a Lebanese immigrant who settled in Fall River in 1929. *A l'ombre des cèdres, ou l'épopée du Liban* (1940) is a moving historical evocation, in alexandrine verse, of his native country's glorious but tragic past. In an annex to this work, the author included articles on "Lebanon During the Great War," on "France, Guardian of the Near East," along with a series of texts on the Franco-Americans, and, finally, an overview of the Maronite and Melkite churches in

America. This work thus reveals a new dimension of the "Franco-American" experience.

Only a few Franco-American novels have been written in French, perhaps a dozen in all, and about half of them were published in the years from 1935 to 1960. This period also marked the birth of the Franco-American novel in English, a genre that would reach its maturity in 1950 with the onset of Jack Kerouac's meteoric career. All of them were mainly social novels, focusing on Canadian immigration and presenting characters from the working-class.

One of the more successful of these was *Canuck*, by Camille Lessard (1883-1972), a native of Sainte-Julie-de-Mégantic who immigrated to Lewiston in 1904. The author gives a realistic and compelling description of the problems caused when, out of sheer economic necessity, people have to leave their beloved country for an unknown land, and the difficulties they encounter in adapting to urban life. Camille Lessard also succeeds in describing the baleful influence that American materialism and creature comforts can have on persons who had previously known only deprivation. Finally, the novelist makes the reader feel the homesickness and the sense of life's monotony that the immigrants endured working in the mills. This eyewitness account of immigration occupies a special place in Franco-American literature.

So, too, does *L'Innocente victime* by Adélard Lambert (1867-1946), the folklorist and polemicist, born in Saint-Cuthbert, Berthier County, Québec, who immigrated to Fall River. He would much later return to settle in Drummondville, Québec, after having spent many years in Manchester. While its plot is that of a detective story, *L'Innocente victime* is in fact a social novel with an axe to grind. Lambert was one of the minority of immigrants who had not succumbed to the appeal of the American dream. He called for a return to the ancestral land to revel in the quiet simplicity of its present and the glory of its past. He believed that the modicum of luxury offered by the United States could only be had at the price of one's personal freedom. Notwithstanding the likely unpopularity of this viewpoint, Lambert had the courage to voice his opinion, deploring the fact that his compatriots had "lost their bearings in these large, foreign cities full of pitfalls, cities that drink the sweat and impoverish the blood of the voluntary slaves who crowd into them."

The only medical novel in Franco-American literature came from the pen of Paul Dufault, M.D. (1894-1969), who was born in Saint-Nazaire d'Acton. In *Sanatorium* (1938), a semi-autobiographical work, the author described the sufferings caused by tuberculosis, partly to alert people to the dangers of this illness. He also recounts how one tubercular patient had been transformed by his illness into a thinker. One of the main characters is afflicted with the disease and is obliged to enter the sanatorium where he slowly recovers. In so doing, he creates for himself a life of the mind, his reflections focusing on the social problems of Canada and the United States. He comes to the realization that the only remedies to these problems that each individual can bring to bear are complete disinterest and self-denial.

Jacques Ducharme's *The Delusson Family* (1939) was the first of the social novels written in English. Amid scenes from the earliest years of Canadian immigration to Holyoke, Massachusetts, the author underscores the important role that traditional values played in the lives of immigrants, though not to the exclusion of their economic progress. The fact that he recognized the importance of the material well-being that immigrants earnestly pursued explains in part why Jacques Ducharme was held in high regard by young Franco-American writers of the 1970s.

In 1954, and in an entirely different vein, Gabriel Nadeau, M.D., published *La Fille du Roy*, a long comical tale. A native of Saint-Césaire-de-Rouville, Gabriel Nadeau (1900-1979) immigrated to

Massachusetts in 1928. In a piquantly archaic idiom, he takes his readers back to the era of New France to recount the misadventures of his hero, François Barnabé dit Barnabé, who refuses to marry the young woman who has been selected for him for the simple reason that she is frightfully ugly. In a succession of comic scenes, the author introduces us to a series of colorful characters. A little-known, small-scale masterpiece, *La Fille du Roy* is one of the jewels of Franco-American literature.

Louis Dantin's posthumous novel, *Les Enfances de Fanny* (1951), belongs to Franco-American literature because this autobiographical work recounts an episode that occurred during Dantin's lengthy sojourn in New England; to wit, his liaison with an Afro-American woman. The author describes Fanny's life of misery in the South prior to her departure for Boston, and he also sketches several scenes of the black neighborhoods of this metropolis. Just below the surface of this novel, one senses a protest against the injustices from which Blacks suffer, as well as a veiled prophecy of racial troubles to come.

In 1950 Jean Louis (Jack) Kerouac (1922-1969), leader of the "Beat" generation and a cousin of Rosaire Dion-Lévesque, produced his first novel, *The Town and the City*. He would publish some twenty volumes of fiction and poetry in his lifetime, and in at least five of his novels he wrote about his ethnic background. In 1957 he achieved international fame with *On the Road*.

The Town and the City is Franco-American in an implicit rather than explicit fashion. In it, the author recounts the breakup of the Martins, a family of eight children at the time of the Second World War. In an interview with Rosaire Dion-Lévesque, Jack Kerouac admitted keeping the Franco-American aspect of his novel in the background "for personal reasons" which he never explained. What is undeniable is that Jack was moved by Yvonne Le Maître's laudatory review in *Le Travailleur,* and he thanked her for it in a letter in which he is quoted as saying: "All my knowledge rests in my 'French Canadianness' and nowhere else."

Doctor Sax (1959) is in part a phantasmagoric evocation of a childhood spent among Lowell's Franco-Americans as well as a parable on the eventual triumph of good over evil. Among the novel's many sources, which include French-Canadian religious beliefs, one is probably that of the legendary "Bonhomme Sept-Heures," the bogeyman, to whom the main character bears some resemblance. Lowell's Franco-American dialect must also be included as a source for the novel as well as one of its themes, several passages being written in this dialect. The book contains wonderful descriptions of Franco-Americans sites, such as Saint John the Baptist Church and the Grotto at the rear of the Franco-American Orphanage with its famous outdoor Way of the Cross. The author also paints some very touching family scenes.

As for the theater, it must be granted that while Franco-Americans were always fond of it as a source of edification and amusement, they published very few plays. In fact, Victor Vekeman (1867-1947), a Belgian immigrant, seems to have been the only writer to have published any dramatic literature during this period. He is especially known for his temperance plays, a typical example being *Un sauveur d'âmes, ou l'Apostolat du père Jacquemet*. The drama revolves around the life of the Dominican priest who founded temperance societies in Fall River at the beginning of the twentieth century. Victor Vekeman also wrote some light plays for entertainment.

This account gives but an idea of the writings which were in circulation in Franco-American circles, especially among the élite, from 1935 to 1960. To complete the picture, the reading habits of the people would need to be studied. We know that readers of Franco-American newspapers enjoyed the serial novels published by them—those of the Baroness Orczy, for instance, and the moral tales of Pierre L'Ermite. The people also liked devotional literature, as can be seen by the many biographies of holy people which they read. Many devotional magazines could also be found in Franco-American homes, especially those published by the important sanctuaries of Québec. In this regard, we should mention the literature inspired by the religious experience of Franco-Americans which includes the musical drama *The Life of a Mystical Rose* by the opera star Yvonne Chalfonte. It was based on the life of Rose Ferron and was performed in Franco-American centers as well as in Québec.

Finally, despite our having written about it at some length, we have failed to do justice to the period's copious historical production. The bibliography of *Abbé* Adrien Verrette alone includes some thirty titles, not counting the compilations, articles, sermons, and speeches. And to our knowledge there is no complete listing of the works of Corinne Rocheleau-Rouleau; many of her writings—for example, her *Laurentian Heritage* which appeared in 1948—served to introduce Quebecers to English-Canadian readers. And many of the articles written by Yvonne Le Maître on the literary or sociocultural events of the first half of the twentieth century still have an undeniable historical value today.

The life of Brother André, a celebrated healer and the moving force behind the conception and establishment of the immensely popular Montréal shrine, Saint-Joseph's Oratory, is one such example. Another is Saint Catherine Labouré, the nineteenth century religious of Saint Vincent de Paul, the originator of the widespread devotion to the "Miraculous Medal" of the Blessed Virgin.

In an article commenting on the congress marking the fiftieth anniversary of the USJB held in Boston in May 1950, Father François-Marie Drouin, a Dominican from Lewiston, wrote as follows about Franco-Americans:

All the Catholic bishops of New England have sung—even in our own language—the heroism of our valiant little people: builders of schools and churches and guardians of the family, society's basic unit. A century of hidden struggles has ended in TRIUMPH, and there is official RECOGNITION of what is exceptionally worthy: that of a people which would not betray its providential destiny.

Bolstered by "encouragements" of this kind and fortified by their own convictions, *patriote* leaders would persist in their efforts to maintain "French culture in the service of God and country," and they would man the barricades for as long as they could. This attitude, which would be dubbed reactionary by the "Young Turks" of the 1970s, was viewed rather as the heroism of perseverance by leaders who had developed a veritable cult of continuity. Did these leaders sense a widening gap between themselves and the people? In an article which appeared in *Le Canado-Américain* in 1948, Adolphe Robert described the anguish he felt over the loss of the rising generation:

Our group's history is barely one hundred years old. . . . We have survived by drawing on our pre-1760 past. But we have reached a period of evolution in which we must formulate a philosophy of life for the future grounded in natural law, historical right, and the social doctrine of the Church. Both our youth, who have no compass to guide them, and the mass of our people, who have lost their bearings, are counting on us to do this. We are one generation late in our efforts to bind today's native sons with yesterday's immigrants. We must also ask ourselves if we do not bear a collective responsibility for what is now occurring in some Franco-American communities. In the absence of a social philosophy that we failed to inculcate in them, they have fashioned one of their own. Tragically, this philosophy does not aspire to the total development of the human personality reflective of the Franco-American as a type. On the contrary, it belittles and diminishes him, robbing him of his rich, age-old French cultural heritage. It is an approach that seeks to subtract rather than to add. It is up to the Comité d'Orientation Franco-Américaine and all who are affected by the problem of our *survivance* to formulate this philosophical doctrine, to reunite the past with the present, and to make it penetrate every level of our society *while there is still time.*

324   The Franco-Americans of New England

This entire chapter has served as a commentary on the situation facing the militant élite in the 1940s and the 1950s and its frame of mind so vividly expressed by the Robert text. It behooves us to underscore the acknowledgement: "We are one generation late. . . ." and we should keep in mind the solution proposed: the elaboration of a philosophical doctrine. Such a reaction overestimated the importance, for a people enamored of materialism and pragmatism, of the life of the mind, of loyalty to the past, and of an old ideal; it also underestimated the impact of the forces of assimilation. This is said without any desire to blame or praise, for in our opinion, by the beginning of the 1960s and even before, assimilation appears to have been almost inevitable. In no way does this diminish the merits of the *patriote* leaders, nor should it be seen as a criticism of the people. To be honest, it is difficult to see how assimilation could have been avoided.

V

ETHNICITY REDISCOVERED
1960-1990

These three decades of Franco-American history were characterized by continuity, a genuine ideological diversity, and new signs of ethnic life. Some observers spoke of a "renaissance" in the life of the group, which they date to 1970, while others saw in various manifestations of ethnic life only a few unanticipated and futile efforts on the eve of total assimilation.

To understand this period, one must first take into account a change in attitude by the American government toward the country's linguistic and cultural minorities. Hostile in 1920 to anything "foreign" and subsequently indifferent to its ethnic groups, the federal government began playing an active role, beginning in 1958, to improve the teaching of what were called "foreign" languages. In the 1960s and 1970s, the government undertook a serious and sustained effort on behalf of bilingual and bicultural education in order to help immigrants adapt to their new country, and this involvement had positive repercussions for Franco-Americans. Other federally-sponsored programs—the 1972 Ethnic Heritage Studies Program in particular—underwrote projects that highlighted the cultural patrimony of the many ethnic groups in the United States. Finally in 1976, the celebration of the country's bicentennial, which had been in the planning stages since the early 1970s and had afterward been extended to 1981, gave ethnic groups the opportunity to publicize the contributions made by their ancestors, and in some cases by their native lands, to the development of the United States.

The very important role played by Afro-Americans on the national scene during the same period must also be kept in mind. By affirming their identity and demanding their civil rights, even to the point of engaging in bloody riots, they succeeded in obtaining, not only their rights, but a recognition of, and even an increased respect for, their culture. At the same time, other minority groups, influenced by them, also experienced a resurgence of ethnic pride.

Franco-Americans took advantage of the situation to assert themselves and increase their visibility. In this, they benefited from the efforts of some young academics and a new generation of activists, militants, writers, and artists who were themselves aided by the establishment of the Maison du Québec in Boston in 1969 and by the coming to power of the Parti québécois in Québec in 1976.

New Élites

From 1960 to 1990, a new group of leaders learned to coexist after a fashion with an old guard which did not readily give up its command posts. Many of the young people of this period were teachers and scholars, unlike the earlier generation of leaders consisting of priests and members of the liberal professions. Some of these university people served the interests of the group by making the Franco-American experience more widely known.

Two of the first who succeeded in doing so in the late fifties and early sixties were Sister Raymond-de-Jésus Dion, whose provincial house was located in Putnam, Connecticut, and Gerard Brault, a university professor. In 1959, Sister Dion published *The Holy Ghost French Series*, textbooks intended for the teaching of French as a second language. Although designed for use in parochial schools, these textbooks were so well received that, in an unprecedented move, a special edition was prepared for the public schools. They were later adapted for the teaching of Spanish, and they were also used in some schools in France where the Daughters of the Holy Spirit had their motherhouse.

Gerard Brault, born in Chicopee, Massachusetts, was a professor of French at the University of Pennsylvania and an internationally-known medievalist when he took a keen interest in the teaching of French to Franco-Americans, as shown by his numerous publications. From 1958 to 1964, he directed summer institutes, first at Bowdoin College in Brunswick, Maine, and then at Assumption College, his *alma mater,* in Worcester. From 1961 on, these institutes were funded by the federal government. The first institute which he directed at Bowdoin enrolled forty Franco-American teachers and sought to serve the national interest by developing the "natural resource" represented by Franco-Americans who were career teachers of French. While recognizing the value of the Franco dialect as a means of communication within the group, the institute also attempted to shift the French spoken by these teachers in the direction of standard French.

The influence of these institutes was felt in several ways. For example, the *Cours de langue française destiné aux jeunes Franco-Américains* that was drafted by Gerard Brault with the help of the participants was revised several times, and it was among the first textbooks to include selections on Franco-Americans. Gerard Brault also had the foresight to collate and publish the *Conférences de l'Institut franco-américain de Bowdoin College*, a series of lectures on Franco-Americans and on language teaching, which is still of value to researchers. Finally, it was a group of institute participants who founded the Association des Professeurs Franco-Américains. Under the skillful direction of Elphège Roy and François Martineau, this association assisted hundreds of members through the meetings, lectures, and workshops that it organized from 1964 to 1980.

It is important to note the inherent wisdom in the position taken by Professor Brault with respect to the French spoken in New England. It recognizes the fundamental value of the Franco-American dialect which it views as the starting point on the road to the mastery of standard French; hence, it is a position that offers the student access to a second linguistic level. It is then up to the student to choose the level most appropriate to specific circumstances: the dialect within the family and standard French in the presence of speakers who are not Franco-American.

Sadly, this kind of tolerance was not shared by teachers of French in public schools. Most of them were Americans who had traditionally considered the French spoken by Franco-Americans as the inferior product of a subculture. Franco-American students came to detest French, in part because of this disdain which helped accelerate assimilation. After they had thus been humiliated, most of these students could hardly wait to rid themselves of a cultural burden they perceived as degrading. And so, not only did the country lose a wonderful possibility to produce bilingual generations, it effectively destroyed that possibility by allowing States like Maine to maintain laws forbidding the use of any language other than English in the schools, except in "foreign-language" courses.

When the United States government began to fund modern language teaching in the late 1950s, the irony of the situation became painfully evident. After having done everything it could for decades to make the country unilingual, it was now—without admitting its past mistakes—spending millions to turn it into a polyglot nation. But this fad would last for only a few years.

In Franco-American New England, the teaching of French was taking place in an environment less and less favorable to the preservation of the cultural heritage and, in particular, the Catholic religion. Confused by the many changes arising out of the Second Vatican Council, the faithful became both increasingly skeptical and less fervent in the sixties. This resulted in a drastic reduction of support for parish activities. With the decline in religious vocations, the drop in enrollments, and the drying up of funding sources, Catholic schools all over the country began to experience a profound crisis. During these decades, more and more Catholic schools reorganized into regional schools in which French had no special standing. Of the 250 or so Franco-American schools in 1950, some seventy-five remained in 1995, either as self-sustaining units or as part of a consolidated school, according to Professor Brault. Some final efforts to reverse this trend were made around 1965, and they need to be pointed out.

Faced with such a distressing problem, the Comité de Vie Franco-Américaine made it the theme of its eighth Congress, held in Manchester, New Hampshire, from October 15 to 17, 1965. In his address to the group, Father Thomas Landry described the "serious, acute, and urgent" crisis in Franco-American schools and the "frightening decline" that was occurring in the teaching of French in these schools. One of the *patriote* leaders most highly respected by the old guard, Father Landry recommended that Franco-Americans accept the fact that what once had been Franco-American schools were now English-language institutions where "religion suffers as a result of its being taught in French, and for that reason, religion could well become less and less loved by young Franco-Americans."

The delegates adopted the solution proposed by Father Landry, demanding that in Franco-American parochial schools French be "a required course in all elementary and high school classes and that it be taught for a *full* forty-five minutes in every complete school day." The Comité de Vie was asked to establish committees in all the dioceses of New England to lobby for Father Landry's proposed solution to the crisis and organize a congress on the same theme the following year.

But neither this second congress—held in Providence, Rhode Island, in 1966—nor the unflagging zeal of the militants, was enough to halt what the elders called the *dégringolade* (collapse) of the teaching of French.

During these same years between 1960 and 1990, a number of American university professors, including some Franco-Americans, discovered or rediscovered Canada and the Franco-Americans. Several of them succeeded in introducing new courses at their respective colleges and universities on the Canadians, both those residing in Canada and those of the diaspora, thereby opening up new areas for research. Additionally, sections on Canada and Franco-Americans were included on a more or less regular basis at meetings of various professional organizations at both the national (Modern Language Association) and regional (Northeast Modern Language Association) levels. Some professors of French, who were also Franco-Americans, developed courses on the French-speaking people of North America. One of the pioneers in this area was Paul P. Chassé who instituted a course on Franco-American literature at Rhode Island College in Providence in the 1960s. This course, which was often repeated, was the source of an imposing number of research papers. Professor Chassé is also to be commended for his doctoral dissertation on Franco-American poets, as well as for producing a considerable number of articles on Franco-American history and on French contributions to the development of the United States.

In the same period, several colleges and universities in the Northeast offered courses on Canada or French-America. University professors who had specialized in one or another aspect of Franco-American studies took on the responsibility for these courses under the typically American system of the law of supply and demand. At the University of Vermont, Professor Peter Woolfson gave a course in anthropology that focused specifically on Franco-Americans; at the University of New Hampshire, Professor Robert LeBlanc studied the

Francos from the viewpoint of human geography, while at Harvard University, Professor Brigitte Lane offered several courses on Franco-American literature.

But it was on the various campuses of the University of Maine that the greatest number of resources were devoted to Canadian and Franco-American studies. As early as the 1960s, the New England/Atlantic Provinces/Québec Center was established at the University of Maine at Orono. In the years that followed, the center increased the number of courses and colloquia while also encouraging research activities. Other campuses of the university offered either programs of bilingual and bicultural studies—the University of Maine at Fort Kent—or a series of seminars on various aspects of the Franco phenomenon—the University of Maine at Farmington—or a program of bilingual and bicultural social services—the University of Maine at Augusta.

Partly because of the funding it received from the federal government, one of the most productive programs to be carried through to its completion by the University of Maine at Orono was the Canadian/Franco-American Studies Project (1979-1981). Teachers from fifteen different school systems in five States enrolled in the project that included courses, colloquia, lectures, and the preparation of two manuals: *Initiating Franco-American Studies: A Handbook for Teachers* by Stanley L. Freeman, Jr. and Raymond J. Pelletier, and *Consider Canada* by Stanley L. Freeman, Jr.

There were too many research studies on Francos produced between 1960 and 1990 to summarize them in a few pages. It should be pointed out, however, that this research was not entirely the work of academics. For example, the New Hampshire Civil Liberties Union published a report around 1979 showing that Francos in that State were victims of both economic and social discrimination, as evidenced by the inequality between Francos and Anglos in the areas of both education and employment. Another study conducted by the Vermont Advisory Committee to the United States Commission on Civil Rights revealed that in 1983 Francos living in Vermont were underrepresented "in institutions of higher education, in certain employment sectors, and in positions of power and influence."

Most of the individual studies on Franco-Americans carried out during this period differed significantly from those done in the past: they did not pay homage to any predecessors, and—more objective in their approach—they were no longer an expression of the author's filiopietistic feelings.

In 1968, the Congress of the United States passed the Elementary and Secondary Education Act, Title VII, authorizing the U.S. Office of Education to fund bilingual education programs in order to teach English to children from homes in which the predominant language was not English. The scope of the law was extended by a Supreme Court decision (Lau v. Nichols, 1974) according to which school systems were required to provide special assistance to young people (ages five to ten) whose competence in English was limited. Both the law and the Supreme Court decision sought to create parity in the schools between minority children and young English-speaking Americans through the use of two languages: the mother tongue of the young immigrants (Spanish-speaking, French-speaking, etc.) and English. Young Americans could also participate in bilingual programs if their parents so wished, since there was a desire to avoid even the appearance of segregation.

The late sixties and the seventies were the golden years of bilingual education: thousands of children of diverse national origin, including hundreds of Francos, were able to take advantage of these programs.

From its very beginnings and to this very day, bilingual education has been the subject of extensive national debate. Opponents argue that it threatens the cultural identity of the United States and that any attempt to preserve "foreign" languages entails the risk that English could be displaced as the country's principal language thereby presenting a threat to the nation's political unity. Many also fear that, in light of the constantly increasing number of Hispanics, Asians, and other minorities pouring into the United States, bilingual education could lead to a fragmentation of the country. Some also maintain that bilingual education marginalizes students and keeps them in transition programs that last too long, thus depriving these students of an education in English which is of critical importance for their future.

Supporters of bilingual education argue that it is essential for young immigrants who do not understand English. They also point out that bilingualism enriches the nation's culture and that it can be very useful in the fields of business and international relations.

The majority of Franco-Americans showed no interest at all in this national debate on bilingual education, either because their children had already mastered English and so the law did not concern them, or because they were no longer interested in issues of language and patrimony. Some Franco-Americans, however, were very much involved. Some members of the old guard saw the law on bilingual education as an unexpected opportunity to make French available to a generation they had viewed as "lost." But others were opposed to any participation by Francos in a program that would underscore their minority status; for them, it was preferable not to participate and to remain full-fledged citizens.

This being said, about ten French-English programs were launched in northern New England—Maine, New Hampshire, and Vermont—between 1969 and 1983. Some ended quickly because of personality conflicts or local political squabbles; others lasted the five years of federal funding, but school districts were not prepared to pay the costs of continuing them. The Saint John Valley project in Maine, established in 1970, was recognized by Washington as a model of its kind and earned a solid reputation at the national level. The communities that benefited from a bilingual education program, due to a high percentage of Franco-Americans living there—often newly arrived from Canada—included Greenville and Berlin, New Hampshire, Caribou, Maine, and Canaan, Richford, and Swanton, Vermont. Each of these programs included a Parent Advisory Council to ensure the necessary collaboration among parents, students, and teachers, and to organize various activities: evening programs, information bulletins, concerts, and workshops.

The federal government also funded some experimental projects. Completed in 1979 by a team from the University of New Hampshire, *The Franco File*, for example, was a television miniseries developed primarily for children; but it was also of interest to adults who might want to learn more about Franco-American biculturalism in the seventies. An episode from the series won an award from the National Academy of Television Arts and Sciences.

The establishment of federally-funded projects led to the creation of a network of centers that could provide them with the services necessary for their smooth operation. Among the services, those devoted to inter-project communication, the training of teachers, the writing of curricula adapted to local circumstances, and the development of teaching materials were assigned the highest priority. At times, area universities assumed these responsibilities, but the United States Office of Education often found it more effective to establish centers whose sole purpose was to assist local projects. The first such Franco-American center, "The Liaison Service for Bilingual Projects in French and English in the United States," was established in Greenville, New Hampshire, in 1971 under the direction of Robert Paris, a young academic. This center was responsible for coordinating bilingual projects in French and English both in New England and in Louisiana. The Liaison Service thus became the first "official" educational and cultural link between New England and Louisiana.

During its five-year existence (1971-1975), the Liaison Service helped implement local projects in several different ways: training of personnel (for example, a number of teachers enrolled in intensive summer courses given at the community college of Jonquière in Québec); exchange programs in New England for teachers from Louisiana and in Louisiana for New Englanders; development of teaching materials; coordination of an annual conference on bilingual education held on an alternating basis in Louisiana and New England; publication of a voluminous *Bulletin du Service de liaison*, helpful not only for specialists but for anyone interested in French-speaking America; and media releases on bilingual teaching in New England as well as in Louisiana.

Meanwhile, Robert Paris and Robert Fournier from the New Hampshire Department of Education were able to persuade Washington that the most serious obstacle that stood in the way of the intended goal was the lack of teaching materials. After a well-organized lobbying campaign, the National Materials Center for French and Portuguese (NMDC) was established in Bedford, New Hampshire, in 1975. The first director, Robert Paris, was succeeded by Normand Dubé who assembled a team of collaborators and led the Center into a period of intensive production. His co-workers—Renaud Albert, Donald Dugas, and Julien Olivier among others—agreed with Dubé that the time had come for Francos to develop their own teaching materials to reflect their contemporary life and values as rural or urban dwellers. Behind this approach one could sense the desire to settle an old score. The NMDC staff deplored, with some bitterness, the fact that in traditional Franco-American schools teaching materials imported from Canada contained nothing that was Franco-American, nor had any attempt been made to adapt these materials to the Franco-American environment. The watchword at the NMDC was "The time has come to change all that."

Because of its determination to produce Franco-American materials and its heavy (almost too much so) publication schedule, the NMDC deserves a special place in Franco-American history. During its seven-year existence (1975-1982), it produced an impressive number of pedagogical materials, including texts for all instructional levels, from the primary school to the university. Of greatest value to researchers is the eight-volume collection, *Franco-American Overview*, a compilation of sociological and historical studies on Franco-Americans, Louisiana's Acadians, and the French Canadians of the West and Midwest. The publication of the nine-volume *Anthologie de la littérature franco-américaine de la Nouvelle-Angleterre,* compiled by Richard Santerre, and the reprinting of ten novels that were no longer in print *(Un revenant, Mirbah, etc.)* were equally valuable contributions. For as long as the NMDC lasted, Franco-Americans could believe that for the first time in their history, they had a publisher they could call their own.

Additional repercussions arising from Franco involvement in bilingual education should also be taken into account because they had an impact on the group's evolution in the 1970s, particularly with respect to the links established with Louisiana, then in the golden period of its French "Renaissance."

The Liaison Service's French-English bilingual projects led to such an increase in exchange programs with Louisiana that in the end, they extended beyond the scope of the bilingual education network. In April 1973, the Council for the Development of French in New

England (CODOFINE) was established in New Hampshire, along the lines of its counterpart in Louisiana (CODOFIL). From the outset, CODOFINE's aim was the organization and coordination of educational and cultural activities in conjunction with the francophone institutions of New England. Generally speaking, CODOFINE sought to extend the use of French in every possible way: increasing the number of bilingual education programs, developing links between New England and French-speaking communities throughout the world, and undertaking projects that would meet the educational and cultural needs of all the Francophones of the region.

These were the programmatic goals developed by a provisional committee headed by Robert Paris, Robert Fournier, and Marron Fort, a language professor at the University of New Hampshire. So as to make it a representative group, the standing committee was composed of two delegates from each of the New England States. Relying as it did for the most part on contributed services, its meetings were hosted by Notre Dame College in Manchester, New Hampshire, a college founded and administered by the Sisters of the Holy Cross. Secretarial functions were divided between the offices of interim president Robert Paris and secretary-treasurer Robert Fournier. The traditional élite seemed dumfounded by the audacity of these Young Turks.

The provisional committee spent several months—from the spring to the autumn of 1973—clarifying CODOFINE's goals and objectives, identifying potential funding sources for their projects, and planning their October 1973 colloquium. The president was also busy answering questions about this new organization that had materialized in a region that already had hundreds of others. Despite repeated assurances from Robert Paris that CODOFINE had no wish to compete with existing groups, both the existing leaders and Franco-Americans in general viewed CODOFINE as a clique of intellectuals bent on taking over the direction of the ethnic group.

The uneasiness associated with the establishment of CODOFINE would never be dispelled; the resistance of the old guard, combined with popular apathy, prevented its survival beyond the difficult organizational period. On its behalf, it must be stated that CODOFINE was a well-conceived entity and that, in spite of opposition from entrenched organizations and public indifference, it did succeed in increasing somewhat the visibility of Franco-Americans. Designed to encourage young people to join the francophone movement so as to prepare them to take over the future leadership of the group, so earnestly called for by previous generations, CODOFINE offered several real advantages: it was democratic in its approach, open to everyone, and it sought to present Franco-Americans as a national resource, rather than as just another uninteresting and needy minority. The fact that it was unable to mobilize the human and financial resources it needed to function properly, this despite its democratic character and religious neutrality—two essential conditions for the rising generation—is a clear indication of just how widespread the assimilation of Franco-Americans had become in the 1970s. Other organizations would subsequently meet with a similar fate.

Another important consequence stemming from Franco-American participation in the bilingual education movement was the series of annual conferences that began in January 1972 in Lafayette, Louisiana. Designed at first for specialists in bilingual education, by 1978 these conferences were opened to the public, the Franco-American public in particular, so as to increase support for bilingualism in the general population as well as among members of Congress in Washington.

These conventions, which attracted between three and four hundred people, were held each year alternately in Louisiana and New England. Although many of those attending were teachers and administrators involved in various bilingual education projects, a large percentage of the participants were individuals who shared a common attachment to one aspect or another of the cultural heritage. Delegates from the American, French, Canadian, Belgian, and Québec governments were on hand to encourage participants in their efforts at promoting bilingualism.

The scope of the conferences was quickly broadened to respond to the interests of a diversified community, and workshops were added on the problems experienced by the Franco-American elderly with social service agencies, on the diverse roles of Franco-American women, and on the future of young people. But the main concerns—shared by all and discussed every year focused on the legislative efforts needed to extend the scope of bilingual education and on the relative lack of visibility of the Franco-American group, that "silent minority."

This series of conferences lasted several years, and although it is difficult to evaluate its results with any accuracy, there were some concrete outcomes. First, the presence at these conferences of Franco-Americans from the Midwest led to a renewed recognition of that region's importance and paved the way for the establishment in 1980 of a new national organization, the Assemblée des Franco-Américains.

However, if the primary goal of these conferences was to create an organized and effective lobby on behalf of bilingual education, it obviously failed to do so. But each conference did provide an opportunity to affirm Franco identity, and as a result of coverage in the media, Franco-Americans became a little less "invisible." Finally, in addition to stimulating the interest of some Francos who had never before participated in the life of the group, the conferences succeeded in identifying the priorities that would need to be addressed if Franco-American life were to continue into the twenty-first century.

With but few exceptions, these conventions were held in an atmosphere of harmony and civility. Ideological differences between the young and the not-so-young were deliberately muted in the debates so as to create the kind of unity the group would need to lobby effectively for bilingualism, especially in the legislative arena. But it would be misleading to pretend that the new leaders and the traditional élite were always in total agreement. A colloquium on "The Franco-Americans: Past Promises and Present Realities," organized in 1976 by Donald Dugas under the aegis of the National Materials Development Center, revealed a conflict of ideas and values that had originated in the 1960s. At the beginning of the colloquium, Robert Paris listed some of the "major issues" which should be addressed by the participants; they included the following, seen by some traditionalists as just so many provocations:

> How can we unify our group without suppressing individual differences and divergent points of view?

> Do we need other institutions, organizations, associations, or committees to take care of our people and represent us publicly?

> How can we prepare new leaders, a new élite, and at the same time develop and increase the active and necessary participation of the *people*?

Questions of this nature, along with the presence at the colloquium of young militants who rejected *survivance* ideology, were viewed as a challenge to the establishment which considered traditional values to be sacred and beyond discussion. The colloquium lasted two days—June 10 to 12, 1976—and nothing seems to have been resolved other than to put on public display the conflict between the old guard and the young moderns that had been simmering for years in Franco-America. It should be noted that on this occasion, the most realistic appraisal was given by Father Thomas Landry. After reminding everyone that the identity of Franco-Americans, now only minimally French, was rapidly evolving, he declared: "Now is the time for new leadership to take over." Speaking on behalf of the traditional élite, he asserted that the new leaders would be given a free hand in reformulating Franco-American ethnicity, and he urged the young not to decree a wholesale ban on anyone—even their elders—who might wish to continue serving the cause. He issued a similar invitation to the watchdogs of old, calling on them to be tolerant and magnanimous and asking that they not wage "futile rear guard battles" whose only result would be to hamper any progress the young might be able to achieve on behalf of the group.

The closing address by Claire Quintal summarized a crucial aspect of the painful drama that the colloquium's participants had just experienced:

> As I listened to Normand Dubé and Paul Paré responding to Father Landry, I could not help thinking that we have once again succeeded in erecting artificial barriers between the generations, between the "leaders" and those who now refuse to be led, between those who, tired of resisting, have accepted the *status quo* and those who want to turn everything upside down and inside out by getting rid of the old in favor of the new. I call these barriers artificial because both sides share the same goal: the personal, cultural, social, and political advancement of our people and, what's more, their happiness as well.

A Cultural Awakening?

During this 1960-1990 period, a convergence of events, social forces, and Franco-American initiatives resulted in what led some observers to believe that perhaps a Franco-American "renaissance" was in the making. This question is worth examinining more closely.

The Reverend Martin Luther King's campaign in favor of civil rights for Afro-Americans led to what was called the "Black Revolution," and the country finally began attempting to grant the truly legitimate demands of the Blacks. Meanwhile, the portrayal of the

Black saga in *Roots* by Alex Haley in 1976, followed by the television series of the same name, aroused the curiosity of the majority of Americans about their own origins.

Even before the publication of *Roots*, the late sixties had produced the phenomenon called the "new ethnicity," an awakening on the part of those "forgotten Americans" who were neither WASPS nor "people of color." They had slowly begun to realize that they, too, had "roots"—a patrimony and a history of which they could be proud. This involved some thirty national groups—perhaps even more—the most numerous and vocal being the Irish, the Italians, the Polish, and the Greeks. Ethnic pluralism blossomed at all levels of American society and expressed itself in popular celebrations as well as in writings of all kinds: autobiographies, local histories, sociological studies, novels, and poetry. With support from organizations like the American Jewish Committee, this movement was analyzed by the philosopher Michael Novak in a key book, *The Rise of the Unmeltable Ethnics*.

The years 1972 and 1973 also marked the start of the preparations for the Bicentennial of the United States; it would be celebrated from 1976 to 1981 so as to recall each historic moment that led to the final victory over the British at Yorktown. Over time, a wider perspective was adopted, and it was decided that the Bicentennial would be an extended celebration of the entire country and its cultural diversity. It was in this spirit that federal and state governments sought to promote both group and individual projects which highlighted the contribution made by ethnic groups to the development of the United States. Franco-Americans took an active part in these commemorative celebrations: they organized parades, gala evenings, and other events. They were particularly proud of the success of the "French Ethnic Days" held at the State House in Boston from May 20 to 26, 1976, during which the Acadian flag was flown in front of the Capitol. May 24th, proclaimed Acadian Day in the Commonwealth, was particularly memorable. Organized by Rev. Clarence d'Entremont, the Acadian historian and educator who lived in New England for some three decades, the day was highlighted by a proclamation from the governor. Exhibits, plays, demonstrations of folk arts and crafts, films, music, and dance attracted crowds of people. In the evening the traditional banquet was attended by dignitaries from the Canadian Maritime Provinces and distant States. Acadians whose ancestors had been deported to Massachusetts in 1755 could hardly believe it was taking place. When Rev. d'Entremont returned to Nova Scotia in the early eighties, he could point with pride to having founded the New England chapter of the Acadian Historical Society and the Federation of Genealogical Societies, comprised of groups in Canada as well as in the United States.

This "ethnic wave," this new climate which encouraged the majority of Americans to take pride in their ancestry, facilitated the creation of various organizations; but other social forces that were also at work in the late sixties and early seventies—especially the counterculture's resort to protest—led to the rise of radical groups. Troubled by the Vietnam War which had come on the heels of political assassinations, the Watergate scandal, and racial riots in American cities, as well as by the upheavals within the Church brought about by the Second Vatican Council, college students began to distance themselves from the previous generation. While some became hippies and dropped out for several years, others organized themselves to transform society. The young people who formed the Franco-American Resource and Opportunity Group (FAROG) at the University of Maine, Orono, in 1971, opted for transformation through protest. They defined themselves primarily as a support group for Franco-American students, who felt like fish out of water in the university's Anglo-American atmosphere, and as a pressure group to sensitize English-speaking Americans to the special situation of Franco-Americans.

The group began its work at the university where it succeeded in gaining official recognition. Despite its leftist leanings and its "we want ours" attitude, the organization won university approval and was granted funding for a number of projects that sought to secure a community-wide recognition of the right of Francos at the University of Maine to be *real* Francos and not just "recycled Anglos"—the right, therefore, to transform the condition of cultural alienation to which they had been consigned in order to assimilate them. The members of FAROG developed their own special orientation program to welcome and guide first-year Franco students from the moment they arrived on campus. They organized new courses and a series of conferences and workshops on Francos besides collecting pertinent materials and opening a counseling center. They forged ties with the Bangor Mental Health Institute where they spoke out in defense of the most destitute Francos: those who suffered from psychological or emotional problems but who could not communicate with their therapists because their English was deficient and the staff did not understand French.

Although founded by two women students, Claire Bolduc and Cécile Collin, the driving force behind the movement was Yvon Labbé, a dynamic community organizer who prided himself on his origins in the Beauce region of Québec. Serving as FAROG's coordinator, he succeeded in widening its scope, winning authorization from the university to hire students in order to expand services. The FAROG was then able to reach a wider Franco-American audience, especially through its publications. For example, in 1973 a member of the team, Céleste Roberge, compiled a selection of texts prepared by specialists for a course on Franco-American culture. The anthology, *Vers l'évolution d'une culture*, contains several selections that are still of interest, including a particularly valuable study by ethnologist Roger Paradis entitled "Franco-American Folklore: A Cornucopia of Culture."

Beginning in September 1974, the group became even better known through the publication of the *FAROG Forum*, in tabloid format. Appearing eight times a year, the paper was combative in tone and deliberately provocative. Beginning with its first issue, it gave rise to the most diverse reactions, ranging from praise to loathing. It usually included a good number of articles, and since the *Forum* never claimed objectivity as one of its strong points, these reports more often than not consisted of criticism of what was happening on the Franco-American scene. The paper often carried a literary page—poems, stories, excerpts from novels—as well as a page devoted to history or genealogy, and there were also reviews of books written about Francos. Although it contained a "Québec" page, the content of the paper was predominantly Franco-American and included not just New Englanders but all Francophones in the United States: New York, Louisiana, the Midwest, etc. Letters expressing every conceivable reaction arrived from readers everywhere, even from France.

Irreverent, rebellious, hypercritical, and excessively sarcastic, the *Forum* irritated its readers by its intolerance of traditional values, its obsession with the negative aspect of things, and an effrontery that sometimes smacked of arrogance. These faults can be imputed to the variety of its correspondents, to whom the *Forum* opened wide its doors, rather than to its editorial staff, since the opinions expressed committed no one but the persons writing the letters or the articles. Nevertheless, because of FAROG's originality and perseverance, this unique phenomenon in Franco-American history requires that we make a special effort to understand what it is seeking to achieve.

From the outset, FAROG's basic "ideological" tenet was its opposition to *survivance* ideology. Influenced by Québec's Quiet Revolution as well as the American counterculture, the members of FAROG began by rejecting both the notion and the reality of an élite, that is, a group whose ideas should determine the beliefs and the behavior of others. Populists at heart, these young people decided to assume responsibility for their own lives and forge their own identity, where patrimony played a part but did not constitute the whole picture. For them, what took precedence was the "self" and its development according to one's own inclination; this cult of the "self" replaced conformity to traditional values.

The partisans of *la survivance* totally rejected this kind of subjectivity which they viewed as anarchistic and leading to chaos. For the *patriote* élite, one's cultural heritage is a *given* that an individual receives at birth, and it constitutes a whole, complete in itself; it defines the individual whose role it is to preserve this heritage and transmit it to posterity. For the "me" generation on the contrary, an individual's heritage is an option: one can take it or leave it, in whole or in part—the choice is up to the individual. And even if one does accept one's heritage, a person does not necessarily accept it as a whole, for to it must be added one's personal experience. Heritage is only a starting point, one aspect of life, one element only of one's individual identity—an identity which must be forged through a lengthy series of choices to which one has freely consented.

Young people associated with FAROG for the last twenty-five years or so would differ from their elders on each of the essential aspects of *survivance* doctrine. They rejected traditional religion because, in their opinion, instead of contributing to an individual's self-development, it crushed him or her. They considered language to be an instrument at the service of the individual and not the opposite. Consequently, it was an instrument that an individual could use in any way he or she pleased. Hence the abundance of "franglais" and Franco dialect in the pages of the *Forum*; these young people wrote as they spoke and considered any distinction between the written and spoken language to be an artificial one. And since an individual must not be enslaved by a language or by the study of that language, mistakes

abound in the *Forum*; they are even welcomed as proof of the author's
"authenticity."

These young people saw the cult of the past as a yoke and so were
less interested in the history of Québec and Acadia than in its dynamic
present. Québec served as a model of refusal—the refusal of traditional
values in its Quiet Revolution and the refusal of second-class
citizenship in its independence movement. But, except for its music
and its movies, these rebels also refused to define themselves in
Québec terms. Franco-American identity, either as an individual
achievement or a group project, could only be pursued and developed
in New England.

A controversial group which knew how to make itself heard,
FAROG was the most expressive wing of the new generation, and it
marked the beginning of an ideological diversity within Franco-
American New England. In the seventies, discussions on the status of
Franco-Americans would often include terms like "awakening,"
"renewal," and even "renaissance." And it is true that the Franco
movement, i.e., the collective effort to preserve the heritage, did at
times create the impression of dynamic expansion during this decade,
especially when compared to the two previous ones.

For example, some "young" Francos—under fifty years of
age—rekindled their interest in their ethnic group while some not so
young returned to the group for cultural, psychological, or other
reasons. Less passive than their predecessors, they sensed the need for
action. This explains the birth of a host of projects—associations,
activities, research—which no one could have predicted during the
period of quiet assimilation from 1950 to 1970.

The most convincing argument proving that the 1970-1980 decade
had witnessed a renaissance was the interest shown in genealogy by a

growing number of people. Genealogy became one of the nation's principal hobbies due to the impetus provided by the United States Bicentennial, and it acted as an extraordinary stimulus for pride in one's origins—national, state, municipal, or individual. The first Franco-American genealogical society, called the American- Canadian Genealogical Society (ACGS), was founded in Manchester in 1973 by Roger Lawrence, a professor at Saint Anselm's College, and Mrs. Lucille Caron-Lagassé. Others, such as Richard Fortin and Jean Pellerin, began working with the founders so as to ensure that it would be an active, dynamic, and up-to-date organization. It made rapid progress, thanks to the dedication and efficiency of its founders who established it on a solid base, especially by insisting that it remain open to everyone, which had not always been the case with Franco-American organizations.

While its founders and directors prided themselves on their spirit of openness, they were equally proud of the services they offered, for these enthusiastic and competent volunteers made themselves available to assist neophytes in genealogical research. Before long, they were able to create an impressive documentation center around which they organized workshops and conferences and published a quarterly magazine, *The Genealogist*. For their part, the Acadian population, after founding its own society in Fitchburg, Massachusetts, and affiliating for a time (1979-1985) with the ACGS, has since then been an independent organization with its own publication, *Le Réveil Acadien.* Although it has a French title, *Le Réveil* is written in English for the most part.

To make the same kind of services available to Franco-Americans in southern New England, a young teacher, Henri Leblond, founded the American-French Genealogical Society (AFGS) at the Foyer Club in Pawtucket, Rhode Island, in 1978. Although written in English, the club's magazine, which is still published, has a French title, *Je me souviens.* Like their New Hampshire colleagues, the Rhode Island genealogists, who later moved their headquarters to Woonsocket, devoted themselves to increasing the knowledge and pride of their members in the past of their family and their people. In the past few years, similar organizations have been founded in Maine, Connecticut, and Vermont, and there existed for a time a Federation of Franco-American Genealogical and Historical Societies. (See Appendix III for a list of these societies and their publications.)

Ethnic pride, unmistakably present in the genealogical societies, manifests itself in different ways. Formerly, it had expressed itself at the Saint John the Baptist Day celebrations. As the feast became less popular—though the Union Saint-Jean-Baptiste and the Association Canado-Américaine continued to observe it—it was replaced by a series of summer festivals.

Beginning in 1971, Lowell Francos were amazingly successful in organizing a "Franco-American Week" whose numerous aspects gave rise to articles in the *Lowell Sun* that resulted in Lowell's Franco heritage being better known. This "Week," which takes place in June to coincide with "La Saint-Jean" on June 24th , opens with a solemn mass in one of the "Canadian" churches of the city and includes a number of events: the raising of the Québec flag over City Hall, the laying of a wreath at the Franco-American monument located on City Hall grounds, a *Soirée canadienne* organized by a local group, the *Equipe du Bon Vieux Temps*, and a proclamation of the "Franco-American Person of the Year." In 1986, the "French Heritage Tour," a guided tour of the city's Franco-American sites led by a member of the National Park Service, was added to the program.

Among the popular celebrations that began in the seventies, Lewiston's was one of the most important because of the number of persons who attended. Lasting an entire week, it included a number of activities: outdoor cafés with Franco foods, exhibits of historical interest, films, craft show, etc. Now and then there would also be an evening of Franco-American poetry or a workshop on Franco-American literature. In 1978 a collection of *catalognes* (woven rag rugs), this little-known aspect of Franco-American material culture, piqued the attention of a larger public.

These events, too numerous to be examined in detail, were sometimes organized by an *ad hoc* committee and sometimes by a more permanent multipurpose organization. The goal of the New Hampshire Franco-American Council, for example, established in 1977, was the development of cultural, social, and educational programs. Among its successes were two festivals entitled *"Arts et Artisanat,"* as well as exhibits of the works of two sculptors: Lucien Gosselin, a Franco-American, and Alfred Laliberté, a Quebecer, many of whose works can be found in New England.

In Vermont, the Société des Deux Mondes, founded in 1977 also, can count several successes among its achievements. In 1978, for instance, its Festival of Two Worlds presented a music and dance program in nine cities of Vermont, New Hampshire, and Maine. This festival was unique inasmuch as it drew francophone artists and groups from Missouri, Louisiana, Maine, Vermont, and Québec. In an outstanding souvenir program, Andrew Wallace and Virgil Benoit assembled a collection of cultural notes on several Franco regions of the United States.

While in the past events of this kind were held in a parish hall or on the grounds of a parish church, today's festivals take place in parks and attract citywide, if not regional, attention. In some cases, as in Barre, Vermont, Somersworth, New Hampshire, and Woonsocket, Rhode Island, Francos work with other ethnic groups to organize multiethnic festivals. Although similar in some respects, these events are far from identical: in Western Massachusetts, for example, the festival organized by the neighboring cities of Holyoke, Springfield, and Chicopee included a tribute to Franco-American War Veterans and to the Franco-American parishes.

One of the most valuable aspects of these celebrations has been the publication of souvenir programs, for they have increased the visibility of Franco-Americans. Sometimes these celebrations serve to shed light on events or documents which historians had overlooked. Such was the case in Western Massachusetts in 1984 when Rev. William Pomerleau published a useful brochure, *Chicopee's Franco-Americans: A New Culture in a New World*, and again in 1986 when he inserted in the souvenir program—*French Heritage Days: Holyoke Heritage State Park, June 7 and 8, 1986*—an article on Canadian emigration to Holyoke written by a British observer in 1885. As a final example, the brochure published for the first annual festival held in Old Town, Maine, in 1978, contained an article on popular remedies and culinary recipes from this corner of Franco-America.

These festivals were also opportunities for singers and musicians to become better known. The Lilianne Labbé and Don Hinkley ensemble from Maine, the violinist Omer Marcoux from New Hampshire, and the Beaudoin family from Vermont, are among those whose live performances of folk songs and traditional dances enriched the cultural heritage. Were it not for these festivals, these artists and many others would be less well known.

The 1960-1990 period was marked not only by public celebrations but also by increased interest in local history. Here again one sees the influence of the American Bicentennial at work, since the federal government had officially encouraged projects in this field. Although they are more objective than had been the traditional writers of history, the authors of this period are no less proud; they also clearly seek to project a positive image of the group, while avoiding the eulogistic excesses of the preceding generations of historians. For instance, the history of Augusta, Maine, that Maurice Violette published in 1976, entitled *The Franco-Americans*, contains a great deal of information taken from reliable sources. One episode among many that he relates refers to the difficulties encountered by Canadian immigrants in obtaining priests of their own nationality; but he tells this story in a much less emotional manner than would have been the case with earlier historians.

Other histories of this kind include *Cotton Was King: A History of Lowell, Massachusetts*, published in 1976 under the direction of Arthur L. Eno, Jr., and *Woonsocket: Highlights of History 1800-1976*, by Alton P. Thomas, M.D., a project underwritten in part by the Bicentennial Commission of the City of Woonsocket. These two works are all the more valuable since they situate the evolution of Franco-Americans in the context of a city's development.

Under the rubric of recent publications, three newspapers should be mentioned. *Observations*, a bilingual newspaper of protest, circulated in Lewiston in 1972. It lasted only six months, not long enough according to its supporters and too long a time for its opponents. Also in Lewiston, *L'Unité* was published from 1976 to 1984 while *Le Journal de Lowell*, a monthly founded by Raymond Barrette in 1975, continued to appear until 1995, edited by Albert and Barbara Côté. In Manchester, Marcelle Martel inaugurated a unique approach to French-language journalism by writing a weekly column in French, from 1974 to 1982—called *En bref*—for the influential *Manchester Union Leader*. Julien Olivier later assumed responsibility for this column which lasted until 1995.

Other new approaches to ethnicity from the 1960-1990 period included one that caused a good deal of commotion. It involved the founding of an umbrella organization that hoped to regroup Francos, both individuals and organizations, so as to facilitate communications and work for the betterment of the group. The idea was so well received that two organizations of this kind were established in 1980. One was national: the Association of Franco-Americans (AFA); the other regional: Action for Franco-Americans in the Northeast (ActFANE). Since the Comité de Vie Franco-Américaine envisioned itself as already serving as a liaison organization, the founding of ActFANE was greeted with some opposition and a great deal of skepticism by the traditional societies and their leaders who had been left out of the loop.

The AFA was born on March 30, 1980, during the third Annual Conference of Franco-Americans held in Lafayette, Louisiana. At its very first plenary session, the AFA adopted a resolution to make French, along with English and Spanish, one of the three official languages of the United States. An executive committee, with Armand Chartier as president, was elected at that same session; other positions were filled by persons from Louisiana, the Midwest, and New England. At the practical level, the immediate objectives of the AFA included sponsoring annual conferences, publishing an information bulletin, and recruiting members, both groups and individuals.

The AFA saw itself as a democratic organization that would be open and responsive to anyone who was interested in the future of the group. Its directors did not wish to impose any specific agenda, doctrine, or approach. They thought it preferable at first to use their newsletter and the annual conferences to build an organization for all Francos in the United States so that, in time, the members themselves could determine how best to use it.

From the outset, the AFA also worked to increase Franco visibility on both the national and local levels. This was one way of supporting the efforts being made to preserve and develop Franco culture. The AFA *Newsletter* was a first step in that direction. It published news of the three major Franco regions on individual and group activities, calendars of cultural events, and recent publications. It also published articles on various regional topics, e.g., the Métis and the Cajuns. The newsletter, although bilingual, was written mostly in English, since it was estimated that a very large percentage of the Franco population did not understand French.

It would be tedious to list all the groups that provided the AFA with moral or financial support at the start, but among them were the Société Canadienne-Française du Minnesota, the Canadian Consulate-General in Boston, the Union des Franco-Américains du Connecticut, the Conseil de la Vie Française en Amérique in Québec, the Québec government, and the Council for the Development of French in Louisiana (CODOFIL).

The AFA's president was part of the group that negotiated to obtain a grant from the Québec government for the establishment of a Franco-American permanent secretariat in New England—created in 1981. Meanwhile, following the AFA's participation at the Rencontre Francophone de Québec (1980), its president, Armand Chartier, became a member of the Commission Consultative de la Corporation des Rencontres Francophones de Québec. Finally, the AFA executive committee helped prepare the fourth national Franco-American Conference held in Burlington, Vermont, from October 14 through 18, 1981, whose primary sponsor was the New England Bilingual Education Service Center located at the University of Vermont. Within two years of its creation, the AFA was thus able to find its niche in the francophone structure of America.

Subsequently, the AFA continued to receive support and encouragement from the three major regions in which it was active and even from the large communities of newly-arrived Quebecers living in California and Florida. Its 1983 Congress, held in the historic Mackinac region of Michigan, gave rise to a controversy in the Québec press on the status of Franco-America. Some observers said it was doomed, judging by the relative absence of young people at the congress and the limited use of French during the deliberations. The old controversy regarding the future of the race on American soil was thus brought to the fore once again.

Among the Elders

Within traditional organizations during this period, discussions often revolved around the topics of a "state of crisis," the "new guard," and the "need for renewal." For the *patriote* old guard, life had become increasingly distressing. The most zealous were traumatized by the effects of an assimilation that was occurring at such a speed that few of them really wanted to know the actual numbers. In addition to the indifference of the people, whose Americanization can be viewed as a normal evolutionary development, the elders now had to contend with long-standing problems: the dispersal of their human resources and the lack of cohesion endemic to the group. In 1965, the leadership, gathered in Manchester for the eighth Congress of the Comité de Vie Franco-Américaine, was put on guard against these problems by a sympathetic observer of the Franco-American scene from Québec, Monsignor Paul-Emile Gosselin, permanent secretary of the Conseil de la Vie Française en Amérique. He declared: "We have deplored—and to be quite frank—we continue to deplore the lack of consensus in viewpoints, attitudes, and efforts. There were, and there still are, many reasons for this fragmentation of your human resources, reasons that you know as well as I do for having analyzed them often."

During this agonizing period of reappraisal, militants realized that they were "losing" the young, but they had no clear idea of how to get them back. In this respect, the remarks of Marie-A. LeBlanc, then president of the Fédération Féminine, were both insightful and typical of the analyses offered by the more perceptive observers: "Have we really planned for new leadership, or are we guilty of having kept our ancestral heritage among a select circle, entrusting it to a mere handful of educated people?" And again, referring to the people and especially to young people: "Where can the reasons for this apathy be found?"

The religious question or "problem," as some call it, is inextricably linked to the ethnic problem, i.e., the uncertain future of *la survivance.* For the traditional élite, the religious problem was caused primarily by the Church hierarchy. Despite the great number of Franco-Americans in all of the dioceses of New England—they even constitute the majority of the Catholics in Maine, New Hampshire, and Vermont—and notwithstanding the respectful requests presented over and over again to the Roman authorities, the Church granted only one bishop to the Franco-Americans in the sixties: Ernest J. Primeau, who was named bishop of Manchester in 1960. Even here, some pointed out that the admittedly brilliant and charming Bishop Primeau was a native of the Midwest and so was not as keenly attuned to the local situation as would have been a New Englander. During the 1960-1990 period, the Church would appoint only five Franco-American bishops. In the minds of the élite, this proportion was so blatantly unjust as to be humiliating; but there was no outcry, since no one wanted to revive the searing conflicts of the Sentinelle era.

The religious problem was aggravated by the decision of Vatican II to replace Latin as the liturgical language with the language of each individual country. "How could anyone imagine that in the United States the language of the country could be anything but English?" queried the pastors for whom *la survivance* was no longer even an issue. In most Franco-American parishes, the use of English spread like wildfire since pastors understood that the participation of the young,

who spoke only English, was essential for the parish's future and that
the loyalty of the elders was assured, despite their displeasure.

Adding to the despair of the *patriotes*, the fraternal or mutual
benefit societies, organizations which in the past could always be
counted upon in the struggle for *la survivance,* were also undergoing
changes, becoming more anglicized and initiating fewer patriotic
activities. To an outside observer, the extension of the use of English
would only have seemed normal and indeed would become more
prevalent since their economic survival depended on it. The newly
elected leaders did not feel quite as obligated to pursue the work of *la
survivance*. They believed that a fraternal benefit society, when
compared to other kinds of insurance companies, has certain
advantages that should be exploited, beginning with its preferential tax
status. To expand their markets, the new directors of these societies
amended their charters which up to then had required that their
policyholders be Catholics of French or French-Canadian descent.

In a word, the fraternal benefit societies were reorganizing,
operating more and more like insurance companies; but in order to
protect their special status, they continued, nonetheless, to contribute
to certain causes. However, with the decreasing interest in cultural
activities that were solely French in character, they began, at the urging
of their membership, to gravitate toward social programs whose impact
was not limited to Franco-Americans. As of 1977, for example, the
USJB developed a special catechetical program for the handicapped.
However, the more "Canadian" oriented ACA made home-office space
available to the American-Canadian Genealogical Society and to
Action for Franco-Americans of the Northeast (ActFANE).

The reactions of the elders to the progressive retreat of the parishes
and the fraternal benefit societies from the front lines of *la survivance*
ranged from outright opposition to quiet resignation. The more

implacable, like Wilfrid Beaulieu, Antoine Clément, and Monsignor Adrien Verrette, used the few remaining newspapers and newsletters to denounce and to plead, pouring out opinions and advice even as they sensed the impending victory of the "powers of the night." Resignation, in their opinion, was a defeatist attitude. These aging *patriotes* knew they were making a last-ditch effort, but it hardly mattered to them. They glorified what they called the "virtue of continuity," and the Comité de Vie Franco-Américaine issued as its watchword in 1964: "Preserve what we have left."

Virtues and watchwords of this kind held little appeal either for the people or for the young in search of something new. In their insistence on the duty to remain faithful to the heritage, the elders invoked reasons that no longer motivated the young, only serving to widen still further the gap between the generations. For the elders, *la survivance* had become an obsession: they desperately wanted to bequeath their heritage to a generation of people who would have none of it, convinced as they were that they did not need it. Wittingly or unwittingly, because of their allegiance to the French language, the elders deprived themselves of that "new guard" that they had talked about for decades. For them, the language was such an integral part of the heritage that without it, the heritage was no longer recognizable. In choosing to remain loyal to French, these elders were convinced that they were fulfilling to the very end a duty that they considered sacred. That the young would refuse French seemed to them incomprehensible and unacceptable. Although some had difficulty recognizing themselves in their own children, they remained adamant.

While maintaining its tradition of holding its congresses in French, the Fédération Féminine Franco-Américaine inaugurated a series of annual youth festivals in 1977 that attracted between fifty and one hundred adolescents each year. The "Fédé" wanted these young people to see themselves as part of a living culture, and it explored every possible avenue to reach its goal: music, discussions, films, cooking, and other resources, including the city of Lowell itself, where the festival took place in 1979. Lowell had been declared a National Historic Park, the first *urban* area in the country to be so designated. In 1980, the "Fédé" managed, with the help of the Québec Delegation in Boston, to hold its youth festival in Québec City.

For traditional organizations, however, the congress was still the best way of coming together to reaffirm one's solidarity and to renew one's enthusiasm for "the cause." This type of patriotic or cultural convention was a custom so ingrained that it had taken on the importance of a quasi-ritual, highly prized by the older generation. For these soul mates, united in a common cause but separated by distance, the congress was a necessity, not a luxury. This was stated very clearly in 1977 by Claire Quintal, then president of the Fédération Féminine Franco-Américaine:

> The very fact that we have come together to participate in a common activity creates in us the possibility of doing even more and of doing it better. It also allows us to renew the ties that must bind us if we wish to extend the range of our activities and create an even larger closely linked network of women standing symbolically shoulder to shoulder throughout New England.

As these large assemblies became less frequent, they became all the more valuable for those who had not ceased their work in favor of *la survivance*. The congress represented a rare opportunity for them to express yet one more time their pride in the achievements of the Franco-American community. They enjoyed calling to mind the memory of the early movers and shakers and the economic strength of the institutions which they had founded, especially the fraternal benefit societies and the credit unions. They deplored the fact that French was being used less and less but consoled themselves with the thought that it was still the language of culture which, for the persons of this generation, was vastly superior to commerce. In their view, French was destined to remain the language of an élite. The older *patriotes* would always hold fast to this belief.

Nor would they abandon the tradition whereby a congress always ended with the adoption of a large number of resolutions. While they might deplore the fact that these resolutions produced almost no results, this did not prevent them from drafting new ones—or from repeating old ones—at the next congress. Not only would it be too facile, it would also be wrong to view this mass of resolutions as mere rhetorical excess; more correctly, they should be seen as reflecting the aspirations, the fervor, the cry of the heart of a generation which had remained loyal to its ideal until the very end and who had tried everything—or nearly everything—so that this ideal would live on after them.

In 1976, a small group found an outlet for its fervor by organizing the francophone participation in the 41st International Eucharistic Congress in Philadelphia. Among those who played a key role in the project were Louis Israël Martel and Gérald Robert of Manchester, Gabriel Crevier and Edgar Martel of Woonsocket, all well-known in Franco-America for their defense of traditional values.

Standing alone to all outward appearances, Wilfrid Beaulieu in fact could count on the support of a small number of staunch *patriotes* to the very end. He, more than most, demonstrated a heroic—some termed it quixotic—perseverance. As *la survivance* continued to lose ground in New England, Beaulieu devoted more and more space in *Le Travailleur* to French-speaking communities around the world and especially to Québec's increasing self-affirmation. *Le Travailleur* thus became the most Québec-oriented of the Franco newspapers of its day as Beaulieu, an ardent supporter of Québec independence, became its indomitable propagandist.

It would be unfair to say that this older generation attempted no creative response to the requirements of a rapidly evolving world. It is useful to recall that during the forties, the principal attempt at renewal had been the creation of the Comité de Vie Franco-Américaine (1947). During the fifties and sixties, the Richelieu International gained a foothold in New England, and each of the New England States established Cultural Commissions to promote exchanges of a cultural nature with French Canada.

Founded in Ottawa in 1944, the Richelieu International is a network of affiliated social clubs known as service organizations. It is the only one of its kind to use the French language and to have a Christian focus. The goal of these clubs, whose motto is "Peace and Brotherhood," is the "total fulfillment of the personality of its members through human relationships," and their humanitarian efforts are undertaken for the benefit of needy children. Their meetings, normally bimonthly, include a business session and a talk.

Franco-American professionals and businessmen, *patriotes* or not, have found the basic principles and method of operation of the Richelieu Club to be to their liking. In addition to providing them with the opportunity to fraternize on a regular basis and contribute to a worthy cause, the Richelieu Club encourages the development of the personality in a social setting which is beyond reproach. Moreover, for Francos who spend their professional lives speaking only English, Richelieu Club meetings offer a rare and valuable challenge, since they are conducted entirely in French. Any member using an English word is subject to a fine, payable on the spot and is beyond appeal. Monies collected in this manner are donated to sick and needy children.

New England's first Richelieu Club was established in 1955 in Manchester under the presidency of Attorney Gérard O. Bergevin. The movement spread, and by 1960, Fall River, Holyoke, and New

Bedford, Massachusetts, as well as Lewiston, Maine, each had its own Richelieu Club. Before long, there were some fifteen clubs in the United States, including one in Hollywood, Florida. There were also Richelieu Clubs for women in Woonsocket, Rhode Island, and Salem, Massachusetts.

The founding of the Manchester group was a key factor in the movement's expansion. Louis Israël Martel, a union official and a politician, was instrumental in the founding of several Richelieu Clubs in the United States and, as international president in 1971, he presented charters to a number of clubs in Canada, the United States, and France—Paris, Rennes, Caen, and Toulouse.

But moments of glory and publicity are brief when compared to the long hours of hidden and thankless toil. Very quietly, Richelieu Club members donate their time and money to help needy children: they organize picnics for orphans, run raffles, launch special fund-raising campaigns, etc. From 1957 to 1980, the Manchester Richelieu Club alone raised over $45,000 in donations.

This spirit of giving is nurtured by a program of social and cultural activities organized around each club's bimonthly meeting. As a rule, neither absenteeism nor passivity are tolerated, and group pressure is brought to bear on each member to attend every meeting and to participate without grumbling in the work of the various "teams" (committees). In any case, the bimonthly meeting is not really a burden; the atmosphere is one of good-natured friendship accompanied by a great deal of humor and gaiety. A typical dinner meeting is punctuated with roars of laughter, teasing, and fines (collected by the person appointed as "the Cardinal" for the evening). Traditional French-Canadian songs, collected in the Richelieu songbook, add life to the gathering and are sung prior to the business meeting which is followed by the talk of an invited guest. The talk can be on any topic, and speakers come from France, Canada, or from a neighboring city.

"Interclub" visits are also part of the sociocultural program; they foster enthusiasm and pride, as do visits by national officers and regional administrators. The anniversary of a club's foundation or the granting of a charter to a new one are occasions for gala evening programs.

In September 1960, the first international congress of the Société Richelieu, held in Manchester—with more than 1600 delegates in attendance—generated an enormous amount of favorable publicity, even in the English-language press. At the banquet, a brilliant address was given by Philippe Armand Lajoie, the "dean of Franco-American journalists." He praised the Richelieu Society, calling it "an élite phalanx [that] rekindles hope in those who desire that—whatever happens—there will always be an élite in New England to maintain a French presence." The speaker drew attention to the fact that the Richelieu Clubs have helped to "preserve the songs and sentimental ballads that delighted our great forebears." And he concluded by quoting from "an unpublished song for male choir," the author of which may very well have been Lajoie himself, a well-known composer and author in his own right:

> Tant que nos voix pourront redire la romance
> Et le joyeux couplet de Québec ou de France,
> Burinés sur nos coeurs, ces mots: "Je me souviens!"
> Font de nous à jamais des fils de Canadiens!

> As long as our voices can echo the romance
> And sing the joyful couplets of Québec or of France
> In our hearts are etched the words "I remember!"
> That make us the sons of Canadians forever!

Abbé Adrien Verrette offered the delegates further encouragement in his sermon in which he praised their "apostolate" and, specifically, the work of the Richelieu Clubs in the field of "social charity." Writing in *Le Travailleur*, Wilfrid Beaulieu, in turn, praised this new method for strengthening the bonds between Franco-Americans and French Canadians.

At a different level, Father Thomas M. Landry, pastor of Saint Anne parish in Fall River, devised the idea of establishing an American and Canadian French Cultural Exchange Commission in the Commonwealth of Massachusetts. He drafted a bill and recruited the necessary sponsors to ensure its passage by the Massachusetts legislature. Constituted in 1968, the Commission was given the mandate of developing cultural ties between French Canadians and Franco-Americans, stimulating interest in the history and culture of both groups as well as in the economic, political, social, and artistic life of Canada and the United States in addition to promoting French-language programs in the schools of Massachusetts. Following Father Landry's lead, Franco-Americans in the other five New England States succeeded in gaining approval from their respective legislatures for similar commissions.

Functioning both as a lobby and as public relations agencies, these Commissions sought at first to make the citizens of their respective States better aware of "the Franco-American presence" in each of them. Although they were pursuing the same goals as many other groups, their activities took on an official character since they had the backing of the State government and access to public funds to underwrite projects. Thus, in their 1969-1970 report, the members of the Massachusetts Cultural Exchange Commission highlighted the "early and heroic presence" of the French in Massachusetts, one that could be traced as far back as Samuel de Champlain's exploration of the New England coastline as far south as Cape Cod, and they included an inventory of Franco-American resources in the State (in the social, cultural, and educational fields) along with a description of their mandated activities. They also advanced some ideas that would be echoed by various other ethnic groups all over the United States as more and more national minorities asserted their own claims to fame and respect. The following statement would come to be seen as particularly prophetic: "A good government must be a representative government, and that representation must be a reflection, not only of political parties, but of ethnic groups as well."

Despite their similarities, these commissions were not alike. Each one developed according to the priorities set by its members and according to the changing political scene. Established in 1974, the American and Francophone Cultural Commission of Connecticut declared itself open to all French-speaking countries and regions rather than just to French Canada. In its inventory of State resources, this Commission estimated that there were some 300,000 Franco-Americans living in Connecticut, and this heretofore little-known fact was subsequently used to justify a request for funds.

These Commissions were active in many fields, all the more so because each one of them defined the term "cultural" as it pleased since it was within its right to do so. One of the important proposals backed by the Massachusetts Commission was the establishment of a program of Canadian studies at North Adams State College in far western Massachusetts. The New Hampshire Commission sponsored performances of Canadian music and theater—Montréal's Théâtre des Pissenlits, the Orphéon of Trois-Rivières, etc.—and the Commission also supported projects which, due to a lack of funds, it could not undertake on its own.

Valuable services were rendered by these Commissions, to the Franco-American community, but also to all of the New England State governments. For example, at the time of the Bicentennial, they guaranteed that Franco-Americans would officially take part in the many projects and ceremonies that honored French and French-Canadian contributions to the country's development. In 1974, the commissions created the Central Committee of Francophone Cultural Commissions in New England so that the different commissions could more easily exchange information, coordinate their activities, and more effectively lobby the federal government on behalf of the continuation of bilingual education programs.

Depending on the initiative of their members and the availability of funds, these Commissions would be more or less active between 1970 and 1990. Despite their official mandate, the commissioners were often forced to contribute their own funds to ensure the success of one project or another. In fact, had it not been for the generosity of its members, all of whom served without remuneration, some of the Commissions would have remained inactive due to lack of funding from the States. In such circumstances, it is not surprising that these organizations were not as productive as they might otherwise have been.

The Presence of Québec

While both France and Canada maintained a more than symbolic presence among Franco-Americans during the 1960-1990 period, Québec was more active, although it was only in the late seventies that it would expand the scope of its activities.

The loosening of the bonds between Franco-Americans and Quebecers that could be observed as early as the Second World War had by the sixties reached such a low point that only a small minority of Franco-Americans were familiar with Québec's Quiet Revolution, while its economic expansion and its growing independence movement were followed by very few of them. Most of those who did so condemned the anticlericalism of the separatists and their "revolutionary ideas." But a minority—journalists, academics, and members of the liberal professions—waxed enthusiastic over what was happening there, inspired by the intense intellectual and cultural ferment and productivity that characterized Québec in the sixties and seventies. They admired "radical" social critics such as Frère Untel (pseudonym of Jean-Paul Desbiens) and Pierre Vallières; after 1976, René Lévesque—the first Québec Premier who favored independence—would also attract a following among Franco-Americans.

At the organizational level, it was the Conseil de la Vie Française en Amérique that best preserved its ties with Franco-Americans. Faithful to its mission, it carefully monitored the evolution of French-speaking groups on the continent, and it remained in contact with the Comité de Vie Franco-Américaine. Five Franco-Americans served as members of the Conseil. At the governmental level, the creation of an agency within the Québec Ministry of Cultural Affairs on behalf of Francophones living outside Canada rekindled the hope of some *patriotes* for assistance with the dwindling *survivance* effort. These hopes were partially fulfilled with the opening in 1969 of a Québec Government Bureau in Boston whose goal was the promotion of the economic and cultural interests of Québec in New England. Its first bureau chief, Jean-Maurice Tremblay, did his utmost to identify possible areas of collaboration. Working with a committee of Franco-Americans headed by the dynamic Paul Blanchette of Lowell, the Québec Bureau succeeded in extending the services of Québec cablevision into the northern part of the region. Despite its modest beginnings, ten years later the network had been made available to over 300,000 homes in New England and in New York State.

In July 1978, Québec began to host a series of annual *Rencontres* (encounters) to which Franco-Americans were invited. The participants were particularly pleased with the spirit that characterized the first meeting: the Québec government had invited spokespersons from all the francophone regions on the continent, not to lecture to them, but to listen to them speak about their problems and their hopes. Hence, the general theme: "Francophone America Speaks to Quebecers" and the sub-theme: "How to Live as a French-Speaking Person in America." This *Rencontre*, the first event of its kind since the Third Congress of the French Language in 1952, successfully combined the joys of celebrating the return to one's roots with the requirements of various study sessions.

New England Franco-Americans were able to observe firsthand the similarities between their situation and that of the French Canadians living outside of Québec, as well as that of Louisiana's Acadian population. Assimilation of the young into the anglophone culture was depriving these three groups of the next generation while the geographical isolation of francophone communities one from the other was threatening the future of French culture and language. The urgent need to establish permanent ties with Québec was obvious to any objective observer.

It was at this 1978 *Rencontre* that Wilfrid Beaulieu, the last great Franco-American journalist, voiced his belief in the need for Québec's independence: "Not only do I not fear a sovereign Québec, my heart rejoices at the prospect." In his opinion, francophone minorities outside Québec would be in a better position to sustain themselves if they could count on a strong Québec, one that could come to their assistance. Another Franco-American, Manchester's Louis Israël Martel, was inducted into the Ordre des francophones d'Amérique, in recognition of the "outstanding nature of his participation in French life in America." Nevertheless, other Franco-Americans would return from that meeting disappointed in not having been offered a valid argument for living in French in an anglophone milieu—the only argument that could persuade young people to resist assimilation.

The 1980 *Rencontre*, entitled *"Questionnement '80,"* committed itself to an overview of the current situation in francophone communities throughout the world. From the Franco-American point of view, this meeting remains memorable for two reasons: first, because of the language difficulties experienced by the young Francos who had been invited to participate. Apparently, in spite of attempts on the part of the organizers to invite only fluent French speakers, these students were unable to communicate with their counterparts from Ontario, Western Canada, or the Maritimes. Some young Canadians protested, objecting to the presence of "English speakers" at a meeting of Francophones. It was a painful moment for both sides, revealing as it did that in becoming an officially unilingual francophone state, Québec had erected a barrier between itself and the great-grandchildren of its 1880 emigrants.

But the aftermath of the 1980 *Rencontre* continued to be felt among Franco-Americans for yet another reason. Having been inducted into the Ordre des Francophones d'Amérique, Claire Quintal, a well-known academic and president of the Fédération Féminine Franco-Américaine, presented a masterly paper entitled, "Le Québec et les Franco-Américains: les limites d'une certaine présence après une si longue absence" (Québec and the Franco-Americans: The Limitations of a Certain Type of Presence After Such a Long Absence). During her presentation, she brought up the rather delicate question: do Franco-Americans and Quebecers really need one another? Answering her own query, she stated: "I truly believe that we need you more than you need us. It must be said clearly and without ambiguity that Québec's presence is absolutely necessary if Franco-American culture is to survive." This declaration provoked an outcry, especially from the

Franco-American Resource and Opportunity Group (FAROG) and its supporters. In their view, this was a humiliating position, one that reduced Franco-Americans to the level of cultural beggars. Worse yet, it threatened to make Franco-America a cultural colony of Québec. According to them, complete parity existed between Quebecers and Francos, and what Franco-Americans offered Québec in terms of friendship, publicity, and cultural artifacts was in no way inferior to what Québec could offer in return.

In 1981 Franco-American participation in the planning for the Rencontres Francophones de Québec was institutionalized through the creation of the Commission Consultative de la Corporation des Rencontres Francophones; its membership included five Francos and five French Canadians from the Maritimes, Ontario, and Western Canada.

Franco-Americans played an active role in the various workshops at the 1981 *Rencontre*, working with Quebecers and francophones outside Québec to maintain what the director of the meetings, the playwright Marcel Dubé, called "a tradition of exchanges, friendship and understanding among francophone cultural communities, for their respective development through a rapprochement that has become increasingly necessary." At sessions devoted to the planning of subsequent meetings, it soon became obvious that the major preoccupations of both the Quebecers and the other French Canadians were the same as those targeted by the Franco-Americans: youth, businessmen, and creative artists. The 1981 *Rencontre* also benefited older Francos with the founding of the Association Internationale Francophone des Aînés (International Association of Francophone Senior Citizens). After 1981, only a relatively small number of Francos would participate in the *Rencontres*, and their participation depended on the topic for that particular year: Youth, The Information Age, Senior Citizens, etc.

In October of 1981, so as to encourage contacts and exchanges from one Rencontre to the next, the Québec government established the Secrétariat Permanent des Peuples Francophones (SPPF). Here is how the then Premier of Québec, René Lévesque, described the agency: "This center will be here to assist you in the preparation of your annual meetings and henceforth will serve at all times as the setting for meetings of study groups, for colloquia, as a site for exhibits, and a clearinghouse for all the information that can be collected, accumulated, and circulated that is of interest to all French-speaking peoples."

The SPPF, located in Québec's Old City, showed its determination to fulfill that role right from the start: immediately following the inaugural ceremonies of October 28, 1981, at which the Premier himself presided, there was a meeting of the SPPF's consultative commission for program planning. The commission included representatives from the Association of Franco-Americans, the Action for Franco-Americans of the Northeast, the Council for the Development of French in Louisiana, the American Midwest, the Québec-California Association, and delegates from several French-Canadian organizations. Its mandate was to present "opinions and helpful recommendations" regarding the content of the annual *Rencontres* and the activities of the new secretariat whose aim was to reflect the sociocultural life of French-speaking peoples throughout the world and especially in North America. For the first time in many years, Franco-Americans had a voice—albeit a modest one—in an agency of the Québec government.

Programs devoted to Franco-Americans and sponsored by the SPPF included the following: an exhibit entitled "Ulric Bourgeois 1874-1963—A Photographer of Québec and New England" (November 1981); a special issue of the magazine OVO on the emigration of Quebecers to New England (May 1982); a new recording of songs by

Josée Vachon entitled "Josée" (September 1983); the founding of the Jack Kerouac Club (1984); and a performance starring Maine artists Lilianne Labbé and Don Hinkley (August 1984). Representatives of the SPPF also attended major Franco-American gatherings throughout the United States.

In April 1980, the Québec government intervened in a decisive manner in Franco-American life: the Ministry of Intergovernmental Affairs invited twelve activists to Québec to review the current status of Franco-America and devise a joint plan of action in the area of cultural cooperation.

"The Twelve," representing the six New England states and active in various professions, especially education, met in Québec to draw up a list of the most pressing objectives. They agreed that their overall goal should take the form of a concerted effort to heighten their compatriots' sense of belonging to Franco-America. They also reached consensus on a first step to be taken: the creation of an umbrella organization that would serve the dual role of *liaison* among the various Franco groups dispersed throughout the region and *negotiator* with the government of Québec in the name of all Francos. To ensure that there would be a follow-up to the Québec meeting, the twelve then constituted themselves as a provisional committee.

Together with the Ministry of Intergovernmental Affairs and its Boston delegation, it was decided that the organization would function as a federation: it would regroup Franco-Americans and their associations and coordinate their efforts at sociocultural development. Its structure would be that of a nonprofit corporation managed by an executive committee and a board of directors whose members would represent the six New England States and the State of New York. It would also be responsible for ensuring that the rights of Francos would be recognized by all participating governments: those of each State in the Northeast, the United States federal government, and the governments of France, Canada, and Québec.

Even prior to its establishment, the projected organization gave rise to varied reactions from within the Franco-American community. Some saw it as redundant in light of the plethora of already existing organizations; others saw only a ploy by the Québec government to extend its political influence and promote its campaign for independence in northeastern United States. These erroneous impressions need to be rectified. This is all the easier since the author of this work himself, as president of the nation-wide Association of Franco-Americans, along with Attorney Robert Couturier of Lewiston, a member of the Conseil de la Vie Française en Amérique, and Normand Dubé, director of National Materials Development Center in Bedford, New Hampshire—all three members of the provisional committee—participated in a series of ministerial meetings held in Québec in December 1980 and January 1981. The purpose of these sessions was to guarantee the cooperation of various government ministries and to explore the feasibility of certain areas of collaboration. During the course of these meetings, many issues were addressed, but none of them related to politics.

The topics broached during these discussions are indicative of the concerns which were shared by both parties and would often be raised again in the future. They included such items as: the preservation of the Franco-American cultural heritage—an offshoot of Québec's patrimony—the training of leaders of social organizations, the cooperation needed between institutions and organizations to promote additional research on the Francos, the distribution of Québec cultural products in the northeastern United States, the loan of staff with technical expertise in areas such as leisure activities, the broadcasting, via cable and satellite, of Québec educational television, and the planning of meetings and exchanges for business people, youth, and teachers. Though not exhaustive, this list clearly indicates that the parties spent a great deal of time on cultural cooperation and none whatsoever on politics.

This series of meetings on both sides of the border culminated in the opening, in July 1981, of the secretariat of Action pour les Franco-Américains du Nord-Est (ActFANE). Located in Manchester, the agency's executive secretary was Paul Paré, at that time a young journalist and advertising man from Lewiston, Maine. Underwritten by the Québec government on condition that it represent *all* Franco-Americans in the region, the new organization was launched through a series of meetings held by its executive secretary who visited the principal Franco-American centers. He used these visits to draw up an inventory of local resources so as to be able to reply to requests for information that began to arrive from everywhere, all the while preparing the publication of a catalog of Franco-American resources, since the last inventory of this kind dated back to 1946.

Subsequently, ActFANE sought in every way possible to increase the visibility of Francos and improve communication among them. One of its major accomplishments was the twelfth Franco-American Congress. Called "Rendez-vous '83," it was held from May 27 to 29 of that year. ActFANE planned these meetings jointly with the Comité de Vie Franco-Américaine, whose previous congress had been held in 1974, and in conjunction with a number of other organizations. It was the first "major" congress—two to three hundred people attended—that was bilingual, with discussions held in either French or English depending on the speaker. The program also embodied the pragmatic approach of the organizers: there were workshops and round-table discussions on topics such as the press, public celebrations, and the leadership role that universities and libraries could play in community activities. These discussions all focused on recent activities, representative of Franco-American life in the eighties.

This 1983 Congress included other signs of the times. For example, there was a seminar on "Planning and Managing Change," according to the methods advocated by the system known as "Facilitative Management." Organized by the Center for Constructive Change of Durham, New Hampshire, this seminar explored ways in which organizations could increase their effectiveness and foster dynamic leadership. Some saw this as the introduction of technology—if not technocracy—into ethnic life.

As the last of the major regional gatherings held to date, this Congress echoed two themes which had become traditional in the life of the group: the need to adapt to the American context without sacrificing one's Franco-American culture, as well as the importance for the group to overcome its passivity and collective self-doubt and finally assert itself as a group. Because some were of the opinion that politics and ethnicity should remain separate, no consensus was reached with respect to political action. The keynote speaker, Jeannine Séguin, president of the Fédération des Francophones Hors (outside) Québec, stressed the fact that minorities would always need to struggle to preserve their heritage and that it was essential for a minority to break out of its isolation and gain recognition as a cultural and political force. Despite the small number of young people in attendance, the fact that the congress was even held was, in the view of the optimists, the sign of a Franco-American resurgence. As if to confirm this viewpoint, the organizers had included in the program the launching of five new publications on the Franco-American experience and an exhibit of Franco-American artists—proof, according to some, of the group's cultural vitality.

Since its founding, ActFANE has served the Franco-American community in several ways. In its role as catalyst, information center, and support organization, it was free to involve itself in any area involving Franco-America, and this it did not hesitate to do. For example, it brought the directors of Franco-American festivals together at its Festival Conference in November 1984. In conjunction with the Canadian Consulate in Boston and the Québec Delegation in New England, it created a scholarship program enabling Franco-American students to study at the University of Ottawa. Its newsletter, *InformAction*, helped spread news of general interest, and, at times, it revealed little-known aspects of the Franco experience, for instance, information on the credit unions. Finally, through its affiliations with the Association of Franco-Americans, the Consultative Commission to the SPPF, and the Conseil de la Vie Française en Amérique, ActFANE guaranteed the preservation of living links with francophone communities outside of the Northeast, all the while contributing to the development of Franco-American awareness at the regional level. Starting with the second Summit Conference of Heads of States using French as an official language, that was held in Québec in 1987, ActFANE coordinated the attendance of a Franco-American delegation at subsequent summits: Dakar, Senegal, in 1989; Paris, in 1991; and Mauritius, in 1993.

A more detailed study of Québec-Franco-American relations would reveal the many ways in which Québec was present in the lives of Franco-Americans between 1960 and 1990. Compared to that of previous periods, it was obviously a reduced presence; nevertheless, it has been more than just symbolic or ceremonial. In addition to the aspects which have already been discussed, one could also study the presence of Québec in the intellectual life of Francos as manifested, for instance, through the activities—colloquia, publications, and exchanges—of the French Institute of Assumption College in Worcester or again in the Québec books and periodicals which circulate among Francos. To complete the picture, one would also have to consider Québec's cultural presence through its artists and folk groups who have performed at various gatherings—festivals, congresses, and colloquia.

Literary Output

During the sixties, elder *patriotes* continued to fight for the cause to which they had devoted their lives. Adolphe Robert, for example, made important contributions to the literature of *la survivance* during the last years of his very full life. Having served as president-general of the Association Canado-Américaine from 1936 to 1956, he was responsible for transforming the organization's bulletin, *Le Canado-Américain,* into a magazine in 1958. Under his guidance as editor until 1966, the year of his death, this periodical, while continuing to feature news of the ACA, became a publication which went beyond this narrow framework. Aided by his many collaborators, Adolphe Robert turned the *Canado-Américain* into a publication of permanent literary and historical value.

Adolphe Robert also published his own best essays in *Souvenirs et portraits* (1965), a valuable personal account of a bygone era. The vignettes and sketches in *Souvenirs et portraits* recall the author's emigration in 1906 and his integration into American life under the banner of *la survivance.* The basic tenets of this ideology are set forth by Father Thomas M. Landry in his book, *Mission catholique et française en Nouvelle-Angleterre,* published in 1962. The book summarizes the essential points of a Canadian ideology adapted to an American context and proposes a course of action for Franco-Americans. Both of these volumes, because of their content as well as their style, seem destined to become classics, not only of *survivance* writings, but of Franco-American literature in its entirety.

Survivance authors can be found in large numbers in the pages of the *Bulletin de la Société Historique Franco-Américaine* which Monsignor Adrien Verrette edited until 1973. The *Bulletin* was replete with articles meant to instill ethnic pride and honor the memory of the group's forebears. From 1960 to 1973, against all odds and aware of the diminishing number of their supporters, they continued, nonetheless, to devote themselves to this labor of filial love, convinced of the sacred nature of their cause. This *Bulletin*, revived by Oda Beaulieu, widow of Wilfrid Beaulieu, began the publication of a different series in 1983 which has continued in an intermittent fashion to this day.

The preponderance of articles on Québec published by Wilfrid Beaulieu in *Le Travailleur* from 1960 to its final issue in 1978 can be explained by the contrast between Québec's rising vitality and the decline of Franco-America. Prior to the referendum of 1980, many believed that Québec was on the road to independence, a prospect that delighted Beaulieu who supported it. Perhaps more of a Quebecer than a Franco-American in his later years—though born in Lowell, Beaulieu was raised and educated in Québec—he continued to serve his ancestral country not only through his extensive coverage of current events such as those of October 1970—when federal troops were sent into Québec to round up all persons suspected of sympathizing with the FLQ (Front de Libération du Québec), responsible for acts of terrorism and kidnapping—and the coming to power of the Parti québécois in 1976, but also by recalling the group's tragic history in the nineteenth century: the ill-fated Rebellions of 1837-1838 and the Métis Louis Riel's execution in 1885 by the Canadian government.

Despite its preoccupation with Québec, *Le Travailleur* continued its reporting on Franco life. Father Thomas Landry, among others, offered further reflections on both the present and the future of Franco-America, as did some younger analysts, including professors Paul Chassé and Claire Quintal. Beaulieu himself continued faithfully to promote Franco-American literature. But one of the paper's main contributions to the group experience of the period was the mutual rediscovery of Francos in New England and those in the Midwest. This reunion was the result of articles written by a new correspondent from

Chicago, Marie-Reine Mikesell, who provided *Le Travailleur* with well-researched studies on the French and French-Canadian contributions to the development of the American West. Her writings would be instrumental in the founding of a nationwide association of Franco-Americans in the eighties.

The role played by the *Bulletin de la Fédération Féminine Franco-Américaine* also needs, in all fairness, to be recognized. In it can be found a considerable number of articles on the condition of Franco-America. The aspirations and setbacks of Francos were described and commented upon in editorials by the most committed of the "Fédé" directors: Alice Lemieux-Lévesque, Marie LeBlanc, Marthe Biron-Péloquin, and especially, the essayist Claire Quintal. A militant on behalf of *la survivance*, the latter offers a wealth of penetrating insights. A keen and gifted observer, adept at analyzing and explaining the Franco-American soul in a clear, rich, spirited, even impasssioned French, she is recognized as one of the best Franco-American writers of her era.

The FAROG *Forum*, published at the University of Maine at Orono since 1973, is in fact an anti-*survivance* publication. Polemical articles abound in this cocky and anti-authoritarian newspaper. Since it also contains poems, excerpts from novels, and texts of all kinds, it also provides historians of Franco-American literature with an abundance of material.

This same period witnessed the continuing development of a modest corpus of scholarly works on the Franco experience. History and sociology were the disciplines of choice, but literary studies also appeared. In 1968 Paul Chassé defended a doctoral thesis at Laval University on "Les Poètes Franco-Américains de la Nouvelle-Angleterre, 1875-1925." In this voluminous and well-documented study, the author covers the principal poets of the emigration, from

Anna-Marie Duval-Thibault to Philippe Sainte-Marie. Chassé provides biographical information on each of them and identifies their major themes which he situates within the overall context of the poet's work. He demonstrates in a convincing fashion the extent to which these poets, despite an exile that was both voluntary and, for most of them, permanent, had remained rooted in Québec. In 1976, Chassé published an *Anthologie de la poésie franco-américaine de la Nouvelle-Angleterre*. In 1973, the French-language Franco-American novel was the subject of an impressive dissertation written by Richard Santerre at Boston College. Santerre subsequently prepared the nine-volume *Anthologie de la Littérature Franco-Américaine,* published by the NMDC and a history of Lowell's St. Jean Baptiste parish which contains valuable information on the Franco-Americans of that city.

Between 1960 and 1990, Franco-American literature became better known both in Canada and the United States. For American academics, Franco-American works formed as much a part of the literature of the United States as those of any other minority group. In Canada, with the growing recognition of the important role that emigration had played in the history of Québec and Acadia, Franco-American literature was perceived both as one of the many North American francophone literatures, along with those of Louisiana, Western Canada, Ontario, etc., and sometimes as forming part of the "Diaspora Literature" of Québec or Acadia. This salvage operation to recover what might otherwise have been lost inspired research groups on both sides of the border and conferred on Franco-American literature its widest recognition to date. The editors of *Ethnic Perspectives in American Literature*, published in New York under the auspices of the prestigious Modern Language Association and containing a dozen overviews of American minority literatures, devoted a chapter to Franco-American literature in New England. Similarly, the directors of the *Dictionnaire des oeuvres littéraires du Québec* included some twenty articles on Franco works. An increasing number of American and Canadian scholarly journals began to give these works the attention they deserve.

While the passion for history, so typical of the preceding generations, may have waned between 1960 and 1990, the field remained an active one with an important difference: for the most part, the historical writings of this period made no attempt to proselytize as had those of an earlier period. History was no longer being used as a weapon.

The more neutral tone of what might be called "the new history" characterized the period's most important historical study, *The French-Canadian Heritage in New England,* published by Professor Gerard Brault in 1986. It was the most complete historical overview since Robert Rumilly's *Histoire des Franco-Américains* (1958). Brault's solidly documented study, written at a serious level for the general reader, reveals the author's deep affection for his ethnic group, but it is entirely free of *survivance* propaganda. Gerard Brault informs, but he does not attempt to convert, and his unbiased judgment is reflected throughout this study.

In fields like ethnology, oral history, and genealogy, the historiography of the years 1960-1990 is more extensive than was that of preceding periods. Here again, the influence of the National Materials Development Center was decisive, especially through the writings of Julien Olivier. Author of *D'la boucane: une introduction au folklore franco-américain de la Nouvelle-Angleterre*, Olivier also published transcripts from oral history—his conversations with the hundred-year-old Jim Caron, with violinist and sculptor Omer Marcoux, and with Maine fisherman Jim Côté. He also published *Souches et racines: une introduction à la généalogie pour les jeunes Franco-Américains*, which is both a manual and a series of personal accounts on various aspects of ethnicity and family history.

While Olivier's works, designed for use in bilingual schools, had a pedagogical dimension, those of Brigitte Lane were read mainly by academics. Her most important work was a masterly and comprehensive doctoral thesis, *Franco-American Folk Traditions and Popular Culture in a Former Milltown: Aspects of Ethnic Urban Folklore and the Dynamics of Folklore Change in Lowell, Massachusetts*, which she defended at Harvard University in 1983. In some 600 pages, she offers the reader a vividly rich tableau of Franco Lowell's folklore, carefully avoiding pure abstraction and unfounded interpretation. One of the principal merits of the work is the great number of examples and firsthand accounts it contains. The study is both a brilliant synthesis and a virtual anthology of the oral history of Lowell's Francos. In addition to stories, songs, popular sayings, jokes, and anecdotes, this volume includes valuable descriptions of a vanished "Little Canada." In a word, this work by Brigitte Lane is a model of its kind and serves as a reliable guide.

Other researchers contributed to the English-language tradition of Franco-American oral history. For example, when Tamara K. Hareven and Randolph Langenbach began the research that led to the publication of *Amoskeag: Life and Work in an American Factory-City*, the many Francos whom they interviewed were able to provide new information on the work experience in Manchester's giant Amoskeag textile company during the first third of the twentieth century. Included in the Hareven and Langenbach study, these accounts add a great deal to what is known of industrial life in general and of Franco attitudes regarding work in the mills.

With respect to the literary output in other genres—poetry, novel, theater—two facts must be noted: the decline of French-language Franco literature and the prominence achieved by novels written in English.

In addition to his previously mentioned thesis and anthology, Paul Chassé also published two collections of poetry: *Et la mer efface . . .* (1964) and *La Carafe enchantée* (1968), in which one senses the influence of several French poets from Leconte de Lisle to Prévert. Rosaire Dion-Lévesque published his last collection, *Quête*, in 1963. In addition to the three editions of his translation of Longfellow's "Evangeline," Rev. Maurice Trottier published several collections of poems on travel, nature, and religious sentiment, from *Envolées* (1965) to his bilingual *Indian Summer/Soleil levant d'automne* (1993). In four volumes published since 1978—*Un mot de chez nous, Au coeur du vent* (both in 1978), *La broderie inachevée* (1979), and *Le nuage de ma pensée* (1981), less populist than his first three collections—Normand Dubé shared his anguish and his dreams, along with those of his people with whom he readily identified. Other poets like Jim Bishop and Paul Marion write in English on both universal and ethnic themes.

This is equally true of the novelists Robert Cormier and Paul Théroux. According to Théroux, who won national recognition in 1975 for his *The Great Railway Bazaar* and who has written a series of novels reminiscent of those by Graham Greene, ethnicity is only a stage through which an individual passes on his way to something more universal. For Robert Cormier, who has become more and more well-known as a writer of young adult fiction, ethnicity is but one element among the many that enter into the creation of his fictional universe. This can be seen especially in his earliest novels, particularly in *Now and At the Hour* (1960) and *Take Me Where the Good Times Are* (1965), both of which take place in a thinly disguised version of Leominster, Massachusetts, where he grew up and continues to live. He has written a great many novels, two of which have been made into films.

The characters in Gerard Robichaud's novels—for example, in *Papa Martel* (1961)—succeed in integrating their Acadian and

American cultures in a seamless fashion. This novelist is able to create very distinctive characters against a background of authentic Acadian family life. These immigrants who have settled in Maine, while having fond memories of their native land, believe in enjoying life rather than being morose. They have also replaced the rigid outlook of traditional Catholic morality with an independent attitude.

A wide diversity of world views can be found in the English-language novel, as is readily shown by a back-to-back reading of Robichaud's *Papa Martel* and *No Adam in Eden* by Grace de Repentigny Metalious. Metalious is a New Hampshire Franco-American whose first novel, *Peyton Place*, caused a scandal even while it became a bestseller of the 1950s. *No Adam in Eden* presents powerfully drawn female characters in complete revolt against traditional Franco-American values. If *Papa Martel* is a novel about love, *No Adam in Eden* is all about rage.

There can be no question, however, that the dominant figure in the Franco-American novel is Jean-Louis ("Jack") Kerouac (1922-1969). After several difficult years, he became famous in 1957 with *On the Road*. Since then, Kerouac continues to find new readers the world over—more attracted to his cycle of "road" novels than to those of his Lowell cycle. It is, of course, especially in the latter group that Kerouac described his Franco-American childhood and youth spent under the kindly eye of a father and mother born in Québec. When the father's once prosperous printing business fails, the family begins its many moves from one of Lowell's "Canadian" neighborhoods to another. In *Visions of Gerard* (1963), Kerouac recalls the last year in the life of his brother Gerard who died at the age of nine when Jack was only four. A precocious and sickly child, Gerard was deeply religious. At first he was both Jack's friend and role model; but Gerard eventually became a symbol of reproach, with Jack coming to see himself as having failed to live up to Gerard's moral and spiritual standards. In this novel, as in

Doctor Sax (1959), the author includes some memorable descriptions of Lowell's Franco-American neighborhoods, in particular the Centralville area with the bustling life of its three-deckers and the mystery surrounding its parish buildings: the church and rectory of Saint Louis de France, the cathedral-like church of Saint John the Baptist, the Grotto and the Way of the Cross on the grounds of the Franco-American Orphanage.

But over and above the scenic descriptions and the passages written in the dialect of Lowell's Francos, these novels are Franco-American both through their characters and the author's depiction of the Franco-Catholic environment that had such a profound influence on him. Preoccupations of a spiritual nature permeated the life and writings of Kerouac, more so than is customarily noted. Haunted by the saintly ideal embodied in his brother Gerard and simultaneously in revolt against the bourgeois conformity of his time, Kerouac, while living the life of a nomad, remained faithful to his origins—family, ethnic group, home town—never letting go of them. Both his loyalty to his origins and his nomadic inclinations are combined in *Satori in Paris* (1966), the story of his trip to France in 1965.

It would be most surprising if Kerouac's works, read the world over, had remained unknown to two other Franco novelists who also write in English. David Plante, a highly successful author, combined three novels—*The Family, The Woods, The Country*—into a single volume titled *The Francoeur Novels* (1983). They are the sad chronicle of a Franco family living in Providence, Rhode Island. Plante is especially successful in recreating the sense of being foreigners—the uprootedness—which Francos in New England long experienced, isolated from the dominant Anglo group by their origins, their language, and their faith, as well as by first names like Oenone and Polidore. His description of the rigid and pessimistic Catholicism inherited from the ancestors is uncannily accurate. Plante makes the reader feel that the French in the United States are living their final hour.

The Questing Beast, the first novel by a talented writer named Richard Hébert, appeared in 1984. To call it a Franco novel in no way detracts from the universality of the author's purpose which is to narrate the search for his own identity by juxtaposing it to the story of his father's painful life journey. Firmly resolved to discover and take possession of his personal and ancestral history, the novelist, a proud descendant of Louis Hébert, New France's first colonist, undertakes a pilgrimage to Québec where he learns the secret of his origins from an uncle. A remarkable stylistic achievement, *The Questing Beast* is a novel of rich complexity in which ethnicity constitutes one of the essential thematic elements.

Ethnicity is central to Robert Perreault's *L'Héritage* (1983), the first Franco-American novel to be published in French since 1938, if one excludes *Les Enfances de Fanny* by Louis Dantin in 1951. Let us first underscore the fact that this young author *chose* to write his novel in French and that he also sought to make of this work "a sort of examination of our collective conscience as an ethnic group in New England." The author invites Franco-Americans to ask themselves what role the enduring cultural heritage should play in their personal lives. This heritage lives on, Perreault claims, even if the majority have little or no awareness of it. *L'Héritage* also captures the admiration that some young Francos have for the strength of character displayed by previous generations. Perreault is the first Franco of his generation to express, in the form of a novel written in French, a respectful, even reverential, attitude toward those who immigrated.

Almost as young as Robert Perreault, the dramatist Grégoire Chabot is also proud of being a Franco-American, but he finds oppressive, even paralyzing, the loyalty to the past and the "excessive" admiration that some Francos have for the culture of France. In two controversial plays, *Un Jacques Cartier Errant* (1977) and *Chère Maman* (1979), the failings of Franco-American establishment figures are placed under a microscope: the lack of self-confidence needed for the creation of an "authentic" Franco-American culture; the inaction and ineffectiveness of organizations whose responsibility was to ensure the preservation of the cultural heritage; the snobbery and exclusivity of these same organizations, which created a chasm between themselves and the people; the slavish adherence to foreign, that is to say, French cultural models, which intensified an already paralyzing inferiority complex among Francos; the excessive conformity to old-fashioned values that hindered the development of an authentic self. Despite the prosecutorial style that characterizes Chabot's plays and other writings, one senses in them a plea for renewal so that, for young people at the end of the twentieth century, French culture would no longer be a dead letter.

During this period between 1960 and 1990, in addition to having published and produced the plays of Grégoire Chabot, the National Materials Development Center did create a certain number of plays for young people. There were also plays produced in various New England regions. In northern Maine, for example, there was a production of Guy Dubay's historical drama, *With Justice For All,* recalling the efforts made by a powerful Anglo-American company to evict Acadian farmers from the Saint John River Valley around 1870. While its subject matter is original, the play is even more so in its dialogue that switches from English to French, depending on whether the scene takes place among the French-speaking farmers or in the offices of American capitalists.

Finally, let us note that a "parish-based" theater flourished here and there throughout New England. It was popular entertainment, often based on a text from the pen of an unassuming amateur, whose goal was either to edify or to amuse parishioners. These productions usually went unnoticed beyond their immediate locality and, all too often, remained unpublished, as was the case for "De la visite originale" which folklorist Roméo Berthiaume wrote in 1975 for a Soirée canadienne in Woonsocket's Saint Louis parish.

Though not abundant, the literature of the 1960-1990 period has at least one characteristic feature: like the society it reflected, it became more pluralistic as it, too, evolved towards assimilation into the dominant culture.

POSTSCRIPT: THE 1990s

Armand Chartier and Claire Quintal

In the quasi-encyclopedic volume entitled *Steeples and Smokestacks: A Collection of Essays on the Franco-American Experience in New England,* painstakingly assembled by Professor Claire Quintal, the sociologist Madeleine Giguère presents a demographic profile of the **French-speaking** Franco-Americans of New England. In her essay, Professor Giguère indicates that, based on the 1990 U.S. Census Report, 1,702,175 individuals in this country speak French at home. Of that number, 360,000 reside in the six New England States. Far more persons claimed **French ancestry** 2,351,368 in New England alone. [See Tables in Appendix I for further details.]

Although more numerous than ever, Franco-Americans remain one of the least visible minorities in this country. For the most part, the public is ignorant of their existence, unaware even that the most famous among them—Will Durant and Jack Kerouac—are of Franco-American origin. It would be beyond the scope of this work to attempt an explanation for this lack of awareness, but it should be pointed out that Franco-Americans for too long settled for a minimal level of formal education, practiced a self-defeating lack of political cohesiveness—which explains their under-representation at all levels of government—and they have been too slow to realize the importance of making known to the world who they are and what they represent for this country. Since the 1980s, the scant attention paid to Franco-Americans by the American or the Canadian media has tended to

390

concentrate on the loss of their language and their gradual disappearance as a separate entity.

Fragmentation and Intermittence

It is now clear that the many efforts at renewal, counted upon by the militants to turn the situation around in the 1970s, were a succession of short-lived projects. Even the most promising initiatives have now lost either most or all of their momentum. However, French New England, although a shadow of its former self, still exists. There are still a few communities in which Franco-American life is less fragmented than in others. Manchester, New Hampshire, is home to the ACA, the only truly independent Franco-American mutual benefit society remaining in New England since the USJB became a division of Catholic Family Life Insurance (CFLI) of Milwaukee, Wisconsin, in 1991; Assomption Mutuelle Vie, now headquartered in Moncton, New Brunswick, but founded in New England for the protection of the region's Acadian immigrant population, no longer maintains its network of local councils in the area; and the Artisans, later known as Les Coopérants, although defunct as an insurance-based institution, lives on in the guise of the "Euclide Gilbert French Language Foundation."

First constituted in 1952 as a French-language competition among Franco-American students in bilingual parochial institutions, the Foundation began reaching out to schools throughout the Northeast, both public and private after its reincorporation in 1984. As many as 42,000 students participated one year. By the nineties, the Foundation had also become the U.S. regional coordinator for the Québec-based *Dictée des Amériques* which seeks to promote competence in the written language. Although currently undergoing a process of transition, the foundation still retains much potential for future involvement in French-language oriented activities.

In 1987, ACA took the lead in producing a television series in collaboration with MediaOne called "Bonjour!" which has now passed the 500th program mark. "Bonjour!" has served as a vehicle for showcasing talented performing artists, especially Josée Vachon, who was also the initial host of the program. Julien Olivier, followed by Paul Paré and Carole Auger, have been its producers. "Bonjour!", which gave much needed visibility and publicity to many performing artists, also became the chronicler of Franco-American life and activities.   By engaging in preliminary discussions with New Hampshire Public Television, "Bonjour!" now hopes to make the transition to another production level.

In July 1998, the Boston Consulate-General and ACA Assurance created the Partenariat pour la Francophonie Franco-Américaine (Partnership for French-Speaking Franco-Americans), the objective of which is to preserve and develop the cultural and linguistic heritage of New England's Franco-Americans.

Manchester also has the Centre Franco-Américain created by ACA Assurance in 1990 as a self-sustaining entity. The priceless Adelard Lambert Collection of Canadiana and Franco-Americana consisting of 30,000 books, many of them rare, along with a museum of French-Canadian and Franco-American art works, gives the Centre Franco-Américain a magnificent resource base. The art collection includes over fifty pieces by the highly regarded Québec sculptor Alfred Laliberté (1873-1953); fourteen portraits and two landscapes by Lorenzo de Nevers (1877-1967), doubtless the best-known Franco-American painter; and works by the New Hampshire-born sculptor Lucien Gosselin (1883-1940), whose creations range from medallions to large-scale public monuments. Increasingly visible in the region, because of its multi-faceted activities, the Centre has undertaken an ambitious program, some components of which are art and historical exhibitions, French language classes for adults and children, Franco-American history classes, lectures, etc. Under the dynamic leadership of Executive Director Adèle Boufford Baker, the Centre produced, in 1996, a memorable exhibit catalogue, *Sur Bois—Wood Carvers of Northern New England.*

Woonsocket, Rhode Island, the original home office of the Union Saint-Jean-Baptiste now houses the regional headquarters of the USJB/CFLI. The Major Edmond Mallet Collection of rare books and manuscripts dealing with French, French-Canadian, and Franco-American contributions to the development of the North American continent is still preserved and maintained in Woonsocket for the use of scholars and genealogists. Since the 1950s, USJB/CFLI leads an annual pilgrimage to the sanctuary of Our Lady of LaSalette in Attleboro, Massachusetts, and devotes resources to summer weekends for young people based upon an ethnic theme. The USJB/CFLI also continues its long-standing practice of assisting needy students through scholarships and loans, in addition to underwriting various programs featuring cultural heritage.

Woonsocket is home to a Museum of Work and Culture, made possible by both public and private funding, which highlights the Franco-Americans as an ethnic group. The museum's permanent exhibit, *La Survivance,* presents a summary view of the transition made by generations of French Canadians whose immigration transformed them into Franco-Americans.

The intensive labor of immigrants from several countries, including Canada, during the 19th and early 20th centuries placed the Blackstone River Valley among the country's top producers of cotton and woolen goods as well as textile machinery. In recognition of this, the U.S. Congress established the Blackstone River Valley National Heritage Corridor in 1986 and has re-authorized the Corridor for an additional ten-year period. Based in Woonsocket, the Corridor extends through twenty-four communities—from the Blackstone River headwaters in Worcester, Massachusetts, to Narragansett Bay in

Providence, Rhode Island—an area covering forty-six miles and 400,000 acres. Franco-Americans settled in very large numbers in the many mill towns located along the banks of the Blackstone River.

The coordinating federal commission which overseas this project has identified seven major priorities: heritage education, recreation development, ethnic and cultural conservation, environmental conservation, historic preservation, land-use planning, and heritage-based economic development. The Blackstone has also recently been designated—by executive order of the President of the United States—as one of this country's fourteen American Heritage Rivers.

An annual *Jubilé* Franco-Américain has been held in Woonsocket each August since 1995. In 1998, *Jubilé* offered more than seventy-five events, such as the "French Marketplace," with strolling musicians, "Jazz sur la rive," a French-Canadian hockey clinic, narrated tours on the Blackstone River with the assistance of performing artists from throughout New England, etc. Created by the Flickers Arts Collaborative, *Jubilé* is made possible by the work of some 250 volunteers and by the sponsorship of organizations like the USJB/CFLI, ACA Assurance, the two Richelieu Clubs of Woonsocket, and Tourisme Québec.

The city of Lowell is an important site in the cultural geography of French New England, especially since the creation in 1978, by the federal government, of a vast museum which encompasses various locations within the city. These sites have been restored to their nineteenth-century appearance in order to commemorate the key role which the city played in the country's Industrial Revolution. Lowell also has a number of Franco-American churches and monuments, some of them immortalized by Jack Kerouac in his Lowell novels. During the past quarter century, people have come by the thousands to take guided tours, visit places described in Kerouac's novels and his grave in Edson Cemetery, or to attend "Franco-American Week." Begun in

1971, this Semaine Franco-Américaine can be credited with having created a trend since it was the first of its kind.

Finally, mention should be made that the last Franco-American newspaper written entirely in French, *Le Journal de Lowell*, was published in this city (1975-1995) and that one of the reading rooms in Lowell's municipal library includes a collection of Canadian and Franco-American books. Called the "Salle Biron," it is so named in honor of the journalist Louis A. Biron, owner-publisher of the highly regarded French-language newspaper *L'Étoile* (1886-1957). His daughter, Marthe Biron-Péloquin, continuing the family tradition, was the editor of *Le Bulletin* of the Fédération Féminine Franco-Américaine for fifteen years, from 1973 to1988. She was also president of the "Fédé" from 1981 to 1986. Lowell is also noteworthy for the fact that, from 1881 to 1995, twenty-three French-language newspapers were published in the city.

Worcester serves as a resource center because of the presence of Assumption College, founded in 1904 by the Assumptionist Fathers, a French teaching and publishing order. The goal of the college was to provide the sons of French-Canadian immigrants with a bilingual high school and college education. This training ensured that French-speaking professionals would be available for Franco-American centers throughout New England. Today, the Institut français/French Institute at the college maintains this tradition through its research and publications on Franco-Americans. At its series of colloquia launched in 1980, academics present papers on various aspects of the Franco-American experience. The Institute has published these proceedings thanks to the seemingly limitless energy and dedication of its esteemed directress, Professor Claire Quintal.

Worcester has also been home to three major Franco-American newspapers: Ferdinand Gagnon's nineteenth century *Le Travailleur,* Wilfrid Beaulieu's newspaper of the same name—twentieth century successor to the first—and Alexandre Belisle's *L'Opinion publique* (1893-1931), all three of which have been described in this book. Franco-Americans helped to celebrate Worcester's sesquicentennial as a city in 1998 with a series of events which lasted a fortnight: various exhibits, Meet the Authors nights, and a mass in honor of St. John the Baptist, the group's patron saint. Marcel Raymond, president of the organizing committee, who has established a Franco-Centre in the city, also hosts a weekly two-hour radio program of music, interviews, and information about France, Québec, and the Acadians.

As a whole, the State of Maine has witnessed some promising developments in the 1990s. Early in the decade, the U.S. Congress, through the National Park Service, funded the creation of the Maine Acadian Culture Project whose dual purpose is the protection and promotion of the Acadian heritage in the St. John Valley area in northern Aroostook County along the New Brunswick border. On a smaller scale, but similar in nature to that of the Blackstone Valley in Southern New England, the Acadian Heritage Project in Maine has resulted in several historical sites being identified and a variety of ongoing cultural and educational programs funded by federal and local sources.

Certain towns in northern Maine—Fort Kent, Madawaska, Van Buren, and Frenchville, to name just four—ensure a French presence in the Maine legislature. Maine is the only State other than Louisiana to represent the United States in the international organization of elected legislators called the Assemblée parlementaire de la Francophonie (APF), founded in 1967. This group has representatives from the legislatures of fifty-nine countries world-wide. Senator Judy Paradis of Frenchville is its American section president.

Since 1990, the University of Maine at Fort Kent houses the Acadian Archives to "document, preserve, celebrate, and disseminate information about the history and cultural heritage of Maine's Saint

John Valley." In 1997, the archives organized a region-wide celebration of the 150th anniversary of the publication of Longfellow's "Evangeline." L'Acadien du Haut St. Jean is a bilingual Two-Way Immersion Program for the towns of Madawaska and Van Buren. In existence since 1995, the program, which now reaches students in grades K through eight, aims "to develop fluency and literacy" in both French and English.

Manchester, Woonsocket, Lowell, Worcester, and the St. John Valley of northern Maine are thus important centers of activity for New England's Franco-Americans, as are Lewiston and Biddeford, Maine. The State of Maine took the initiative in creating the national U.S. chapter of the Forum Francophone des Affaires. Based in Lewiston, its goal is to develop business linkages between New England's French-speaking entrepreneurs and their francophone counterparts the world over. Also in Lewiston, the Lewiston-Auburn College of the University of Southern Maine has added yet another dimension to Franco-American cultural maintenance by taking custody of and enriching the collection of the Centre d'Héritage Franco-Américain, created in the 1970s and housed for a time in private facilities. With this as a base, the college has built a strong research facility centered upon local Franco-American culture. It is an active participant in area Franco-American activities and hosts a series of regularly scheduled popular events.

Biddeford's MacArthur Library contains the Francophone Collection originally established at St. Francis College in that city by three Franco-American professors of French—Normand Beaupré, Robert Parenteau, and Hervé Poissant. Both Lewiston and Biddeford have justly earned praise for their summer festivals: "La Kermesse" in Biddeford has maintained its popular and financial success and the "Festival de Joie" in Lewiston has revitalized the Franco-American festival tradition in that city. In addition to the activities mentioned above, all of these cities, which already attract tourists, historians, and genealogists, have churches, mills, and the remnants of "Little Canadas" which await discovery by historians of architecture, art, and urban planning.

Fragmentation and intermittence have also begun to characterize the relations between Franco-Americans and Québec. With the passage of time, the network of personal ties—family and school friendships, in addition to institutional relationships via religious and patriotic organizations—has been eroded by the indifference resulting from assimilation and diverging historical paths. Most Franco-Americans know as much about Québec as do Americans in general, that is very little. Following the lead of the Anglo-American media, and generally unaware of the issues, Franco-Americans say that they are happy that Québec twice voted against independence—in 1980 and 1995—and that everything is "back to normal." Only a tiny minority recognizes that this issue will not "go away," regretting the results of these referenda and hoping for a resurgence of what others have called the "specter" of independence. It should be added that the closing, in 1996, of the Québec Delegation in Boston has removed a valuable, dynamic resource from the regional cultural and economic scene.

Only a few other links remain between Québec and French New England. The Richelieu Clubs, founded in Ottawa, and ACA Assurance come to mind. A large proportion of the ACA's members are Francophone Canadians living in Québec, New Brunswick, and Ontario. Québec also remains a focus for a few scholars and other Quebecophiles. For the elders, however, Québec remains a Mecca for pilgrimages to shrines that still welcome a considerable number of visitors each year—Saint Joseph's Oratory in Montréal and the sanctuaries of Notre-Dame-du-Cap near Trois-Rivières and Sainte-Anne-de-Beaupré near Québec City.

During the past decade, the French government, through the French Consulate-General in Boston and the Cultural Services of the

French Embassy, has continued to demonstrate its encouragement of the Francos as a result of the interest manifested for the group by Alain Decaux, the first Minister Designate for Francophone Affairs in the government of French President François Mitterrand. Franco-American participation at the summit meetings of the francophone world is a consequence of this interest. Maurice Portiche, during his stay in Boston as French consul-general, while maintaining the traditional activities of his office, also supported two major new initiatives, the Forum Francophone des Affaires/USA (1997) and the Partenariat Accord (1998) between ACA Assurance and the French government for the preservation and enhancement of the cultural and linguistic heritage. One of the tangible results of this Accord was the promotion of Franco-American participation and representation at the "Festival de l'été indien" held in France in 1999 to highlight the existence of Franco-Americans and their group culture maintained through the generations against great odds.

French television, via TV 5 and Radio France Internationale, provides additional "windows" on France, as do the excellent weekly newspaper *France-Amérique,* published in New York, and the monthly *Journal Français,* published in San Francisco since 1965.

Another linkage with France began to materialize in 1994 when Professor Joseph Garreau, of the University of Massachusetts Lowell, and others, organized a colloquium at the Université d'Angers on the presence and influence of western France on North America. The following year, representatives of the University of Maine at Orono and the Université d'Angers signed an agreeement creating academic and cultural ties between the two institutions. A second colloquium, coordinated by Jim Bishop of the University of Maine, on the topic "Cultural Identity in French America," took place in Bar Harbor, Maine, in 1996. Community members participated in these proceedings alongside scholars from American and Canadian universities as well as the French universities of Angers, Orléans, Nantes, and Le Mans.

Moreover, Franco-Americans are now better known in France, thanks to the books, articles, and public appearances of two academics, Louise Péloquin-Faré and François Weil.

In Orono, the Franco-American Center has been given an expanded role within the University of Maine, and Franco-American studies are fully integrated into the university's academic programs. A new interest in contemporary Franco-American theater is also evident on campus.

As a consequence of its fragmentation, Franco-American life has increasingly become a local phenomenom, as evidenced by the many groups, both large and small, which present lectures, films, and concerts here and there throughout New England. Festivals, featuring music and dance as well as traditional foods, are very popular because of the joyous atmosphere they succeed in creating. In addition to Woonsocket's "*Jubilé*," Lewiston's "Festival de Joie," Biddeford's "La Kermesse," there is also Madawaska's "Festival Acadien" which has been honoring a specific family from the region since its foundation. Since 1995, FrancoFest—under the auspices of the Union des Franco-Américains du Connecticut—asks each of the Union's affiliated clubs throughout the state to organize an event during the month of October. These various manifestations, which are community-based, connote a resurgence of sorts. Thus, in Franco-American cities throughout New England, ethnic life, although no longer as concentrated nor as many-sided as it had been until the early sixties, continues to show signs of vitality.

Continuities and Discontinuities

Traditional *survivance* was perceived by the younger generations as stark, idealistic, inflexible, and uncompromising. Such an ideology seemed too restrictive to the generations that have come of age in the past three or four decades. With the self-assurance of the young, these generations rebuffed the *patriotes* of old either by assimilating totally or, in a few instances, by selecting what they wished to retain from the traditional *survivance* values. This was in fact the case for those who in the 1970s and 1980s developed a "new" *survivance,* especially the group affiliated with the Franco-American Center located at the University of Maine, Orono. Dogmatism gave way to eclecticism, and the long-held belief that conventional *survivance* was the only way to combat the disappearance of a people and a culture was repudiated.

The old *survivance* might have fared better at the hands of the young had there been less emphasis on some aspects of the French-Canadian and Franco-American cultures—long viewed as essential—such as traditional religion with its sense of the redemptive value of suffering, counterpoint to the triumphalism of feast days. This attitude can still be observed today in the pessimistic approach of the elderly to the practice of Catholicism. This attitude is often linked with the worship of the past and its attendant nostalgia for a golden age when, from cradle to grave, life could be lived in French within the confines of a Little Canada.

Young and middle-aged Franco-Americans rebelled against this cult of the past which entailed explaining the present in terms of a bygone era. In addition, most Franco-Americans who can still recall anything about Canadian history remember it as three distinct periods of struggle ending in loss: the heroic period of New France, the defeat of 1760, and the sad exodus of the migration. It seemed to the young that the only models worthy of emulation were to be found either in the Gospels or in New France while the sole purpose of life was "to earn entrance into heaven at the end of one's days."

Loyalty to such a past, that was viewed as somehow better than the present, did not appeal to a generation that defined itself by rebelling against all that belonged to another time and place. This perspective minimized the importance of the present and the immediate future, the main concerns of the young. Although this approach may well have satisfied the spiritual or intellectual aspirations of its elders, the "me" generation rejected such an attitude and the self-abnegation required of its "true believers."

Survivance, perhaps misunderstood or badly taught or simply deemed irrelevant, was seen by the young as an outmoded dead-end that left no room for self-expression. The very terminology in use at the time was problematical: the word "cause," for example, with its implied submission of the individual will to that of the group, was abhorrent to young people. Members of this new generation refused to adopt such a narrow focus, opting instead for self-fulfillment.

The few who created a new *survivance* acted less out of a sense of moral obligation than of love for the cultural heritage or a need to be loyal to something, perhaps even out of a sense of nostalgia for Canada or France. These individuals, whether professionals or non-professionals, preserve the positive values that stem from tradition, beginning with the sense of belonging to an ethnic and cultural community that has its roots in a distant time and place. For them, the past was and is a source of inspiration and is not necessarily synonymous with irrelevance or oppression. They agree with the statement by the Québec historian, Canon Lionel Groulx: "Many are the dead who survive in us, the living, explaining who we are." Those who live according to this new concept of *survivance* form a more flexible and open community than did their predecessors. Rigid moralism and cultural dogmatism have become obsolete.

The new *survivance* is eclectic, tolerant, and pluralistic. Moreover, without abandoning moral principle, its adherents are prepared to accept religious indifference, the use of the Franco-American dialect, and a lack of awareness of the collective past by members of the group. In an effort to be inclusive, they no longer brand individuals as "traitors of the race" for not speaking French or not practicing their religion.

They view assimilation into mainstream America as having been inevitable in the long run. Proponents of this modernized form of *survivance* consider themselves to be full-fledged American citizens and are quite aware that they are swimming upstream when they attempt to preserve and even enrich a cultural heritage that is not Anglo-American. This new *survivance,* however, has at least one important thing in common with the old: it appeals as much—if not more—to the heart as to the mind.

This latter-day mentality is an individual matter rather than a social phenomenom since the institutional framework has all but disappeared or been transformed beyond recognition. For instance, today one can hardly speak of "national" parishes. Language and faith, inseparable in the past, have become distinct realities. For most Franco-Americans, the French language no longer has anything to do with preserving the Catholic faith, even if, in the 1980s and early 1990s, some elderly Franco-Americans, left anglicized Franco-American parishes to join one where there was still at least one Sunday mass in French. But one can anticipate that ethnic parishes will not outlive today's older generation of Francophones, largely because of changing demographics. While Franco-Americans have moved to the suburbs, the inner cities and their parishes have been occupied by growing numbers of Hispanic, Portuguese, and Southeast Asian immigrants.

These demographic changes have also caused bishops to merge French "national" parishes with territorial ones or to close "French" parishes completely, a move met with varying degrees of opposition from Franco-Americans affected by such episcopal decisions. In some instances, parishioners felt inner devastation and helplessness when their bishop not only closed the parish, but razed the church building, as was the case in Holyoke and Fall River, Massachusetts, where in the late 1980s, both Precious Blood, the "mother" parish of Holyoke's Franco-Americans, and St. Mathieu, in Fall River's Bowenville section, were erased from the map. In other instances, parishioners organized and protested. No protest movement in recent years has equaled that which centered on St. Joseph parish in Worcester, Massachusetts. For over a year, beginning in 1992, the church was occupied by parishioners and sympathizers in a defiant response to the bishop's order that the parish be closed because it needed costly repairs. The group, whose church had played a vital role in their lives and in those of their parents and grandparents, maintained a round-the-clock vigil for some thirteen months to ensure that the church they cherished would stay open. St. Joseph was eventually closed for some months until a new bishop allowed the church to reopen in 1996. For the time being, however, the parish remains "technically" merged with Worcester's "mother" parish of Notre Dame des Canadiens.

The eclecticism and tolerance that characterize French New England today are also in evidence with respect to language issues. In this regard, attitudes range from considering French as being of little importance to viewing it as chic. This range of perception includes total rejection by some who consider the French language to be synonymous with the immigrant status and resulting poverty of their forebears. Given the milieu in which they reside, it is not surprising that the majority of Franco-Americans do not speak French; what *is* surprising is that thousands continue to use it. While once, during the period of immigration, people spoke it because they knew no English and insisted that their children speak it out of loyalty, today, if the young speak it at all, it is by choice, either out of a sense of ethnic belonging or for cultural reasons. Some also recognize that French constitutes a "visceral bond" with their ancestral past.

Some young people, particularly at the Franco-American Center of the University of Maine, Orono, defend the use of the Franco dialect; it is, they say, the true expression of the popular soul. For them, the use of the dialect is a question of authenticity. Today, one seldom hears the contention that the use of French is one of the prerequisites to being considered a Franco-American. Clearly, individuals can be and are Franco-American whether or not they speak French. The numerous Franco-American genealogical societies, whose activities are carried on in English, offer eloquent testimony to the existence of a sense of ethnic identity regardless of language. This pride in one's origins is repeatedly expressed by many for whom French is the tongue spoken not by them but by their forebears. This new spirit was well articulated by Marie-Reine Mikesell, a Franco-American from Chicago, Illinois, who served as coordinator of the Sixth National Franco-American Congress held in Michigan in August 1983. Referring to Franco-Americans who had attended the Congress but who did not speak French, she aptly stated: "These are not just any unilingual Anglophones; they are *our* Anglophones. And if they chose to be with us today it is because their hearts have remained French."

This openness has long been a common practice among other American minorities like the Irish, the Italians, and the Jews whose members, while loyal to their ethnic heritage, no longer speak the language of their ancestors. After decades of discussion, most Franco-Americans recognize that it would be unfair to exclude from their ethnic group those who have French blood in their veins, who recognize a shared history and ancestry, and who consider themselves to be Franco-Americans. Without denying the vital role that language plays in any culture, it is no longer realistic to make it a *sine qua non* for membership in an ethnic group in the United States, especially since the original language is no longer a mother tongue and is not spoken by most American "ethnics."

An Uncertain Future

Opinions remain divided concerning the future of Franco-American New England. Some say that it has no future, having already ceased to exist. It is true that its human resources are gravely diminished and that assimilation, one of the fears dogging Franco-American *survivance* ideology for more than a century, has made huge inroads, with no effective countervailing force. In support of the most somber predictions, one could cite the demise of the old *survivance* and the fact that the diminishing number of people who are interested in their French or French-Canadian patrimony are dispersed throughout New England. The rather ironic truth is that, despite the growing ease of communication and travel of the present era, Franco-American activity on a regional scale is less vibrant today than it was fifty years ago. But Franco-American life still has some strong points that might carry it beyond the first decades of the twenty-first century.

True, there are far fewer Franco-Americans who believe that they need to know or cherish their heritage than there are who remain oblivious or indifferent to it. For the majority, *la survivance,* whether old or new, is a form of romanticism to be stored away in the subconscious ethnic memory. Nevertheless, there are Franco-Americans who are constantly rededicating themselves to the task of developing the heritage. These people make room in their lives for what Ferdinand Gagnon called "the psychological homeland." They devote their talents and energies to preserving the heritage and making it better known; some even succeed in enriching it. Far from seeing it as atrophied or stagnant, they view the Franco-American experience as an important cultural phenomenon, one that needs to be elucidated and made known.

At the regional level, the more important traditional groups still hold regular functions. In addition to a discussion of pertinent issues, the social dimension of this sort of gathering allows people who have come from different areas of New England to fraternize and thus preserve a minimal sense of community on a regional level. The genealogical societies are very active, and gatherings of writers and artists were held in various locations from 1981 to 1996. There are also some French-language radio broadcasts which maintain at least a musical connection between New England's Franco-Americans and their Québec and Acadian counterparts.

The organization called Action for Franco-Americans in the Northeast (ActFANE) achieved success in several different areas, including its media campaign to correct the error made by the U.S. Postal Service when it neglected to recognize the role played by Canadians and Franco-Americans in the creation and development of the credit union movement in the United States. ActFANE helped score several legislative victories in the "English only" debate. It also worked diligently in various city halls to ensure the continued broadcasting of Québec television programs.

At the international level, Franco-Americans were present at the francophone summit in Paris (1986), thanks to the initiative of Alain Briottet, French consul-general in Boston until 1990. ActFANE, acting in concert with the French Consulate-General in Boston, organized the Franco-American delegations to the Québec Summit Conference in 1987 and those of Dakar in 1989 and Mauritius in 1991. Observers agree that these meetings, by increasing Franco-American visibility, create windows of opportunity vis-à-vis the international francophone community, eventually resulting in more frequent contacts and exchanges in both cultural and economic spheres. Despite its limited resources, during the time that it was active, ActFANE was a key player in making the new *survivance* both appealing to the young and acceptable to the old. Although never officially disbanded, ActFANE today can no longer claim to be playing a vital role in Franco-American circles.

For individuals and organizations active in preserving or contributing to their ethnic heritage, Québec and France remain critical sources of sustainment. Some also stay in contact with Acadia, Ontario, and Western Canada where the situation is somewhat analogous to that of the Franco-Americans. At the same time, there is greater receptivity within the Franco community to the good will of Francophiles and Francophones who are not of Québec or Acadian descent.

Most Franco-American organizations have recognized the need to become bilingual without abandoning their dedication to the French language. As a general rule, they welcome within their ranks persons who share their goals, beginning with those who have been neglected for too long: unilingual Franco-Americans. But, if the Franco-American community is to have a future, the number of individuals willing to devote time and energy on behalf of group solidarity—in exchange for greater personal growth—must increase appreciably. In this era of seemingly optional ethnicity, the future of Franco-American New England depends on those who *choose* to live bicultural lives and to make the required commitment.

Franco-American activists and militants also want young people to understand that a cultural heritage does not impoverish—it enriches. The more enterprising among the activists would like to explore the phenomenon of "latent ethnicity" to see if organizations might not reach, and perhaps even attract, the thousands of Franco-Americans who, while having remained apart from the group, have nevertheless inherited traditional Canadian virtues: loyalty, perseverance, pride in workmanship, etc. "These people were born with a Franco-American psyche. Is it possible that nothing is left of it?" they ask. These are the forgotten ones who are not even aware that there is within their reach a biculturalism that could enhance their lives. Those, however, who have rediscovered their ethnicity—by means of genealogy, for instance—have recognized the potential for personal growth that it represents. Many Franco-Americans dispersed throughout the United States have experienced a *rapprochement* with regard to their French and French-Canadian roots via the Franco-American genealogical societies. Some have even gone on to serve the group by becoming directors of Franco-American organizations. To rediscover one's ethnic group and return to one's roots are, of course, no guarantee of perfect bliss. And there is no denying that activists and militants are weary—weary of soul-searching about the effectiveness of their activities, tired of discussions on the "ideal" role of Québec and France in helping to preserve the heritage, and other similar questions.

But, one might ask, even in this new climate of tolerance, pluralism, and eclecticism, how does one live a Franco-American life now that so many ethnic organizations have disappeared or been assimilated and that there is no support for the militants from "the people"? Several paths are open: volunteering in an organization committed to cultural heritage activities, developing an interest in research at the family, parish, municipal, or regional levels, or drawing on ethnic themes if one is a writer or an artist.

In this sense, many genealogists offer excellent role models. Indeed, involvement in genealogy has led more than one Franco-American to the dedicated pursuit of family and ethnic history, while making the acquaintance of like-minded souls in the process. While traditional Franco-American organizations are faring less well than one might hope, the robustness and continued growth of interest in genealogical societies augur well for the future. Genealogists of the American-Canadian Genealogical Society of Manchester and the American-French Genealogical Society of Pawtucket/Woonsocket, among many others, are emphatic about the fundamental needs filled by these groups. According to their elected officers, the pursuit of one's ancestry not only helps individuals identify their forebears, it also yields facts about one's family history along with an understanding of their place in the history of France, Canada, and the United States. "Genealogy is not just a search for the dead," they say, "it is a way of connecting with the living." Ever more sophisticated in their methodology, these societies—many of them founded in the 1970s—very much give the impression that they are here to stay. [See Appendix III for a list of these societies and their publications throughout the United States].

The above statements apply to all the Franco-American genealogical societies in New England and upstate New York. However, as a consequence of the friendly rivalry among them, these societies also strive for and achieve a certain degree of uniqueness. The Manchester group, for example, is proud of the building they own. Founded in 1973, the ACGS celebrated its 25th anniversary in 1998, and is justly proud of its seniority among these societies. The society has entered into a contract with Archiv-Histo of Montréal for access to the *Parchemin* database of the acts of the notaries who practiced in Québec during the period 1635-1775. In 1997, the American-French Genealogical Society (AFGS) of Pawtucket/Woonsocket announced with pride its purchase of research materials from the venerable Institut de Généalogie Drouin in Montréal, which ceased operations in the early 1990s. The principal components of the Drouin Collection include a 3,000-volume library consisting of rare books on family, parish, town history, and related subjects; the register of nearly all the marriages having taken place in Québec between 1608 and 1940; and several hundred reels of microfilmed church records from the foundation of a parish to *circa* 1940.

Journals published by these societies, while steadily improving in quality, have yet to receive the praise they have rightly earned. Whereas many articles focus of necessity on topics such as "Direct Line Ancestors," "Vital Records," "Biographies," "Members' Forum," etc., individuals who write for these journals often move beyond the strict confines of genealogy to social, cultural, political, and military history. They are thus making contributions to the history of the United States, Canada, and France. It would therefore be unconscionable to write Franco-American history without consulting these increasingly rich sources.

An exemplary instance of collaboration between historians and genealogists is the imposing book of nearly 600 pages entitled *The Beginnings of the Franco-American Colony in Woonsocket, Rhode*

Island by Marie Louise Bonier. Translated from the original *Débuts de la colonie franco-américaine de Woonsocket, Rhode Island*—the 1920 French version—the book was edited by the ever-productive Professor Claire Quintal, directress of the Institut français at Assumption College. Professor Quintal was assisted by genealogists Roger and Sylvia Bartholomy and local historian Raymond H. Bacon in this monumental enterprise. This opus constitutes a splendid addition to regional history and could well serve as a model of this genre. Professor Quintal's substantive Preface and Conclusion, as well as the volume's copious notes, combined with Marie Louise Bonier's original research, make this work an essential item for any Franco-American bibliography. Also noteworthy is the ongoing updating—by AFGS senior researcher Robert Pelland—of the family charts of the first 117 French-Canadian families listed by Bonier.

In point of fact, the most fortunate Franco-Americans are probably those who live their ethnicity as intellectuals or artists. In addition to the resources available in the documentation centers of the genealogical societies and in various libraries, they have at their disposal the libraries of ACA Assurance, the Union Saint-Jean-Baptiste/CFLI, and the Institut français of Assumption College in Worcester which remains in the forefront of Franco-American research. Under the direction of Claire Quintal, an experienced academic, the Institute supports both research and discussion in various ways, especially through its colloquia, its publications, and by means of special projects. As well-served as they are by these resources, researchers, historians, writers, and artists also benefit from an increasingly tolerant climate that characterizes this particular period of Franco-American history. If researchers and writers felt stifled in the past, this restraining influence has now disappeared, and today they enjoy almost limitless freedom. The remaining limitations will disappear when all the archives pertaining to Franco-American history have been unlocked and examined.

Regrettably there is at present a shortage of researchers. Luckily, some French, Québec, Acadian, and Anglo-American scholars have recognized that a substantial part of their history has taken place in New England and New York State and have added to the public's knowledge of the Franco-American experience. American scholars have also contributed greatly to this body of information. A lack of research has prevented further study in some areas, especially the arts. For example, too little attention has been paid to the splendid art work to be found in Franco-American churches. Similarly, the day-to-day Franco-American experience during the past one hundred and fifty years remains open to ethnologists as do the group's material culture and folklore. Professor Brigitte Lane's brilliant thesis on the Franco folklore of Lowell, Massachusetts, offers a striking illustration of what can be done. Only after a substantial number of similar empirical studies have been completed will it become possible to approach larger issues, such as comparative ethnicity.

It is, of course, impossible to predict with any certainty that Franco-Americans have any long-term future outside the realm of folklore. Those who currently seek to elicit support for the preservation or enrichment of the heritage may well feel like the mythical Sisyphus, condemned forever to push his boulder back to the top of his hill, only to have the boulder roll back downward when the summit is near. Others, more fortunate, have been able to transform their ethnic experience into a source of enrichment for their inner life.

The Fédération Féminine Franco-Américaine continues to meet on an annual basis and, although having lost a great deal of ground, it has made serious efforts at maintaining itself. For its part, the FAROG *Forum* has become less polemic in outlook. It is now called simply *Le Forum,* and its articles tend to be more serious and substantive than had previously been the case.

Although it seems that *la Franco-Américanie* is near the twilight of its history, the past decade has yielded some pleasant surprises. In 1993, Professor Eloïse Brière, of the State University of New York at Albany, began creating an electronic database of "people active in Franco-American cultural life in the information age." Professor Brière defines "cultural life" broadly. Her database includes persons involved in traditional cooking, weaving and needlework, woodcraft, music, dance, stories, healing, and cures. Participants in the arts and the professions are also part of the databank. She and her assistants continue to "gather information widely hoping thereby to help people form new connections."

LIFRA, a work group on Franco-American writing, under the direction of Elizabeth Aubé, also deserves to be mentioned. Interested in the practice, criticism, and theory of writing, LIFRA is seen as "a means of encouraging Franco-American literature, its creation, its circulation, and its study."

Another unexpected development occurred with the 1996 founding of the Maine-based Franco-American Women's Institute by Rhéa Côté Robbins, Lanette Landry Petrie, Kristen Langellier, Katie Bossé, and Amy Bouchard Morin. The purpose of this Women's Institute is to facilitate the development of "programming, panels, presentations of gifts and talents" and to leave a record of these activities. The group also publishes an electronic magazine, *The Initiative.* This on-line magazine contains substantive articles on women's issues, first-person accounts of ethnic life, poetry, and other genres.

The much hoped-for cohesiveness of the Franco-American community as well as the involvement of large numbers of its people in the pursuit of a collective goal, so ardently pursued by the activists of the seventies—especially those who gathered on the outskirts of Manchester, N.H., in 1976, at the invitation of Professor Robert Paris, the first Director of the National Materials Development Center—have, however, remained an elusive dream. The organizations now serving the community function for the most part without the widespread support of the critical mass needed to ensure optimal effectiveness.

The ongoing, dynamic involvement of ACA Assurance in ethnic life—highlighted by the signing of the Partenariat d'Accord with France—along with the constant outreach of the Institut français of Assumption College, particularly through its ever-expanding publication ventures—all of these point to Franco-American diversity, vitality, and increased visibility. In the cultural sphere, especially in literature and history, a few Franco-Americans have achieved both popular and critical success. Jack Kerouac and Will Durant are still the best-known among them. Novelists David Plante and Robert Cormier have achieved international renown as have the Pulitzer Prize winner Annie Proulx and the novelist and travel writer Paul Théroux.

As the millennium approaches, many of New England's nearly three million descendants of French-Canadian ancestry are so well integrated into mainstream American society that most of them, especially the young, are only faintly aware of their ethnic heritage. Assimilated or not, these descendants of the 900,000 French Canadians who crossed the border into the United States have made and continue to make contributions to the economic and cultural life of the United States in every field of human endeavor. It may not be too presumptuous to believe that those who, some three or four generations ago, left French Canada in search of their livelihood, might look with pride upon the achievements of their millions of descendants now scattered throughout this country.

It is also worth remembering that some of their forebears explored this continent, made friends very early on with Native American tribes, that they scouted and named this land, long before Lewis and Clark appeared upon the scene, and some two hundred years before so many of their offspring spilled over the Canadian border in successive waves

to become workers in New England and New York State's textile and
shoe industries.

Appendix I

FRENCH* SPOKEN AT HOME: NEW ENGLAND STATES, 1990
Persons five years of age and over

Maine	81,012
New Hampshire	51,284
Vermont	17,171
Massachusetts	124,973
Connecticut	53,586
Rhode Island	31,669
Total	**359,695**

* Language Category includes: French, Walloon, Provençal, Patois, French Creole, Haitian Creole, and Cajun.

Source: 1990 Census of Population and Housing - Summary Tape File 3A.

Compiled by Madeleine D. Giguère, Professor emerita, University of Southern Maine, 6/94

The statistics listed on the next page were presented by Dean Louder, professor of geography at Laval University, at the French Institute's 1994 colloquium on "The Franco-Americans." The sources of these statistics are Table ED 90-6, Languages Spoken at Home by Persons 5 Years and Above, by State: 1990 Census 1990 CPH-L 96 and USA 1980, Bureau of the Census: Chapter C-Tables: 60 and 172. We publish them here with Prof. Louder's permission.

States	Population of 5 Years and + 1990	French-Speaking 1990	French Ancestry 1990	Population of 5 Years and + 1980	French-Speaking 1980	French Ancestry 1980
Alabama	3 759 802	17 965	108 069	3 322 234	9 819	94 165
Alaska	495 425	2 030	30 031	355 723	1 710	23 012
Arizona	3 374 806	13 115	183 658	2 505 455	9 264	154 539
Arkansas	2 186 665	8 210	86 244	2 111 214	4 908	83 056
California	27 383 547	132 657	1 207 805	21 969 013	112 760	1 307 235
Colorado	3 042 986	12 855	173 337	2 670 872	11 249	175 992
Connecticut	3 060 000	53 586	371 274	2 922 810	59 788	326 483
Delaware	617 720	3 753	22 427	553 319	2 326	22 749
District of Columbia	570 284	9 783	10 450	604 289	8 779	10 467
Florida	12 095 284	194 783	630 540	9 180 230	71 924	484 904
Georgia	5 984 188	34 422	183 573	5 049 559	18 543	140 420
Hawaii	1 026 209	3 921	25 650	857 400	3 936	26 437
Idaho	926 703	2 839	53 704	850 632	2 463	54 792
Illinois	10 585 838	43 070	405 863	10 586 633	35 438	486 724
Indiana	5 146 160	20 578	231 135	5 071 880	13 563	267 338
Iowa	2 583 526	7 941	114 793	2 768 363	5 483	151 103
Kansas	2 289 615	7 851	122 931	2 393 102	5 770	140 959
Kentucky	3 434 955	13 543	102 707	3 462 290	7 730	107 668
Louisiana	3 886 353	261 678	1 069 558	3 845 505	263 387	934 237
Maine	1 142 122	81 012	336 227	1 046 188	94 225	266 096
Maryland	4 425 285	39 484	148 782	3 945 488	26 129	154 728
Massachusetts	5 605 751	124 973	946 630	5 400 422	135 033	838 509
Michigan	8 594 737	39 794	828 557	8 577 824	33 673	871 877
Minnesota	4 038 861	13 693	283 632	3 764 209	10 026	303 682
Mississipi	2 378 805	13 215	103 539	2 305 754	8 132	95 155
Missouri	4 748 704	20 135	289 050	4 563 086	12 831	340 026
Montana	740 218	2 572	51 088	721 613	2 379	54 124
Nebraska	1 458 904	4 135	61 445	1 447 251	3 036	77 834
Nevada	1 110 450	5 464	71 112	744 698	3 509	54 912
New Hampshire	1 024 621	51 284	324 569	858 108	61 846	237 140
New Jersey	7 200 696	52 351	189 010	6 893 400	32 448	213 913
New Mexico	1 390 048	3 402	51 538	1 191 276	3 205	48 034
New York	16 743 048	236 099	783 209	16 429 011	165 158	834 742
North Carolina	6 172 301	37 590	166 589	5 559 813	22 900	134 210
North Dakota	590 839	1 998	32 144	662 049	2 153	33 917
Ohio	10 063 212	46 075	401 474	10 011 580	32 728	464 366
Oklahoma	2 921 755	8 328	133 722	2 792 986	6 617	151 980
Oregon	2 640 482	10 854	191 189	2 435 197	8 336	195 957
Pennsylvania	11 085 170	45 515	296 616	11 117 862	34 072	336 177
Rhode Island	936 423	31 669	206 971	890 643	40 563	178 710
South Carolina	3 231 539	22 339	102 546	2 884 059	15 320	84 072
South Dakota	641 226	1 228	27 843	632 385	1 056	30 936
Tennessee	4 544 743	20 444	130 483	4 267 445	12 021	112 532
Texas	15 605 822	64 585	737 234	13 034 594	47 520	673 565
Utah	1 553 351	6 684	60 028	1 271 285	5 467	60 281
Vermont	521 521	17 171	165 697	475 452	19 906	144 528
Virginia	5 746 419	40 353	216 954	5 008 578	27 903	191 712
Washington	4 501 879	19 883	320 579	3 826 416	15 180	315 136
West Virginia	1 686 932	7 695	43 798	1 804 171	4 904	49 633
Wisconsin	4 531 134	14 242	295 039	4 358 993	10 468	323 759
Wyoming	418 713	1 558	25 079	424 510	1 560	26 396
USA TOTAL	230 445 777	1 930 404	13 156 122	210 426 869	1 549 144	12 890 949

Appendix II

Resources

Readers will find below a list of resources—both organizations and individuals—capable of providing them with additional information on the Franco-Americans of the Northeast.

Acadian Cultural Exchange of Northern Maine
RFD # 2 - Box99
Madawaska, ME 04756
1-207-728-4272
Contact person: Mrs. Géraldine Chassé
A valuable source of books and other materials. Inquiries should be accompanied by a stamped, self-addressed envelope.

Bilingual Historical Calendar
c/o Marie Reine Mikesell
1155 East 56th Street
Chicago, IL 60637
(773) 643-7865

Blackstone River Valley National Heritage Corridor Commission
One Depot Square
Woonsocket, RI 02895
1-401-762-0440 or 1-401-762-0250
The commission's numerous publications include a high quality newsletter, *Revolutions.*

Centre Franco-Américain
52 Concord Street
Manchester, NH 03101-1806
Adèle Boufford Baker, Executive Director

Le Forum
Centre Franco-Américain
University of Maine
164 College Ave.
Orono, Maine, 04473-1512
1-207-581-3764 e-mail: yal@umefarog.maine.edu
A bilingual newspaper of opinion and creative writing.
Yvon Labbé, Director

Franco-American Database
Professor Eloïse Brière
Department of French Studies
State University of New York (Humanities)
235-1400 Washington Ave.
Albany, NY 12222
Tel: 518-442-410 e-mail: EAB13@cnsvax.albany.edu

Franco-American Women's Institute (FAWI)
641 South Main St.
Brewer, Maine 04412-2516
Tel/Fax: 1-207-989-7059 e-mail: FAWI 1200@aol.com
Rhéa Côté Robbins, Director

La Librarie Populaire
18 Orange Street
Manchester, NH 03104
1-603-669-3788
A source of French, French-Canadian, and Franco-American books,
cassettes and CDs

LIFRA
Work group on Franco-American Writing: Practice, Criticism, Theory,
"...A means of encouraging Franco-American literature, its creation, its
circulation, and its study."
Elizabeth Aubé, Director
49 Moberly Ave. Toronto, Ontario, M4C 4A9 Canada
Tel: 1-416-698-7804

Museum of Work and Culture
Market Square
Woonsocket, RI 02895
1-401-769-WORK The only museum dealing with French-Canadian
immigration and FrancoAmerican history.

Quintin Publications
28 Felsmere Ave.
Pawtucket, RI 02861-2903
1-401-723-6797
Publishes genealogical books of interest to Franco-Americans and
French Canadians.

Therrien, Lucie
P.O. Box 4721
Portsmouth, NH 03802-4721
Tel: 603-430-9524

Union Saint-Jean-Baptiste
A Division of Catholic Family Life Insurance
P. 0. Box F
Woonsocket, RI 02895-0989
1-800-225-USJB or 1-401-769-0520
Louise Champigny, Vice-President for Fraternal Affairs

Vachon, Josée
CeVon Musique
P.O. Box 2235
Amherst, MA 01004
Tel: 413-253-2315

For additional addresses consult:
Répertoire de la Vie française en Amérique
150 Boul. René-Levesque Est rez-de-chaussée
Québec, QC, GIR 2B2 Canada
Directeur: Guy Lefebvre
(418) 646-9117   e-mail: www.cvfa@cvfa.ca

Appendix III

Franco-American Genealogical Societies and Their Journals

Franco-American Genealogical Societies and Public and State Library Collections of Franco-American Genealogical Material in the Northeast, the Midwest, and California.

California
French-Canadian Interest Group
Southern California Genealogical Society, 417 Irving Drive, Burbank, CA 91504 (818) 843-7247
http://home.earthlink.net/~djmill/

Connecticut
French-Canadian Genealogical Society of Connecticut (1981).
P.O. Box 928, Tolland, CT 06084 (860) 872-2587
http://ourworld.compuserve.com/homepages/rlcarpenter/frenchca.htm

Journal, *Connecticut Maple Leaf*, semi-annual, summer and winter. First issue-June 1983. Editor: Albert J. Marceau
This society was the subject of an article in the January 21, 1996 Connecticut edition of *The New York Times.*

French-Canadian Genealogical Society of Connecticut Annex
Killingly Historical and Genealogical Society
P.O. Box 6000, Danielson, CT 06239-6000 (860) 779-7250
Holds 230 duplicate copies of books owned by FCGSC. All other books at this location owned by the Killingly Historical and Genealogical Society.

The Bisaillon Collection
Connecticut State Library, History and Genealogy Unit
231 Capitol Ave., Hartford, CT 06106 (860) 566-3690,
http://www.cslnet.ctstateu.edu
The Bisaillon Collection consists of 900 books, originally owned by
Robert Bisaillon, which were donated to the Connecticut State Library
in December 1994 after his death.

Kentucky
Acadian Genealogy Exchange
863 Wayman Branch Rd., Covington, KY 41015-2250
(606) 356-9825
Journal: *Acadian Genealogy Exchange*

Maine
American-Canadian Genealogical Society, Father Léo Bégin Chapter
P.O. Box 2125, Lewiston, ME 04240

Franco-American Genealogical Society of York County (1982)
P.O. Box 180, Biddeford, ME 04005-0180
Holdings kept at the McArthur Public Library, 270 Main St.,
Biddeford, ME 04005-2413
Telephone 207 284-4181   Fax: 207 284-6761
President: Celeste Steele, RFD # 1 Box 293, Alfred, ME 04002-3151
Recording Secretary: Rena Payeur Côté, 210 West St.
Biddeford, ME 04005-9753   Telephone (207) 282-9173
Journal : *Maine's Franco-American Heritage*
First issue, November 1984.

Massachusetts
Acadian Cultural Society
P.O. Box 2304, Fitchburg, MA 01420-8804

Holdings at the Fitchburg Public Library, 610 Main St., Fitchburg, MA 01420
Telephone: (978) 345-9635
President: Paul A. Cyr, 671 County St., New Bedford, MA 02740-6718
Telephone: (508) 992 3535
Editor: Dennis Boudreau, Centredale, R.I.
Publicity: Lucille A. Langlois, P.O. Box 47, Quinebaug, CT 06262-0047 http://www.angelfire.com/ma/1755
Journal: *Le Réveil Acadien,* quarterly

French-Canadian-American Genealogy
Genealogy and Local History Department
Springfield Public Library, 220 State St., Springfield, MA 01103

Michigan
French-Canadian Heritage Society of Michigan
P.O. Box 10028, Lansing, MI 48901-0028
http://fp-www.wwnet.net/~dulongj/fchsm.Fchsm.html
Mount Clemens Public Library, 150 Cass Ave., Mount Clemens, MI 48043-2297
(810) 469-6200   Fax (810) 469-6668
Journal: *Michigan's Habitant Heritage,* quarterly, January, April, July, and October
There are three chapters of the French-Canadian Heritage Society of Michigan: the Detroit Chapter, the Traverse City Chapter, the Mid-Michigan Chapter. Of the three, only the Detroit Chapter publishes any material.

French-Canadian Heritage Society of Michigan, Detroit Chapter
c/o Burton Historical Collection
Detroit Public Library, 5201 Woodward Ave., Detroit, MI 48202
Publication: *French Connection*

Minnesota
La Société Canadienne-Française du Minnesota
4020 Reservoir Blvd., Minneapolis, MN 5421-3150
Publication: *Chez Nous*

NorthWest Territory French and Canadian Heritage Institute
Section of the Minnesota Genealogical Society
P.O. Box 16069, St. Paul, MN 55116
Newsletter: *Cousins et Cousines*

NorthWest Territory Canadian and French Heritage Center
P.O. Box 29397, Brooklyn Center, MN 55429-03997
Journal, quarterly, from *circa* 1974 to Summer 1994—*Lost in Canada?:
Canadian-American Genealogical Journal*
Journal as of Spring 1995: *Canadian-American Journal of History and
Genealogy for Canadian, French, and Métis Study*

New Hampshire
American-Canadian Genealogical Society (September 1973)
P.O.Box 6478, Manchester, NH 03018-6478
(603) 622-1554; http://www.acgs.org/
Journal, quarterly, first issue May 1975.
American-Canadian Genealogist, formerly titled *The Genealogist*
The ACGS has leased from the Mormons a series of CD ROMs entitled
"Family Search," a compendium of world-wide indices giving
members access to information on virtually countless individuals.
Access to a new research tool called *Parchemin* is also available.
ACGS has recently entered into a contract with Archiv-Histo of
Montreal for access to the *Parchemin* database of the acts of the
notaries who practiced in Québec during the period 1635-1775. To
date, abstracts have been prepared for some 250,000 notarial acts that
have been examined. The topics range from marriage contracts to land

concessions, to purchase and sales agreements, to the payment of debts, liens and mortgages, to work contracts (*engagement ouest*), to property inventories, to the partition of goods, to last wills and testaments, to *donations*, etc.

L'Association généalogique et historique acadienne de la Nouvelle-Angleterre (1979-1985)
P.O. Box 668, Manchester, NH 03105
Journal/newsletter 1981—*L'Étoile d'Acadie* (1981-1985). It is presently a section of *American-Canadian Genealogist*.

New York
La Societé des Filles du Roi et Soldats du Carignan, Inc.
9 Croydon Dr., Merrick, NY 11566-2303
http://users. deltanet.com/~ms900/Kings/members.html
Wvbx90a@prodigy.com
Treasurer: David Toupin   Dtoupin@juno.com
(516) 867-5680.
Journal/newsletter: *Sent by the King*, semiannual, first issue December 1994

Northern New York American-Canadian Genealogical Society (1983)
P.O. Box 1256, Plattsburgh, NY 12901-0120
Holdings at the Community Center, Main St., Keeseville, NY
Telephone: (518) 834-5401
President/Librarian - Barbara Sequin—(518) 236-7567
Journal: *Lifelines,* semi-annual. First issue, Spring 1984
Editor: Elizabeth N. Botten—(518) 563-2709.

Rhode Island
American-French Genealogical Society (1978)
P.O.Box 2113, Pawtucket, RI 02861-2113
(401) 765-6141, http://users.ids.net/~afgs/afgshome.html

Journal: *Je me souviens*, first issue September 1978.

Vermont
French-Canadian Genealogical Society of Vermont (1996)
P.O. Box 65128, Burlington, VT 05406-5128 Fax (802) 656-8518,
http://members.aol.com/vtfcgs/genealogy/index.html
President: Paul Landry—e-mail: landrypr@aol.com
Journal: *Links,* first issue, Fall 1996
First Editor: J. André Senécal—e-mail: asenecal@zoo.uvm.edu

Wisconsin
French-Canadian-Acadian Genealogists of Wisconsin
4624 W. Tesch Ave., Greenfield, WI 53220
French Canadian-Acadian Genealogists of Wisconsin Quarterly

Alphabetical Listing of Current Journals published by Franco-American Genealogical Societies in the United States

Acadian Genealogy Exchange—Acadian Genealogy Exchange,Covington, KY

American-Canadian Genealogist—American-Canadian Genealogical Society, Manchester, NH

Chez Nous—La Société Canadienne-Française du Minncsota, Minneapolis.

Canadian-American Journal of History and Genealogy for Canadian, French, and Métis Study—NorthWest Territory Canadian and French Heritage Center, Brooklyn Center, MN (Name of journal before Spring 1995—*Lost in Canada ?*)

Connecticut Maple Leaf—French-Canadian Genealogical Society of Connecticut, Tolland, CT

Je me souviens—American-French Genealogical Society, Woonsocket, RI

Le Réveil Acadien—Acadian Cultural Society, Fitchburg, MA

Lifelines—Northern New York American-Canadian Genealogical Society, Plattsburgh New York.

Links—French-Canadian Genealogical Society of Vermont, Burlington, VT

Maine's Franco-American Heritage—Franco-American Genealogical Society, Biddeford, ME

Michigan's Habitant Heritage—French-Canadian Heritage Society of Michigan, Lansing, MI

Sent by the King—La Société des Filles du Roi et Soldats du Carignan, Merrick, New York

Genealogical lists compiled by:
Albert J. Marceau
Editor, *Connecticut Maple Leaf*

BIBLIOGRAPHY

OUTLINE

1. Reference

    a. Bibliography

    b. Other

    c. Newspapers, Periodicals, and Audio-Visual Materials

2. General

3. History

4. History: Regional & Local listed by State and City

5. Biography & Autobiography

6. Ethnology & Folklore

7. Religion: General & Miscellaneous

8. Sociology & Anthropology

9. Language & Linguistics

10. Literature

1. REFERENCE

a. Bibliography

Anctil, Pierre. *A Franco-American Bibliography: New England.* Bedford, N.H.: National Materials Development Center, 1979, 137 p. The 800 titles listed in this work make it an essential tool for serious researchers.

Catalogue de la Bibliothèque de l'Union St-Jean-Baptiste d'Amérique. Collection Mallet. Woonsocket, R.I.: USJB, 1935, 2nd ed., xiii, 303 p. Particularly useful for its listings of rare books, pamphlets, manuscripts, etc., contained in the Mallet Collection.

Chartier, Armand B. "A Selective and Thematic Checklist of Materials Relating to Franco-Americans." *Contemporary French Civilization* II, 3 (Spring 1978), pp. 469-512. The first bibliography on this subject to appear in a U.S. scholarly journal. Many of the titles in this checklist have been incorporated into the present bibliography.

Quintal, Claire, et al. *Répertoire des 90 ans d'études et de conférences de la Société Historique Franco-Américaine.* Marthe Péloquin, ed., Manchester, N.H.: Imprimerie Lafayette,1991. An essential tool for serious students.The volume also contains the texts of lectures by Arthur L. Eno, Esq., and Jean Duquette.

Roby, Yves. "Un Québec émigré aux États-Unis: bilan historiographique." In *Les rapports culturels entre le Québec et les États-Unis,* Claude Savary, ed., Québec: Institut québécois de recherche sur la culture, 1984, pp. 103-144. Franco-American history as seen by a Quebecer. This article is followed by the "Commentaires" of Pierre Anctil and Claire Quintal.

b. Other

———. *Le Guide Français de la Nouvelle-Angleterre des États du Maine, New Hampshire, Vermont, Massachusetts, Rhode Island et Connecticut.* Première édition. Lowell, Mass.: Harrington Frères, 1887, 320 p.

Bélanger, Albert A., ed. *Guide franco-américain des États de la Nouvelle-Angleterre,* Fall River, Mass.: A. A. Bélanger, 1916, 828 p. This *guide* ("established in 1899," according to the title page) contains the names and addresses of Franco-American professional and business persons. Renamed *Guide officiel des Franco-Américains,* it was revised and updated for each of the thirteen editions published between 1916 and 1940. The last edition (1946) was compiled by Lucien and Thérèse Sansouci (Woonsocket, R.I.)

Bourbonnière, Avila. *Le Guide français de la Nouvelle-Angleterre.* Lowell, Mass.: La Société de Publications Françaises des États-Unis 1887. A "Who's Who" of the early years. Later editions are entitled: *Le Guide français de la Nouvelle-Angleterre et de l'État de New York* (1889) and *Le Guide français des États-Unis* (1891), 960 p.

Coulet du Gard, René. *Dictionary of French Place Names in the U.S.A.* N.p., Éditions des Deux Mondes et Slavuta, 1986, 431 p. The compiler of this dictionary "covers" every state, though not exhaustively.

Dion-Lévesque, Rosaire. *Silhouettes franco-américaines,* Manchester, N.H.: Association Canado-Américaine, 1957, vi, 933 p. A compendium of 300 biographical sketches of some better- and some less well-known Franco-Americans.

Freeman, Stanley L., and Raymond Pelletier. *Initiating Franco-American Studies: A Handbook for Teachers.* Orono, Me.: University of Maine, Canadian/Franco-American Studies Project, 1981, 284 p. Contains course outlines and lists of pedagogical resources.

Quintal, Claire. *La toponymie française de la Nouvelle-Angleterrre.* In François Beaudin, ed. *450 ans de noms de lieux français en Amérique du Nord.* Québec: Les Publications du Québec, 1986, pp 397-402.

Senécal, André, comp. *Inventaire Franco-Américain (INFA), ongoing compilation of the Franco-American Bibliographic File of Newspapers, Monographs, and Periodicals (1609-1989).* Burlington: University of Vermont. Available on CD-ROM from the compiler at the Canadian Studies Program (802) 656-3062. Fax : (802) 656-8518.

[Verrette, Adrien]. *La Vie franco-américaine* 1937-1953. The author has chronicled numerous activities of the many Franco-American organizations at the regional (New England) and at the local level.

c. Newspapers, Periodicals, and Audio-Visual Materials

The most important collections of newspapers and periodicals are housed in the archives of the A.C.A. in Manchester, N.H., and the U.S.J.B. in Woonsocket, R.I. As to Audio-Visual Materials, the Dimond Library at the University of New Hampshire contains an abundance of material, both audio and video. La Librairie Populaire in Manchester, N.H., also has a considerable inventory.

2. GENERAL

————. *The Chinese of the Eastern States.* Manchester, N.H.: L'Avenir National, 1925. A collection of articles and letters dealing with the Franco-American participation in the labor force.

Anctil, Pierre. "La Franco-Américanie ou le Québec d'en bas." In *Cahiers de Géographie du Québec,* vol. 23, no. 58, April 1979, pp. 39-72.

Association Canado-Américaine. *Les Franco-Américains peints par eux-mêmes.* Montréal: Éditions Albert Lévesque, 1936. An overview of the social situation of the Franco-Americans during what has been called "the golden age."

Benoit, Josaphat. *L'Âme franco-américaine.* Montréal: Éditions Albert Lévesque, 1935. Concentrates on the reasons for and obstacles to the survival of the Franco-Americans as an ethnic group.

Breton, Raymond, and Pierre Savard, eds. *The Quebec and Acadian Diaspora in North America.* Toronto: The Multicultural Society of Ontario, 1982, xix, 199 p. Proceedings of a colloquium on the Franco-Americans, the Acadians, the Franco-Ontarians, and the French Canadians of Western Canada.

Breton, Roland J.-L. *Géographie de la Franco-Américanie.* 25e Congrès International de Géographie sur l'Amérique française, Paris, August 1984.

Chaput, Donald. "Some *Rapatriement* Dilemmas." In *Canadian Historical Review,* no. 49, Dec. 1968, pp. 400-412.

Chartier, Armand. "Franco-Americans and Québec: Linkages and Potential in the Northeast." In *Problems and Opportunities in U.S.-Quebec Relations.* Hero, Alfred A. Jr., and Marcel Daneau, eds. Boulder, Colorado: Westview Press, 1984, pp. 151-68. A critical systematic analysis of Québec-Franco-American relations, past and present, with recommendations for the future.

Demers, Normand J. *Revolution in Quebec: A Past Rejected, A Future in Doubt.* Portsmouth, N.H.: Peter E. Randall Publisher, 1995, xviii, 192 p. From the title-page: "An American Reflects on the Dynamic but Divided Society of His Heritage." The author, a close observer of contemporary Québec, arrives at some debatable conclusions.

Desaulniers, G. L., ed. *Précieux pêle-mêle franco-américain.* Woonsocket, R.I.: G. L. Desaulniers, ed. 1922, 236 p. This collection of articles is intended to encourage Franco-Americans to be loyal American citizens while preserving their French Catholic heritage.

Eno, Arthur L. *French Trails in the United States.* Manchester, N.H.: S.H.F.A., 1940.

Foley, Allen B. "From French-Canadian to Franco-American." Ph.D. dissertation, Harvard University, 1940.

Forget, Ulysse. *Les Franco-Américains et le "Melting Pot". Onomastique franco-américaine.* Fall River, Mass.: Imprimerie de l'Indépendant, 1949. Discusses the impact of inter-ethnic marriages on Franco-American assimilation. Part 2 lists French surnames which have been anglicized.

Les Franco-Américains. Montréal: Maison de Radio-Canada, Service des Transcriptions, 1983, 2 vol. Interviews with some twenty

Francos, aired on the program "Actuelles," January 17-21 and January 24-28, 1983.

Francophonies d'Amérique [1991-]. An annual scholarly journal, ably edited by Professor Jules Tessier of the Department of French Literature, University of Ottawa. Recent issues on a specialized topic, e.g., Women, have been edited by various francophone Canadian specialists. Each issue usually contains one or more articles on Franco-Americans.

Garff, Dennis. "Heirs of New France: An Ethnic Minority in Search of Security." Ph.D. dissertation, Tufts University, Fletcher School of Law and Diplomacy, 1970.

Ham, Edward B. "French Canadians in the U.S." In *Writings on Canadian-American Studies,* 1966.

Hamelin, Rev. Hormidas. *Lettres à mon Ami sur la Patrie, la Langue et la Question franco-américaine.* Montréal: Imprimerie des Sourds-Muets, 1930, 255 p. In defense of assimilation.

Jannin, Valérie. "The Franco-American Cultural Survival in New England (1840s-1992)." Master's thesis, Université de Paris IV-Sorbonne, 1992.

Landry, Thomas M., O.P. *Mission catholique et française en Nouvelle Angleterre.* Québec: Éditions Ferland, 1962, 262 p. A collection of speeches and essays by one of the last and certainly one of the staunchest advocates of *survivance.*

Leblanc, Robert G. "The Acadian Migrations." *Cahiers de Géographie du Québec,* vol. 11, no. 24, December 1967, pp. 523-541.

————. "Regional Competition for Franco-American Repatriates: 1870-1930." In *Quebec Studies,* vol. 1, 1983, pp. 110-129.

Louder, Dean R., and Eric Waddell, eds. *Du continent perdu à l'archipel retrouvé: le Québec et l'Amérique française.* Québec: Presses de l'Université Laval, 1983, xviii, 292 p. Translated by Franklin Philip. *French America: Mobility, Identity, and Minority Experience Across the Continent.* Baton Rouge: Louisiana State University Press, 1993, xviii, 371 p. A collection of substantive essays on the various francophone regions of North America.

Louder, Dean, ed. *Le Québec et les francophones de la Nouvelle Angleterre.* Sainte-Foy, QC.: Presses de l'Université Laval, CEFAN, 1991, xiii, 309 p. This major work covers several topics, including literature and historiography: it also includes personal *témoignages.*

Olivier, Julien. *Souches et racines: une introduction à la généalogie pour les jeunes Franco-Américains.* Bedford, New Hampshire: National Materials Development Center, 1981, 175 p. Methods, personal accounts, and resource guide.

Paquet, Gilles. "L'émigration des Canadiens Français vers la Nouvelle-Angleterre, 1870-1910. Prises de vues quantitatives." *Recherches sociographiques,* vol. 5, Sept.-Dec. 1964, pp. 319-370.

Parker, James Hill. *Ethnic Identity: The Case of the French-Americans.* Lanham, Md.: University Press of America, 1983, 67p.

Péloquin, Marthe, ed. *La Femme francophone aux États-Unis.* Manchester, N.H.: Imprimerie Lafayette, 1984, 82 p. Proceedings of the 16th biennial Congress of the Fédération Féminine Franco-Américaine held at Rivier College, Nashua, New Hampshire, 27, 28, and 29 April 1984.

Péloquin-Faré, Louise. *L'identité culturelle: les Franco-Américains de la Nouvelle-Angleterre.* Paris: Didier-Crédif, 1983, 159 p. An optimistic description of contemporary Franco-American life.

Perreault, Robert, et al. *Magazine Ovo,* vol. 12, no. 46, 1982, 48 p. This issue, entitled *Du Québec à la Nouvelle-Angleterre,* "illustrates" immigration through text and rare photographs.

———. "Ulric Bourgeois artiste-photographe: des images retrouvées du temps perdu." In *Liaison,* no. 42, Spring 1987, pp. 28-31.

Poulin, Eugena, R.S.M., and Claire Quintal. *The French Experience in North America: An Activities Packet.* Providence, R.I.: The Rochambeau Education Committee and the Rhode Island Heritage Commission, 1981, iv, 151 p. A revised edition entitled *The French Experience - Classroom Activities* appeared in 1987 under the auspices of the American and Canadian French Cultural Exchange Commission of the Commonwealth of Massachusetts. This compilation of elementary and junior high level activities contains data which would benefit adult readers as well.

Quintal, Claire. "An Unrecognized Minority: New England Franco-Americans." In *Contemporary French Civilization,* vol. V, no. 3, Spring 1981, pp. 381-388. An insightful essay in social psychology.

———. "Les Petits Canadas de la Nouvelle-Angleterre." *Héritage francophone en Amérique du Nord.* Actes du Colloque de Vancouver, 1983. Bernard Andrès, Vital Gadbois and Claude LeGoff, comp. *Québec français* and FIPF, 1984.

———. "Les institutions franco-américaines: pertes et progrès." *Le Québec et les francophones de la Nouvelle-Angleterre.* Dean

Louder, ed. Québec: Les Presses de l'Université Laval, CEFAN, 1991, pp. 61-84.

The River Review/La Revue Rivière is a "bilingual, multidisciplinary journal of arts and ideas," published annually by the University of Maine at Fort Kent since 1995.

Roberge, Céleste, ed. *Vers l'évolution d'une culture.* Orono, Me.: University of Maine, Franco-American Resource Opportunity Group, 1973, 131 p. Essays on various socio-cultural topics, including a particularly useful paper on folklore by ethnologist Professor Roger Paradis. (Cf. Part 6, Ethnology and Folklore), pp. 43-87.

Robert, Gérald. *Musée de l'Association Canado-Américaine.* Manchester, N.H.: Association Canado-Américaine, 1987, 180 p.

Therriault, George F. "The Franco-Americans of New England." In *Canadian Dualism: Studies of French -English Relations*, Mason Wade, ed. University of Toronto Press, 1960, pp. 392-411.

Truesdell, Leon. *The Canadian Born in the United States.* New Haven: Yale University Press, 1943. A demographic analysis.

Vicero, Ralph D. "Immigration of French Canadians to New England, 1840-1900: A Geographical Analysis." Ph.D. dissertation, (Geography), University of Wisconsin, 1968, xii, 449 p. Perhaps the definitive work on the demography of emigration.

Wright, Davidson Carroll. "The Canadian French in New England." In *The Thirteenth Annual Report of the Massachusetts Bureau of Statistics of Labor.* Boston: Rand, Avery & Co., 1882.

3. HISTORY

Anctil, Pierre. "Chinese of the Eastern States, 1881." In *Recherches sociographiques*, vol. XXII, no. 1, January-April 1981, pp. 125-131.An analytical study of this controversy.

―――. "L'identité de l'immigrant québécois en Nouvelle-Angleterre: le Rapport Wright de 1882." In *Recherches sociographiques,* vol. XXII, no. 3, September-December 1981, pp. 331-360. Continues the previous article.

Belisle, Alexandre. *Histoire de la presse franco-américaine et des Canadiens-Français aux États-Unis.* Worcester, Mass.: Les Ateliers de l'*Opinion Publique*, 1911, xvi, 456 p. Indispensable early history, not only of the press, but also of the people, with fascinating sketches of many leading figures.

―――. "French Canadians in the Development of the United States." *Proceedings of the Worcester Society of Antiquity*, vol. 23, 1907, pp. 4-20.

Benoit, Josaphat. *Catéchisme d'histoire franco-américaine.* Manchester, N.H.: La Société Historique Franco-Américaine, 1939. A brief (57 p.) outline-history of the French and the French Canadians in the U.S. in question/answer form.

Bilodeau, Rev. Georges-Marie. *Pour rester au pays.* Québec: l'Action Sociale, 1926. A study of the French-Canadian emigration to the U.S., its causes and possible remedies, written by an opponent of emigration.

Blewett, Mary H. *The Last Generation: Work and Life in the Textile Mills of Lowell, Massachusetts, 1919-1960.* Amherst, Mass.:

University of Massachusetts Press, 1990, xxiii, 330 p. This work contextualizes the oral histories of several Franco-American men and women.

Brault, Gerard J. *The French-Canadian Heritage in New England.* Hanover, N.H.: University Press of New England, 1986, xiii, 282 p. A broad overview of the Franco-American experience, with a chapter on the Brault family in North America.

Bulletin de la Société Historique Franco-Américaine. Published in the years: 1906; 1935 through 1954; 1955-1973; 1983, 1988, 1990, 1992-93. Each of these issues contains substantive material.

Chartier, Armand B. *Histoire des Franco-Américains de la Nouvelle-Angleterre, 1775-1990.* Sillery, Québec: Éditions du Septentrion, 1991, 435 p. The most comprehensive history to date.

—————. ed. *Littérature historique populaire franco-américaine.* Manchester, N.H.: National Materials Development Center, 1981, 108 p. Choice of texts and presentation of ten historians.

Clément, Antoine, comp. *Les quarante ans de la Société Historique Franco-Américaine* (1899-1939). Manchester, N.H.: L'Avenir National, 1940, 878 p. A collection of lectures and speeches presented *in extenso* or in summary form, given before the S.H.F.A. from its beginnings to 1939.

Daignault, Elphège-J. *Le vrai mouvement sentinelliste en Nouvelle-Angleterre, 1923-1929 et l'Affaire du Rhode Island.* Montréal: Éditions du Zodiaque, 1936, 246 p. Pro-sentinellist version of the movement. See the book by Foisy on this same topic.

D'Andrea, Vaneeta. "The Women of *Survivance*: A Case Study of a Franco-American Women's Group in New England." Ph.D. dissertation in sociology, University of Connecticut, 1986. An overview of this subject by an author not involved in *survivance.*

Deuxième Congrès de la Langue Française au Canada. Québec: Imprimerie du Soleil, 1938. (Compte-rendu, 517 p.; Mémoires: 3 vols.). The second in a series of three "Congrès" which brought together large delegations from each of the many French-speaking regions of North America.

Doty, C. Stewart. *The First Franco-Americans: New England Life Histories from the Federal Writers' Project 1938-1939.* Orono, ME.: University of Maine at Orono Press, 1985, 163 p. This collection of oral histories, gathered in the 1930s and published here for the first time, suggests the nature of Franco-American life at the level of the "common man"—and woman.

Ducharme, Jacques. *The Shadows of the Trees.* "The Story of French-Canadians in New England." New York: Harper, 1943. Impressionistic, anecdotal "history" of the Franco-Americans.

Foisy, J.-Albert. *Histoire de l'agitation sentinelliste dans la Nouvelle-Angleterre, 1925-1928.* Woonsocket, R.I.: La Tribune, 1928, 427 p. Anti-sentinellist version of the controversy. See. Daignault's book on this topic.

A Franco-American Overview. Cambridge, Mass.: Lesley College, National Assessment and Dissemination Center, 1979-1982, 8 vol. This collection of scholarly texts explores the nature and extent of the "Franco," French-Canadian, and French experience throughout the United States.

Gatineau, Félix. *Historique des Conventions générales des Canadiens français aux États-Unis, 1865-1901.* Woonsocket, R.I.: L'Union Saint-Jean-Baptiste d'Amérique, 1927, 500 p. Indispensable for the study of the nineteenth century, this volume contains the proceedings of these large gatherings which brought together delegates from the various French-speaking communities of the Northeast and the Midwest.

Ham, Edward B. "French Patterns in Quebec and New England." *The New England Quarterly*, 18, Dec. 1945, 435-47.

Hamon, Edouard, S.J. *Les Canadiens-français de la Nouvelle-Angleterre.* Montréal: Éditions du 45e Parallèle Nord, 1982, xv, 484 p. Reprint of the 1891 edition (Québec: Hardy). One of the first general histories, this study remains useful for the author's comments on nineteenth century "French" parishes and parishioners.

Hareven, Tamara. *Family Time and Industrial Time: The Relationship Between the Family and Work in a New England Industrial Community.* Cambridge: Cambridge University Press, 1982, 474 p. and Lanham, Md.: University Press of America, 1993.

Hendrickson, Dyke. *Quiet Presence.* Portland, Maine: Guy Gannett Publishing Company, 1980, ix, 266 p. This volume contains twenty-eight oral histories of persons from diverse milieux and ages; especially useful for the modern period.

Lafleur, Normand. *Les "Chinois" de l'Est ou la vie quotidienne des Québécois émigrés aux États-Unis de 1840 à nos jours.* Montréal: Leméac, 1981, 108 p.

Lapointe, Jacques and André Leclerc. *Les Acadiens: État de la recherche.* Québec: Conseil de la vie française en Amérique, 1987, 259 p. Contains, among others, texts by Claire Quintal,

"Situation de la recherche sur les Acadiens de la Nouvelle-Angleterre," pp. 67-72, and by John Martin, "Les Acadiens en Nouvelle-Angleterre: Au-delà de la *Survivance*," pp. 243-48.

Lavoie, Yolande. *L'Émigration des Québécois aux États-Unis de 1840 à 1930.* Québec: Éditeur officiel du Québec, Documentation du Conseil de la langue française, 1981, édition revue et augmentée, 68 p. This demographic study seems definitive.

Leblanc, Robert G. "The Francophone 'Conquest' of New England: Geopolitical Conceptions and Imperial Ambition of French-Canadian Nationalists in the Nineteenth Century." In *The American Review of Canadian Studies,* 15, no. 3, Autumn 1985, pp. 288-310.

Magnan, Rev. D.-M.-A. *Histoire de la race française aux États-Unis.* Paris: Charles Amat Éditeur, 1913, 2nd edition revised and corrected, xvi, 386 p. This panorama of the French presence in North America since 1504 has never been duplicated.

Podea, Iris Saunders. "Quebec to 'Little Canada': The Coming of the French-Canadians to New England in the Nineteenth Century." *New England Quarterly,* 23, (1950), 365-80. A brief description of the early experiences of Franco-Americans in New England.

Poteet, Maurice, ed. *Textes de l'exode. Recueil de textes sur l'émigration des Québécois aux États-Unis (XIXe et XXe siècles).* Montréal: Guérin, 1987, 505 p. An excellent choice of texts on the emigration and its aftermath.

Premier Congrès de la Langue Française au Canada. Québec: Imprimerie de l'Action Sociale, 1913. (Compte-rendu, 693 p.;

Mémoires, 636 p.), 1914. Proceedings of the first, in a series of three, French-language *Congrès.*

Quintal, Claire, and André Vachon, eds. *Situation de la recherche sur la Franco-Américanie.* Québec: Conseil de la vie française en Amérique, 1980, 100 p.

Quintal, Claire. "Le Québec et les Franco-Américains: les limites d'une certaine présence après une longue absence." *Bulletin de la Fédération Féminine Franco-Américaine,* vol. 28, nos. 3 et 4, été-automne 1980, pp. 10, 12 et 13, and Poteet, *Textes de l'exode,* see above.

Quintal, Claire, ed. *L'Émigrant québécois vers les États-Unis: 1850-1920.* Québec, QC.: Conseil de la vie française en Amérique, 1982, 122 p.

———. *The Little Canadas of New England.* Worcester, Mass.: Assumption College, French Institute, 1983, x, 119 p.

———. *L'Émigrant acadien vers les États-Unis; 1842-1950.* Québec, QC.: Conseil de la vie française en Amérique, 1984, 177 p. An indispensable contribution to the history of Acadians in New England.

———. *Le patrimoine folklorique des Franco-Américains.* Québec, QC.: Conseil de la vie française en Amérique, 1986, 276 p.

———. *Les Franco-Américains et leurs institutions scolaires.* Worcester, Mass.: Institut français, Assumption College, 1990, 363 p.

———. *La littérature franco-américaine: écrivains et écritures Franco-American Literature: Writers and Their Writings.*

Worcester, Mass.: Institut français, Assumption College, 1992, iii, 185 p.

————. *Religion catholique et appartenance franco-américaine/ Franco-Americans and Religion: Impact and Influence.* Worcester, Mass.: Institut français, Assumption College, 1993, iii, 202 p.

————. *La femme franco-américaine/The Franco-American Woman.* Worcester, Mass.: Institut français, Assumption College, 1994, iii, 216 p.

————. *Steeples and Smokestacks: A Collection of Essays on the Franco-American Experience in New England.* Worcester, Mass.: Institut français, Assumption College, 1996, iii, 683 p. In this monumental work, Claire Quintal brings together for the first time in English, thirty-seven essays dealing with topics ranging from emigration, Franco-American communities, Religion, Education, Literature, Journalism, Folklore, Franco-American Women, Franco-Americans today to *témoignages* by authors as varied in outlook as Arthur Milot, Lucien Aubé, David Plante, and John Dufresne. The volume also contains several titles dealing with the Acadians. A *must* for any reader interested in ethnicity or in any one of these numerous topics.

Quintal, Claire. "La Fédération Féminine Franco-Américaine ou Comment les Franco-Américaines sont entrées de plain-pied dans le mouvement de la survivance." Estelle Dansereau, ed. *Francophonies d'Amérique*, Université d'Ottawa, 1997, pp. 177-191.

Ramirez, Bruno. "French Canadian Immigrants in the New England Cotton Industry: A Socioeconomic Profile." In *Labour,* vol. 11, Spring 1983, pp. 125-142.

——— and Jean Lamarre. "Du Québec vers les États-Unis: l'étude des lieux d'origine." In *Revue d'Histoire de l'Amérique française,* vol. 38, no. 3, Winter 1985, pp. 409-422. Describes various perceptions of the immigrants and explains their genesis and evolution.

Robert, Adolphe. *Mémorial des Actes de l'Association Canado-Américaine, 1896-1946.* Manchester, N.H.: Imprimerie de l'Avenir National, 1946, 486 p. Summarizes the principal contributions of this important "société."

Robert, Gérald. *Mémorial II des Actes de l'Association Canado-Américaine.* Manchester: Ballard Bros, Inc., 1975, 496 p.

Roby, Yves. *Les Franco-Américains de la Nouvelle-Angleterre (1776-1930).* Sillery, Québec: Éditions du Septentrion, 1990, 434 p. A rigorously scientific and indispensable work.

———. "Les Canadiens Français des États-Unis (1860-1900): Dévoyés ou missionnaires?" In *Revue d'Histoire de l'Amérique Française,* vol. 41, no.1, Summer 1987, pp. 3-22. Describes various perceptions of the immigrants and explains their genesis and evolution.

Rocheleau-Rouleau, Corinne. *Laurentian Heritage.* Toronto: Longmans Green and Co., 1948, xi, 178 p. A vivid introduction to rural Quebec in the 1870s, this book deserves republication and broad dissemination.

Rouillard, Jacques. *Ah les États! Les travailleurs canadiens-français dans l'industrie textile de la Nouvelle-Angleterre d'après le témoignage des derniers migrants.* Montréal: Boréal Express, 1985, 155 p. As the title indicates, this work describes the life of French Canadians in the New England textile industry, based on oral histories of the last immigrants.

Rumilly, Robert. *Histoire des Franco-Américains.* Woonsocket, R.I.: L'Union Saint-Jean-Baptiste d'Amérique, 1958, 552 p. This "classic" work is especially useful for a history of Franco-American institutions and ethno-religious conflicts.

Schriver, Edward, ed. *The French in New England, Acadia and Québec.* Orono, Maine: New England, Atlantic Provinces, Quebec Center, University of Maine, 1973. Proceedings of a 1972 conference. Includes articles on the Acadians, the French-Canadian immigration, oral tradition in New England and French Canada, etc.

Tétrault, Maximilienne. *Le rôle de la presse dans l'évolution du peuple franco-américain de la Nouvelle-Angleterre.* Marseille: Ferran, 1935, 143 p. This updates the Belisle *Histoire de la presse...* bringing the study of the subject to the 1930s.

Vachon, André and Claire Quintal, eds. *Situation de la recherche sur la Franco-Américanie.* Québec: Conseil de la vie française en Amérique, 1980, 100 p.

Verrette, Adrien. Monsignor Adrien Verrette has published some 30-40 volumes on Franco-American life. Unfortunately, an exhaustive list of his writings does not exist. Developing such a list lies beyond the scope of the present work. We therefore include here only a few of what some experts consider his most important works.

Verrette, Rev. Adrien. *La Croisade franco-américaine.* Manchester, N.H.: L'Avenir National, 1938, 500 p. This account of the Second French-Language Congress, held in Quebec City in 1937, summarizes the state of the Franco-American community in the 1930s and also the aspirations of the militant elite.

──────. *Centenaire Franco-Américain 1849-1949.* Manchester, N.H.: Ballard Frères, 1950, xv, 643 p. An invaluable collection of articles. There exists another edition of this work with a Preface by Adolphe Robert and Rev. Thomas M. Landry, O.P., and an *"Avant-propos"* by Msgr. Verrette. Manchester: l'Avenir National, 1950, xiv, 274 p.

──────. *La Vie franco-américaine.* Troisième Congrès de la Langue Française. Manchester N.H.: Ballard Frères, 1953, xi-xv, 568 p. The comments made above concerning the Second French-Language Congress also apply to this work on the Third French-Language Congress.

──────. "Les Acadiens aux États-Unis: 1755-1955." *Bulletin de la Société Historique Franco-Américaine,* Nouvelle Série, 1, 1955, 75-85. A brief look at an often neglected group of French-speaking Canadian immigrants.

Viatte, Auguste. "Les Franco-Américains de la Nouvelle-Angleterre." In *Renaissance,* 1945.

Wade, Mason. "French and French-Canadians in the United States." In *The New Catholic Encyclopedia,* Vol, 6, New York: McGraw-Hill, 1967. Concise historical survey with due emphasis given to Franco-American religious life.

Weil, François. *Les Franco-Américains, 1860-1980.* Paris: Belin, 1989, 251 p.

Wilson, Bruno. *L'évolution de la race française en Amérique*: *Vermont, New Hampshire, Connecticut, Rhode Island*. Montréal: Beauchemin, 1921. Contains insights not found elsewhere.

Winks, Robin. "Un point d'histoire controversée." *Le Canado-Américain I,* February-March 1960, 33-43. An important article on the French-Canadian participation in the American Civil War, followed by an exchange of letters between the author and Adolphe Robert.

4. HISTORY—REGIONAL, LOCAL, PAROCHIAL

Images of America Series. Arcadia Publishing. One Washington Center, Dover, NH 03820: In the growing list of works published by Arcadia, one finds a number of titles of Franco-American interest. Lowell, Pawtucket, Woonsocket, New Bedford are among the titles in this series. Usually, the name of the city is the title of the book.

Connecticut

Histoire et Statistiques des Canadiens-Américains du Connecticut: 1885-1898. Worcester, Mass.: Imprimerie de l'Opinion Publique, 1899, 357 p. Proceedings of the conventions of Connecticut's Franco-Americans.

French in Connecticut: A Cultural and Historical Guide. The French Guidebook Committee, American Association of Teachers of French, Connecticut Chapter, 1979, 88 p.

Hartford

Dutelle, Lorena. *French History.* Hartford: Mayor's All American Committee, 1978.

Taftville

Dugas, René, Sr. *The French Canadians in New England, 1871-1931: Taftville, (The Early Years)*, n.p., 1995, 237 p. Despite the title, this book summarizes the author's reminiscences about his long life in Taftville.

Waterbury

Bisaillon, Robert R. *Franco-American Biographies of the Greater Waterbury Area.* Waterbury, Conn.: Waterbury Printing Co., 1993, vi, 239 p. Because so little has been published on the French in Connecticut, this is a welcome addition to the general Franco-American bibliography. The work also contains more than the title suggests: information on the social life of the area's Francos.

———. *Saint Anne Parish and Its People, Waterbury, Connecticut, 1886-1986.* New Jersey: Jostens, 1986.

Maine

Brault, Gerard J. "The Franco-Americans of Maine." *Maine Historical Society Newsletter,* 12, Summer 1972, Special No., 4-27.

Searles, James W. *Immigrants from the North.* Bath, Maine: Hyde School, 1982, xi, 63 p. Brief review of the French-Canadian immigration to Maine based on oral histories.

Maine - Northern

Albert, Gilbert. *Les champs et les forêts.* Durham, N.H.: National Materials Development Center for French, Dept. of Media Services, Dimond Library, University of New Hampshire, 1985, 29 p. Collection of short narratives about North Country woodsmen.

Brassard, Francis. "The Origin of Certain Public Schools in the St. John Valley of Aroostook County, Maine." Master's thesis, University of Ottawa, 1967.

Craig, Béatrice. "Kinship and Migration to the Upper St. John Valley, Maine-New Brunswick." In *Quebec Studies,* vol. 1, no. 1, Spring 1983, pp. 151-163.

Cyr, Marguerite, S.M. *Mémoires d'une famille acadienne de Van Buren, Maine.* Madawaska, Me.: Saint John Valley Bilingual Education Program, 1977, 264 p. This "family album," abundantly illustrated, contains ethnological elements about a relatively unknown region.

Doty, C. Stewart. *Acadian Hard Times: The Farm Security Administration in Maine's St. John Valley, 1940-1943.* Orono, Maine: University of Maine Press, 1991, xiv, 186 p. A superb edition of these period photographs with excellent commentary.

Lebel, Louis-A. "Évocation du cheminement national des Acadiens du Madawaska." *Vie française,* vol. 38, nos. 1-2-3 (in one volume, pp. 28-36). A historical sketch of the region.

Michaud, Guy R. *Brève histoire du Madawaska: débuts à 1900.* Edmundston, N.B.: Les Éditions GRM, 1984, 206 p.

Paradis, Roger. "Henriette, la capuche: The Portrait of a Frontier Midwife." In *Quebec Studies*, vol. 1, no. 1, Spring 1983, pp. 130-150.

Perreault, Gene N. *Memories Grow on Trees—L'arbre des mémoires.* Durham, N.H.: University of New Hampshire, Department of Media Services, Dimond Library, 1986, vii, 79 p. The author describes her work as "the folk history of the logging business in northern Maine."

Pozzuto, Cécile Dufour. *Madoweskak, 1785-1985: A Pictorial History.* Madawaska, Maine: Madawaska Historical Society, 1985, 258 p. Valuable for its iconography. This volume also contains historical sketches of the region's institutions and organizations.

Maine - Central and Southern

Allen, James P. "Migration Fields of French-Canadian Immigrants to Southern Maine." In *Geographical Review*, no. 62, July 1972, pp. 366-383.

Biddeford

Guignard, Michael J. *La Foi, La Langue, La Culture: The Franco-Americans of Biddeford, Maine*, n.p., xvi, 191 p., 1982. Revised version of a Ph.D. dissertation (History), Syracuse University, N.Y., 1972.

Lewiston

Frenette, Yves. "La genèse d'une communauté canadienne-française en Nouvelle-Angleterre: Lewiston, Maine, 1800-1880." Ph.D. dissertation (History), Laval University, 1988, 392 p.

Historic Lewiston: Franco-American Origins. Lewiston, Maine: Historical Commission, 1974, 47 p. Despite its brevity, this volume is valuable for its text, written by Charlotte Michaud, Adelard Janelle, and James S. Leamon, as well as for its photographs.

Parker, James Hill. *Ethnic Identity: The Case of the French Americans.* Washington, D.C.: University Press of America, 1983, 67 p. Although the focus of this study is Lewiston, many of the author's findings are true for other New England cities and towns with a substantial Franco-American population.

75th Anniversary of the Founding of St. Mary Parish (1907-1982). Lewiston, Maine: St. Mary's Parish, 1983, 50 p.

Massachusetts

Petrin, Ronald A. "Ethnicity and Political Pragmatism: The French Canadians in Massachusetts, 1885-1915." Ph.D. dissertation (History), Clark University, 1983, 486 p. An in-depth analysis of the subject.

———. *French Canadians in Massachusetts Politics, 1885-1915: Ethnicity and Political Pragmatism.* Philadelphia: Balch Institute Press; London: Associated University Press, 1990, 234 p.

Rimbert, Sylvie. "L'immigration franco-canadienne au Massachusetts." In *Revue canadienne de géographie,* vol. 8, July-October 1954, pp. 75-85.

Adams

Hamelin, Rev. H. *Notre-Dame-des-Sept-Douleurs ou Une paroisse franco-américaine.* Montréal: Arbour et Dupont, Imprimeurs-Éditeurs, 1916, 362 p.

Chicopee

Assumption of the Blessed Virgin Mary Centennial Jubilee 1885-1985. Chicopee, Mass.: Assumption of the Blessed Virgin Mary Parish, 1985, 40 p.

Pomerleau, Rev. William A. *Chicopee's Franco-Americans: A New Culture in a New World.* Chicopee, Mass.: n.p., 1984, 35 p.

Weil, François. "Du Québec en Nouvelle-Angleterre: Les Franco-Américains de Chicopee, Massachusetts 1860-1980." Master of Arts thesis, University of Paris IV-Sorbonne, 1983, 125 p. Short but insightful.

Fall River

Coelho, Anthony. "A Row of Nationalities: Life in A Working Class Community: the Irish, English, and French Canadians of Fall River, Mass. 1850-1890." Ph.D. dissertation (Ethnology), Brown University, 1980, 301 p.

Diamond Jubilee, The Brothers of Christian Instruction in the Diocese of Fall River. Fall River, Mass.: Msgr. Prevost High School

Alumni Association, 1987, non-paginated. Contains a short history of the Frères de l'Instruction Chrétienne in Fall River.

Le Guide Français de Fall River, MA, contenant l'histoire de la colonie et l'almanach des adresses avec illustrations. Fall River: L.J. Gagnon, 1909, 862 p.

Lachance, Pierre, O.P. "Les Dominicains à Fall River." In *Le Rosaire,* nos. 843-844, juin-juillet-août 1969 (special double issue),55 p.

————. *History of Our Parochial Schools and Educational Activities from the Foundation of Saint Anne Parish to This Day.* Fall River, Mass.: Paroisse Sainte Anne, 1975, non-paginated.

Lemaire, Hervé B. "Les Franco-Américains de Fall River." In Gerard J. Brault, ed., *Les Conférences de l'Institut franco-américain de Bowdoin College, Brunswick, Maine,* 1961, pp. 39-48.

Notre-Dame-de-Lourdes Memorial Book. Fall River, Mass.: Paroisse Notre-Dame, 1983, 42 p. This souvenir album was published shortly after the magnificent parish church was destroyed by fire in May of 1982.

Silvia, Philip T. " 'The Flint Affair': French-Canadian Struggle for *Survivance.* " In *Catholic Historical Review,* vol. 65, 1979, pp. 414-35.

————. "The Little Canadas of New England: French-Canadian Immigrants vs. Trade-Unionism in Fall River, Massachusetts." *The New England Social Studies Bulletin*, vol. 42, no. 1, Fall 1984-1985 (sic), pp. 12-24.

———. "Neighbors From the North." In *Steeples and Smokestacks.* Worcester, Mass.: Institut français, Assumption College, 1996, pp. 145-163.

———. "The Spindle City: Labor, Politics and Religion in Fall River, Massachusetts, 1870-1905." Ph.D. Dissertation (History), Fordham University, 1973, 2 vol., 896 p.

Thank you, Dominicans: 90 Years of Community Service to Fall River. Fall River, Mass.: Paroisse Sainte Anne, 1978, 100 p. Includes a short history.

Fitchburg

Robbins, Jeffrey Paul. "The French Canadians of Fitchburg. *Survivance* and Industry." Middlebury, VT: Middlebury College, 1980.

Holyoke

Bilodeau, Thérèse. "The French in Holyoke (1850-1900)." *Historical Journal of Western Massachusetts,* vol. III, no. 1, 1974, pp. 1-12.

Haebler, Peter. "*Habitants* in Holyoke: the Development of the French-Canadian Community in a Massachusetts City, 1865-1910." Ph.D. Dissertation (History), University of New Hampshire, 1976. Ann Arbor, Michigan: University Microfilms, 1977.

———. "Educational Patterns of French Canadians in Holyoke, 1868 to 1910." *Historical Journal of Western Massachusetts,* vol. X, no. 2, 1982, pp. 17-29.

Lowell

Blewett, Mary H., ed. *Surviving Hard Times: The Working People of Lowell.* Lowell, Mass.: Lowell Museum, 1982, xii, 178 p. Includes much material on Franco-Americans.

Early, Frances H. "French-Canadian Beginnings in an American Community: Lowell, Massachusetts, 1868-1886." Ph.D. dissertation (History), Concordia University, 1979, xxii, 282 p.

————. "The French-Canadian Family Economy and Standard of Living in Lowell, Massachusetts, 1870." In *Journal of Family History,* vol. 7, no 2, 1982, pp. 180-199.

————. "The Settling-In Process: The Beginnings of the Little Canada in Lowell, Massachusetts, in the Late Nineteenth Century." In *Steeples and Smokestacks.* Worcester, Mass.: Institut français, Assumption College, 1996, pp. 89-108.

Eno, Arthur L., Jr., ed. *Cotton Was King: A History of Lowell, Massachusetts.* Lowell, Mass.: Lowell Historical Society 1976, xv, 312 p. History of a major Franco-American city.

Lane, Brigitte M. "Franco-American Folk Traditions and Popular Culture in a Former Milltown: Aspects of Urban Folklore and the Dynamics of Folklore Change in Lowell, Massachusetts." Ph.D. dissertation (Folklore), Harvard University, 1983, vii, 593 p. New York: Garland Publishing, 1990, 599 p. A brilliant synthesis, a model of the genre. Contains a mini-anthology of Lowell's French-language oral literature.

Lowell: The Building Book. Lowell, Mass.: City of Lowell, Division of Planning and Development, 1982, 3rd edition, 71 p. Describes the urban environment of the Franco-Americans of Lowell.

Quintal, Claire. "Lowell – le rêve et la réalité." *Francophonies d'Amérique,* Jules Tessier, ed. Université d'Ottawa, 1996, pp. 159-170.

Santerre, Richard. *The Franco-Americans of Lowell, Massachusetts.* Lowell, Mass.: Franco-American Day Committee, 1972, 27 pp.

———. *La paroisse Saint-Jean-Baptiste et les Franco-Américains de Lowell, Massachusetts, 1868 à 1968.* Manchester, N.H.: Éditions Lafayette, 1993, 311 p. A "leisurely" social and religious history of this former Franco-American parish.

New Bedford

Chartier, Armand B. *French New Bedford.* Manchester, N.H.: Association Canado-Américaine and New Bedford, Mass.: La Ligue des Présidents, 1993, 39 p. Sub-title: "A Historical Overview of Franco-Americans of New Bedford, MA." First synthesis of this subject.

Quintin, Doris C., and Jeanne Weaver Swiszcz. *Saint Anthony of Padua, New Bedford, Massachusetts: A Parish History 1895-1995.* New Bedford, Mass.: Saint Anthony of Padua Church, 1996. Edited by the author of the present volume. This study contains many rare photographs.

Pittsfield

Notre Dame du Bon Conseil: History of 100 years... Pittsfield, Mass.:
Notre Dame Church, 1967, 40 p.

Southbridge

Gatineau, Félix. *Histoire des Franco-Américains de Southbridge,
Massachusetts.* Framingham, Mass.: Lakeview Press, 1919.

LePain, Albert N. *The Franco-American Ethnic Heritage.* Southbridge,
1979.

Notre Dame Parish, Southbridge, Massachusetts. South Hackensack,
New Jersey: Custombook, 1969, 40 p.

Springfield Area

Burns, Kathryne A., et al. *Springfield's Ethnic Heritage: The French
and French-Canadian Community.* Springfield: Bicentennial
Committee, 1976, 46 p.

Carvalho, Joseph III, and Robert Everett. "Statistical Analysis of
Springfield's French Canadians." *Historical Journal of Western
Mass.,* vol. 3, Spring 1974.

Fréchette Arvantely, Marcelle. *Le Festival.* Springfield, Mass.: Comité
du Festival Franco-Américain, Inc., 1985, 120 p. This souvenir-
program contains useful information and iconography on
western Massachusetts, one of the least well known Franco-
American regions.

————. *French Heritage Days.* Springfield, Mass.: Comité du Festival Franco-Américain, Inc., 1986, 100 p. Remarks made relative to the previous item apply here.

St. Joseph Church, Springfield, Massachusetts, 1873-1973. South Hackensack, New Jersey: Custombook, 1974, 56 p.

Swansea

St. Michael's Church, Swansea, Massachusetts, 50th Anniversary Publication (1922-1972). Swansea, Mass.: St. Michael's Parish, 1972, 30 p. This multicultural parish—long considered to be French—is located in the Ocean Grove section of Swansea.

Souvenir Album, St. Louis de France Parish, (1928-1978). Swansea, Mass.: St. Louis de France Parish, 1978, 44 p.

Worcester

Belisle, Alexandre. *Livre d'or des Franco-Américains de Worcester, Massachusetts.* Worcester: Compagnie de Publication Belisle, 1920, 363 p.

Chandonnet, Rev. T. A. *Notre-Dame-des-Canadiens et les Canadiens aux États-Unis.* Montréal: Georges E. Desbarats, Imprimeur, 1872, xvi, 171 p. English-language version: same title.Translated by Kenneth J. Moynihan. Worcester, Mass.: Assumption College, 1977, revised 1979, viii, 132 p.

Desautels, Kenneth. *History of Saint Joseph Parish: 1820-1992, Worcester, Massachusetts.* Worcester: Domus Mariae Inc., 1997, 538 p.

Gagnon, Richard L. *Holy Name of Jesus Parish: 100 Years in South Worcester.* Worcester, Mass.: Community of Teresian Carmelites, 1993, 101 p.

―――. *A Parish Grows Around the Common: Notre Dame des Canadiens,1869-1995.* Worcester, Mass.: Domus Mariae Inc., Community of Teresian Carmelites, 1995, x, 164 p.

Marion, Raymond J. *An Historical Look at Assumption College, 1904 to 1964* . Worcester, Mass.: Assumption College, Department of History, 1995, 54 p.

Moynihan, Kenneth J., trans. *Le Worcester Canadien (1888-1907) and Le Guide Français de Worcester 1916-1917.* Worcester, Mass.: Assumption College, Community Studies Program, 1979, 160 p. Compilation of extracts from these guides translated into English, and 10-page Name Index. Originals in the Worcester Room, Worcester Public Library.

New Hampshire

Doane, Ashley W., Jr. *Occupational and Educational Patterns for New Hampshire's Franco-Americans.* Manchester, N.H.: New Hampshire Civil Liberties Union, 1979, 76 p.

Samson, Gary. *The Merrimack Valley, New Hampshire.* Norfolk, Va.: Donning Co., Publishers, 5659 Virginia Beach Blvd, Norfolk VA 23502, 1989, 208 p.

Hudson

Presentation of Mary Academy: Golden Jubilee 1926-1976. Hudson, N.H.: Presentation of Mary Academy, 1976, 112 p.

Manchester

Hareven, Tamara K., and Randolph Langenbach. *Amoskeag: Life and Work in an American Factory-City.* New York, N.Y.: Pantheon, 1978, xiii, 395 p. A major work on the subject indicated in the title. Contains much oral history.

Hareven, Tamara K. *Family Time and Industrial Time: The Relationship Between the Family and Work in a New England Industrial Community.* Cambridge: Cambridge University Press, 1982, and Lanham, Md.: University Press of America, 1993, 474 p.

Kanzler, Eileen M. "Processes of Immigration: The Franco-Americans of Manchester, N.H. 1875-1925." Ph.D. dissertation, Illinois State University, 1982, 277 p.

Parent, Louise, C.S.C. *The First Twenty-Five Years of Notre Dame College, Manchester, N.H.* Notre Dame College, n.d., 91 p. Covers the period 1950-1975.

Trottier, Rev. Maurice. *Paroisse Sainte-Marie: le centenaire d'une Étoile de Dieu, 1880-1980.* Manchester, N.H.: Éditions Lafayette, 1980, 173 p. Contains many comments on the aesthetic merits of this parish church. Numerous photographs. See following item.

Verrette, Rev. Adrien. *Cinquantenaire de la Paroisse Sainte-Marie, Manchester, N.H. 1880-1930.* Manchester, N.H.: n.p., 1931, 416 p. A masterful study by one of the key figures in the *survivance* effort. Illustrated. See previous entry.

Nashua

Thériault, George French. *The Franco-Americans in a New England Community: An Experiment in Survival.* New York, N.Y.: Arno Press, 1980, vi, 569 p. The author's study of *survivance* goes well beyond the boundaries of Nashua, N.H.

Rhode Island

Aubin, Albert K., ed. *The French in Rhode Island: A Brief History.* Providence, R.I.: Rhode Island Heritage Commission, 1988.

Bouvier, Leon F., and Inge B. Corless. *An Ethnic Profile of the State of Rhode Island.* Kingston, R.I.: University of Rhode Island, 1968. Statistical data on the ethnic composition of the State's cities and towns, based on the 1960 census.

Chassé, Paul-P. *Rhode Island's Franco-Americans in Our Pluralistic Society.* Somersworth, N.H.: Éditions de l'Abbaye de Thélème, 1973. Historical survey of the French presence in R.I. from the sixteenth century to the twentieth.

Oswald, Denise Bissonnette. "Health Care for the Franco-American Community in Rhode Island - 1900-1925." Master's thesis, Sarah Lawrence College, 1996.

Working Water: A Guide to the Historic Landscape of the Blackstone River Valley. Providence, Rhode Island: Department of Environmental Management and Rhode Island Park Association, 1987, 49 p. This valley extends from Worcester, Mass., to Providence, R.I. Thus it crosses many cities, towns, and villages having substantial Franco-American populations.

Central Falls

Central Falls, Rhode Island. Providence, Rhode Island: Historical
Preservation Commission, 1978, 78 p., "Statewide Historical
Preservation Report Collection," P-CF-1.

Notre Dame Church, Central Falls, Rhode Island. South Hackensack,
N.J.: Custombook, 1974, 36 p.

Pawtucket

Saint Cecilia's Parish (1910-1985). Pawtucket, R.I.: St. Cecilia
Parish,1985, 96 p.

St. Godard, Rev. Edward G. *Our Lady of Consolation Church:
Yesterday, Today and Tomorrow.* South Hackensack, New
Jersey: Custombook, 1975.

————. *St. John's Parish, 1884-1978.* Pawtucket, R.I.: St. John
the Baptist Parish, 1978.

West Warwick

St John the Baptist Church, West Warwick. South Hackensack, New
Jersey: Custombook, 1974, 52 p.

Woonsocket

Anctil, Pierre. "Aspects of Class Ideology in a New England Ethnic
Minority: The Franco-Americans of Woonsocket, R.I. (1865-
1929)." Ph.D. Dissertation (Anthropology), New School for

Social Research, 1980. Issues discussed in this work go well beyond local history.

Bellemare, Marcel. "Social Networks in an Inner-City Neighborhood: Woonsocket, Rhode Island." Ph.D. dissertation (Sociology), Catholic University of America, 1974, 260 p.

Bellerose, Robert R. *Triomphe et Tragédie: A Guide to French, French-Canadians, and French-Huguenot Historic Sites in Woonsocket, Rhode Island.* P. O. Box 1053, Slatersville, RI: Robert R. Bellerose, 1998, 70 p. Offers a useful inventory of sites and structures of cultural significance.

——————. *Precious Blood Cemetery, Woonsocket, Rhode Island.* Slatersville, R.I.: Robert R. Bellerose Bookseller, P. O. Box 1053, 1998, 33 p. This unusual guide book contains biographical information about thirty-two Franco-American notables — and some lesser known figures, along with the locations of their final resting place.

Bonier, Marie Louise. *The Beginnings of the Franco-American Colony in Woonsocket, Rhode Island.* Translated and edited by Claire Quintal, with additional notes by Raymond H. Bacon and the technical assistance of Sylvia and Roger Bartholomy. Worcester, Mass.: Institut français, Assumption College, 1997, xxxv, 560 p. This is a greatly augmented English-language edition of Marie Louise Bonier's classic 1920 study, *Débuts de la colonie franco-américaine de Woonsocket, R.I.*

Bourget, Paul A., ed. *Towers of Faith and Family: St. Ann's Church, Woonsocket, Rhode Island, 1890-1990.* Woonsocket, R.I.: St. Ann's Church Corporation, 1990, 312 p. This history could well serve as a model of its genre.

Church of the Precious Blood, Woonsocket, R.I. South Hackensack, New Jersey: Custombook, 1975, 32 p.

Fortin, Marcel P., ed. *Woonsocket, Rhode Island: A Centennial History, 1888-1988.* Woonsocket, R.I.: Centennial Committee, 1988, 252 p. An excellent work about a city in which Franco-Americans have played a leading role.

Gerstle, Gary. *Working-Class Americanism: The Politics of Labor in a Textile City, 1914-1960.* Cambridge, England and New York : Cambridge University Press, 1989, xii, 356 p.

Ribes, Christophe. "Interactions Between the Emergence and Decline of Industrialism and the Rise and Fall of a French-Canadian Community in Woonsocket, Rhode Island, Since the 19th Century." Master's thesis, Université d'Orléans, 1996.

Sorrell, Richard. "Sports and Franco-Americans in Woonsocket." *Rhode Island History,* 1972.

Thomas, Dr. Alton P. *Woonsocket. Highlights of History 1800-1976. A Bicentennial Project for the City of Woonsocket.* Providence, R.I.: Globe Printing Co., 1976, v, 107 p.

Wessel, Bessie Bloom. *An Ethnic Survey of Woonsocket, Rhode Island.* Chicago: University of Chicago Press, 1931; New York: Arno Press, 1970.

Vermont

Franco-Americans in Vermont: A Civil Rights Perspective. Vermont Advisory Committee to the U.S. Commission on Civil Rights. Washington, D.C.: U.S. Government Printing Office,

1983, 53 p. On the inequalities between Francos and Anglos in education and in the workplace.

Senécal, André J. "Studies on Vermont/Québec Relations: The State of the Art." In Peter A.Woolfson and André J. Senécal, *The French in Vermont: Some Current Views*, "a series of occasional papers." Burlington, Vt.: University of Vermont, Center for Research on Vermont, 1983, pp. 27-36. Contains an abundant bibliography.

Woolfson, Peter. "The Rural Franco-American in Vermont." In *Vermont History*, vol. 50, no. 3, 1982, pp. 151-162.

—————. "The Franco-Americans of Northern Vermont: Cultural Factors for Consideration by Health and Social Services Providers." In Peter A. Woolfson and André J. Senécal, *The French in Vermont: Some Current Views*, "a series of occasional papers." Burlington, Vt.: Center for Research on Vermont, 1983, pp.1-26.

—————. "Cross Cultural Families: Franco-American Elders." In *U.S. And Canadian Perspectives*, Greenwood Press, 1988.

Barre

Beavin, Daniel, et al. *Barre, Vermont: An Annotated Bibliography.* Barre, Vt.: Aldrich Public Library, 1979, iii, 80 p. Situates Franco-Americans in the local multicultural context.

Burlington

Keenan, Robert G., and Rev. Francis R. Privé, eds. *History of Saint Joseph Parish, Burlington, Vermont, 1830-1987.* Burlington,

Vt.: Saint Joseph Church, 85 Elmwood Ave., Burlington, VT 05401, 1988, xi, 91 p. and more than 150 p. of Appendices, each paginated separately. This is both a scholarly work and a labor of love. It is particularly important since this parish, along with those established in Maine's St. John Valley, are the first French-American parishes.

Winooski

Blow, David J. "The Establishment and Erosion of French-Canadian Culture in Winooski, Vermont, 1867-1900." In *Vermont History,* vol. 43, no. 1, 1975, pp. 59-74.

Woolfson, Peter. "The Heritage and Culture of the French-Vermonters: Research Needs in the Social Sciences." In *Vermont History,* 1976.

5. BIOGRAPHY/AUTOBIOGRAPHY

Biographies

Amaral, Anthony. *Will James, the Last Cowboy Legend.* Reno: University of Nevada Press, 1980, xiv, 174 p.

Aubé, Mary Elizabeth. "Mes entretiens avec Mémère." Ph.D. dissertation (French), Brown University, 1985, v, 343 p. A fascinating example of "conversational history," inter-generational, and critically scrutinized in terms of form and content.

Bell, William Gardner. *Will James: The Life and Works of a Lone Cowboy.* [a.k.a., **Dufault, Joseph Ernest Nephtali** (1892-

1942)] Flagstaff, Arizona: Northland Press, 1987, xix, 130 p. A substantial and well illustrated biography of this western writer and artist.

——————. **Dufault, Ernest or Will James**: "Will James, Inevitable Cowboy." *American West*, vol. 20, no. 1, 1983, pp.36-43.

[Benoit, Josaphat]. *Ferdinand Gagnon: Biographie, éloge funèbre, pages choisies.* Manchester, N.H.: Imprimerie de l'Avenir National, 1940, 279 p. This is one of two book-length presentations on the subject, the founder of Franco-American journalism and a major figure in Franco-American history.

Capistran, Armand. "**Adélard Lambert** (1867-1946), Folkloriste-Bibliophile." *Bulletin de la Société Historique Franco-Américaine,* 1954, 70-75. A sympathetic portrait of one of the rare Franco-American folklorists.

Chapdelaine Gonzalez, Rosemarie. *Chappy: A Youthful Biography of **Arside Joseph Chapdelaine**.* Manchester, N.H.: Entre Amis, 1994, 73 p. Episodes from the life of a young French-Canadian immigrant as told by his daughter.

Dozois, Charles H. *Le bon père Bolduc: Biography of **Father Émile Bolduc**, O.M.I.* Manchester, N.H.: Lafayette Press, 1989. Bilingual edition: 74 & 78 p. and several unnumbered pages of photos.

Kennedy, Ambrose. *Quebec to New England: The Life of **Monsignor Charles Dauray**.* Boston: Humphries, 1948. Biography of a prominent Rhode Island ecclesiastical leader.

Lacerte, Roger V. "**Antoine Clément**: sa vie et son oeuvre." Master's thesis, Université Laval, Québec, 1963, xiii, 79 p.

Ledoux, Denis. *Turning Memories Into Memoirs: A Handbook for Writing Life Stories.* Lisbon Falls, Maine: Soleil Press, 95 Gould Road, ME 04252, 1993, 206 p. An intelligent, "user-friendly" guide to this subject.

Lilyestrom, Betty. "**Archibald R. LeMieux.**" *Le Canado-Américain,* IV, April-May 1965, 13-24. Biographical sketch of a prominent Franco-American industrialist and philanthropist.

Martin, Marie Thérèse Beaudet. *My Grandmother's Face/Le visage de ma grand'mère.* Wilton, Maine: Wilton Publishing, 1990, 96 p. Topics include history, genealogy, gastronomy, geography, etc.

Parent, Louis-Marie, O.M.I. *Un coeur sur la main: **Jean-Louis Collignon, O.M.I,** Évêque des Cayes* [Haiti]. Montréal: Centre Missionnaire Oblat, 8844, Notre-Dame Est, 1988, 347 p.

Quintal, Claire. *Herald of Love, **Father Marie Clement Staub, A.A.*** Sillery, Québec: Sisters of Saint Joan of Arc Motherhouse, 1984, 217 p. Its French translation by the author is entitled *Héraut de l'Amour.* Québec: Anne Sigier, 1989, 295 p. Rev. Staub is the founder of the Soeurs de Sainte Jeanne d'Arc. The community was founded with Franco-American recruits in Worcester, Mass. on Christmas Day 1914.

Robert, Adolphe. "**Philippe Armand Lajoie.**" *Le Canado-Américain,* I, Dec.-Jan. 1959-60, pp. 21-23. Biographical sketch of an important Franco-American journalist.

Roby, Yves. "**Ferdinand Gagnon**." In *Dictionnaire biographique du Canada,* vol. XI, 1982, pp. 362-364. A substantive article on a major Franco-American leader.

Rocheleau-Rouleau, Corinne. *Heritage of Peace: Land of Hope and Glory.* Cumberland, R.I.: Jemtech Digital Publishing, 9 Elmwood Drive, Cumberland, RI 02864, 1996. A historical narrative based on the life of **Wilfrid Rouleau**. Edited by Louise Lind, 204 p.

Sansouci, Lucien C. "**Philippe Armand Lajoie**." *Le Phare*, vol. 1, nos. 7-8, August-September 1948, pp. 3-4.

[Tonnancour, Godfroy de]. *Ferdinand Gagnon: sa vie et ses oeuvres.* Worcester, Mass.: C.F. Lawrence, 1886, 250 p.

Autobiographies

Albert, Felix. *Immigrant Odyssey: A French-Canadian Habitant in New England.* Orono: University of Maine Press, 1991, ix, 179 p. A bilingual edition of *Histoire d'un enfant pauvre.* Introduction by Frances H. Early. Translated by Arthur L. Eno, Jr. One of the very few Franco-American "rags-to-riches" stories. The locale is Lowell, Mass.

Bissonnette, Georges, A.A. *Moscow Was My Parish.* New York: McGraw-Hill, 1956, 273 p. An account of the author's two-year stay in Moscow in the 1950s. *Moscou ma paroisse.* Translated by Jacques Mignon. Paris: Éditions du Centurion, 1958, 302 p.

Blaise, Clark. *I Had a Father.* Reading, Mass.: Addison-Wesley Publishing, 1993, xi, 204 p. "A Post-Modern Autobiography."

Durant, Will. *Transition: A Sentimental Story of One Mind and One Era.* New York: Simon and Schuster, 1927, 352 p. The celebrated author of *The Story of Civilization* recalls his coming-of-age in Massachusetts and elsewhere. He refers to his family and to himself as "French-Canadian." Cf. Dion-Lévesque, Rosaire. *Silhouettes franco-américaines* for a substantial article on Durant.

Harnois, Albert J. *Growing Up With Guilt.* Cumberland, R.I.: Alsis Publishing, 1996, ix, 221 p. With much good humor, the author describes his life, from his earliest years through elementary and high school, his seminary years and beyond.

Lagassé, Julie de Champlain. *Incidents de ma vie.* Fall River, Mass.: Privately printed, 1952.

Lambert, Adélard. *Journal d'un bibliophile.* Drummondville, Québec: Imprimerie "La Parole", 1927, 140 p
.

James, Will (pseudonym of Ernest Dufault). *Lone Cowboy. My Life Story.* Illustrated by the author. New York and London: Charles Scribner's Sons, 1946, 421p. First published 1930. Re-issued Missoula, Montana: Mountain Press Publishing Co., 1996, XI, 431 p.

Milot, Arthur. *Childhood Memories.* N.p., 1992. "With introduction, translation and notes by Claude Milot, his son." Available from Claude Milot: 3440 Charlwood Dr., Rochester Hills, MI 48306.

Robbins, Rhéa Côté. *Wednesday's Child.* Brunswick, Maine: Maine Writers and Publishers Alliance, 1997. 1997 Winner of the Maine Writers and Publishers Alliance Chapbook Award for Creative Non-Fiction.

Robert, Adolphe. *Souvenirs et portraits.* Manchester, N.H.: Imprimerie Lafayette, 1965. A collection of reminiscences and autobiographical vignettes by a major figure in 20th century Franco-American life.

Savarin, Jules. *Mémoires d'un soldat français de 1914 à 1919.* Lewiston, Maine: Éditions du Messager, 1928, 158 p. A moving first-person account of a young Frenchman's involvement in World War I. The author was also a journalist in Waterville, Maine.

Tremblay, Rémi. *Pierre qui roule. Souvenirs d'un journaliste.* Montréal: Éditions Galand, 1923.

6. ETHNOLOGY - FOLKLORE

Beaupré, Normand R. *L'enclume et le couteau: The Life and Work of Adelard Côté Folk Artist.* Manchester, N.H.: National Materials Development Center for French & Creole, 1982, xvii, 98 p. Bilingual text.

Brûlé, Dorilla. "Le folklore français à Central Falls [Rhode Island]." Master's thesis, Boston College, Department of Romance Languages, August 1951.

Hample, Henry. "Swing la tabatière au fond d'une boîte à bois. The Contemporary Franco-American Quadrille in Rhode Island." Master's thesis, Brown University, 1998.

Lane, Brigitte M. "Franco-American Folk Traditions and Popular Culture in a Former Milltown: Aspects of Urban Folklore and the Dynamics of Folklore Change in Lowell, Massachusetts."

Ph.D. dissertation (Folklore), Harvard University, 1983, vii, 593 p. New York and London: Garland Press, 1990, xiv, 599 p. This may well be the most brilliant piece of work ever done on Franco-Americans. It draws part of its strength from its focus on "the common man"... and woman, a category regrettably under-represented in Franco-American studies.

_____. "De la culture immigrée à la culture ethnique: la chanson populaire d'expression française et l'expérience franco-américaine en Nouvelle-Angleterre. *Études de linguistique appliquée.* Foyer Francophones aux États-Unis. Louise Péloquin, ed., vol. 70 April-June 1988, pp. 51-64.

Olivier, Julien, *D'la boucane: une introduction au folklore franco-américain de la Nouvelle-Angleterre.* Cambridge, Mass.: Lesley College, National Assessment and Dissemination Center, 1979, vi, 142 p. A precious collection of essays and first-person accounts.

Paradis, Roger. "Franco-American Folklore: A Cornucopia of Culture." In Céleste Roberge, ed. *Vers l'évolution d'une culture.* Orono, Maine: Franco-American Resource Opportunity Group (at the University of Maine), 1973, pp.43-87. A useful survey, particularly with regard to Northern Maine.

————— . *Gilbert O. Roy, peintre populaire de la vallée Saint-Jean.* Cambridge, Mass., Lesley College: National Assessment and Dissemination Center for Bilingual/Bicultural Education. Lesley College, 1979, xvi, 98 p.

Parent, Michael, and Julien Olivier. *Of Kings and Fools: Stories of the French Tradition in North America.* Collected, translated, and retold by Parent and Olivier. Little Rock, Arkansas: August House Publishers, 1996, 206 p.

Perreault, Gene N. *Memories Grow on Trees/L'arbre des mémoires* (sic). Durham, N.H.: National Materials Development Center for French, Dimond Library, University of New Hampshire, 1986, 79 p. According to the author, this collection of narratives represents the folk history of the lumber industry in northern Maine according to the author.

Quintal, Claire. "Dans les villes des États..." *Ethnologies francophones de l'Amérique et d'ailleurs.* Desdouits, Anne-Marie and Laurier Turgeon, eds. Québec: Les Presses de l'Université Laval, 1997, pp. 197-214.

Reif, Christine. "Franco-American Music in New England: Portrait of Three Contemporary Composers/Performers." Master's thesis, University of California, 1992.

Sur bois: Franco-American Woodcarvers of Northern New England. Manchester, N.H.: Centre franco-américain, 1996, 48 p.

7. RELIGION

NOTE: This section may seem unduly short, but users of this bibliography will note that the subject of religion occurs in other sections, such as history, biography, literature, and others.

Bonin, Jeanne Savard, *Une stigmatisée: Marie-Rose Ferron.* Montréal: Éditions Paulines, 1987, 248 p. English edition translated by the

author, under the title *A Stigmatist. Marie-Rose Ferron.*
Sherbrooke, QC: Éditions Paulines, 1988, 265 p.

Cheney, Liana. *Religious Architecture of Lowell.* Lowell, Mass.:
Landmark Printing Co, 1984, 2 vol. In vol. 1, the author devotes
a chapter (pp. 62-104) to "French-Canadian" churches.

Paradis, Rev. Msgr. Wilfrid H. *Upon This Granite. Catholicism in New
Hampshire. 1647-1997.* Portsmouth, N.H.: Peter E. Randall
Publisher, 1998, 379 p. This book by a Franco-American native
of New Hampshire contains much that is pertinent to the
religious history of Franco-Americans in a diocese where they
constitute the majority of Catholics.

Perreault, Robert B. *Elphège J. Daignault et le mouvement sentinelliste
à Manchester, New Hampshire.* Bedford, N.H.: National
Materials Development Center, 1981, ii, 243 p.

Wade, Mason. "The French Parish and *Survivance* in Nineteenth
Century New England." In *The Catholic Historical Review,* vol.
36, no. 2, July 1950, pp. 163-189.

RELIGIOUS COMMUNITIES: What follows is a very short list of
histories of religious congregations. Similar works can be found
under the parish histories (*cf. supra*). It is also true that an
exhaustive bibliography of this subject is long overdue.

Augustinians of the Assumption

Guissard, Rev. Polyeucte, A.A. *Un siècle d'histoire assomptioniste,
1850-1950.* Worcester, Mass.: Collège de l'Assomption, 1950,
144 p.

Daughters of the Holy Spirit, D.H.S.

Dion, Anita, D.H.S. trans. *Gleanings From Our Early Days: Daughters of the Holy Spirit, Plerin-Saint-Brieuc,* n.p., n.p., 1975, 100 p.

——————. "Since They Must Be Filled With Love. . .": *Daughters of the Holy Spirit – Our Mission in the Church,* n.p., n.p., 1979, 111 p.

——————. *The Spirituality of the Daughters of the Holy Spirit.* Putnam, Conn., n.p., 1975, 74 p.

Little Franciscans of Mary, P.F.M.

Garceau, Michelle, P.F.M. *Par ce signe tu vivras. Histoire de la Congrégation des Petites Franciscaines de Marie (1889-1955).* Baie-Saint-Paul: P.F.M., 1955, 539 p. English translation: *By This Sign You Will Live.* Worcester, Mass.: P.F.M., 1964, 491 p.

Presentation of Mary, P.M.

Bouchard, Isabelle, P.M. *Marie Rivier, son coeur et sa main: son ardente vie apostolique d'après sa correspondance.* Rome: Imprimerie Sped Im-Monte Compatri, 1985, 367 p.

Sisters of Saint Anne, S.S.A.

Cantwell, Sister Margaret, S.S.A. In collaboration with Sister Mary George Edmond (Lucienne Babin), S.S.A. *North to Share – The Sisters of Saint Anne in Alaska and the Yukon Territory.* British Columbia: Sisters of St. Anne, 1992, 308 p. Many Franco-American women were involved in this missionary activity opening and staffing schools and hospitals which served the native tribes.

Mailloux, Christine. *Une femme dans la tourmente.* Lachine: Les Editions Sainte-Anne, 1992, 530 p.

Marie-Jean de Pathmos, S.S.A. *Les Soeurs de Saint-Anne: Un Siècle d'Histoire,* Tome I, 1850-1900. Lachine: Les Soeurs de Sainte Anne, 1950, 640 p. English translation: Sister Marie Anne Eva (Mondor), *A History of the Sisters of St. Anne,* vol. 1, 1850-1900. New York: Vantage Press, 1961, 364 p.

Nadeau, Eugène, O.M.I. *Martyre du Silence - Mère Marie-Anne.* Lachine: Editions Sainte Anne, 1956, 429 p.

Poudrier, Anita, S.S.A. *A Tradition Unfolds - The Sisters of Saint Anne in the United States.* Lachine: Les Editions Sainte-Anne, 1997, 299 p.

Roy, Louise, S.S.A. *Les Soeurs de Sainte-Anne: Un Siècle d'Histoire,* Tome II, 1900-1950. Montréal: Editions Paulines - Soeurs de Sainte-Anne, 1992, 556 p.

Sisters of the Assumption of the Blessed Virgin Mary, S.A.S.V.

Lesage, Germain, O.M.I. *The Origins of the Sisters of the Assumption of the Blessed Virgin.* Nicolet,QC: Editions S.A.S.V., 1957. English translation by Sister Marie Janelle, D.H.S., 1981, 241 p.

Mignault, Alice, S.A.S.V. *Vingt ans d'expansion chez les Soeurs de l'Assomption de la Sainte Vierge, 1874-1894.* Nicolet, Québec: Éditions S.A.S.V., 1985, 430 p.

Sisters of the Holy Cross, C.S.C.

Parent, Louise, C.S.C. *A Mosaic to the Glory of God: The History of the Sisters of the Holy Cross and of the Seven Dolors in the New England States 1881-1980*, n.p., n.p., n.d., 214 p.

Sisters of Saint Joseph [of Le Puy, France], S.S.J.

Aherne, Consuelo Maria, S.S.J. *Joyous Service: The History of the Sisters of Saint Joseph of Springfield.* Holyoke, Mass.: Sisters of Saint Joseph, 1983, 318 p.

8. SOCIOLOGY - ANTHROPOLOGY

Adrian, Patricia Wood. "Ethnic and Class Differences in Definitions of Mental Health and Deviance." Ph.D. dissertation, Catholic University of America, 1970. A study of third generation Franco-American and Italo-American communities in Rhode Island.

Anctil, Pierre. "Aspects of Class Ideology in a New England Ethnic Minority: The Franco-Americans of Woonsocket, Rhode Island (1865-1929)." Ph.D. dissertation (Anthropology), New School for Social Research, 1980, ix, 340 p.

Benoit, Josaphat. "Attitudes des Franco-Américains en politique." In Gerard J. Brault, *Les Conférences de l'Institut Franco-Américain de Bowdoin College,* pp. 7-19, Brunswick, Maine, 1961.

Bouvier, Léon. "La stratification sociale du groupe ethnique canadien-français aux États-Unis." In *Recherches Sociographiques,* vol. V, no. 3, Sept.-Dec. 1964, pp. 371-379.

Chevalier, Florence Marie, S.S.A. "The Role of French National Societies in the Sociocultural Evolution of the Franco-Americans of New England from 1860 to the Present: An Analytical Macro-Sociological Case Study in Ethnic Integration Based on Current Social System Models." Ph.D. dissertation (Sociology), The Catholic University of America, 1972, vi, 386 p. This scientific study of Franco-American fraternal societies is clearly the most complete on this subject.

Hareven, Tamara K. "The Dynamics of Kin in an Industrial Community." In *Historical and Sociological Essays on the Family*. Chicago, Ill.: University of Chicago Press, 1978, pp. 151-182.

Paquet, Gilles, and Wayne R. Smith. "L'émigration des Canadiens-Français (sic) vers les États-Unis, 1790-1940: problématique et coups de sonde." In *L'Actualité Économique*, vol. 59, 1983, pp. 423-453.

Péloquin, Louise. "Longue présence, récente reconnaissance... l'institutionnalisation de la Franco-Américanie." *Études de linguistique appliquée*. Foyers francophones aux États-Unis. vol.70, April-June 1988, pp. 103-114.

Péroncel-Hugoz, Jean-Pierre. "Recherche et découverte des Français de Nouvelle-Angleterre." Études de linguistique appliquée. Foyers francophones aux États-Unis. vol 70, April-June 1988, pp. 115-118.

Sorg, Marcella, "Genetic Demographic of Deme Formation in a Franco-American Population 1830-1903." Ph.D. dissertation (Sociology), Ohio State University, 1979, 192 p.

9. LANGUAGE AND LINGUISTICS

Bernard, Irene Mailhot. "Some Social Factors Affecting the French of Lewiston, Maine." Ph.D. dissertation (French), 1982, Pennsylvania State University.

Brault, Gerard J. "Le français en Nouvelle-Angleterre." In *Le français hors de France*. Paris: Honoré Champion, 1979, pp. 75-91.

——————— , et al. "Cours de langue française destiné aux jeunes Franco-Américains." Fall River: Association des Professeurs Franco-Américains, 1969, 261 p.

——————— . *Essais de philologie franco-américaine.* Worcester, Mass.: Assumption College, 1958.

d'Arles, Henry. "Le français dans nos écoles." La Ligue du ralliement français en Amérique, Tract no. 2, 1920, 11 p.

Darbelnet, Jean-Louis. "Étude sociolinguistique des contacts entre l'anglais et le français au Canada et en Nouvelle-Angleterre." *The French Language in the Americas.* Modern Language Association Annual Bulletin, December 1970, no. 16, pp. 26-32.

Fischer, Robert A. "A Generative Phonological Description of Selected Ideolects of Canadian French in Lewiston, Maine." Ph.D. dissertation (Linguistics), Pennsylvania State University, 1975.

Fox, Cynthia A. "Une communauté franco-américaine dans l'État de New York: étude préliminaire sur le Français à Cohoes." *Francophonies d'Amérique,* no. 3, 1993.

Garreau, Joseph. "Quelques caractéristiques lexicales du parler français en Nouvelle-Angleterre." *Études de linguistique appliquée.* Foyers francophones aux États-Unis, Louise Péloquin, ed., vol.70, April-June, 1988, pp. 65-74

Kelly, Henry E. "Phonological Variables in a New England French Speech Community." Ph.D. Dissertation (Linguistics), Cornell University, 1980, 222 p.

Kloss, Heinz. *Les droits linguistiques des Franco-Américains aux États-Unis.* Québec: Presses de l'Université Laval, 1970. Succinct study of the legal status of the French language in New England and Louisiana.

Lemaire, Hervé B. "Franco-American Efforts on Behalf of the French Language in New England." In *Language Loyalty in the United States,* Joshua Fishman, ed. The Hague: Mouton, 1966, pp. 253-279.

—————— . *The French Language in New England.* Washington, D.C.: Language Resources Project, 1963, 60 p.

Locke, William. "Pronunciation of the French Spoken at Brunswick, Maine." Publications of the American Dialect Society, no. 12, 1949.

Pousland, Edward. *Etude sémantique de l'anglicisme dans le parler franco-américain de Salem, Massachusetts.* Paris: Droz, 1933.

Quintal, Claire. "Langue française et identité culturelle pour les Franco-Américains de la Nouvelle-Angleterre." In *Identité culturelle et francophonie dans les Amériques* (III). Québec: Université Laval, Centre international de recherche sur le bilinguisme, 1980.

Robert, Adolphe. "Le bilinguisme franco-américain et ses différents aspects." In *Le Canado-Américain,* I, February-March 1960, pp.5-10.

Veltman, Calvin. *L'avenir du français aux États-Unis.* Québec: Éditeur officiel du Québec, 1987.

10. LITERATURE

a. Literary History and Criticism
b. Anthologies
c. Journalism
d. Theater
e. Fiction in French: Individual Works and Literary Biography or Criticism
f. Fiction in English: Individual Works and Literary Biography or Criticism
g. Poetry in French: Individual Works and Literary Biography or Criticism
h. Poetry in English: Individual Works and Literary Biography or Criticism

a. Literary History and Criticism

Chartier, Armand B. "The Franco-American Literature of New England: A Brief Overview." In *Ethnic Literatures Since 1776: The Many Voices of America,* edited by W.T. Zyla and W.M. Aycock. Lubbock, Texas: Texas Tech Press, 1978, Vol. 1, pp.193-215. Although superseded by my "Franco-American Literature: The New England Experience," this revised version of a paper delivered at a Comparative Literature symposium at Texas Tech University began the process of lifting Franco-American literature out of scholarly obscurity.

————— . "Pour une problématique de l'histoire littéraire franco-américaine." In *Situation de la recherche sur la Franco-Américanie*. Québec: Conseil de la vie française en Amérique, 1980, pp. 81-100. A short discussion of the questions raised by the study of this literature.

————— . "Franco-American Literature: The New England Experience." In Di Pietro, Robert J. and Edward Ifkovic, eds. *Ethnic Perspectives in American Literature*. New York: Modern Language Association, 1983, pp. 15-42. As the most prestigious of our professional organizations, the M.L.A., by publishing this work, has vastly increased the "visibility" of U.S. ethnic literatures. This volume represents a major step toward the rewriting of American literature.

————— . "La littérature franco-américaine de la Nouvelle-Angleterre: origines et évolution." In *Revue d'histoire littéraire du Québec et du Canada Français,* vol. 12, 1986, pp. 59-81.

————— . "La situation littéraire chez les Franco-Américains de la Nouvelle Angleterre à la fin du 20e siècle." Presented at a state-of-the-art colloquium on the French in North America. Québec Université Laval, June 16, 1990. Published in Dean Louder, ed. *Le Québec et les francophones de la Nouvelle-Angleterre.* Sainte-Foy: Presses de l'Université Laval, 1991, pp. 23-51.

Dubé, Normand. "The Franco-American Presence: A New England French Literature." In *Francophone Literatures of the New World.* Denver, Colorado: University of Denver, Department of Foreign Languages and Literatures, 1982, pp. 71-81. A mostly bibliographic overview.

Poteet, Maurice. "The Image of Québec in Franco-American Fiction of Immigration and Assimilation (in English, from 1934 to 1974)." Ph.D. Dissertation, University of Montréal, 1980.

Robert, Adolphe. "Essai sur l'apport franco-américain à la littérature des États-Unis." In *Le Canado-Américain*, V, Oct.-Nov.-Dec. 1967, pp. 23-29.

Santerre, Richard. "Le Roman franco-américain de la Nouvelle-Angleterre, 1878-1943." Ph.D. dissertation (French) Boston College, 1974, iv, 352 p.

Therriault, Sister Mary Carmel, S.M. *La littérature française de Nouvelle-Angleterre.* Montréal: Fides, 1946, 325 p. This literary history has been updated in part by my own article in *Revue d'histoire littéraire du Québec et du Canada français. (Cf. supra).*

Trottier, Rev. Maurice. *Les interprètes du beau.* Manchester, N.H.: Éditions Lafayette, 1983, 104 p. Includes essays on Franco American writers.

b. Anthologies

Chassé, Paul P., comp. *Anthologie de la poésie franco-américaine de la Nouvelle-Angleterre.* Providence, R.I.: Rhode Island Bicentennial Commission, 1976, viii, 293 p.

Ledoux, Denis. *Lives in Translation: An Anthology of Contemporary Franco-American Writings.* Lisbon Falls, Me.: Soleil Press, (95 Gould Road 04252), 1991. Thirteen authors: A. Poulin, Jr., Bill Tremblay, Daniel Campion, John Dufresne, David Rivard, Susann Pelletier, David Plante, Michael Parent, Dorianne Laux,

Paul Marion, Steven Riel, Jackie Giasson Fuller, Denis Ledoux. The only anthology of Franco-Americans who write in English.

Marion, Paul, ed. *French Class: French Canadian American Writings on Identity, Culture, and Place.* Lowell, Mass.: Loom Press (P.O. Box 1394, 01853), 1999, x, 54 p. The notes on this book's back cover best summarize the intent and scope of this work: "Writing about spirituality, family, work, language, and food, the authors show how we can move beyond memory and make our past a meaningful part of an evolving life."

Poteet. Cf. Poteet, in **General** (above).

Roche, François. *Les Francos de la Nouvelle-Angleterre: anthologie franco-américaine (XIXe et XXe siècles).* Le Creusot, France: LARC et Centre d'Action Culturelle (Diffusion: Les Belles Lettres), 1981, 220 p.

Santerre, Richard, ed. *Anthologie de la littérature franco-américaine de la Nouvelle-Angleterre.* Bedford, N.H.: National Materials Development Center, 1980, 9 volumes.

c. Journalism

Beaulieu, Oda, ed. *Actes du Symposium tenu à l'occasion de l'ouverture des Archives Wilfrid Beaulieu — Le Travailleur,* [Boston Public Library]. Manchester, N.H.: Imprimerie Lafayette, n.d., 64 p. Also published as "Cahier no 1," 1983 of the Société Historique Franco-Américaine.

Belisle, Alexandre. *Histoire de la presse franco-américaine et des Canadiens-Français aux États-Unis.* Worcester, Mass.: Les Ateliers de l'Opinion Publique, 1911, xvi, 456 p.

Chartier, Armand B. "Yvonne Le Maître chroniqueuse franco-américaine." In *Les autres littératures d'expression française en Amérique,* edited by Jules Tessier and Pierre Vaillancourt. Ottawa: Presses de l'Université d'Ottawa, 1987, pp. 113-25. The first study of this author.

Guillet, Ernest B. *Essai de journalisme* [sic]. Bedford, N.H.: National Materials Development Center, 1981, 78 p. Study of Franco-American journalism in Holyoke, Mass.

Ham, Edward B. "Journalism and the French Survival in New England." *The New England Quarterly,* vol. 11, March 1938, pp. 89-107.

Heyman, Denise Tanya. *"Wilfrid Beaulieu Defender of the French Language and Culture in New England."* Master's thesis, University of Paris VII, Institut d'anglais Charles V, June Session 1983, 111 p.

Perreault, Robert B. *La presse franco-américaine et la politique: l'oeuvre de Charles-Roger Daoust.* Bedford, N.H.: National Materials Development Center for French, 1980, ix, 102 p. Presentation of this author and excerpts from his writings.

Quintal, Claire, ed. *Le journalisme de langue française aux États-Unis.* Québec: Conseil de la Vie Française en Amérique, 1984, 162p.

Rabin, Stéphanie. "The Franco-American Press in New England (1865-1929)." Master's thesis, University of Paris IV-Sorbonne, 1995.

Robert, Adolphe. "Correspondance avec Yvonne LeMaître." In *Bulletin de la Societé Historique Franco-Americaine*, New series: vol.

I, 1955, pp. 89-93. Excerpts from previously unpublished letters written by a well-known Franco-American journalist.

Roy, Elphège E. "Les causes du déclin de la presse franco-américaine." Master's thesis, Rivier College, Nashua, N.H., 1965.

Tétrault, Maximilienne. *Le rôle de la presse dans l'évolution du peuple franco-américain de la Nouvelle-Angleterre.* Marseille: Ferran, 1935, 143 p.

Vincens, Simone J. "L'évolution de la presse franco-américaine." In *Contemporary French Civilization,* vol. IX, no. 1, Fall/Winter 1985, pp. 1-17.

d. Theater

Chabot, Grégoire. *Un Jacques Cartier Errant. Jacques Cartier Discovers America.* Three plays: "Un Jacques Cartier Errant," "Chère Maman," "Sans Atout/No Trump." The original North American French texts with English translations by the author. Orono, ME.: University of Maine Press/Le Centre Franco-Américain, 1996, xvii, 291 p. A bilingual edition of plays on Franco-American life.

Guillet, Ernest B. "Un théâtre francophone dans un milieu franco-américain." Bedford, N.H.: National Materials Development Center for French, 1981, 52 p.

Rocheleau, Corinne. *Françaises d'Amérique: Esquisse historique.* Montréal: Beauchemin, 1940, 125 p. "Quelques faits vécus sur la vie des principales héroïnes de la Nouvelle-France." A collection of scenes in which several prominent women of New France share something of their individual lives.

e. Fiction in French

Beaugrand, Honoré. *Jeanne la fileuse: Épisode de l'émigration franco-canadienne aux États-Unis.* Montréal: Fides, Collection du Nénuphar, 1980, 312 p. An excellent edition, containing a lengthy "Introduction," "Chronology," and Bibliography" by Roger LeMoine. Another edition was published by the National Materials Development Center, Bedford, N.H., 1980, 188 p. It includes the poems of the first (1878) edition. This novel has a special meaning for Franco-Americans because it was the first to deal with the controversial issue of emigration which the author defends.

On Beaugrand:

Schick, Constance Gosselin. "Jeanne la fileuse et le rapatriement des immigrés." In *The French Review,* May 1998.

Senécal, André. "The Economic and Political Ideas of Honoré Beaugrand in *Jeanne la fileuse.* " In *Québec Studies*, vol. 1, no. 1, Spring 1983, pp. 200-207.

Beaupré, Normand R. "Un roman de filiation: la formation d'un écrivain franco-américain." *Études de linguistique appliquée.* Foyers francophones aux États-Unis. Louise Péloquin, ed., vol.70, April-June 1988, pp.8996.

Ben-Haim, Aharon. *Akiouin'j: La fleur de lys ne se fane pas.* Montclair, N.J.: 4-N Language Publishers (230 Park St., 07042), 1989, x, 216 p. Novel about a military incident involving New France in the 18th century.

Chapdelaine, Henri. *Au nouveau pays de Maria Chapdelaine. Suite du roman de Louis Hémon.* Manchester, N.H.: Éditions du Chèvrefeuille, 1988, 98 p. One of the two French-language Franco-American novels published since the 1940s.

——————. *Le St. Laurent coule dans le Merrimack.* Manchester, N.H.: La maison aux cinq pignons (180 Oakland Ave. 03109-4408), 1993, 111 p. A splendid collection of essays and short stories.

Crépeau, Georges. *Bélanger, ou l'histoire d'un crime.* Bedford, N.H.: National Materials Development Center, n.d. First published in 1892.

Dantin, Louis (pseudonym of Eugène Seers). *Les enfances de Fanny.* Montréal: Cercle du Livre de France-Poche Canadien, 1969, 181 p. Translated into English as *Fanny.* Montréal: Harvest House, 1974. Autobiographical novel by the controversial French-Canadian expatriate poet and literary critic.

Dufault, Paul. *Sanatorium.* Manchester, N.H.: National Materials Development Center for French and Creole, 1982, 153 p. First published in 1938. The only known "medical" novel in Franco-American literature.

Duval-Thibault, Anna. *Les deux testaments: esquisse de moeurs canadiennes.* Bedford, N.H.: National Materials Development Center for French, 1979, 204 p. First published in 1888.

Gastonguay, Alberte. *La jeune Franco-Américaine.* Bedford, N.H.: National Materials Development Center for French, 1980, 65 p. First published in 1933.

Lambert, Adélard. *L'Innocente victime.* Bedford, N.H.: National Materials Development Center, 82 p. First published in 1936.

——— . *Dans le jardin d'autrui. Contes ... Légendes... Récits.* Manchester, N.H.: 1919, 125 p.

Lessard-Bissonnette, Camille. *Canuck.* Bedford. N.H.: National Materials Development Center for French, 1980, 119 p. First published in 1936.

Malouin, Reine. *Où chante la vie.* Québec, QC: Éditions de l'Action catholique, 1962, 170 p. *Roman à thèse,* which advocates *survivance.*

Nadeau, Gabriel. *La Fille du Roy, Conte drôlatique.* Trois-Rivières: Éditions du Bien Public, 1954.

Perreault, Robert B. *L'Héritage.* Durham, N.H.: University of New Hampshire, Dimond Library, Department of Media Services, 1983, 256 p.

Port-Joli, Emma (pseudonym of Emma Dumas). *Mirbah.* Bedford, N.H.: National Materials Development Center for French, 1979, 247 p. First published in 1910-1912.

Tremblay, Rémi. *Un revenant: épisode de la Guerre de Sécession aux États-Unis.* Bedford, N.H.: National Materials Development Center for French, 1980, 348 p. First published in 1884.

f. Fiction in English

Archambault, Albéric. *Mill Village.* Boston: Bruce Humphries, 1943. A novel on the integration of French-Canadian immigrants into mainstream American life.

Bélair, Richard. *The Road Less Traveled.* Garden City, N.Y.: Doubleday, 1964, 192 p.

————— . *Double Take.* New York: Dell Laurel Leaf, 1979, 191 p.

————— . *The Fathers.* Boston, Mass.: Brandon Publishing, 1991, 243 p. A novel about a family divided by the *Sentinelliste* controversy of the 1920s.

Blaise, Clark. *Lusts.* Markham, Ont.: Penguin Books Canada, 1984 (First published by Doubleday, 1983), 253 p. "Clark Blaise is a born story-teller and an easy writer to like, to savor." *The New York Times Book Review,* quoted on the back cover.

————— . *Resident Alien.* Markham, Ont.: Penguin Books Canada, 1986, 184 p,
Short stories and autobiographical fragments.

—————

Cormier, Robert. Several of this prolific author's novels have been categorized as works for "Young Adults." While young adults may read them with profit, so too may adult readers. What follows is merely a sampling taken from Cormier's lengthy bibliography.

————— . *Now and At the Hour.* New York: Coward-McKann, 1960. Re-issued: Dell-Laurel, 1988. "Dignified and touching," according to *Time* magazine (back cover of book).

————— . *A Little Raw on Monday Mornings.* New York: Sheed & Ward, 1963. Re-issued by Dell, 1992, 217 p. This is one of the author's "adult books."

—————— . *Take Me Where the Good Times Are.* New York: Macmillan, 1965.

—————— . *The Chocolate War.* New York: Pantheon Books, 1974, 253 p. Released as a movie in 1989.

—————— . *I Am the Cheese.* New York: Dell Publishing, 1977, 221 p. Adapted for the movies, 1983.

—————— . *After the First Death.* New York: Pantheon Books, 1979.

—————— . *Eight Plus One* (short stories). New York: Pantheon Books, 1980.

—————— . *The Bumblebee Flies Anyway.* New York: Pantheon Books, 1983.

—————— . *Beyond the Chocolate War.* New York: Knopf, distributed by Random House, 1985, 275 p. Sequel to *The Chocolate War.*

—————— . *Fade.* New York: Dell Publishing, Laurel-Leaf. Contemporary Fiction, 1988, 293 p. New York: Delacorte Press, 1988, 310 p. A most intriguing work.

—————— . *Other Bells for Us to Ring.* New York: Delacorte Press, 1990. 137 p. Illustrated by Deborah Kogan Ray.

—————— . *We All Fall Down.* New York: Delacorte Press, 1991.

—————— . *I Have Words to Spend: Reflections of a Small-Town Editor.* New York: Delacorte Press, 1991, xiv, 210 p. Edited and with a Preface by Constance Senay Cormier. A wonderful assemblage of short, human-interest pieces, culled by

Constance Cormier, the author's wife, from the more than 900 articles which the author wrote for various periodicals. A book to savor.

—————. *Tunes for Bears to Dance to.* New York: Delacorte Press, 1992.

—————. *In the Middle of the Night.* New York: Delacorte Press, 1995.

—————. *Tenderness.* New York: Delacorte Press, 1997.

—————. *Heroes.* New York: Delacorte Press, 1998, 135 p. This latest Cormier novel will, very likely, be considered as one of his most powerful and thought-provoking.

On Cormier

Campbell, Patricia J. *Presenting Robert Cormier.* Boston, Mass.: Twayne Publishers, Updated edition, 1989, xiv, 189 p.

—————

Ducharme, Jacques. *The Delusson Family.* New York: Funk & Wagnalls, 1939. A novel on immigration and the American dream.

Dufresne, John. *Love Warps the Mind a Little.* New York: W. W. Norton, 1997, 315 p.New york: Plume (Penguin Putnam, Inc),1998 "A funny, tenderhearted book marinated in a keen sense of the absurdities of everyday life. Dufresne rises to considerable literary heights." *New York Times,* as quoted on the back cover of the book.

Gosselin, Henri. *George Washington's French-Canadian Spy.* Available from the author: P.O. Box 1305, No. 104, Brunswick, ME 04011, 1998. Fascinating. "A good read."

.James, Will (pseudonym of Ernest Dufault). *Cowboy Stories.* New York: Charles Scribner's Sons, 1951, 243 p. Illustrations by Will James. This collection contains some of his best stories.

——— . *Home Ranch.* Cleveland: World Publishing Co., 1945, xvii, 346 p. Illustrated by the author. Realistic novel of ranching life in the 1930s and 1940s.

Kerouac, Jack

NOTE: Listed here are the "Lowell novels" and *On The Road* of Jack Kerouac. In addition to these, he has written many novels in which he makes references to his ethnicity, but which could not be called "ethnic novels." Also, there is a constantly increasing body of literature on Kerouac's life and work. Some of the more significant studies are listed here.

Kerouac, Jack. *The Town and the City.* New York: Harcourt Brace Jovanovich, 1950. Novel of a Franco-American family uprooted from its Massachusetts home and transplanted to New York.

——— . *On The Road.* New York: Viking Press, 1957. This phenomenally successful novel has remained in print since its first publication.

—————— . *Doctor Sax.* New York: Grove Press, 1959. Vivid portrayal of a Franco-American adolescence, the mysteries and terrors of which are explored and evoked with unusual skill.

—————— . *Maggie Cassidy.* New York: Avon Books, 1959.

—————— . *Visions of Gerard.* New York: Farrar, Strauss & Co., 1963. One of several works in Kerouac's fictional autobiography, this short book provides insights into the Franco-American way of life and death in the 1920s.

On Jack Kerouac

Beaulieu, Victor-Lévy. *Jack Kérouac.* Montréal: Éditions du Jour, 1972. Contains many perceptive remarks on Kerouac's Franco-American background.

Jack Kérouac et l'imaginaire Québécois, Special issue of *Voix et Images: Littérature québécoise,* vol. XIII, no. 3, Spring 1988. A significant contribution to Kerouac studies.

Chartier, Armand B. "Jack Kérouac, Franco-Américain." In *Revue d'Histoire Littéraire du Québec et du Canada Français,* vol. 12, 1986, pp. 83-96. This is the first in-depth study of the influence of Kerouac's ethnicity on his work.

Chiasson, Herménégilde. "Le grand Jack: une lecture qui devient un film..." In *Liaison,* no. 44, September 1987, pp. 7-8.

Dickson, Robert. "Ti-Jean, Patrice, Robert et les autres..." In *Liaison,* no. 44, September 1987, pp. 5-6.

Fortin, Andrée. "Vision de Jack." In *Nuit Blanche,* December 1987-January 1988, pp. 32-34.

Kerouac-Harvey, Raymonde. *L'Album.* Beauceville, Québec: L'Éclaireur, 1980, 141 p. History of the Kerouac family.

Moody Street Irregulars. "French Connection Issue." No. 11, Spring/Summer 1982, 24 p.

Nicosia, Gerald. *Memory Babe: A Critical Biography of Jack Kerouac.* New York: Grove Press, 1983, 767 p. This is the most complete of the many biographies of Jack Kerouac.

N'importe quelle route: Bulletin du Club Jack Kérouac. Québec, QC: Secrétariat permanent des peuples francophones, 1987.

Perreault, Robert B. *Au-delà de la route: le côté franco-américain de Jack Kérouac.* Québec: Secrétariat permanent des peuples francophones, 1987, 28 p.

Poteet, Maurice. "The Images of Quebec in Jack Kerouac's Fiction." *Les Avant-Dire de la Rencontre internationale Jack Kerouac.* Québec: Secrétariat permanent des peuples francophones,, 1987.

Quintal, Claire. "Franco-American Literature: The Case of Jack Kérouac." In *Le FAROG Forum,* January 1988, pp. 18-20.

——————. "Mémère Kérouac ou la revanche du berceau en Franco-Américanie." In *Voix et Images,* Université du Québec à Montréal, no. 39, Spring 1988.

Sorrell, Richard S. "Jack Kérouac, French Canada and France." In *American Review of Canadian Studies,* vol. 10, no 2, 1980, pp. 16-25.

—————— . "Kerouac's Lowell: 'Little Canada' and the Ethnicity of Jack Kerouac." Essex Institute Historical Collection, vol. 117, no 4, 1981, pp. 262-282.

—————— . "Novelists and Ethnicity: Jack Kerouac and Grace Metalious as Franco-Americans."*MELUS*, vol. 9, no 1, Spring 1982, pp. 37-52.

—————— . "The Catholicism of Jack Kerouac." *Sciences Religieuses/Studies in Religion,* 11/2, Spring 1982, pp. 189-200.

Tardif, Richard, "Un écrivain sous influence." In *Nuit blanche,* December 1987-January 1988, pp. 37-39.

Woolfson, Peter. "The French-Canadian Heritage of Jack Kerouac as Seen in his Autobiographical Works." University of Vermont. Unpublished paper available from the author.

———————

La Salle, Peter. *Hockey sur glace.* New York: Breakaway Books, 1998. First published in 1996, 189 p. According to the *New York Times Book Review*, quoted on the back cover of the book, these short stories "all take weight from a powerful retrospect, from a lost time that was both troubled and blessed."

Ledoux, Denis. *What Became of Them, and Other Stories from Franco-America.* Lisbon Falls, Maine: Soleil Press, 1988, 103 p.

————— . *Mountain Dance and Other Stories.* Thomaston, Maine: Coastwise Press, 1990, 58 p. Winner, 1990 Maine Arts Commission Chapbook Competition.

————— . *Cf. also* **Anthologies:** *Lives in Translation.*

Metalious, Grace

Metalious, Grace. *No Adam in Eden.* New York: Pocket Books, 1967. A novel about the disintegration of traditional values in a Franco-American family, by the author of the controversial *Peyton Place.*

On Metalious

Perreault, Robert B. "In the Eyes of her Father: A Portrait of Grace Metalious." *Historical New Hampshire,* vol. 35, no. 3, Fall 1980, pp. 318-328.

Sorrell, Richard S. "A Novelist and Her Ethnicity: Grace Metalious As a Franco-American." In *Historical New Hampshire,* vol. 35, no. 3, 1980, pp. 284-317.

Toth, Emily. *Inside Peyton Place: The Life of Grace Metalious.* Garden City, N.Y.: Doubleday, 1981, viii, 395 p.

————— . "Fatherless and Dispossessed: Grace Metalious As a French-Canadian Writer." In *Journal of Popular Culture,* vol.15, no. 3, 1981, pp. 28-38.

Nadeau-Single, Lee. *Annette: The Story of a Pioneer Woman.* New York: Vantage Press, 1990, 138 p. A historical novel about a pioneer woman in Northern Maine in the 18th century.

Parsons, Vivian La Jeunesse. *Not Without Honor.* New York: Dodd, Mead & Co., 1941. Deals with the interaction between Franco-Americans and Italian-Americans in a Michigan mining community. An unjustly neglected novel, as is the author's *Lucien.*

Plante, David

Plante, David. *The Francoeur Novels.* New York: Dutton, 1983. Contains: *The Family* (1978); *The Country* (1981); *The Woods* (1982), each of which has also been published separately.

————— . *The Foreigner.* New York: Dutton, 1986.

————— . *The Accident.* New York: Ticknor and Fields, 1991.

————— . *Annunciation.* New York: Ticknor and Fields, 1994, 343 p. This work "offers his most complex and powerful novel to date" according to the jacket blurb.

————— . *The Age of Terror.* New York: St. Martin's Press, 1999. The review in the *New York Times Book Review* (24 January 1999, pp. 10-11) suggests the complexity of this work.

On Plante

Aylward, Susan L. "'Accidents of Terrain': The Native and Foreign Worlds of David Plante." Ph.D. dissertation (English) University of Rhode Island, 1998.

———

Proulx, Annie. *Heart Songs and Other Stories.* New York: Harper & Row, 1988, 152 p.

————— . *Postcards.* New York: Charles Scribner's Sons, 1992, 309p

————— . *The Shipping News.* New York: Charles Scribner's Sons, 1993, 337 p. This novel won both a National Book Award and a Pulitzer Prize. In 1999, a screen adaptation was shot in Nova Scotia and Maine.

————— . *Accordion Crimes.* New York: Scribner, 1996, 381 p.

_____. *Close Range: Wyoming Stories.* New York: Scribner, 1999, 285 p. Watercolors by William Matthews. *The New York Times* has called this collection of stories "powerful" and "great writing."

———

Robichaud, Gérard. *Papa Martel.* Garden City, N.Y.: Doubleday, 1961. All Saints Press, 1962.

————— . *The Apple of His Eye.* Garden City, N.Y.: Doubleday, 1965, 277 p.

On Robichaud

Aubé, Mary Elizabeth, and Yves Frenette. "Le difficile accommodement: culture paysanne et changement socioculturel dans *Papa Martel.*" In *Francophonies d'Amérique,* Université d'Ottawa, vol. 2, 1992.

g. Poetry in French

Boucher, Georges-A. *Chants du Nouveau Monde.* Montréal: Beauchemin, 1946.

————. *Je me souviens.* Montreal: Arbour & Dupont, 1933.

————. *Sonnets de guerre.* Montréal: Beauchemin, 1943.

Chassé, Paul P. *Poèmes.* Dover, N.H.: Odyssey Press, 1995, 221 p. Preface by Rémi Gilbert. Introduction by Armand Chartier.

————

Dantin, Louis. The Poet (pseudonym of Eugène Seers)

Dantin, Louis. *Chanson intellectuelle.* Montréal: Éditions Albert Lévesque, 1932.

————. *Le Coffret de Crusoé.* Montréal: Éditions Albert Lévesque, 1932.

————. *Poèmes d'outre-tombe.* Trois Rivières: Éditions du Bien Public, 1962. Collection "Les Cahiers Louis Dantin." Preface by Gabriel Nadeau.

Dantin, Louis: The Literary Critic

Dantin, Louis. *Gloses critiques* (First series). Montréal: Éditions Albert Lévesque, 1931. (Second series: ibid., 1935).

————. *Poètes de l'Amérique Française*. (First series). Montréal: Louis Carrier & Co, (Les Éditions du Mercure), 1928. (Second series, Montréal: Éditions Albert Lévesque, 1934).

————. "Préface" d'*Émile Nelligan et son oeuvre*. Montréal: Éditions Édouard Garand, 1925, xxxix, 166 p.

————. *La Vie en Rêve*. Montréal: Librairie d'Action Canadienne-Française, 1930.

On Dantin

Chassé, Paul P. "Les Cahiers Louis Dantin." In *Le Canado-Américain*, V, April-May-June 1968, 39-40. Review-essay of an important collection.

————. "La correspondance de Dantin." In *Le Canado-Américain*, IV, June-July 1964, 36-39.

————. "Miré dans un étang d'opale." In *Le Canado-Américain*, III, June-July 1963, 32-36.

Garon, Yves, A.A. *Louis Dantin.* Montréal: Fides, 1968.Collection "Classiques canadiens."

Nadeau, Gabriel. *Louis Dantin - Sa vie et son oeuvre.* Manchester, N.H.: Éditions Lafayette, 1947, 252 p.

——————— . *Dantin parmi les Nègres. Dantin et l'Universel Bureau.* Trois-Rivières: Éditions du Bien Public, 1968, 109 p.

———————

d'Arles, Henri. (pseudonym of Rev. Henri Beaudé)

——————— . *Pastels.* New York: Daniel V. Wien, 1905.

——————— . *Essais et Conférences.* Québec: Laflamme et Proulx, 1909. Literary criticism.

——————— . *Eaux-fortes et Tailles-Douces.* Québec: Laflamme et Proulx, 1913. Literary criticism.

——————— . *Arabesques.* Paris: Dorbon-Aîné, 1923.

——————— . *Laudes.* Paris: Paul Lefebvre, 1925.

——————— . *Estampes.* Montréal: Bibliothèque de l'Action française, 1926. Literary criticism.

——————— . *Miscellanées.* Montréal: Les Éditions du Mercure, 1926. Literary criticism; includes a chapter on Ferdinand Gagnon.

——————— . *Horizons.* Montréal: Librairie d'Action Canadienne-Française, 1929.

——————— . "Journal intime." In *Bulletin de la Société Historique Franco-Américaine,* Nouvelle serie: vol. II, 1956, pp. 132-142. Suite: *Bulletin,* 1958, pp. 133-44; *Bulletin,* 1959, vol. V, pp. 129-57. Although censored, these pages offer some insights into the soul of one of the most intriguing Franco-American writers.

On Henri d'Arles

Parenteau, Irène, C.S.C. "Henri d'Arles, styliste." Master's thesis, University of Montréal, 1960, 102 p. Extracts published in *Le Canado-Américain,* II, February-March 1962, 35-39.

Robert, Adolphe. "Henri d'Arles." In *Bulletin de la Société Historique Franco-Américaine,* 1942, 19-33.

——— . *Henri d'Arles: Étude critique.* Québec: L'Action, 1943, 31 p.

———

Daoust, Charles-Roger

Daoust, Charles Roger. *Au Seuil du Crépuscule.* Shawinigan Falls, Québec: La Compagnie de Publication du Saint-Maurice, 1924.

———

Dion-Lévesque, Rosaire

Dion-Lévesque, Rosaire. *En égrenant le chapelet des jours.* Montréal: Louis Carrier, Les Editions du Mercure, 1928. Preface by Henri d'Arles.

——— . *Les Oasis.* Rome: Desclée & Cie., Éditeurs Pontificaux, 1930.

——— . *Petite Suite Marine.* Paris: Éditions de la Caravelle Franco-Américaine, 1931, 16 p. Four poems with illustrations by Camille Audette.

————. *Walt Whitman.* French translation of selected poems from *Leaves of Grass.* Montréal: Les Elzévirs, 1933. Preface by Louis Dantin.

————. *Vita.* Montréal: Éditions Bernard Valiquette, 1939.

————. *Solitude.* Montréal: Chanteclerc, 1949.

————. *Jouets.* "Poems inspired by childhood." Montréal: Chanteclerc, 1952.

————. *Quête.* Québec: Éditions Garneau, 1963.

On Dion-Lévesque

Chassé, Paul P. "La terre et la mer étant des exils." In *Le Canado-Américain,* III, December 1963-January 1964, 28-33.

LaPierre, Michel. "Rosaire Dion-Lévesque (1900-1974) et la littérature franco-américaine." Master's thesis, University of Montréal 1983, vii, 179 p.

————. "Rosaire Dion-Lévesque, Poet and Translator of Walt Whitman." *Steeples and Smokestacks.* Worcester, Mass.: Institut français, Assumption College, 1996, pp. 401-411.

Nadeau, Gabriel. "Silhouettes Franco-Américaines: Appréciation." In *Bulletin de la Société Historique Franco-Américaine.* Nouvelle Série: vol. IV, 1958, 111-13. More than a review of this indispensable biographical dictionary, the article is also a mini-portrait of Dion-Lévesque, the poet.

Dubé Normand

Dubé Normand. *Un mot de chez nous.* Bedford. N.H.: National Materials Development Center, n.d., 80 p.

——— . *Au coeur du vent.* Bedford, N.H.: National Materials Development Center, 1978, vi, 96.

——— . *La broderie inachevée.* Cambridge, Mass.: National Assessment & Dissemination Center, 1979, vi, 88 p.

——— . *Le nuage de ma pensée.* Bedford, N.H.: National Materials Development Center, 1981, vi, 91 p.

_____ "M'entendez-vous écrire? *Études de linguistique appliquée.* Foyers francophones aux États-Unis. Louise Péloquin, ed. Vol. 70, April-June, p. 97-102

———

Duval-Thibault, Anna-Marie. *Fleurs du Printemps.*   Preface by Benjamin Sulte. Fall River, Mass.: Société de Publication de l'Indépendant, 1892.

Eid, Rev. Joseph. *A l'Ombre des Cèdres* ou *L'Épopée du Liban.* Fall River, Mass.: Privately printed, 1940, 222 p.

Fecteau, Edouard. *Intimes* (Mini-Poems). Manchester, N.H.: Ballard Frères, n.d.

———

Girouard, Joseph-Amédée. *Au fil de la vie.* Lewiston, Maine: Imprimerie du Messager, 1909.

On Girouard

Chassé, Paul P. "Joseph-Amédée Girouard." In *Le Canado-Américain,* V, April-May-June 1969, 10-17.

———

On Laferrière, Joseph

Perreault, Robert B. *Joseph Laferrière, écrivain lowellois.* Manchester, N.H.: National Materials Development Center, 1982, iv, 186 p.

———

Lemieux, Alice

Lemieux, Alice. *Heures effeuillées.* Québec: Imprimerie Ernest Tremblay, 1926.

——— . *Poèmes.* Montréal: Librairie d'Action Canadienne-Française, 1929.

Lemieux Lévesque, Alice. *L'Arbre du Jour.* Québec: Éditions Garneau, 1964.

——— . *Silences.* Québec: Éditions Garneau, 1962.

———

Nolin, Louis Alphonse, O.M.I. *Poèmes détachés.* Unpublished manuscript kept in the Archives of Oblate Fathers, Lowell, Mass., 1922.

─────── . *Vers les Cimes.* Lowell, Mass. Unpublished manuscript kept in the Archives of the Oblate Fathers, Lowell, Mass., 1924.

Paris, Robert L. "Dreams of Time and Space." Electronic visual and musical setting for poems, 1968.

─────── . *"'Le Voyage.'"* Electronic musical interpretation of a poem by Charles Baudelaire, 1967.

───────

Roy, Joseph Hormidas. *Voix étranges.* Lowell, Mass.: Imprimerie de l'Étoile, 1902.

On Roy

Chassé, Paul P. "Joseph-Hormidas Roy." In *Le Canado-Americain*, V, October-November-December 1968, 66-71. Biographical and critical presentation.

───────

Sainte-Marie, Philippe. *En passant.* Paris: Imprimerie d'Art "Le Croquis," 1924.

Tremblay, Rémi. *Boutades et Rêveries.* Fall River, Mass.: Société de Publication de l'Indépendant, 1893.

————— . *Caprices poétiques et chansons satiriques.* Montréal: Filiatreault, 1883.

————— . *Coups d'aile et coups de bec.* Montréal: Imprimerie Gebbart-Berthiaume, 1888.

————— . *Vers l'Idéal.* Ottawa: n.p., 1912.

Trottier, Maurice. *Envolées.* Montréal: Beauchemin, 1960, 1965.

————— . *Songs of my Youth/A la fleur de l'âge.* Manchester, N.H.: Éditions Lafayette, 1981.

————— . Trans. Homer's *Odyssée.* Songs I to XII and songs XII to XIV. Worcester, Mass.: Éditions de l'Institut français, 1992, iii, 220 p.

————— . *Soleil levant d'automne/Indian Summer.* Worcester, Mass.: Institut français, Assumption College, 1993, 119 p. Most of the poems in this collection are in French.

————— . *Évangeline.* Manchester, N.H.: Entre Amis, 180 Oakland Ave. 03109-4408, 1995, 78 p. This 4th edition was published posthumously by Henri Chapdelaine and Rev. Jean-Marie Rondeau, of Saint-Laurent, Québec.

On Franco-American Poetry

Chassé, Paul P. "Les poètes franco-américains de la Nouvelle-Angleterre 1875-1925." Ph.D. dissertation (Lettres françaises), Laval University, 1968, L, 408 p. This is *the* major work on this subject.

Quintal, Claire. "Survol de la poésie franco-américaine." *Lettres et cultures de langue française.* Paris: ADELF, 1987.

Therriault, Sister Mary Carmel. "La Poésie française en Nouvelle-Angleterre." In Gerard J. Brault. *Les Conférences de l'Institut Franco-Américain de Bowdoin College*, pp. 53-63, Brunswick, Maine; 1961.

h. Poetry in English

Bishop, Jim. *Mother Tongue.* Portland, Me.: Contraband Press, 1975. Unpaginated.

Marion, Paul. *Strong Place: Poems 1974-1984.* Lowell, Mass.: Loom Press, P.O. Box 1394, Lowell, MA 01853, 1984, 57 p.

————. *Apples and Oranges.* Lowell, Mass.: Loom Press, 1986. Unpaginated.

————. *Middle Distance.* Lowell, Mass.: Loom Press, 1989, 51 p.

Pelletier, Susann. *Immigrant Dreams and Other Poems.* Lisbon Falls, Me.: Soleil Press, 1989, 33 p.

Poulin, A. (Jr.) *A Momentary Order: Poems.* St. Paul, Minnesota: Graywolf Press (P.O. Box 75006, St. Paul, MN 55175), 1987, 141 p. A. Poulin has published several collections of poems.

Rivard, David. *Torque.* Pittsburg, Penn.: University of Pittsburgh Press, 1988, 63 p.

Tremblay, Bill. *Crying in the Cheap Seats.* Amherst, Mass.: University of Massachusetts Press, 1971, 106 p. Of special interest to Franco-American readers is the sequence "Jack Kerouac's Funeral."

————— . *Duhamel: Ideas of Order in Little Canada.* Brockport, N.Y.: BOA Editions, 1986, 67 p.

————— . *The June Rise. The Apocryphal Letters of Joseph Antoine Janis.* Logan, Utah: Utah State University Press, 1994, x, 233 p. Janis, a fur trader and early settler of Colorado's Cache La Poudre River Valley, tells his life story, as imagined by the author. The work offers a substantial contribution to our knowledge of French and Native American life in the Western United States in the 19th century.

INDEX

Y

Z